# FIFTH EDITION

# Talking Sociology

## Gary Alan Fine

*Northwestern University*

## David Shulman

*Lafayette College*

D1516155

Boston   New York   San Francisco
Mexico City   Montreal   Toronto   London   Madrid   Munich   Paris
Hong Kong   Singapore   Tokyo   Cape Town   Sydney

**Series Editor:** *Jeff Lasser*
**Editor in Chief, Social Sciences:** *Karen Hanson*
**Editorial Assistant:** *Andrea Christie*
**Marketing Manager:** *Judeth Hall*
**Editorial-Production Administrator:** *Annette Joseph*
**Editorial-Production Service:** *Holly Crawford*
**Composition Buyer:** *Linda Cox*
**Electronic Composition:** *Peggy Cabot, Cabot Computer Services*
**Manufacturing Buyer:** *Megan Cochran*
**Cover Designer:** *Kristina Mose-Libon*

For related titles and support materials, visit our online catalog at www.ablongman.com.

Between the time Website information is gathered and then published, it is not unusual for some sites to have closed. Also, the transcription of URLs can result in unintended typographical errors. The publisher would appreciate notification where these errors occur so that they may be corrected in subsequent editions.

**Library of Congress Cataloging-in-Publication Data**

Fine, Gary Alan.
    Talking sociology.—5th ed. / Gary Alan Fine, David Shulman
      p.  cm.
    Includes bibliographical references.
    ISBN 0-205-34270-1
      1. Sociology.  2. Social problems.  3. United States—Social policy.
    I.  Shulman, David.  II. Title.

HM585 .F56 2003
  301—dc21

                          2002021598

*To*
*Christina Jeffrey*
*and the brave band of conservative academics*
*fighting for diversity on college campuses*

*Free speech and free minds*

# Contents

# ▪ CHAPTER TWO

## Socialization: Should Parents Be Allowed to Hit Their Children However They Wish?    36

# ▪ CHAPTER THREE

## Deviance and Social Control: Should Drug Use Be Legalized?    53

# ▪ CHAPTER FOUR

## Human Sexuality: Is Adultery Wrong?    70

# ■ CHAPTER FIVE

## Economy and Stratification: Is Global Free Trade Harmful?     89

# ■ CHAPTER SIX

## Gender Roles and Sexual Stratification: Is Marriage Detrimental to Women?     111

# ■ CHAPTER TEN

## Work and Organizations: Should Employers Investigate Their Employees' Private Lives?    189

# ■ CHAPTER ELEVEN

## Health: Are Americans Too Fat?    209

# ■ CHAPTER TWELVE

## Social Movements/Collective Behavior: Can Civil Disobedience Be Justified?     228

# Acknowledgments

With each subsequent edition, the number of individuals who deserve thanks for bettering a manuscript grows, as a new book arises on the ruins of the old. Ira Reiss, D. Stanley Eitzen, Ramona Asher, Albert Chabot, Dennis Teitge, Maurice Garnier, Michael Bassis, Ira Cohen, Charles Ogg, Meg Wilkes-Karraker, Ben Noah, T. S. Schwartz, John Taylor, Rick Hargraves, Rene Wildermuth, Melvyn Fein, Michael Lovaglia, and Stephanie Shanks-Meile helped improve this work through their comments. Judith Ann Williams, Randy Stoecker, Sari Fried, Nancy Wisely, Kendra Butler, Lori Ducharme, Christopher Vacek, Kerry Smith, Shun Lu, and Peter Fine have served ably as research assistants sniffing out clever quotations as if they were truffles—a metaphor that pays heed only to their powers of investigation and not to any porcine resemblance. The second author would also like to acknowledge the intellectual and personal support of Lucy Millman, Kent Grayson, Sheldon and Sherry Blackman, and Susan Shulman. Completing this edition was facilitated by a research leave received by the second author from Lafayette College. We also thank Holly Crawford for her copyediting skills, guarding against the wayward comma. Finally, thanks to Al Levitt, formerly of Allyn and Bacon, who convinced the first author, over several fine dinners, to write this book, and, later to Karen Hanson and Jeff Lasser, who persuaded us that revisions were in order.

# INTRODUCTION

# Murder and Martyrdom

- *What would you die for?*
- *What would you kill for?*

■ Before reading on, spend a few moments pondering your answers. Is there anything for which you would either give up your life or take the life of another?

Would you be willing to die to prevent your child from dying? Would you kill to prevent your sister from being raped? Would you lay down your life to prevent a terrorist attack on an American skyscraper? Would you murder an oppressor to end brutality against your ethnic, racial, or religious group? Would you place yourself in the path of a fellow student with a rifle? Or, might you be that student, inflicting vengeance on your tormentors? Around the world, young people, in most respects identical to you, are choosing to die and to kill for their beliefs. Americans were willing to die and to kill to gain independence from the British, to defeat the Nazis, to control the Viet Cong, to prevent massacres in Kosovo, and to search out Al Qaeda fighters in the caves of Afghanistan. We have died in struggles for union rights and civil rights. We have executed convicted murderers, lynched those accused of crimes, and knifed members of rival gangs.

Yet, if you compose a list of what you would die or kill for, the list is likely to be short. If you are like most students we have asked, the only answer that you will give has to do with individuals for whom you have intense personal feelings. You might kill someone who attacks you or your family. You might choose to risk your life to give birth to a child. Of course, not everyone would assent to these hypothetical emergencies, but many would. Some would agree that they would pick up arms and lay down their lives for the sake of national defense against a hostile enemy, if asked by our government, and after September 11, 2001, more students are surely supportive of counterterrorist operations and military intervention.

Few of you will name a *cause* that you might kill or die for. Americans today do not care enough about causes, even those they deeply believe in, to take or give a life. Yet, when we read the newspapers we learn that people around the world are doing just that. Whatever you might think about the morality of terrorism, admit that these terrorists have an overwhelming passion for their causes. One striking aspect of the attack on the World Trade Center and the Pentagon is that men were willing to give up their lives for a cause that would not benefit them—except, perhaps, in an afterlife. These kamikazes needed no immediate social pressure to engage in their acts; they were living in American communities for months, privately stoking their fiery beliefs. When confronted with the attacks on the United States, we are reduced to explaining it as "evil," and have great difficulty trying to figure out why nearly two dozen competent young men would care so much for their beliefs to kill and to die. We simply cannot put ourselves in the heads of members of Al Qaeda. Around the world we look at Kosovo, East Timor, Sri Lanka, Gaza, Peru, Haiti, Northern Ireland, Chechnya, the Sudan, Sierra Leone, and Columbia, and see essentially the same phenomenon. People do care enough to kill and be killed, even when, from the view of outsiders, their deadly crusades are pointless. Because we cannot identify with intense nationalistic, ethnic, or religious impulses, most Americans see this violence as silly, futile, tragic, and destructive. One of the goals of American foreign policy is to encourage the rest of the world to think about political problems in the pragmatic fashion that we prefer, draining disputes of physical force. In the immediate aftermath of the bombing of the Federal Building in Oklahoma City, it was "naturally" assumed that the terrorists involved *must* have been foreigners, most likely Arabs. While some measure of racism was surely involved in this supposition, it also spoke to the assumption that no "real" American could possibly have felt that explosives belonged in political debate.

Consider two important American political issues: the Equal Rights Amendment and legalized abortion. The fight over the passage of the Equal Rights Amendment is history. That constitutional amendment, which meant so much to so many women, was defeated by enough state legislatures to prevent its passage. Significantly, during the decade in which the Equal Rights Amendment was a political battleground, no one was killed and no one took her or his own life over this proposed amendment. Although the passage of the amendment was vital to many women, women did not feel justified to assassinate state legislators who opposed them and no woman saw fit to become a gasoline-soaked martyr for the cause. This political moderation contrasts sharply to the battles for suffrage in Great Britain and the United States during the first two decades of the twentieth century, when these campaigns included acts of violence. Although it may be repulsive to consider the tactical value of a well-placed bomb, terrorists know that violence focuses debate.

The civility shown by those who hold strong beliefs applies not only to progressive causes. Many members of the pro-life (antiabortion) movement believe that each year some 1.5 million babies are being *murdered* in the United States. Surely such genocide—as some have termed it—is ample reason for direct political action. Yet, the pro-life movement, with rare exceptions, has worked within the conventional political rules with few overtly violent acts. Only in the last decade have a few pro-life extremists started to use some of the tactics common to other violent social movements. These actions have been widely condemned, both inside and outside this movement. Despite the high profile bombing of the 1996 Olympics in Atlanta, which has been attributed to fugitive pro-life extremist Eric Rudolph, only a handful of doctors have been murdered and clinics firebombed. Mass civil disobedience is more common than it used to be—through the activities of militant groups like Operation Rescue—but is still infrequent. For now, most within the movement stay within the boundaries of conventional social action, letting thousands of "innocent babies" die without putting their own lives and freedom on the line. Why?

Suggesting that Americans do not see murder and martyrdom as acceptable political alternatives does not imply that we should. We are not politically deficient because we lack a tradition of organized political terrorism. Presumably this relative (but not total) lack of collective violence is a reason for our political stability. Americans are largely pragmatic and centrist in political outlook. We vote overwhelmingly for two parties that often seem to have not "a dime's worth of difference" between them. Perhaps this is a reason for the low intellectual level of our political campaigns. Our level of political passivity is particularly striking when we consider the broader range of political beliefs that are acceptable in Great Britain, France, or Canada. While we should not ignore the real differences between the Democratic and Republican parties, their basic values and policies are similar. Neither Al Gore nor George W. Bush provoked grand passions, which perhaps explains that despite the concluding confusion of the election of 2000, there was little chance of governmental chaos. Both candidates claimed to believe in a strong national defense, a social security system, aid to the needy, tax relief, control of nuclear weapons, environmental protection, and free enterprise. The candidates differed in the level of funding for these programs and in the way specific programs are administered; however, when we think of the range of possible alternative political policies, our two politicians were huddled very much in the center. Each wished to convince voters that it is the real centrist party, the party of moderation. When a third party nominates a Pat Buchanan or a Ralph Nader, he is overwhelmingly defeated at the polls. Socialist, nativist, populist, and libertarian parties have had little success in selling their nostrums to the American people.

Because of the success that the two parties have had in making the United States strong at home and abroad, most voters feel the general centrist positions of the major parties are correct. Furthermore, most Americans accept the idea that compromise and civil discussion are more effective than forcing their opinions on others. Americans typically are pragmatic in their political orientations and avoid all-encompassing ideologies, despite strong opinions on many issues. We seem more concerned with getting the job done than in the larger questions that surround the immediate problem. Americans tend not to be much concerned with what former president George Bush called "the Vision Thing." Perhaps the existence of extremist militia groups and the pockets of Aryan Nation activity will make terror more likely, but the history of the Klan, Weathermen, Black Panthers, and other groups tends to suggest that American terrorism burns itself out quickly, particularly when agents of social control take the threat seriously.

Of course, there are many good reasons for not wanting to kill—and be killed. Some accept the principle that nothing is as valuable as life and that there is no excuse for shortening it. In the days of the Cold War, some claimed that it was better to be Red than dead. No political issue, these thinkers believe, can take priority over the destruction of human life—a point emphasized by the Indian revolutionary Mahatma Gandhi and his present-day followers, who feel that nonviolent demonstrations and civil disobedience can achieve the same end. The popular response to the August 1991 Soviet coup cheers those who believe that massive peaceful protest can defeat tyrants, although the 1989 repression at Tiananmen Square in Beijing indicates that such victories are by no means certain. In theory, most agree with this approach, but whether we believe it is effective depends on our view of human nature. Debates over the death penalty reveal this strain—many people would prefer not to have the state involved in the killing business, but others feel that executions are necessary to protect the rest of us.

We used killing and being killed as an opening gambit to indicate how strongly some people feel about social issues and political ideology. (We have no desire for students to raise arms.) Yet, we wonder whether our American lack of ideological concern is a good thing. How far can political pragmatism be pushed before it becomes a willingness to accept any policy so long as it is nicely packaged? We have written this book to expose students to the philosophical bases of social life. Sociology is the proper place to begin to understand underlying questions of social order.

People are better off when they are consciously aware of their basic principles—that is, those general beliefs and values that structure how they view the world. In the terms of social critic Thomas Sowell, in his book *A Conflict of Visions,* these constitute "visions" of society. From these basic principles, attitudes toward particular issues can emerge in logical and consistent ways, to the extent that psychology allows. People may not have strong feelings about human nature or about the general role of the government in individual affairs. We assume that many students have never considered these two issues in any detail, even though most students do have beliefs about particular social problems. Since we believe that these two issues, human nature and government intervention, are at the heart of all sociological understanding, they deserve to be considered in detail.

Richard Feynman, the noted physicist, once criticized students for memorizing and reciting the content of physics textbooks perfectly without being able to apply the books' concepts to explain what happened when he rolled a ball off a table. How social forces affect individuals and how natural laws affect physical objects can both be perceived only as abstractions. We are as adamant as Richard Feynman that students appreciate the practical applicability of ideas and emphatically urge you to consider how being aware of sociological ideas and different visions of society helps in analyzing the world.

Over three centuries ago, the British moral philosopher Thomas Hobbes raised an intriguing and important question that continues to haunt sociologists: How is social order possible? In other words, why, in a world of individuals with their own potentially conflicting needs and personalities, is society as orderly as it is? Just as the physical world rarely fools us, the social world (perhaps a little less consistently) rarely surprises us. We usually know what to expect from our fellow citizens. How, in a world of over six billion people, do we so neatly fit our personal routines together? The answer that a person gives to this puzzle of social order depends on how he or she evaluates human nature, and from this answer we can draw conclusions about how people should be governed.

People do not go through their daily routines constantly aware of these fundamental questions; people generally act on the basis of immediate circumstances and options. While this is fine for small decisions, such an approach presents difficulties when we confront momentous decisions. These decisions may be erratic or inconsistent since they derive from immediate concerns and not from basic principles. Some critics suggest that U.S. economic and foreign policies lurch from position to position to position, depending on what the public is most clamoring for and how close the nation is to an election. We try to control inflation just when inflation is subsiding, only to push the country into a recession; we deal with rising unemployment by establishing social welfare programs, which increase inflation; or we stimulate the economy by cutting taxes, which leads to increased deficits, which we solve by raising taxes. Conservatives support high deficits and an expansion of government programs when doing so is in their political interest; liberals support massive arms buildups and restrictions on civil liberties when this is what the public wishes to hear.

A dilemma inherent in this pragmatic approach is one of morality. The pragmatist may wish to correct troubles in the immediate setting but often without concern for the long-term consequences. Some solutions may be morally wrong, even though they are more effective than others. For example, sterilizing "genetically deficient" individuals might decrease the incidence of mental retardation; yet, many who believe this policy is possible would reject it on moral grounds. Forced sterilization is wrong, even if it works. Ethics may take precedence over technical efficiency.

Finally, by considering issues only pragmatically, we are prone to ignore universal sociological principles. Sociology strives for insights with general relevance. What sociology can tell us applies to more than narrow, local problems, but rather addresses a wider range of concerns. As we shall discuss later, the sociological perspective of *functionalism* allows us to understand many social spheres. The same can be said of an alternative approach—*conflict theory*.

Do not make too sharp a distinction between decisions based on principles and those based on the needs of the moment. Many sociologists believe the world is too complex to be completely dominated by any single set of principles or ideologies. No theory can account for "every sparrow's fall."[1] We should be sensitive to each of the sometimes contradictory principles that are widely held. Many claim that no single set of beliefs can possibly hold all the answers. Whether or not this is true, political reality typically means that some principles must be compromised. Politics is, after all, the art of the possible, of learning to make adjustments to the wishes of others. Although you should be aware of your principles in making decisions, this does not mean you should always blindly and coldly act on these principles. Pragmatism is not a dirty word: In a democracy, rather, it is essential in reaching consensus.

## The Social Order

Many possible prescriptions exist for how society should be ordered. Each society, each tribe, each nation has at least one, sometimes several, ways of seeing the world. In this book we will examine three of the most prevalent views in American life: libertarianism, conservatism, and social democracy. We do not claim that these are the only three perspectives that Americans hold, but they do have several things in common that make them good subjects. First, each presents a reasonably consistent and complete view of human nature. Second, each contains within it the principles by which a government could make policy. Third, each of these views is accepted by a significant number of Americans, and elements from each have penetrated the general, pragmatic political view. Finally, each perspective described here is consistent with democratic government. Certain important philosophies that are not readily amenable to democracy are not considered: communism (Marxist-Leninism), fascism, or benevolent monarchy. In addition, we consider only "Western" political philosophies here; those of the great empires of China, Japan, India, Persia, Mexico, Arabia, Peru, and West Africa are ignored.

We do not pretend to discuss all the details of the three approaches that we have selected. Each is a complicated view with many nuances of thought and objective. No single, correct interpretation of any of them exists. We only try to capture their basic ideas. Keep in mind while reading the following descriptions that few people are "true believers"; most individuals pick and choose the best ideas from each philosophy. Furthermore, it will be helpful for you to read these points of view sympathetically. In other words, try to see the world from each perspective. After reading, ask yourself which view you find most appealing and why. Why do the other two approaches seem wrong? Ask your study partners and classmates the same questions.

This book will not assert that one approach is more correct than any other. If we can give you something to think about, something to argue about, and something to help you understand the buzzing, booming social order a little better, then we will have accomplished our purpose. Ultimately, we hope to prod you into thinking about your basic assumptions, your visions about the world, and how your assumptions lead to positions on important contemporary issues. Although sociology is, in some measure, a science grounded in empirical investigation, it is also a branch of social philosophy.

## The Libertarian Point of View

Of the three approaches, the libertarian perspective is probably the easiest to describe, as libertarians pride themselves on their logical consistency and principled positions (which reaches absurdity in the eyes of critics). Libertarians hold individual freedom as their highest value. They believe that each person should have the right to do what he or she wishes if it does not directly coerce or interfere with the freedom of others. The libertarian strives to uphold individual rights in all ways. Although we tend to think of a single liberal/conservative dimension, libertarianism falls outside of this schema with its belief in governmental nonintervention in all realms of human affairs, economic as well as social.[2]

Although many social democrats and conservatives hold public office, few strict libertarians do. One reason is that libertarians are often perceived as extremists who are unwilling to compromise. This stems from their reliance on pure logic—cold logic, some might call it—to make their case. For instance, the 2000 Libertarian Party platform endorsed the following programs, which most Americans would find difficult to accept: (1) eliminating all restrictions on firearms and weapon ownership (presumably, although not explicitly, including nuclear and chemical weapons), (2) eliminating all restrictions on immigration, (3) eliminating all antipornography legislation, (4) ending all government operation and subsidy of schools, (5) abolishing the Border Patrol, Consumer Product Safety Commission, Environmental Protection Agency, Federal Aviation Administration, and Food and Drug Administration, (6) ending all "protective" labor legislation for women and children, and (7) terminating U.S. membership in and financial support for the United Nations. In conventional political terms, libertarians are very conservative on economic issues (ultimately opposing all government regulation of businesses) and very liberal on social issues (allowing any and all acts that do not directly harm another person). How have libertarians come to adopt such views?

These positions are derived from the libertarians' understanding of human nature, especially the belief that individuals are responsible for their own actions. If people are successful, it is because they have the skills that enable them to be successful: They have chosen to be successful. They are hard-working, sincere, honest, diligent, and educated. These traits are ones that are not inherited but are acquired through personal effort and moral strength. Of course, the libertarian would not deny that some things are hereditary, but those are seen as less important. Likewise, the libertarian does not deny that some individuals have social handicaps—race, parents' income, sex; however, the libertarian believes that in a fair society discrimination would not exist and, anyway, people should be able to overcome these obstacles without government help. This view may strike some as naive, but it follows from a belief in free will. (We would do well to recall in all the philosophies we examine matters of degree, rather than absolutes.) The libertarian believes that people are rational decision makers, relatively free to do what they wish; success or failure in this life is due to each individual's own efforts. The libertarian believes you are free to get an "A" or "D" in this course, and the fact that you attended a poor high school, just split up with your lover, or your grandmother recently died does not alter your own responsibility for the grade you receive. The libertarian, of course, has no objection to voluntary charity and other forms of communal support, but these forms of aid cannot be coerced.

From this belief in individual effort follows the libertarian's view of government. The libertarian assumes, in Henry David Thoreau's words, "that government is best which governs least." Since people have the knowledge and ability to make themselves happy and successful (if they choose), it follows that government can best serve its citizens by maximizing their freedom. This position derives from the writings of eighteenth- and nineteenth-century British liberals, such as Adam Smith, John Stuart Mill, and Jeremy Bentham, who mistrusted the power of the state. These thinkers, and others who followed them, raised the individual to a pinnacle of power in the social universe. They also believed reason would ultimately provide the means by which human beings could live happily with each other. If everyone would try to maximize his or her own happiness, without infringing on the rights of others, the world would be a congenial place in which to live.

The greatest sin for the libertarian is coercion. Although libertarians recognize that some people can coerce other people (muggers or rapists, for instance), libertarians' primary concern is the power that is taken away from individuals by the government. Although at first this concentration of power might seem innocent—someone has to provide for national defense and for a police force to prevent anarchy—power can easily be misused. As the American revolutionary Thomas Paine wrote in *Common Sense* (1776): "Society in every state is a blessing, but government, even in its best state, is but a necessary evil; in its worst state, an intolerable one." Libertarian economist Murray Rothbard used the metaphor of the state as "a criminal band" to explain the libertarian philosophy.[3]

As a result, the libertarian believes passionately that the government should not entangle itself in the private lives of its citizens. If a person wishes to have sexual relations with a (willing) sheep, so be it. If someone chooses to use heroin or commit suicide without involving others, that is no cause for concern. The government should not protect people from themselves. Thus, rape is not a crime against the social order but rather a crime that violently eliminates the right of a woman to refuse intercourse. All crimes are crimes against individuals, not against society—an argument to which the conservative would object.

One problem in libertarian theory concerns the boundaries of coercion. When are a person's rights infringed? A libertarian believes people should be allowed to play music if they wish, but suppose they do this at 3:00 in the morning in your dormitory. Are they infringing on your rights? There are no easy answers to these conflicts of rights. The libertarian, more than the conservative or the social democrat, is likely to side with the actor, rather than with the person that the act inconveniences.

In the realm of economics, the libertarians' position is *laissez-faire* (translated from the French: "leave it alone"). This concept, derived from the writings of the eighteenth-century Scottish economist Adam Smith, refers to the theory that the government should not attempt to manipulate the economy. The economy is best stabilized through the laws of supply and demand. When more people want something, its price increases. Price increases will typically increase the supply (because of the hope of greater profit) and will decrease the demand, and this increased supply and decreased demand will, in turn, decrease price. When the government subsidizes a product or action by interfering with the free market, such as through tax breaks, more will be produced than can be justified by the demand. The economy should operate by the rational decisions of free people. This assumes a "free" market, not one artificially controlled by large monopolies or cartels. Social democrats are likely to object to laissez-faire economics and government nonintervention on this point because, they claim, the market is not truly free.

Another problem with libertarian theory is its border with anarchy. Indeed, anarchy is closely related to libertarianism, with the primary difference being that libertarians accept the fundamental right to property, whereas most (left-wing) anarchists do not. In prioritizing freedom, the libertarian places less emphasis on equality and order. The libertarian would qualify this by saying that with rational human beings working together for their common ends, order will emerge, and that equality means only equality of opportunity, rather than equality of outcome. Equality of opportunity is always present in libertarian theory because of the free will inherent in life. The great virtue of libertarians is their lust for freedom; their great failing is their cold-hearted lack of compassion for their neighbors who simply cannot keep up.

## The Conservative Point of View

Ambrose Bierce, in his *Devil's Dictionary,* defined a conservative as "a statesman who is enamoured of existing evils, as distinguished from the liberal, who wishes to replace them with others."[4] There is some truth in this sardonic comment. Conservatives do have a high regard for the tried and true, and fret about the new and untested.

The term *conservative* is derived from French political thought during the Napoleonic era and refers to a guardian of principles of justice and the nation's civilized heritage. Conservatism largely originated from opposition to the radical changes brought about by the French Revolution. Sociologist Robert Nisbet, in tracing the history of sociological thought, made a cogent case that sociology is derived from conservative political thought with its love for community, order, and authority, although relatively few sociologists today would define themselves as politically conservative.[5]

Russell Kirk, a leading conservative theorist, argued that conservatism is not really a political system or an ideology.[6] He made this claim because conservatives are in favor of preserving what has come before—that is, whatever has worked for a society in the past. Thus, a Peruvian conservative would legitimately differ from a Swiss conservative, who would differ from a Kenyan conservative. Unlike the libertarian, who has the same principles wherever she or he might be, the conservative's policies are based on the society in which he or she lives. As Alexander Hamilton noted: "What may be good in Philadelphia may be bad at Paris and ridiculous at Petersburgh."[7] If an innovation (e.g., Social Security or enforced racial equality) has proven successful, despite the original opposition of the conservative, the conservative will now support it. Conservatives do not suggest that any single set of policies is necessarily superior.

Kirk, making particular reference to British and American conservative writings, pointed to a set of "first principles" that are shared by most conservatives.[8] We shall draw heavily on his analysis.

Unlike the libertarian who sees human beings as fundamentally rational and basically decent, conservatives believe that humans are imperfect. Human nature is faulty and, as a result, no perfect social system can ever be devised. The conservative sadly concludes that all we can hope for is a reasonably happy, just, and fair society. Finding absolute goodness is no more likely than finding a unicorn. The human lot (perhaps due to "original sin") is to live in a world where some evil, misery, and unfairness exist. We can't eliminate pain; we can only hope to control it. The conservative perspective is most likely to present human beings in an unflattering, pessimistic fashion. Conservatives are apt to agree to some extent with the seventeenth-century British moral philosopher Thomas Hobbes that human beings without government to control them are destined to live a life that is "solitary, poor, nasty, brutish, and short." [9] This belief in the weaknesses of human nature leads the conservative to accept the rightful place of a variety of social institutions to control these excesses.

Most conservatives include God in their social equation. That is, they accept the existence of a "transcendent moral order"—moral authority that cannot be challenged by other people.[10] Conservatives reject the libertarian credo that individuals should do their own thing. They believe in a moral authority that is set by divine principle or "natural law," an issue that emerged in the appointment of senator John Ashcroft to be attorney general of the United States.

Conservatives also accept the value of social continuity—preferring the devil they know to the one they are yet to meet. They believe most changes are for the worse, and so changes should be made gradually, cautiously, and often not at all. The church serves in some regard as the model for the state. Just as theology changes very slowly—after all, it is supposed to be God's will—so should secular law. The radicalness of revolution, particularly the French and Russian Revolutions, is profoundly frightening to conservatives. Implicit in conservative thought is a deep respect for the past. The wisdom of the past has been replaced by the foolish babble of the present. This romanticism for what has come before leads some to claim that conservatives are reactionary. Yet, it is not so much that conservatives revere particular historical figures; rather, they revere the trial-and-error learning to which they are heir. In eighteenth-century conservative philosopher Edmund Burke's words: "The individual is foolish, but the species is wise." [11]

Finally, conservatives share with libertarians the belief that everyone should not be treated equally. While social democrats wish to minimize class divisions, conservatives believe that classes produce a healthy diversity in a society. Leveling social classes leads to a stagnant society. If all people are equal, there is no need for anyone to exert himself or herself to do better; motivation is lost. Furthermore, conservatives cherish the existence of other social institutions besides government. They see the church, the community, and the family as particularly important social forces that have authority equaling or surpassing that of the government. The state, on the other hand, is a secondary or artificial institution, not derived from the natural relations of human beings.

For the conservative, government is not the evil that it is for the libertarian; it is just secondary. When other social institutions have failed, then government must intervene. As a result, conservatives often believe government involvement should staunch the tide of moral decay and, as long as the economic system is functioning, allow businesses to operate without government regulation. The conservative is not afraid of the facts that some people are poor and some people fail; these unfortunate facts simply represent the natural diversity of a social system.

Unlike social democrats, who admire a just and strong government, and libertarians, who mistrust all government, conservatives are neutral toward government. It is simply not the most important thing in society. While government is needed to preserve order, it is weakened by the frailty of human nature and doesn't compare with natural, primary organizations. Conservatives' greatest virtue is order, and, according to Russell Kirk, their particular vice is selfishness—the desire to let things rest in a way favorable to them. Despite popular stereotypes, conservatives are no more anachronisms than social democrats are long-haired firebrands.

## The Social Democratic Point of View

Of the three philosophies, the broadest and least clear is what we have termed *social democracy*. Although some Americans are proud to call themselves libertarians and conservatives, few Americans call themselves social democrats. In the United States, such people will typically refer to themselves as liberals or progressives and will be called by their opponents leftists, left-liberals, or socialists. *Liberal,* once a term of honor, has become scorned by many as the dreaded "L-word." None of these terms really do justice to this social and political approach. Perhaps liberal comes closest, but the history of the word is so muddled with libertarianism that it confuses more than enlightens. (Some of the founders of libertarianism were known as liberals.) So, we have chosen to use a European term to refer to this group of Americans. In Germany, the major left-liberal party is known as the Social Democratic Party. In other European countries, the leading party on the noncommunist left is a social democratic party— committed to democracy but also to a strong, involved government. Although this term does not precisely fit the situation in the United States, it is the best available. We have combined an uneasy blend of contemporary liberalism, welfare-state economics, democratic socialism, and progressivism. More than the other two approaches, the social democratic perspective casts a wide net, possibly slightly too wide.

Unlike conservative theory, social democratic philosophy accepts the possibility of the betterment of human beings. It is not that people are naturally good, but that they can be made to be good. Social policies can bring out the best in people. This perspective can be seen most clearly in the social democrat's fight for civil rights legislation. The social democrat starts with the assumption that all people have been created equal and that they should be treated equally. Of course, in the tough, cold, real world they are not always treated in this way. Thus, in the early 1960s, social democrats vigorously and successfully fought to have the United States Congress pass a civil rights law that would outlaw discrimination in restaurants and other places of public accommodation. They believed that by preventing whites from segregating racial minorities, they could increase toleration among the races. Social democrats believed that changing laws would eventually produce a change in attitudes—that "stateways" precede folkways. In this case, at least, the philosophy worked. For example, white southerners, forced by law to eat at the same coffee shops as black southerners, discovered the moral order of society did not come crashing down. Southern politicians, such as George Wallace, discovered when they were forced to desegregate that they really did not mind blacks as much as they claimed they would. Civil rights legislation provides a textbook case of how government involvement led to positive moral outcomes and a presumed improvement in human nature.

Perhaps most central to the social democrat's philosophy is the positive role of government. President Andrew Jackson provided a wonderful metaphor that captures the social democrat's attitude toward government: "There are no necessary evils in government. Its evils exist only in its abuses. If it would confine itself to equal protection and, as Heaven does its rains, shower its favors alike on the high and the low, the rich and the poor, it would be an unqualified blessing."[12]

State power need not necessarily be scary; it can increase human happiness. Likewise, change need not be the fearsome foe pictured by the conservative. Although some changes can be harmful (no one is in favor of every possible change), other changes, even radical ones, are sometimes for the best. The social democrat sees a multitude of crimes committed by a multitude of governments as not necessarily characteristic of every strong government. The obligation of the government to promote equality and justice must take priority. In this desire for equality, the social democrat parts company with the libertarian and the conservative who welcome the diversity of a class system, a social system in which some succeed and others fail.

Behind this belief in equality lies a distinct view of motivation. Social democrats believe that people will work hard because that is the right thing to do. Unlike conservatives who are constantly complaining about the many people who try to cheat on welfare and try to get by without working, the social democrat believes that few people think that way. Most people have strong internal moral compasses, and while they are not perfect, they do have good hearts. The social democrat ultimately paints a rosier picture of human beings than does the conservative. The problems for the social democrat are those traditional social arrangements that prevent people from living happily and equally: racism, social inequality, gender discrimination, and prejudice against old people, and people of a different nationality, sexual orientation, or religion.

Ultimately, the primary problem for the social democrat is poverty; poverty destroys human dignity. In the words of former Democratic presidential candidate Adlai Stevenson: "A hungry man is not a free man."[13] This reflects the attitude of the social democrat, who is concerned with insuring that government takes an active role in preventing these offenses to human dignity and in working against poverty.

One of the problems with such a broad category as the social democratic perspective is that adherents have different attitudes about what the appropriate governmental response to poverty should be. Some (welfare-state liberals) wish to restrain the government's effect on the market to as little as is necessary to cure the symptoms of poverty. Such individuals favor a constellation of welfare programs to help those who are disadvantaged because of their social position. They also believe government should play an active role in combating the excesses of business. In contrast, some democratic socialists consider it appropriate for the government to manage large segments of the essential industrial and service economy of the nation. Thus, in Great Britain, the government controls areas of public transportation, much heavy industry, medical practice, and other areas of concern to the people as a whole. Some areas are left to private industry, but often these are not the most central industries and services. Critics have noted inadequacies of government intervention in all its forms and wonder whether an efficient government is ever possible.

In the area of morality, the social democrat often stands with the libertarian, although some who are called neoliberals or communitarians have begun to sound more like some conservatives. Since private institutions of religion and the family have no special position in social democratic thought (as they do for the conservative), the government should allow a full flowering of lifestyles. Morality is personal and relative, while economic insufficiency is public and objective. Morality is a matter of individual choice, whereas economic position is related to the social structure. Since morality has no special place in society, the social democrat thinks it unwarranted that some groups suffer discrimination by others because of differing beliefs and practices. For example, the social democrat finds it easy to support legislation prohibiting discrimination against homosexuals. Discrimination poses a structural barrier to the well-being of these citizens. A group's right to protection takes priority over an individual's freedom to discriminate.

The leading virtue for the social democrat is equality. Social democrats believe in the equality of opportunity, and many believe in the equality of outcome as well. There is a point below which a society should never let its citizens slip—a view not shared by the extreme libertarian or conservative. Just as equality is the social democrat's virtue, envy is the weakness. Some say that social democrats are envious failures, who wish to grab from the successful those rewards they have not been able to achieve through personal efforts. Social democrats who are personally successful may be accused of being naively optimistic, painting too rosy a picture of those they wish to aid. Redistribution of wealth is particularly appealing to those who have little; just as the status quo is appealing to those with much to lose.

## The Structure of the Text

In the remaining chapters, we use these three major standpoints to examine twelve controversial social issues. The issues were selected to reflect major sociological concepts, those found in most textbooks for introductory sociology and social problems courses. Each chapter emphasizes a major sociological concept and addresses a contemporary question that reflects on that concept. So, for example, when discussing culture, we ask whether violent content in entertainment harms people.

Each chapter begins with a short discussion of how the relevant concept has been treated in sociological writing. This does not replace the discussion in a larger textbook or in class but rather provides a basis for the discussion that follows. We try to present the major concept in a straightforward and simple fashion. In order to provide continuity among the concepts, we typically include in each chapter some discussion of the three major theoretical approaches to sociology: functionalism, conflict theory, and interactionism.

*Functionalists* see society as similar to a living creature. By this they mean that all of the systems (or "organs") of society are interrelated. The life of that society is a result or "function" of the interplay of these systems (for example, religion, the family, the economy, culture). The functionalist is likely to emphasize consensus and stability in a society. A smoothly functioning society is a stable society, which is a happy society. While functionalists do not totally ignore change, they de-emphasize it and see it as a threat to the functioning of the society, something that disturbs the systems in society. The functionalist believes that each system helps to preserve the society and that, when functioning properly, each system's form is best suited for its tasks. Furthermore, systems should mesh without conflict. For the functionalist, conflict should be avoided if possible. Conflict is perceived as dysfunctional because it undermines the smooth order of society. Thus, it is easy to see why functionalism is often defined as a conservative approach to society, although as a group of talented young sociologists (labeled *Neofunctionalists*) argue, this conservative bias is not inevitable.

Of course, it is not always easy to determine what the function of a social system is; as a result, functionalists distinguish between *manifest* and *latent* functions. The manifest functions are those that are easily observable. The family has a manifest function in providing for the systematic moral socialization of children. Latent functions are those which may be unintended and unseen. Some suggest the family has the latent function of preserving the sexual division of labor, of keeping women out of the work force. The problem with this approach is that one person's latent function may be another's oppression. Functionalism with its orientation toward the status quo may be charged with having an ideological bias in favor of the dominant classes.

*Conflict theory* presents a sharp contrast to functionalism. Contemporary society for the conflict theorist leaves a sour taste. Just as consensus is basic to the functionalist, struggle and change are central for the conflict theorist. This approach emphasizes that the existence of rival groups with contrary interests is inevitable and even healthy by preventing a stagnant society. The world can be a fierce place in such a view.

The conflict theorist is prone to ask: Who gains from current social arrangements? How are opposing groups trying to change systems or society? In practical terms, these sociologists tend to side with those whom they see as oppressed, so the conflict approach can easily be linked to the social democratic philosophy in its desire for change. In the conflict perspective, power is central, and because the wealthy and those with the greatest amount of resources hold power, they tend to run society in their own interest, unless others stand up against this social control.

*Interactionism*, the third major theoretical approach in sociology, is less overtly political than the other two. Interactionism focuses on the relations among individuals and the meanings these relations have for participants. It suggests that society has no inherent meaning but that individuals give meaning to events. A gunshot, for example, means nothing by itself; whether it is part of a murder, a prank, a hunting expedition, or a suicide depends on the context. Likewise, a minister and a drill sergeant will define a "curse" in very different terms; it would be the same word but with very different significance, provoking dissimilar reactions. The interactionist believes that meanings change over time and in negotiation with others. In the recent past, two men hugging in public would have been censured; today, such behavior is tolerated. Even those who might condemn this action if they assumed that the two men were gay, would quickly revise their attitudes if assured that the two were long-lost brothers. Behavior is subject to change in interpretation at a moment's notice.

Crucial to interactionist theory is the belief that human beings have the power to define their world. Unlike the functionalist and the conflict theorist, who both emphasize structure, the interactionist is likely to point to the power of individuals to create their own sets of meanings. Because of this emphasis on the power of the individual, we can liken interactionism to libertarianism; although, in this case, because of the generally apolitical stance of interactionism, the connection is tenuous.

After the examination of each broad sociological concept, there is a general examination of the chapter question. We present background material that will allow you to make sense of the fuss. Each question is controversial, and, while it cannot be dealt with in as much detail as the disputants might provide, we sketch a brief description of the basic issue. That section is followed by a discussion of how proponents of the libertarian, conservative, and social democratic points of view address the question. We have chosen to present the approaches in no particular order, choosing as the first perspective that which seems to be the most vehement about the issue under discussion. This is fair because the order in which one makes an argument affects how readers respond. By changing the order of discussion, we provide some semblance of balance.

We do not pretend to have provided an exhaustive treatment of any of these subjects; we hope only to give you enough material for debate and controversy and to make you consider the basis of your own beliefs. We do not encourage you to accept any particular perspective or, for that matter, any of the perspectives. We recognize that Marxism has not been adequately covered; neither have many non-American ideologies. Because of the breadth and diversity of each philosophy, some who hold that view may disagree with portions of our discussion. This may, in part, be due to our errors of understanding, and, may, in part, be attributed to the difficulty of describing a complex philosophy in simple terms. In presenting these issues, we have attempted to draw from a wide variety of sources, some of which rarely appear in reputable sociology textbooks. We have chosen quotations that are written in a lively fashion and capture the essence of an argument in a memorable way. Some of the sources make strange bedfellows, but at least we try to change the sheets frequently.

We then turn to a research case study that relates to the question being discussed. Our goal is to demonstrate how various styles and methodologies of research can be used to examine these theoretical questions. While the studies selected represent a variety of approaches to social problems, each is respectable. Even though the assumptions of each will be held up for scrutiny, they represent a collection of the best research that sociologists have to offer. (You might wish to read the original version of each of them.) Our point is that the debates are not mere idle speculations, but constitute empirical questions that researchers can study. Although the research does not provide a solution, it helps us recognize the dimensions of the problem.

The final section of each chapter connects the sociological concept with the particular question that we have addressed. Here we raise the basic issues that underlie the specific question. So, in the chapter that deals with race relations, we ask the possibly horrifying question: What is so wrong with discrimination? It is our belief that unless we understand the foundations of our beliefs, we cannot hold them strongly and steadfastly. While these broad questions are not destined to be answered totally satisfactorily, at least they have been raised, to fester or flower in your mind and in discussion. Remember that sociology ultimately is based on questions of human nature and addresses questions of how the social order should be organized. With that in mind, "Let the wild rumpus start!"

## For Further Study

### Conservative

Buckley, William F., and Charles R. Kesler, eds. *Keeping the Tablets: Modern American Conservative Thought*. New York: Harper & Row. 1988.

Hodgson, Godfrey. *The World Turned Right Side Up: A History of the Conservative Ascendancy in America*. Boston: Houghton Mifflin. 1996.

Kirk, Russell, ed. *The Portable Conservative Reader*. New York: Penguin, 1982.

Nisbet, Robert. *Conservatism*. Minneapolis: University of Minnesota Press, 1986.

### Libertarian

Bergland, David. *Libertarianism in One Lesson*. 3rd ed. Costa Mesa, CA: Orpheus Publications, 1986. (Available from Libertarian Party headquarters).

Friedman, Milton. *Capitalism and Freedom*. Chicago: University of Chicago Press, 1962.

Hazlitt, Henry. *Economics in One Lesson*. New York: Arlington House, 1979.

Machan, Tibor R., ed. *The Libertarian Reader*. Totowa, NJ: Rowman and Littlefield, 1982.

### Social Democratic

Bellah, Robert N., Richard Madsen, William M. Sullivan, Ann Swidler, and Steven M. Tipton. *The Good Society*. New York: Knopf, 1991.

Putnam, Robert. *Bowling Alone: The Collapse and Revival of American Community*. New York: Simon & Schuster, 2000.

Wolfe, Alan. *Moral Freedom: The Search for Virtue in a World of Choice*. New York: Norton, 2001.

## General

Nisbet, Robert. *The Sociological Tradition.* New York: Basic Books, 1966.
Sowell, Thomas. *A Conflict of Visions.* New York: William Morrow, 1987.
Wolfe, Alan, ed. *America at Century's End.* Berkeley: University of California Press, 1991.

## *Notes and References*

1. Thomas Sowell, A *Conflict of Visions* (New York: Morrow, 1987), p. 15.
2. "All That's Not Left Is Not Right," *Reason* (October 1986): 16.
3. Mark Paul, "Seducing the Left: The Third Party Wants *You*" *Mother Jones* (May 5, 1980): 47.
4. Ambrose Bierce, *The Devil's Dictionary* (New York: Dover, 1958), p. 24.
5. Robert Nisbet, *The Sociological Tradition* (New York: Basic Books, 1966). See also Everett C. Ladd, Jr., and Seymour Martin Lipset, *The Divided Academy: Professors and Politics* (New York: McGraw-Hill, 1975), pp. 107–115, 369.
6. Russell Kirk, ed., "Introduction," *The Portable Conservative Reader* (New York: Penguin, 1982), p. xiv.
7. Quoted in Thomas Sowell, *A Conflict of Visions* (New York: William Morrow, 1987), p. 34.
8. Ibid., pp. xv–xviii.
9. Thomas Hobbes, *Leviathan* (New York: Collier, 1962; original ed., 1651), p. 100.
10. Kirk, *The Portable Conservative Reader,* p. xv.
11. Ibid., p. xvi.
12. President Andrew Jackson's message to Congress vetoing the Bank Bill, July 10, 1832. *Bartlett's Familiar Quotations,* 13th ed. (Boston: Little, Brown, 1955), p. 399.
13. Adlai Stevenson, campaign speech, September 6, 1952, Kasson, MN. *Bartlett's Familiar Quotations,* 13th ed. (Boston: Little, Brown, 1955), p. 1086.

# CHAPTER ONE

# Culture: Is Violent Entertainment Harmful?

■ Few concepts have had the longevity and significance in social science writing as has culture. Culture reflects our humanity; it differentiates us from other animals. But what do we mean by *culture?* Among the many hundreds of definitions put forth, anthropologist Melville Herskovits defined culture in this general fashion: "Culture is essentially a construct that describes the total body of belief, behavior, knowledge, sanctions, values, and goals that mark the way of life of any people. That is, though a culture may be treated by the student as capable of objective description, in the final analysis it comprises the things that people have, the things they do, and what they think."[1]

This vastly broad definition suggests that culture is fluid. Within a society, culture includes material artifacts (such as the flag or works of art), behaviors (handshaking or kissing), or social expectations (the concept of honor). This last category has two important aspects—norms and values. *Norms* refer to rules that specify appropriate and inappropriate behavior, *shared expectations* that people have of each other. *Values* refer to the *shared conceptions* people use to evaluate the desirability or correctness of objects, acts, feelings, ideas, or events.

People should not assume norms and values are universally agreed upon or that people consciously think of them when they act. According to interactionist theory, both values and norms are abstractions. People, say the interactionists, do not behave as they do because they are consciously or deliberately attempting to follow a set of rules; rather, they do what seems best in the specific situation in which they find themselves. Although the concepts of values and norms are useful for social scientists searching for regularities in behaviors (for instance, people behave *as if* these things exist), they may not tell us *why* people behave as they do.

Culture is not an innate part of human nature; it must be learned, even though it is made possible by our biological equipment. Socialization, the process of learning a society's rules and expectations, is critical to human development. From about age two to about age fourteen, a child is transformed from an egocentric savage to a responsible, civilized human being—a most remarkable change in only a dozen years. Learning a language, religious values, gender appropriate behaviors, social traditions such as sharing, eating with a knife and fork, finding and maintaining friendships all constitute a daunting amount of cultural information for individuals to absorb.

Another remarkable aspect of culture is its diversity. Behaviors and norms that are appropriate in one society are inappropriate in others. As an example, what people happily eat in one country can be anathema elsewhere. While most people in the United States might recoil at eating grasshoppers, some Mexicans eat them like potato chips. Most women in the United States do not marry at fourteen, but some young women in India do. Male friends hold hands in Italy, but would attract glances or worse for doing so in Indiana. Some societies accord twins a place of honor; other societies see twins as a curse. These marked differences between societies raise an important issue: Are any cultural traditions universally moral, or are particular cultural traditions right for each society? This is the distinction between *cultural absolutism* and *cultural relativism*. Is racism or infanticide absolutely wrong, or should we refrain from making these judgments? If we cannot say that another culture is acting immorally, how can we set standards for ourselves? If everything is right, then, by implication, nothing is wrong.

At one extreme, *ethnocentrism* refers to a tendency to believe that one's own culture is vastly superior to others, an assessment usually made from evaluating other cultures using our own culture's standards. At the other extreme, a *cultural relativist* argues that every culture must be judged on its own terms and beliefs. Although most social scientists would grant that different societies have different traditions, few deny all standards of moral propriety.

No aspect of culture is more important than language. One of the most tragic stories in the Bible is that of the Tower of Babel, in which the previously monolingual humanity was transformed into hundreds of groups of people who spoke mutually incomprehensible languages. Historically, we have had only modest success trying to understand each other.

The study of language suggests that it shapes the ways in which people see the world. This approach to the social effects of language on thought and perception is known as the *linguistic relativity hypothesis,* or the *Sapir-Whorf hypothesis,* after the two American linguists who stated it the most emphatically.[2] Any group develops specialized vocabulary for topics that are important to it. Here are some simple examples of how culture and language are related: While many outside the snow belt have a limited vocabulary for talking about "this white stuff," the Central Alaskan Yupik Eskimos have at least a dozen words for snow (or several dozen if one is liberal about what counts).[3] The Hanunoo people in the Philippines have names for ninety-two different varieties of rice. Different groups divide even the color spectrum very differently.[4] Linguistic relativists suggest people admit some things to their consciousness (they "see" them) while filtering out other things for which they do not have words. According to this theory, language is not only a basic means by which culture and information are communicated, but it also structures the way in which we experience the world.

Sometimes cultural objects or traditions may be the subject of considerable dispute. Societies—particularly modern, industrial societies—are far from homogeneous. Take the case of works of art. Sociologist David Halle found that most people place objects on their walls and that they appreciate the "aesthetic" qualities of these objects.[5] Yet, there is much divergence on what is beautiful. What is considered high art by cultural elites may be scorned as ugly, boring, or obscene by others. Critics, in turn, may sneer at art that achieves mass popularity, decrying it as "bourgeois" or "lowbrow." Aesthetic power is in the eye of the beholder, but also may be involved in political battles within a society. These divisions are frequently linked to educational level or social class.

Just as some individuals are wealthier than others (with all that this permits them to achieve), French sociologist Pierre Bourdieu suggested that people differ in their *cultural capital*.[6] Those with a rich cultural background, in terms of elite aesthetic traditions, have advantages over those whose background is more limited. Communicating well with different kinds of people is important, but the ability to impress influential people is crucial. If people associated with powerful organizations value some cultural information highly, typically that associated with being an "educated person" or a "good citizen," then having that cultural knowledge is vital. Knowledge of Shakespeare is valuable not only in itself, but also because it allows you to present yourself as a person of sophistication and distinction.

# ▪ Question:

*Is violent entertainment harmful?*

> *The culture of carnage surrounding our children is turning some of them into killers.*
> —Sen. Joseph Lieberman (D-Conn.)

Technological innovations alter cultures by giving rise to new artistic expressions and an unprecedented ability to deliver those cultural objects to masses of consumers. We reside in what communication theorist Marshall McLuhan referred to as a "global village." Mass media can now simultaneously reach almost everyone in the world. The Internet, movies, musical recordings, television and videogames, all relatively recent phenomena, have transformed society into a vast audience and market for cultural products. People now have an unprecedented array of cultural objects from which to choose.

Among the most popular and commercially successful cultural products are those that depict the harming of a person: violent entertainment. Rapper Eminem, whose albums rank among the best-selling of recent years, writes many songs depicting violent images, such as the charming and subtle "Still Don't Give a Fuck," where he raps about wanting to "crush your skull 'till your brains leaks [sic] out of your veins/and bust open like broken water mains."[7] Kid Rock, Snoop Doggy Dogg, and Marilyn Manson might be sympathetic. Professional wrestling, with its staged violence, has been the most watched program on cable television. The wildly popular computer games *Quake III* and *Unreal Tournament* involve people competing to see who kills virtual versions of other players in the greatest numbers. Two recent films, *Crouching Tiger, Hidden Dragon* and *Gladiator*, both with heavy doses of violence, received artistic kudos and commercial success and were leading competitors for best picture Oscar. Critics rave over *The Sopranos* on HBO. What is wrong with us?

Although Americans have many diverse and nonviolent cultural tastes, the undeniable popularity of violent entertainment should give us pause. If you are like most students, you have had teachers who have impressed on you their belief that the appreciation of art, film, literature, and music has the power to make you a better person. Does it not then follow that some cultural forms can also make you a lesser person? Many historical and contemporary battles are fought over how "culture works against people." One side advocates that some art, literature, and films should be banned, censored, or restricted because they promote values that lead to harmful patterns of behavior. Others believe that a society's character can be judged by the extent to which diverse artistic and cultural expressions are allowed to flourish, including ones that are morally, politically, and sexually controversial.

Interest in the potential harmful effects of violent entertainment surged in the wake of reports that the teenagers responsible for the infamous murders of their fellow students at Columbine High School were influenced in part by exposure to violent video games and song lyrics. The 2000 presidential campaign featured political candidates trying to outdo each other in offering harsh condemnations of violent entertainment. Senators Lieberman and McCain—a Democrat and a Republican—introduced a bill in the U.S. Senate, the Media Violence Labeling Act of 2000, "to provide for the development, use and enforcement of an easily recognizable system in plain English for labeling content in audio and visual media products and services."[8]

The Media Violence Labeling Act of 2000 proposed increasing the government's role in regulating the production and consumption of American culture beyond the existing voluntary movie, recording, television, and videogame ratings systems. Debating whether violent content in entertainment harms people, as well as what to do about it, raises two significant questions: First, at a general level, what responsibility do government and individual citizens have for cultural values in society? Second, what actions should government and individuals take, if any, to define certain cultural expressions as harmful, such as violent entertainment, and to restrict them?

James Davison Hunter has written that U.S. society is a battlefield of "culture wars," in which progressives and traditionalists tussle over appropriate values and their dissemination.[9] The conflict theorist approaches this issue by examining how different social groups compete over what cultural objects and values to promote or restrict. The conflict theorist also attends to how powerful interests, such as business, organized religion, and government officials weigh in on such debates, and how artists are treated as a consequence. The functionalist looks to culture as a mechanism for socializing people to values that help society to function well. Some cultural forms may be perceived as threatening because they undermine the smooth working order of society. To the extent that some cultural expressions, such as violent entertainment (or, historically, comic books and rock music), are viewed as promoting harmful behaviors in youth, functionalists are concerned by the impact these might have on social stability. Interactionists center their analyses on how people construct the meanings of the cultural objects they consume. Interactionists believe cultural meanings change over time and in negotiation with others, which requires investigating how people define a cultural object as "violent" or as "promoting harmful behavior."

Other nations provide diverse examples of managing the perceived potential of culture to work against people. For example, in countries governed under *Shaaria*, or Islamic religious law, most western television programs are banned because they display cultural values that conflict with ones promoted under *Shaaria*. Some Western democracies, such as Canada and the United Kingdom, force broadcasters to restrict the ages of viewers and the hours that violent content can be screened or televised much more strictly than the United States presently does. More authoritarian countries go to the extreme of limiting media freedom, and censoring and punishing artists whose cultural products are believed to produce harmful and potentially rebellious behaviors. Alternatively, millions of American television viewers watch comedy routines on late night talk shows that sharply criticize and mock the nation's most powerful government figures. Such satirical exercises demonstrate an amazing liberty in a world where in some countries, overheard criticisms or jokes about political leaders can lead to beatings, imprisonment, or worse.

Some people assume only very conservative organizations try to censor "harmful" culture. Protests by "family values" groups—like Reverend Donald Wildmon and the American Family Association—against the "moral indecency" of programs such as Howard Stern's radio broadcasts and *South Park* have been heavily publicized. As former mayor of New York, Rudy Giuliani attempted—without success—to force publicly funded art museums to refrain from funding or showing works that offend large numbers of citizens. Yet, some feminists and left-wing activists also attempt to ban cultural expressions they find objectionable or "politically incorrect." As an example, several college newspapers recently printed a full-page advertisement by conservative activist David Horowitz that vigorously rejected the idea that the U.S. government should pay reparations to African Americans for slavery. After the ad ran at Brown University and the University of Wisconsin-Madison (among others), student protesters demanded that the newspapers' editors resign, and they also removed copies of newspapers that had not yet been distributed and destroyed them.[10] Gay activists have attempted to have Dr. Laura's talk radio show canceled because of views that they find objectionable. These activists are surely not her regular listeners; they simply wish others to be unable to hear her positions. People from diametrically opposed political perspectives are willing to censor or outright ban cultural expressions that they do not consider morally decent.

## The Conservative Point of View

Have you ever read a book, viewed a painting, or seen a film you found so hurtful or offensive, you would gladly prevent others from being exposed to it? For the conservative, encountering such objects is a reminder of the saying "Don't be so open-minded that your brains fall out."[11] From this perspective, allowing harmful culture to go unimpeded is foolish. According to Senator Sam Brownback (R-Kansas), in a statement jointly backed by the American Medical Association, the American Psychological Association, the American Academy of Pediatrics, and the American Academy of Child and Adolescent Psychiatry, "the verdict on violent entertainment is now in . . . well over a thousand studies point overwhelmingly to a causal connection between media violence and aggressive behavior in some children."[12] If violent entertainment produces harmful behaviors in the real world, particularly in children, the state must recognize and prevent that danger. Conservatives believe that government has a role in promoting positive, healthy values, which may require restrictions on violent entertainment, especially its availability to youth—to you. This is particularly evident if we come to believe that audiences may be moved by the messages, inspired to become violent themselves. As "morality czar" William Bennett put it, "in the matter of the protection of our children, nothing should be off-limits." Should people "develop, market, promote and sell something regardless of how degrading or destructive it is?"[13]

However, whether research studies actually demonstrate that exposure to violent entertainment produces aggression, particularly violent acts by teenagers, is very much in dispute. The Federal Trade Commission's report *Marketing Violent Entertainment to Children* recognizes that "exposure to violence in entertainment media alone does not cause a child to commit a violent act and that it is not the sole, or even necessarily the most important, factor contributing to youth aggression."[14] We investigate the inconclusiveness of research on the effects of violent entertainment later in this chapter. Some researchers do conclude, however, that existing data demonstrate "a high correlation in youth between exposure to media violence and aggressive, and at times violent behavior . . . as well as increased acceptance of violent behavior in others."[15] Culture has effects on people. For conservatives, any such evidence confirms a need for government action.

The Media Violence Labeling Act of 2000 requires labeling content and legally enforcing minimum ages for purchase and viewing of entertainment products of all stripes. Implicit in this policy is establishing criteria that correlate a particular level of violence with an age appropriate for viewing that violence. Producers of films, television, and videogames have voluntarily established their own ratings of the level of violence in their products, fearing that if they failed to do so, the government would issue more forceful and binding definitions than industry would on its own. Hence, we have the present system of ratings we see when attending a film, buying a videogame, or watching television.

Because they urge that violent entertainment should be condemned and restricted in both content and sales, conservatives are accused of censorship and thereby ignoring first amendment rights to free speech. It is important to remember the designation "conservative" here includes both Democrats and Republicans. Members of both parties are on record as supporting a conservative view that harmful culture should be staunched by legislative action. While censorship is a word with harsh implications, as a practical matter, the idea is also more mundane than we normally think. Often it implies selection by those with the authority to make decisions: such as giving librarians the authority to decide what books to purchase. In addition, we ask people not to swear or discuss controversial or adult matters in front of children, and more than a few parents cover their children's eyes, both metaphorically and physically, to conceal problematic content. Try explaining the explicit details of the Monica Lewinsky/Bill Clinton scandal to an inquisitive five year old—or to your grandparents!

Is there, however, at the governmental level, any proper use of censorship and/or restrictions on culture and entertainment? The conservative point of view offers a defense for such actions, as Irving Kristol wrote:

> We all know, and social scientists too, that the ways in which we use our minds and imaginations do shape our characters and help define us as persons. That those who certainly know this are nevertheless moved to deny it merely indicates how dogmatic resistance to the idea of censorship can—like most dogmatism—result in a mindless insistence on the absurd. . . . For the plain fact is that none of us is a complete civil libertarian. We all believe that there is some point at which the public authorities ought to step in to limit the "self-expression" of an individual or a group, even where this might seriously be intended as a form of artistic expression, and even where the artistic expression is between consenting adults. A playwright or theatrical director, might in this crazy world of ours, find someone willing to commit suicide on the stage, as called for by the script. We would not allow that—any more than we would permit scenes of real torture on the stage, even if the victim were a willing masochist. And I know of no one, now matter how free in spirit, who argues that we ought to permit gladiatorial contests in Yankee Stadium, similar to those once performed in the Coliseum at Rome, even if only consenting adults were involved. The basic point is one that Walter Berns has powerfully argued: No society can be utterly indifferent to the ways its citizens publicly entertain themselves. . . . The desirability of self-government depends on the character of the people who govern. It should not permit people to capriciously corrupt themselves.[16]

Conservatives are embroiled in a culture war. The oft-used expression "family values" is a sincere battle cry to instill cultural expressions that affirm educational, religious, and traditional values over "degenerative" ones. The stakes here, for conservatives, are enormous. Cultivating in children cultural values that instill love for community, faith, and order is imperative. If cultural institutions such as entertainment businesses contribute to moral decay, then government must intervene to counter the threat. Conservatives acknowledge that some adults choose to consume destructive culture and perceive this decision as evidence of the absence of strong moral fiber. The willingness of businesses to supply consumers with the violent culture they seek is evidence of a society lacking moral resolve.

## The Social Democratic Point of View

While social democrats acknowledge the potential harmfulness of some cultural expressions (here they differ from libertarians who reject any mandatory labeling or restriction of culture), they are ambivalent about placing restrictions on culture. Violent entertainment does test the social democrat's commitment to an unrestricted freedom of cultural expression. Social democrats do not advocate making violent entertainment easily available to children, and both conservatives and social democrats offer equally vociferous condemnations of violent entertainment's content. But though both might bash Eminem's lyrics (although they disagree on what they find most repulsive), they differ in what to do about them. For the social democrat, censoring culture is a slippery slope. If not used carefully, such actions can be used to stifle political criticism and social action, enshrining the status quo against those who are pushing for change. Consider the range of the 1934 Legion of Decency's Production Code Administration that regulated what content movies of that time could depict.

> The production code did more than clean up dirty movies . . . the code also prohibited the questioning of social institutions and norms. No Hollywood picture could ridicule a religious figure or faith, and the flag could not be shown disrespectfully. The court system could never appear unjust. The sanctity of marriage and home had to be upheld, divorce could never be positive and adultery could never seem exciting. . . . The existence of drug trafficking, homosexuality, miscegenation, prostitution, and venereal disease couldn't be depicted.[17]

Making moral judgments is a matter of individual choice, something that should be personal and relative, as long as there are no clear limitations on the rights and dignity of others.

Yet, a key concern for social democrats in considering censorship is whether the cultural images support or undercut issues of equality, and, thus, social democrats do not oppose all forms of government censorship. For example, are all depictions of violence the same? Are depictions of violence against men as serious as depictions of violence against women? Are depictions of violence against gays particularly dangerous? What about depictions of violence that might lead to racial and ethnic violence? Isn't there some legitimate right to protect the most vulnerable groups from harm? We sometimes speak of this as involving "identity politics" or "political correctness," but this recognizes that culture can have different effects depending on the power arrangements of society. The bloody female body might carry no more horror than a bloody male body, but in a society in which males are typically the source of violence, and females often their victims, the consequences of these images may differ, and as a result government action might need to differ. Hate speech legislation is such an example: Insults can depend on their context, and context should matter, says the social democrat. Social democratically inclined feminists often argue for limitations on sexualized portrayals of women, particularly when these images are linked to violence, seeing in this "pornography" the potential for attacks on women. It is the vulnerable who are the special responsibility of the State.

It is well to remember that an urge to sanitize the world can mean neglecting to mention institutional sources of inequality, such as the court system or the economy. Social democrats are concerned with the capacity of cultural depictions to divert attention away from solving real problems of injustice. Violent content in entertainment might hurt people in the abstract, but actual violence hurts real people concretely and immediately. Clear causes of real violence demand action in more urgent ways than wishing away their depictions in entertainment media. As one pundit noted "the real danger to society isn't imaginary violence in music or movies. Youth violence is nearly always a response to brutalization—by families, by peers, by police or by punitive "zero tolerance" juvenile crime laws . . . but that is reality, not politics."[18]

Some violent entertainment, like rap, also depicts the reality of violence in artists' lives. To vilify this "storytelling" without considering the truth in the stories constitutes "a form of empty moral grandstanding, a shameful attempt by politicians to earn political favor and ride a public frenzy about crime while at the same time remaining unable and often unwilling to tackle the real problems that plague America's cities and their poorest black children."[19] The social democrat's great passion is ending inequality. For the social democrats, controversial cultural expressions can awaken people from their sleep, express the reality of violence in some everyday lives, and spur people to alleviate sources of social and economic dispossession that help produce that violence.

Yet, censorship doesn't derive from government alone. Social democrats, unlike libertarians, are troubled by the prospect that private business will respond to pressure by censoring products themselves:

> Few people understand that censorship isn't limited to governmental entities; that large corporations are deeply and continuously engaged in censorship of movies, TV programs and magazines, as well as music . . . that when retail outlets as large as Wal-Mart or Blockbuster Video refuse to sell certain kinds of CDs or movies, those CDs and movies are less likely to get made in the first place. Few people realize how large corporations—using marketing, legal and other constraints—work to limit our creative, informational, and cultural offerings by pursuing safe noncontroversial content. One of their many side effects is that smaller retailers who will sell more diverse kinds of creative offerings are driven from business, making the things Wal-Mart and Blockbuster don't like unavailable not only in their chain outlets, but everywhere.[20]

Should we let a thousand flowers bloom, even if some are weeds? A society where culture is inhibited and dictated by a controlling government and big business is too dangerous to individual and group freedoms to risk. The social democrat is torn between the earnest desire to protect and mistrust for the motives of those who might do the protection.

## The Libertarian Point of View

Libertarians decry the state taking away peoples' power to make their own decisions. Government should not mandate tastes or restrict in any way what artists make available to the marketplace. Cultural products, violent or not, ought to be freely available if consumers want them, without the government building walls. If an individual "does not care for what popular culture has to offer, just turn the TV *off.*"[21] But government should not turn TVs off or limit available channels. The marketplace of ideas can do that.

For the libertarian, a mandated ratings system is not acceptable. If a business wishes to provide such ratings, hoping to gain an audience, so be it. Libertarians would question whether we need a uniform set of moral standards that are enforced on all consumers.[22] Defending efforts to censor under the guise of protecting children from harm infringes on the rights of parents and businesses—and children (often meaning you). First, what a child sees is a parent's responsibility, not the government's. As an example, according to the Interactive Digital Software Association, 97 percent of people who purchase computer games and 87 percent of those who purchase console games are over eighteen.[23] If parents buy games for their children (or for themselves), they are responsible for evaluating those purchases.

Further, many parents vehemently reject the idea of mandatory standards on what their children can see. As Art Hilgart remarked pungently: "Of all the crybabies demanding government protection from their own free will, the parents wanting ratings of television programs deserve to spend hell watching the *Jetsons*. By their standards, Americans are utterly irresponsible parents."[24] Are children, including adolescents and teenagers, simply puppets who hopelessly mimic everything that they observe and thus must never be allowed to think or observe the range of the human condition? Libertarians reject the sentiment that government restrictions offer a welcome or needed protection. Libertarians abhor sacrificing any freedom to the government to make decisions for individuals, even if violent content is potentially problematic.

> Even if there were evidence that letting teens watch TV could make them ill tempered, that doesn't really suggest that the ultimate solution lies in a Senate hearing room. After all, look as you might, you won't find an "unless it makes the kids jittery" exception to the First Amendment.[25]

Libertarians also prize the free market and view government imposition of standards on industry as an unnecessary restraint on commerce. Industry officials interpret Washington's message as "censor yourselves, or we'll do it for you."[26] The Media Violence Labeling Act of 2000 involves

> prohibiting the sale of any audio or visual product or service to an individual whose age in years is less than the age specified as the minimum age in years for a purchaser or consumer, as the case may be, under the labeling system issued or prescribed by the Federal Trade Commission.[27]

If a sophisticated thirteen year old wants to purchase a videogame deemed appropriate for a fourteen year old or see a documentary depicting violence, under this law, the child and his or her parents are prohibited from acting on their own best judgment. Industry is also punished for selling them such products, which restricts the marketplace. Kmart, Wal-Mart, and smaller chains, such as Camelot, now simply refuse to sell any music that is "too hot to handle," and some companies refuse to sponsor artists and products that will run into commercial restraints.[28] Libertarians are against any such handcuffs on the free market. Libertarians also doubt government assertions that compliance with ratings schemes will be "voluntary." Steve Kurtz pointed to the Canadian case.

> "While compliance with the code is officially voluntary," the Canadian Radio-Television-Telecommunications Commission said, "it will make compliance with the code a condition of license for all privately owned television stations and networks when renewing their licenses." We've seen this drama before, the one in which government officials make a group an offer they can't refuse.[29]

People and business should have an unlimited choice to consume or produce violent entertainment. If you want to read or write a book like *How to Be a Hitman*, you should have the right to do so. If you kill someone afterwards, that is your choice, and not the fault of the author or publisher, and you should be held accountable for it. Government has no place deciding that some culture works against people and should be kept from them.

## Violent Entertainment and Social Research

Does violent entertainment harm individuals? This fateful question is the precursor of calls for government regulation. Does violent entertainment plant seeds of aggression in children that bloom into increasingly violent acts as teenagers and adults? Or are children, like adults, wise enough to differentiate fantasy wrongs and real ones? If so, why is the persistent use of commercials to sell products effective, particularly in children? Don't media images sometimes influence an audience's actions, even unintentionally, such that viewers want to wear their hair the way a sitcom character does, mimic a comedian's witticisms endlessly, or duplicate fighting moves from martial arts movies or professional wrestling matches?

Discovering what effects, if any, violent media have on public behavior is problematic. Killers and rapists surely differ from lawful persons on more than their reading and viewing habits. Nor are potential killers or rapists likely to candidly reveal their inner secrets to prying social scientists. Yet, the difficulty of researching the effects of violent entertainment has certainly not deterred investigators. At the national level, the Surgeon General of the United States, congressional committees, and the National Institute of Mental Health have each commissioned comprehensive research studies of the effects television violence has on children. In the business world, network executives at ABC, CBS, and NBC have also commissioned studies by their in-house research departments into the effects of televised violence. University-based scholars, often psychologists, have produced dozens of independent studies.

This abundant research has failed to produce any uniform conclusions. Naysayers argue:

> the causes of violence are well known. Unfortunately, they are not conveniently located in the television tube where they could be easily eradicated. The causes of real-world violence—rather than laboratory produced aggression—are to be found in the

childhood experiences of known violent offenders with the real persons in their early lives.[30]

On the other side, proponents argue consistent findings show that "scenes of violence sometimes had some effects on certain types of viewers in certain specific cases."[31] Richard Felson, a well-known criminologist and expert on aggressive behavior, in reviewing this literature, concluded one consistent effect may be to "direct a viewer's attention to novel forms of violent behavior they would not otherwise consider," meaning violent media can inspire acts of copycat violence, but in itself, do not routinely produce higher levels of aggression in viewers.[32]

Investigations by network researchers contradict the findings of government-sponsored commissions.[33] This research concludes that violent content does not cause aggressive behavior; government researchers, who support policies restricting violent content, argue a causal link does exist. This disagreement encourages scrutiny as to whether the vested self-interest of investigators may affect their findings and methodologies. Consumers of research—you—must consider whether research by individuals and organizations that advocate a particular point of view is fair-minded and avoids stacking the deck to favor a preordained conclusion.

By what actual evidence and method do experimenters draw conclusions about the possible harmfulness of violent entertainment? Most research on the effects of violent entertainment involves laboratory experiments on children or college students. One such example is research by Craig A. Anderson and Karen E. Dill, entitled "Video Games and Aggressive Thoughts, Feelings, and Behavior in the Laboratory and in Life," published in the *Journal of Personality and Social Psychology*.[34] First, this article offers a representative and up-to-date example of the experimental research methods many social scientists use to discover whether violent entertainment is harmful. Second, the popularity and profits of video games will soon overtake those of the movie industry. Videogames thus merit attention as an increasingly important form of violent entertainment among children and teenagers. What conclusions are researchers drawing about the potential harmful effects of this medium? How do they even define harm in their investigations? Third, innovations in technology are currently making videogames increasingly realistic. Are more powerful graphics and a videogame's capacity to allow players to participate directly in simulated violent acts contributing to aggressiveness?

Anderson and Dill's article reports the results of two psychological studies on videogames and aggressive thoughts that use college students as subjects. Many of you may have participated in these types of experiments in order to receive extra credit in psychology courses. Experimental social psychologists like Anderson and Dill often report the results of multiple studies in their papers. The assumption in such research is that each experiment leads to the next as the experimenter tests related and linked questions—the results of one study provide questions for the next. Each experiment further refines the experimenter's theory and eliminates hypotheses that are demonstrated to be false. Thus, experimental research is in many respects closer to the model of "physical sciences" than any other sociological methodology.

In their first study, Anderson and Dill collected data from 227 male and female undergraduates. These data included measures of each student's past experience playing both violent and nonviolent videogames. Anderson and Dill used this information to make predictions about the levels of aggressive behavior and delinquency student subjects would report. The subjects' self-reported levels of aggression and delinquency were gathered from their responses to surveys asking them to rate questions such as "Some of my friends think I'm a 'hothead'" and "How many times in the past year have you purposely damaged or destroyed property belonging to a school?" They assume that these "self-report" data provide an adequate picture of the lives of these students.

Anderson and Dill used a "Delinquency Scale," which asked subjects to identify the number of times they engaged in forty-five specific delinquent-type behaviors over the last year. The intuitive logic of scales is that a subject's responses will fall into patterns that indicate high or low levels of delinquency, hence the idea that the measure provides a range, or scale, that indicates how delinquent someone is. Anderson and Dill's first study is correlational, meaning that they examined whether reports of exposure to videogame violence in particular is correlated to high self-reports of aggression and delinquency. Anderson and Dill found that playing violent videogames was, indeed, correlated to higher self-reports of delinquency, as well as to receiving lower grades. Whether watching too much TV, playing videogames frequently, or reading too many "trashy" magazines is harmful is a familiar question, but a different one from asking whether violent entertainment causes people to become more aggressive.

In their second study, Anderson and Dill investigated the immediate short-term effects of playing violent videogames. Would subjects who just played a violent videogame show more subsequent aggressive behavior in a laboratory experiment than people who just finished playing a nonviolent game? The nonviolent videogame was *Myst*, a best-selling videogame in which players must solve puzzles. The violent videogame was *Wolfenstein 3D*, a game in which players use guns, knives, and flamethrowers to kill enemy soldiers. Subjects were told they were taking part in a study of how people develop skills at motor tasks involved in videogame playing. Subjects in many psychological experiments are often deceived or kept "blind" about the actual research goals. This deception is justified based on the experimenters' concern that subjects will depart from how they normally act if they know what behaviors actually interest the researchers. Hence, experimental studies must be plotted intricately—the experimenters must develop and implement a plausible cover story and the actual underlying experiment simultaneously. For example, these experimenters set up wires between the videogame unit and a VCR to make it appear as if "skill development" was being recorded. The experimenters' control over the situation is a potent advantage in this methodology. However, we never learn exactly what the subject *believes* he or she is experiencing in connection with the game and her or his subsequent acts and potential behaviors. By focusing on the experimenters' view of the world, rather than the subject's, this methodology is alien to interactional methods. Subjects were randomly assigned to either the *Myst* or *Wolfenstein 3D* videogame, which they played for fifteen minutes. Each subject then completed "state hostility" and "trait irritability" scales.

Subjects played their game for another fifteen-minute period and were asked to return in a week. After a week, subjects played their game again for fifteen minutes. They then played a "competitive reaction time" game, in which they competed against another subject to see who could push a button faster. The winner was told he or she could administer a "noise blast" of the intensity and duration of their choice to the loser. A computer fixed the actual intensity and duration of the blast at a modest level; however, the winner thought he or she chose the length and time of the administered noise. Anderson and Dill found that people who played the violent videogame behaved more "aggressively" toward opponents than did students who played a nonviolent video-game. Based on their two studies, Anderson and Dill offered the following conclusions:

> Playing violent video games is positively related to aggressive behavior and delin-
> quency. That relation was stronger for individuals who are characteristically aggres-
> sive, and for men. Laboratory exposure to a graphically violent video game increased
> aggressive thoughts and behavior. Exposure to violent video games will increase ag-
> gressive behavior in both the short term (e.g., laboratory aggression) and the long term
> (e.g., delinquency).[35]

As consumers of scientific research, you should maintain a critical but open pos-
ture to these conclusions. Consider how research is designed in order to measure behaviors of interest. Ask yourself, based on the research design, How persuasive do you find
the conclusions? Clearly, a laboratory measure of aggression, such as a willingness to
direct a noise at someone, hardly simulates real acts of criminal violence or brutality.
But blasting noise does represent an act of some hostility. In addition, the researchers
found correlations between reports of time spent playing violent videogames and
higher self-reports of harmful behaviors. These laboratory studies offer evidence—but
not definitive proof—of violent entertainment having harmful effects on people.

# Culture and Violent Entertainment

Americans share common symbols and events: apple pie, the Fourth of July, the image
of the United States as a melting pot, Abraham Lincoln, and our beloved Constitution.
Within this broad cultural umbrella, there are numerous subcultures, based on race, age,
region, education, gender, occupation, and so forth. Together, these comprise what we
mean by American culture. What is the place of violent entertainment in that culture?

Many politicians who criticize violent lyrics turn around and praise "traditional"
movie heroes Clint Eastwood, Harrison Ford, or Arnold Schwartzenegger who blast
away bad guys. Americans are devoted fans of boxing, football, and hockey, all contact
sports with a high degree of controlled violence. James Bond punching, a hockey
player swinging, a professional wrestler pantomiming a punch, and a boxer connecting
all involve a fist hitting another person, but they are not necessarily given the same
moral equivalence. The definition of violent entertainment itself is no easy matter, as a
collector of videotapes of hockey fights, a deer hunter, a *Quake* fan, an aficionado of

Jackie Chan films and hip-hop lyricists might all disagree about what to call violent or harmful entertainment.

Some violent entertainment may be *intended* to be artistic—a distinction speaking to the creator's motivation and the audience's reaction. *Crouching Tiger, Hidden Dragon* received critical praise for visually stunning displays of choreographed sword fighting. Yet, even if violent entertainment is artistically valid, does that negate any harm that the depicted violence might cause? Is the aesthetic value an artistic depiction of violence supplies greater than the potential harm done by its distribution? Are artistically rendered depictions of violence still properly labeled violent entertainment?

The mass availability of entertainment allows individuals voluntarily to choose which entertainment to consume. A great many people voluntarily pay to see bullets, knives, pipes, cars, fists, and boots strike other human beings. People also purchase videogames that allow them to carry out those actions themselves. People condemn violent entertainment but the marketplace—itself made up of people—eagerly consumes it. Social science research on violent entertainment is inconclusive, but these studies often do not address why, regardless of harm, violent entertainment is so popular.

The consumption of violent entertainment appears to be more a male phenomenon than a female one. There are recognizable popular distinctions between "chick flicks" and "films for guys." The former usually emphasize dialogue and romance and the latter, fights, car chases, and automatic weapons. Male children may greet one another with a headlock and an ensuing wrestling match; female children fight physically less often than boys do, and girls play with less violent toys. Men and women both possess traits of assertiveness and aggression—yet male children are certainly socialized to be more physically aggressive than are women. As noted, many feminist thinkers believe violent entertainment victimizes women by making men more aggressive in general and by depicting women as possible targets for subsequent violent behavior. If violent entertainment causes harm, the feminist recognizes the perpetrator as typically male, and the female as a common victim. A debate over whether violent entertainment harms people must take into account that one gender is disproportionately likely to do both the harming and consuming.

The conservative and functionalist view is that culture, at its best, brings Americans together as a people and strengthens our character. Conservatives see the debate over violent entertainment as a battle over values, part of the culture war. Conservatives see limitations on violent entertainment as appropriate and as a legitimate step in safeguarding American culture against decay.

Social democrats, more open to the legitimacy of conflict in society, see various strains in culture as healthy. Culture should not be monolithic; a plurality of tastes and views are necessary to accommodate citizens. Some violent entertainment, like rap, can even help people question and change existing social conditions. Social democrats may disagree intensely with some violent entertainment—in that feeling, they are close to the conservative; yet, social democrats are more likely to believe in having a plurality of values, even if they have to hold their noses to do it. Violent entertainment, however distasteful, can ironically demonstrate tolerance and societal belief in diversity. It is only in the case of violent pornography, which debases women and perhaps leads to violence, and in depictions of violence against racial groups and those with differing sexual orientations that the social democrat begins to suggest the need for government involvement to protect the vulnerable.

The libertarian, of course, tolerates no enforced restrictions on culture. No controversy should exist about violent entertainment or indecent art, because there is no public interest involved in its creation or dissemination. Individuals will consume or produce that product according to their desires and resources. The libertarian has no qualms about violent entertainment, as long as there is no coercion involved in its creation or distribution. Perhaps more than partisans of the other approaches, libertarians feel that cultural tastes have little social impact—at least not to the extent that governmental involvement is warranted. Whether a violent movie inspires an individual to start a fight or not is irrelevant. For whatever reason, a person chooses to fight, and they, not their culture, should be punished.

In sum, the conservative, libertarian, and social democratic visions offer different prescriptions for people's relation to a larger culture. For the conservative, potential harms justify restricting the opportunity for culture to work against people. The social democrat holds open the possibility that violent entertainment may be harmful in some circumstances, but sees restricting cultural tastes as more dangerous, essentially arguing that some violent entertainment is a necessary evil in order to preserve free expression and speech, unless the vulnerable are being attacked. Finally, the libertarian rejects any infringement whatsoever on culture. What is important is protecting individuals' autonomy to consume the culture of their own choosing. Although violent videogames might just be seen as debris from a culture out of control, one might also argue that such games are, in an important way, a form of political philosophy.

## Questions

1. Why is violent entertainment so popular?

2. Can cultural objects make you a better person? A lesser person? Why?

3. Does violent content in entertainment harm people?

4. What circumstances, if any, justify censoring?

5. Have you ever snuck into an R-rated movie or played an extremely violent videogame? Why, or why not?

6. Do you agree with current voluntary ratings systems?

7. Should the federal government restrict or ban violent entertainment? If so, which forms?

8. Should society be more concerned about sexual images or violent images?

9. How would you research whether violent entertainment harms people?

10. Should entertainment producers offer fewer products with violent content, even if they are the most successful commercially?

11. Do males prefer violent entertainment more than females? Why?

## For Further Study

Anderson, Craig A., and Karen E. Dill. "Video Games and Aggressive Thoughts, Feelings, and Behavior in the Laboratory and in Life." *Journal of Personality and Social Psychology* 78 (2000): 772–790.

Bennett, William. *The De-Valuing of America: The Fight for Our Culture and Our Children.* New York: Summit, 1992.

Dworkin, Andrea. *Pornography: Men Possessing Women.* New York: Perigee, 1981.

Felson, Richard. "Mass Media Effects on Violent Behavior." *Annual Review of Sociology* 22 (1996): 103–129.

Gans, Herbert. *Popular Culture and High Culture.* Rev. Ed. New York: Basic Books, 1999.

Hunter, James D. *Culture Wars.* New York: Basic Books, 1991.

Newton, David E. *Violence and the Media: A Reference Handbook.* Santa Barbara, CA: ABC-CLIO, 1996.

## Notes and References

1. Melville J. Herskovits, *Man and His Works* (New York: Knopf, 1948), p. 625.
2. See Edward Sapir, *Selected Writings in Language, Culture, and Personality* (Berkeley: University of California Press, 1949); Benjamin Whorf, *Language, Thought, and Reality* (Cambridge: MIT Press, 1956).
3. Geoffrey K. Pullum (*The Great Eskimo Vocabulary Hoax* [Chicago: University of Chicago Press, 1991], pp. 159–171) provides an amusing and provocative discussion of this claim. Whatever the precise number of "snow-related" words among the Inuit and the rest of us, there is no doubt that peoples who specialize tend to create more terms for what they specialize in.
4. Verne F. Ray, "Techniques and Problems in the Study of Human Color Perception," *Southwestern Journal of Anthropology* 8 (Autumn 1952): 251–258.
5. David Halle, *Inside Culture* (Chicago: University of Chicago Press, 1993).
6. Pierre Bourdieu, *Distinction* (Cambridge: Harvard University Press, 1984).
7. Eminem, *The Slim Shady LP.*
8. Media Violence Labeling Act of 2000, S 2497 IS 106th Congress, 2d Session S. 2497.
9. James D. Hunter, *Culture Wars* (New York: Basic Books, 1991).
10. Eric Zorn, "College editors running scared over running ad," *Chicago Tribune* (Thursday, March 22, 2001): Section 2, page 1.
11. Attributed to philosopher Richard Rorty.
12. Jacob Sullum, "Phantom Studies," *Reason* 32 (December 2000): 15.
13. William Bennett, "Marketing Violence to Children." Statement delivered before the Senate Committee on Commerce, May 4, 1999.
14. United States Federal Trade Commission Report, *Marketing Violent Entertainment to Children: A Review of Self-Regulation and Industry Practices in the Motion Picture, Music Recording & Electronic Game Industries.* Executive Summary, September 2000, p. 1.
15. Ibid., p. 2.
16. Irving Kristol, "Liberal Censorship and the Common Culture," *Society* (September 1999): 8.
17. Steven Kurtz, "Deja Viewing," *Reason* (February 1994): 45.

18. "Holy Joe! A Culture War! Al Gore and Joe Lieberman fight violent entertainment," *The Nation* (October 9, 2001): 13.

19. Tricia Rose, "Rap Music and the Demonization of Young Black Males," *USA Today* (Magazine) (May 1994): 42.

20. Jon Katz, "Son of Wal-Mart." Wired News Media Awareness Network, http://www.media-awareness.ca/eng/news/news/columns/walmart.htm

21. J. D. Tuccille, "Paging Mr. Zappa." Free-Market.net Spotlight/spotlight/mediaspeech

22. Tom Russo, "Games Grow Up But Is the Rest of the World Ready?" *Next Generation* (February 2001): 56.

23. Russo, "Games Grow Up But Is the Rest of the World Ready?" p. 57.

24. Art Hilgart, "Stuff a Gag in the V-Chip (Censorship of Television)," *The Humanist* (September–October 1997): 3.

25. J. D. Tuccille, "Paging Mr. Zappa."

26. Jacob Sallum, "Minor Problem," *Reason Online* (November 8, 2000).

27. Media Violence Labeling Act of 2000.

28. Jon Katz. "Son of Wal-Mart."

29. Kurtz, "Deja Viewing," p. 47.

30. David E. Newton, *Violence and the Media: A Reference Handbook* (Santa Barbara, CA: ABC-CLIO, 1996): 157.

31. Ibid.

32. Richard Felson, "Mass Media Effects on Violent Behavior," *Annual Review of Sociology* 22 (1996): 103.

33. Newton, *Violence and the Media*, p. 157.

34. Craig A. Anderson and Karen E. Dill, "Video Games and Aggressive Thoughts, Feelings, and Behavior in the Laboratory and in Life," *Journal of Personality and Social Psychology* 78 (2000): 772–790.

35. Craig A. Anderson and Karen E. Dill, "Video Games and Aggressive Thoughts, Feelings, and Behavior in the Laboratory and in Life," p. 72.

# CHAPTER TWO

# Socialization: Should Parents Be Allowed to Hit Their Children However They Wish?

■ Could Tarzan ever exist? Could a child, raised by apes, but without any human contact, reach puberty, be found by humans, take a crash course in Civilization 101, and then fall into place in society? On rare occasions, children have been discovered in the wild who have survived on their own since infancy. Imagine the vast amount of information that these children have to learn once they are found—just learning how to speak and overcome their aggressiveness are tremendous undertakings. Dubbed *feral children,* only with great difficulty do they eventually attain even a minimal level of social skills, such as acquiring basic language or using a knife and fork. There is too much for feral children to learn—without early assistance and nurturance from other humans in the first few years of life, attempts at socialization meet with limited success. Fortunately, most children have other human beings around to guide them through this process.

At birth, when we enter this complex and confusing world, we are nothing but a bundle of cute and complex biological mechanisms—we are not social beings. We arrive "uncivilized" and must be trained to live in a world in which we have been placed without our consent. The British folklorist Douglas Newton once remarked, "The worldwide fraternity of children is the greatest of savage tribes, and the only one which shows no signs of dying out."[1] Despite the affront to our vanity, Newton's point helps clarify how sociologists view the process by which human beings mature. Socialization refers to the process through which an infant human child is shaped into a responsible, mature adult. Primary socialization occurs largely, although not entirely, during childhood and is learning that occurs through core social institutions, most particularly the family. Secondary socialization typically refers to more specific, formal training—such as learning one's occupation or how to behave properly in some public association.

Socialization is the result of a complex interplay of biological and social factors. Often children are unable to learn a task or skill until they are biologically ready. Most parents at some time or another become frustrated raising their children because a child will seem unwilling to master something the parents are sure the child "should" be able to do. Ask any parent about toilet training. Despite parental frustration, the child is probably not so much unwilling to learn as he or she is just not yet ready to learn. Experts in child development look at this biological readiness in terms of a series of stages through which each child passes. These stages do not only involve obviously biological factors, such as bladder control, but intellectual skills as well. The Swiss child psychologist Jean Piaget argued that children must pass through a series of intellectual or cognitive stages. For instance, until children reach approximately the age of seven, it is difficult to teach them that the larger of two objects need not be the heavier (a pound of feathers versus a pound of lead).[2] When children reach the appropriate stage (what Piaget terms the "concrete operational stage"), this connection becomes obvious.

Socialization also teaches children who they are as individuals. They become familiar with the core of personality: the self. The self is what a person believes makes them special, different from everyone else, uniquely themselves. Development of the self-concept is too complicated to explain completely here, but some aspects should be mentioned. Perhaps most important from a sociological viewpoint is recognizing that the development of the self is a social process. The American social psychologist Charles Horton Cooley recognized that we come to know ourselves after we know others. In other words, our self-concept is a function of the "reflection" of us that we see in others. We discover how others view us and eventually see our self in the same or similar ways. If others see us as great beauties or unendurable prigs, we will use these attitudes to build our own self-concept. Cooley referred to this aspect of socialization as the *looking glass self*.[3]

George Herbert Mead, a prominent American philosopher and social psychologist, extended this idea by emphasizing the importance of *role taking*.[4] This process enables children to internalize the expectations that others have of them. By understanding how others see them, children can shape their behavior so as to be perceived in a favorable light. Later, children expand their role taking to include the expectations of large groups or of the entire society; Mead called this skill "taking the role of the generalized other."[5] Acquiring these skills helps people present themselves in desirable ways—a technique that sociologist Erving Goffman labeled "impression management."[6] This skill is largely mastered by the time a child reaches adolescence, although it has roots much earlier, stretching back to infancy.

Many aspects of our eventual social identities are also fixed for us at birth. Known as *ascribed characteristics,* social categories such as gender, race, religion, and nationality help define how we are perceived, treated, and expected to act. For example, boys and girls learn to meet specific expectations associated with their genders; children born into different castes in Indian society are socialized into distinct ways of life. Our guardians, usually our parents, confront the formidable challenge of molding us into responsible Americans, or Britons, Croatians, Dominicans, Nigerians, or Vietnamese. Within these nationalities, we learn to be black Americans, Scots, Moslems, Hottentots, socialists, upper class, and so forth.

Although all children undergo socialization, they do so under dramatically unequal conditions. Some children grow up with hunger, crime-ridden neighborhoods, family violence, and woefully undersupplied schools, all of which affect their transformation into adulthood. The opportunities these children have pale in comparison to those afforded children who grow up in physical security in resource-rich environments. Perhaps the most contentious difference between the conflict and functionalist theories lies in their radically different approaches to this inequality. Viewing society as a competitive battleground over social resources, the conflict perspective emphasizes the long-term societal consequences of having large numbers of people be unsuccessful competitors for social resources. Since one generation's poverty diminishes the succeeding generation's chances of achieving better opportunities in life, perpetual social inequality results, with the built-in disadvantages of being at the bottom of the economic ladder generally forcing people to stay there. To the conflict theorist, such enduring inequality is unconscionable, especially in bequeathing limitations to innocents—children. Wrath against a social system that renders poor children with disproportionate handicaps in their socialization explains the affinity conflict theorists have for social democrats and their view that government intervention is needed to remedy social inequities.

The functionalist, while regretting the toll inequality takes, nevertheless views some social inequities as a necessary evil. Social resources must be allocated inequitably to reward individuals who perform the most important social functions, such as captains of commerce and doctors. People who perform the most important social functions simply warrant more rewards, many of which they use to provide their children with a more advantaged upbringing (which also functions to secure their replacement in future generations). This functionalist view resonates with the conservative and libertarian conviction that individuals meriting great rewards earn and deserve any advantages that those rewards confer. If you have the ability to live in a wealthy neighborhood (and school district) or to pay for private schooling, why shouldn't your children reap those benefits? Why is it also your responsibility to pay to educate other people's kids at the same level as your own? To the victors rightfully belong the spoils—inequality is an inevitable (and some would say desirable) outcome of important differences in individual merit and ability. To the conflict theorist, however, this inequality is not a product of a meritocracy but of unfair social engineering.

## ▪ Question:

*Should parents be allowed to hit their children however they wish?*

Socialization requires teaching children how to behave. Parents constantly orchestrate a dance of treats and punishments to manipulate their children's behavior, including applying physical force. Parents strive to set up reward/cost systems so that it is in the child's interest to do what the parents want. The idea that children consider the consequences of their actions, and eventually internalize rewards and punishments, supports a behaviorist understanding of how socialization works. Many people believe that using spanking as a reinforcement technique does change behavior and is an especially effective form of socialization.

All studies of U.S. child rearing practices indicate that corporal punishment has been and remains a common form of discipline. Survey data show that 55 percent of American adults approve of spanking children as a form of discipline.[7] More than 90 percent of parents of toddlers admit to having punished their children physically. Spanking or corporal punishment continues through adolescence with over half of all parents hitting children at age twelve, a third at age fourteen, and 13 percent at seventeen.[8] Hitting children is clearly part of the American way; parents who claim *never* to have hit their child are either saints or, more likely, liars, and are certainly deviants.[9]

The statutory laws of all fifty states have a "parental exemption" for corporal punishment of their children.[10] Some feel the legality of corporal punishment is a slippery slope; its pervasive use may presently be or escalate into the physical abuse of children. For example, many sociological studies attempting to measure child abuse or violence in the family use broad definitions that include any kind of physical action, including slapping and shoving, which are also normal forms of corporal punishment. Consider one mother's account of what happens when this "normal" behavior gets out of control, becoming child abuse:

> I started abusing my boy because he was an accident and a screamer. When he was four months old, I hit him so hard my engagement ring carved a deep bloody furrow across his soft face. His screams shattered my heart. I sank to the floor with self-loathing. Then I held him tightly in my arms, so tight he turned blue. I told him he had to do his share. Why didn't he stop screaming? Deep down, I knew he couldn't understand. But I also thought he was doing it on purpose.[11]

This account makes you want to cry for and strangle this woman all at once. The publicity accorded to the sadistic death of six-year-old Lisa Steinberg in a filthy apartment in a fashionable New York City neighborhood by a father who was an attorney and a mother who was a children's book editor remind us that child abuse is not limited to the impoverished but can occur across social classes.

As anyone who reads the newspaper knows, there is a staggering amount of child abuse in the United States. Statistics on its extent vary so widely that we do not know how widespread the problem is nor do we know if it has increased in recent years. Figures for the number of abused children each year range from 650,000 to a million to six million. In 1998, 2.8 million children were reported abused or neglected, and 903,000 of those reported cases were substantiated.[12] We do not know the extent of the "abuse" in these cases and whether the investigations into them were adequate. On the other hand, we do not know how many cases were missed. We simply do not have very good ways of measuring the problem, nor is there agreement on how to define "child abuse." Of course, if even one child dies because of the neglect or abuse of a parent (and according to the U.S. Department of Health and Human Services, the figure for 1998 was 1,100),[13] this is cause for alarm.

Although much remains to be studied, we do know some things about violence in families. First, there is a cycle of violence; those who had violent and abusive childhoods have an increased probability of being violent and abusive as parents and of engaging in violent crimes. Second, family violence is directly related to the amount of stress on a family and to the extent of its social isolation. Although both strict discipline and child abuse are found in all economic classes, both are relatively more common among poor families.[14]

Some researchers would include any form of corporal punishment as family violence, which would label most parents as abusers; others accept causing deep welts and bruises as part of normal, strict parental discipline. Broad definitions, while alerting us to the possibility of serious abuse in families, equivalent to legal definitions of assault, also suggest to some that figures on child abuse are so inflated that they approach being meaningless. Is it really child abuse if a parent slaps the back of a child's hand to keep him or her from touching something dangerous? Alternatively, is deliberately hitting a child with a belt or rod simply another form of corporal punishment or is it really child abuse?

In general, the last thirty years have seen a philosophy of strict and humiliating corporal punishment move out of favor, to be replaced by a philosophy emphasizing permissiveness, discussion, and the control of anger.[15] Nevertheless, we face a cruel paradox. As civilized people, we react with disgust when we hear of any atrocity, violent or sexual, that has been perpetrated on a child. And we can all agree with Sergeant Dick Ramon, head of the sex-crimes division of the Seattle police department, when he said, "Child abuse is the ultimate crime, the ultimate betrayal."[16] However, most Americans do hit their offspring and were hit themselves by their parents, and many people believe corporal punishment is valuable in teaching children right from wrong.

Many parents also see corporal punishment as a responsibility, an act based in love and the obligation to raise "a good kid." Further, some also suggest that today's parents epitomize a new era of gutlessness, of docile parents allowing misbehaving, disrespectful children to walk all over them, producing an unprecedented modern crisis of discipline. Hence, there is now some revisionism about the wisdom of parental permissiveness. Some recent research data also show that nonabusive spanking is the most effective method for getting children under thirteen to comply with their parent's wishes, with nonabusive spanking also not causing children any lasting harm.[17] However, a significant amount of research also exists suggesting the exact opposite.

Most of us accept that there may be a hazy, wobbly line that divides disciplinary guidance from villainy. Americans agree that child abuse is a crime. However, is spanking child abuse? Should American laws go as far as the Swedish law, passed in 1979, that says: "The child should not be subjected to corporal punishment or other humiliating treatment?"[18] Or should we restrict, as much as possible, the intrusion of the state into family decision making? Is corporal punishment an important means of socialization or is it an outdated form of barbarism? Where shall we draw the line, and on what grounds?

# The Social Democratic Point of View

The social democrat wishes to insure that the rights of all groups are protected, particularly those of children, who cannot easily protect themselves. When a social democrat hears of a problem, he or she is likely to suggest that the government step in, even if this action infringes on the "rights" of individuals and families. Government intrusion may be necessary to protect a greater right—that of not allowing a child to be beaten. Irene Barth wrote about her views on this issue:

> The public has been treated to accounts of a 5-year-old snuffed out by means of a plastic bag placed over her head, a 3-year-old boy beaten to a pulp with a bat and a 2-year-old shaken into the hereafter with bare hands. Another 3-year-old, a girl, according to police, was shredded with a belt because she showed too little interest in arithmetic flash cards. . . . Because of increased public awareness, the number of tips [to social service agencies] is up. Now comes a suit charging that social workers caused $6.5 million worth of "anguish and humiliation" to a family by looking into an unfounded allegation of child abuse. Richard and Dee-Ann Marrone complain that they were asked personal questions and that their children were undressed by a child-welfare worker looking for bruises. The family doctor, friends and school officials are said to have been told of the investigation. . . . Even if the plaintiffs are the tenderest of parents and the accusation against them was malicious, their suit has terrifying implications. . . . What is worse than the anguish visited upon innocent parents is the anguish visited upon the innocent children of guilty parents. . . . In an ideal world, all parents would receive thoughtful instruction in child rearing and all homes housing young children would be visited at least once or twice by family experts. . . . Children's rights to protection from cruel and unusual punishment should outweigh adults' right to secure their houses against searches.[19]

Barth made a strong and coherent presentation of the social democratic position. She argued that the rights of vulnerable individuals take priority over the property and privacy rights of parents. That individual parents might be hurt is more than offset by preventing child abuse. There is no way to know how many parents will be hurt by this intervention versus how many children spared pain, but social democrats know on which side they prefer to err.

Barth was explicit about her "ideal world." Parents would be thoughtfully trained in child rearing (presumably by the government), and "family experts" would visit every home. The U.S. Advisory Board on Child Abuse and Neglect has supported this view, proposing in a government report that health-care workers should visit new parents and instruct them in childcare.[20] This aid, however, is not everyone's idea of utopia. Conservatives and libertarians would react with horror to this army of bureaucratic intruders. Some might see thoughtful child-rearing instruction as ideological manipulation by an all-powerful state. While proponents are sincere about the beneficial role of a caring government, state intervention in child rearing would be a living hell for critics.

One social democrat, former Philadelphia judge, Lois Foner, argued that we have gone too far in our attempts to "preserve the family":

> I suggest that it is time for us to demand that government provide permanent, well-run orphanages for the more than 2 million abused children who are de facto orphans. . . . Public institutions are answerable to the public. They can be inspected regularly by public officials.[21]

When social democrats suggest that the government organize "orphanages" for children whose parents are incapable of caring for them, they speak as big-government proponents of child welfare. This view implies the government is ultimately a parent for its citizens, a form of the legal doctrine of *parens patriae* ("the parenthood of the state").

Whatever position you adopt may relate to the faith you have in families and governments. The more you see a capacity for individual parents to be ignorant, apathetic, or primitive, the more likely you are to grant a place for the thoughtful, altruistic government official. The rhetorical cases that advocates of large-scale government intervention make attempt to paint this picture. For example, what kind of a world do we live in when a father could "shred" his three-year-old daughter with a belt for not caring about mathematics? On the other hand, there are horror stories of bumbling, incompetent bureaucrats. Do-gooders may intrude on your family espousing their own narrow ideology of parenting and discipline or blindly following government regulations to the letter.

To understand where this government concern with the health and well-being of young children might lead, let us turn to Sweden. In 1979, this progressive Scandinavian nation passed a law making spanking, slapping, locking in a closet, or in general humiliating a child illegal. This law added to strong Swedish laws providing stiff punishment for child abuse. The law was not designed to be punitive but educational. As a Swedish Ministry of Justice spokesperson put it: "We hope to use the law to change attitudes. If we launched a big campaign on the subject, it probably would be forgotten in a year. But the law stays, and it enters the public consciousness."[22] In the first decade since the law was enacted, only one Swede was taken to court.[23] Still, even if it is unlikely to send parents who swat their kids to jail, the proposal does have the force of law. The Swedish politicians who passed this legislation believed that the state has a legitimate role to insure "proper" child-rearing practices. A majority were convinced that children who are hit or threatened do not respond positively and being convinced of this, they acted. The premise is not only preventing present harm, but future harm as well.

Of course, this social democratic legislation has been subject to heated attacks and ridicule by those with a more conservative bent. Jim Klobuchar, a popular Minneapolis newspaper columnist, imagined satirically the length to which government interference might go:

> My cousin [from Sweden] said the family had torsk the other day, or whatever the Swedes call cod, and the kid refused. The wife tried all the gentle, loving approaches and when that didn't work, the guy ordered the kid to eat the torsk. The kid angrily refused. He said he was studying to be a vegetarian and the old man was intruding on his right of choice. When the predictable impasse developed, the old man said Ingemar couldn't go outside to play. The kid then went into his room and came out with a

banner four feet high, which he put in the picture window, announcing: "This house practices grounding and other methods first used by the Spanish Inquisition." The guy might go to jail.[24]

As silly as this scenario seems, the social democrat does believe that government has a place in the home. The family is not seen as a sacred institution, but government and its ideas as represented in laws are. The social democrat believes that through legislation, people can be made happier and more moral. When they see child abuse or any social wrong, they have no difficulty in correcting the problem by the most direct and universal solution—putting a law in place. Government must right wrongs. As Bob Greene wrote, "children are not property; parents are not owners . . . children must be made to know that there are adults who they can turn to when they are being hurt—adults who will listen and help them."[25] Having a "big brother" does not always frighten social democrats; sometimes big brother is not there to watch you, but to watch out for you.

# The Conservative Point of View

Although no conservatives celebrate beatings, you are more likely to find a conservative approving of corporal punishment than a member of the other two groups. Conservatives believe that these tried and true methods of discipline offer the best tools for socialization. They believe along with the Bible that "He that spareth his rod hateth his son: but he that loveth him chasteneth him early" (Proverbs 13:24). They believe like Odin, the Norse God of War and Wisdom, that "He who goes without corporal punishment will go lawless and die without honor." The conservative is far less likely to agree that reason is a guiding force of child development. A child must learn to accept and obey legitimate authority. Physical discipline is a forceful means of impressing the power differential between child and adult on the former in an emotional, rather than a rational, way. A nineteenth-century minister put it this way:

> [Corporal punishment] must be viewed not as simply the pain produced, but pain as the expression of disapprobation of a moral governor; and the dread of it, or the appeal made to fear, must be on account of the association it recalls of the displeasure of the beloved parent. To fear such displeasure, is a proof of affection; and the appeal made to such a feeling, even by means of external infliction, has no tendency to produce or cherish slavish submission . . . the family is a monarchy, though not a despotism; the father and mother, considered as one, are invested with patriarchal authority: and we carry out our idea still further; for we say that a holy family is in a sense a Theocracy.[26]

The authority of the family is central for conservatives, who would agree with philosopher Herbert Fingarette's claim:

> In terms of child abuse, [critics of corporal punishment] include the notion that it is wrong for the parent to use, or even to have authority to use, any kind of disciplinary

action that involves what we call corporal punishment, which means laying a hand on the child. Now, if that is child abuse, then it is something which many people over the ages, and many people today . . . are well-convinced is a perfectly reasonable way to run a family. [When] you deal with the family, you are dealing with an institution . . . that is the one fundamental opportunity for intimacy in a little community, a kind of peculiar, special intimacy, one which is rooted in eons of traditions. We don't know what we are fiddling with when we fiddle with that. It is an enormously valuable thing that a family should have a certain kind of intimacy.[27]

Of course one should not caricature this position by pushing it too far. As conservative columnist William F. Buckley wrote: "It is sometimes difficult to draw the line, but a line simply can and must be drawn between domestic discipline and domestic savagery."[28]

Fingarette was particularly concerned about the possibility of legislation damaging the integrity of the family. Rather than emphasizing the problem of child abuse, he focused on a totally different problem: that of preserving and strengthening the family. The strength of the traditional family is considered a foundation of Western society, but conservatives believe the family is being attacked from all quarters: delinquency, feminism, sex education, divorce, and premarital intercourse. Of course, when conservatives speak of the family, they are likely referring to the traditional nuclear family (two parents and their offspring). This structure has never been as common as its staunchest defenders imply. Throughout history, numerous family forms have existed—extended, single-parent, and communal. The conservative, then, is protecting an ideal, rather than a universal reality. To the conservative, however, working to preserve this ideal is a noble end: to maintain the social order in one's family is a microcosm of preserving the larger social order.

This moral privileging of the family makes little sense to the extreme libertarian or social democrat. They view the family as a contract among consenting individuals. Admittedly, children do not consent to this contract at birth and must be slowly given rights; still, they see nothing particularly sacred about the nuclear family structure. It may be efficient, but not *especially* moral, and so does not deserve to be specially protected by tradition or by law. The rights of individuals or protected classes are more relevant. One critic of Fingarette reminded him that the same argument he made about parents and children might be made about plantation owners and slaves.[29] A conservative would counter this by saying the family has a special status that did not apply to antebellum cotton plantations.

Whereas the social democrat is concerned with the "epidemic" of child abuse, the conservative is equally concerned with an "epidemic" of permissiveness. Conservatives attribute the "moral decline" of the United States to the permissive child-rearing techniques of the past few decades, and to the shunning of the basic and traditional values of society. For the conservative, the best response to the new permissiveness is to return to corporal punishment. Certainly preventative discipline is preferable to a subsequent onslaught of problems like delinquency, drug use, and premarital sex. Walter Williams summarized this view using the example of violence in schools:

Do we Americans, as parents, teachers, principals and others in positions of authority have the guts and willpower to control our youngsters? Or are we going to play costly games, such as having metal detectors at school entrances, video monitors, locked classrooms, hallway guards, teacher panic alarms and accept a jail-like atmosphere in our schools. . . . If the punishment for bringing a weapon to school were five lashes on the 6 o'clock news, there'd be an end to weapons being brought to school.[30]

Despite focusing on moral laxity, conservatives do not support harsh discipline for its own sake. No one argues that children should be hit as an end in itself. Conservatives emphasize that pain and love should be mixed and that corporal punishment is only a last resort and a sign of parental concern. Children, for their own good, need to be told "no" in a forceful enough way to stop detrimental behaviors. It is a sad commentary on the chasm between attitudes and behaviors that many parents who share these reasonable beliefs find they engage in unloving, brutal behavior.

## The Libertarian Point of View

The debate over whether parents should be allowed to hit their children is primarily between social democrats and conservatives. For libertarians, the debate offers two undesirable alternatives. Corporal punishment is alien to the spirit of libertarian child rearing, which attempts to maximize the freedom and dignity of the child. Many child-rearing books of the postwar era generally agree with the libertarian emphasis on the child as an individual worthy of respect and responsibility. One libertarian child-rearing manual advises parents that "Children are rational and logical within the context of their limited experience. Making allowances for their lack of experience, we should treat children exactly as we treat adults."[31]

To hit an adult is assault—should it be any different when done to a child? Bernice Weissbourd, president of a Chicago area agency that provides drop-in centers for parents of young children, suggested that "A child learns many lessons from being spanked, but responsibility is not necessarily one of them. He learns that there are forces in his world to be feared. . . . He learns that the bigger and stronger you are, the more power you have. He learns that hitting is a way to express feelings and solve problems."[32] Libertarians consider such lessons harmful because they undermine the personal respect and rationality a free society requires. Likewise, corporal punishment demeans the parent. From a libertarian position, it really does "hurt me more than it does you."

Lillian Katz, a professor of early childhood education, warned about the dangers of spanking: "Overall, spanking can best be thought of as something we use against our better judgment. It is something we do in 'hot' (as opposed to 'cold') blood. To spank in the heat of the moment is not recommended; but, once in a while, it is inevitable and forgivable. But to spank in cold blood, as a matter of deliberate, premeditated policy, is sadistic."[33] Violence is outside the pale of libertarian thought because it denies the validity of a society based on rationality.

Libertarians also share the conservative's concern with government intervention in child rearing. A tenet of their philosophy is the right of privacy. Consider the comments of John Maher, the founder of San Francisco's Delancy Street Foundation, a self-help foundation for drug addicts and criminals:

> Children's rights seem like something I would like to be in favor of. On the other hand . . . my fear of intervention in my family by the kind of clowns I find in our juvenile justice system would increase the possibility of violence in our culture. I would be outraged. On the other hand, the concept of children's rights sounds like something I should support. But I can't get my teeth in it. Does this mean we simply add rights for children to the Constitution, or do we create intervention agencies that we must then deal with?[34]

Unlike for the true conservative, the idea of children's rights is not offensive to libertarians; the problem is rather the government's enforcement of these rights. The libertarian rejects the legal doctrine of *parens patriae*—the belief that the state is a parent to its citizens—and spins fantasies of state control, as in an article titled "Family Abuse":

> The police often strike at night. Your children are seized and taken to a secret location. They are placed in the hands of state doctors who strip them down and give them thorough examinations, focusing attention on their genitalia. Meanwhile, you are hauled into court to face an inquisitorial hearing into your character. . . . Your guilt is essentially assumed. . . . Even among those who, against all odds, manage to prove their innocence and recover their children, many escape only by agreeing to state-directed psychological counseling, where therapists work to restructure one's mind and values.[35]

The images libertarians use could not be more at odds with the ones social democrats use. Indeed, some libertarians even suggest that programs in schools about child abuse prevention teach children rhetoric to use in private family disputes, bringing state agencies on their side.[36]

As is true for conservatives, most libertarians grit their teeth and agree that the government has a right to be involved in cases of extreme child abuse—one legitimate role of any government is protecting its citizens from harm. This does not imply that the libertarian is happy with the government's involvement in personal relations. Even though the family does not have the same sacredness for libertarians that it does for conservatives, the specter of government intervention deeply concerns them.

# Spanking and Social Research

Despite the fact that spanking is unfashionable among experts in child development, it is widely practiced. Many Americans feel they are what they are because of child-rearing practices that included corporal punishment. For their part, sociologists investigate the scope, prevalence and effects of corporal punishment. They ask, How much spanking occurs in American families? And what are its long-term effects? Murray Straus, a leading scholar of family violence and corporal punishment, wrote *Beating the Devil Out of Them: Corporal Punishment in American Families* (with Denise A. Donnelly) to address these questions. This book analyzes the practice and effects of corporal punishment using survey data from thousands of respondents.

Survey research strives to collect systematic information about attitudes, behaviors, and experiences across thousands of respondents. The goal is to identify broad patterns of behavior, to make predictions, and to test and refine theories. But to do this, one must start with a definition. Straus defined corporal punishment as "the use of physical force with the intention of causing a child to experience pain, but not injury, for the purpose of correction or control of the child's behavior."[37] Straus used data from the 1975 and 1985 National Family Violence Surveys to measure the prevalence of corporal punishment. The 1975 survey had 2,143 respondents; the 1985 survey had 4,032. The assumption in this research, and in most survey research, is that these people—a small part of the population—stand for all of us, because they were randomly selected to participate in the research. The fact that some people decline to participate is assumed not to bias the results.

Straus counted any incident in which a parent reported having thrown something at a child, or pushed, grabbed, shoved, slapped, or spanked a child as corporal punishment. As with any definition, one must ask if this definition is adequate, or might it be too broad? Any reported act involving more serious violence—for example, burning, scalding, hitting with objects, threatening with a knife or gun—was not counted as corporal punishment but as physical abuse.[38] Most surveys attempt to draw a representative sample of respondents so that the researchers can generalize the survey results from that sample to the population as a whole. Straus extrapolated nationwide patterns in applying corporal punishment from these survey data, assuming that the patterns found here would also be found in the larger population. Straus found that most American parents hit toddlers—often repeatedly—and young children. More than half of all parents continued using corporal punishment into the child's early teen years, and about a quarter continued until the child left home.

Straus predicted that corporal punishment would have long-term negative consequences on children. To address this question, Straus used "adult recall data" collected from 5,452 adults. Each respondent was asked: "Thinking about when you yourself were a teenager, about how often would you say your (mother, stepmother, father, stepfather) used corporal punishment, like slapping or hitting you? Think about the year in which this happened the most. Never, Once, Twice, 3–5 Times, 6–10 Times, 11–20 Times, More than 20 Times." The peak ages of experiencing such punishment as teenagers were thirteen and fourteen.[39] These respondents were also asked about their current well-being as adults. Straus found that respondents who reported being punished physically as children also reported experiencing more negative outcomes as adults. For example, the more the respondents were hit by their parents, the higher their scores were on an index measuring depressive symptoms, and the more likely they were to think about committing suicide. In sum, this research suggests that children who are spanked are more likely to report becoming depressed or suicidal, to develop drinking problems, to have difficulty attaining a high-level occupation and high income, and to engage in violent behavior as adults.[40]

Survey data yield quantifiable results that allow researchers to use *statistical control.* Suppose you believe that being spanked doesn't explain being depressed as an adult, but that witnessing your parents using violence against each other does. To test this idea, a researcher can exercise statistical control and hold a variable "constant." The researcher can sort all the people who witnessed their parents being violent into one group, and examine whether the people in that group who experienced corporal punishment still report more depression as adults than the people who did not experience corporal punishment. Straus found that regardless of one's sex, socioeconomic status, drinking problems, experience of marital violence, or witnessing violence between parents, when other explanations are held constant, corporal punishment on its own was a cause of adult depression. The theory behind this particular idea is that being punished physically for multiple years during childhood, releases hormones associated with stress that are linked to depression and that alter brain chemistry so as to produce depression.

Straus did not flinch from identifying some weaknesses in his research design. For example, asking one group of adults to describe how they use corporal punishment but a completely different group of adults about their memories of being spanked implies a comparison between two groups of unrelated data. A better but unrealistic method would have been to do a longitudinal study, in which people were observed being spanked and then tracked over the course of many years to see what outcomes were associated with having been spanked. It is also possible that the relationship between being spanked and later negative outcomes as an adult is purely spurious and explained better by some other variable, such as one's number of friends or educational attainment—variables that were not measured. People may also have erroneous memories of their childhood experiences, and surveys of reported behaviors are always vulnerable to misrepresentations by respondents.

Many people are spanked and do not become violent criminals—but this point, which Straus reported is often cited to refute his arguments, does not then imply that corporal punishment is harmless. Yet, surely it suggests that corporal punishment does not always have these negative effects, even if it serves to predispose people in negative ways. Straus acknowledged that he has not "proven" an absolute cause and effect relationship between corporal punishment and negative outcomes, such as depression and attaining low-income work. Yet, he argued strongly that his findings provide a compelling argument for reconsidering the use of corporal punishment and for investing in further research to provide more evidence about consequences of corporal punishment.

Straus noted that it is difficult to admit that our own parents did something wrong and that we might be doing something wrong to our own children—hence, it is difficult to accept that spanking is a counterproductive and brutal behavior. Yet, for Straus, it is also inconceivable that spanking's potential negative consequences have not raised an alarm. He wrote that millions of children are experiencing corporal punishment, are suffering currently, and are being placed at risk of future suffering. Straus is personally outraged by spanking, repeatedly asking how it can be illegal to slap an adult but perfectly legal to slap a weaker and defenseless child? As a result, one might wonder whether he is able to separate his personal beliefs from his research aims, even while admitting that the strength of his beliefs may be a result of his research. For Straus, the adverse consequences of spanking justify its condemnation. His argument is even embedded in the book's rhetoric, where he sometimes substituted the word *attack* for spanking. This is a choice that might not sit well for many readers, who may feel the term *attack* is better reserved for deliberate attempts to physically injure someone rather than to discipline them through what many parents see as loving, but firm action.

Because Murray Straus is an outspoken critic of corporal punishment, *Beating the Devil Out of Them* is an example of integrating advocacy and social science research. Straus did more than just seek to describe "objective reality"; he used his research data to urge parents to stop using corporal punishment and to call for public policies to that end. Straus's advocacy raises an age-old question for sociologists: Should they use their research to advocate for particular behaviors and public policies? Or is the proper scientific choice to avoid politics for fear of injecting bias into the research process? Straus emphasized what he considered the serious impacts corporal punishment has on society, and suggested that immediate actions need to be taken; as a result, he falls closest to the social democratic point of view.

## Spanking and the Socialization Process

The type of discipline parents select is a major factor in how their children develop. Parents are the primary role models for their children. Children are likely to define their morals by what they see their parents do. If a child is spanked by a loving parent, he or she could feel that, in some circumstances, inflicting pain is morally right. If parents insist that children obey them, this may lead children to have respect for authority. If children receive love from their parents or guardians, they will probably be accepting of others and contented with the justice of the social order.

Children see their reflection in the actions of their parents. Interactionists explain that parents are the primary "looking-glass self" in our culture, allowing the child to "create" his or her own identity through that of the parents. The faults children resent in their parents, their own children will likely resent in them. Those things children most admire about their parents, their children will likely admire in them. Children, in other words, are the products of the parents who socialize them. This is why family violence is so troubling. One of the strongest predictors of child abuse is whether the adult was abused as a child. Child abuse is not only a social problem, but also a self-perpetuating one.

Yet, a completely undisciplined child poses problems as well. Children are, alas, not "naturally" obedient; parents must, somehow, impress their will on their offspring. If we choose not to accept corporal punishment, this leaves the problem of how to teach children to follow appropriate behavior. Perhaps the discipline used in the home will also reflect itself in the courts of law and in the prisons of society. The larger question this chapter raises involves whether the choice of child-rearing discipline is best left up to parents or to the community.

Social democrats believe there is a moral imperative to protect the vulnerable members of society—our children. The government in some sense serves as the child's advocate. In contrast, the libertarian is more willing to let children fend for themselves in the rough and tumble of family life. To the libertarian, the government's power to decide for the child is as abhorrent as the potential tyranny of the family. For the conservative, there is no contest; the family is a "natural" institution whose autonomy must be protected. The family, rather than the government, prevents society from breaking down. These views reflect the philosophies of socialization that each perspective has. The conservative looks to the family, the social democrat counts on the society, and the libertarian stresses the autonomy of children, mothers, and fathers.

## Questions

1. Do you believe that in some circumstances parents should spank their children?
2. What lessons do children learn from being spanked?
3. Are all forms of corporal punishment "child abuse"? What is child abuse?
4. What is the appropriate punishment for a parent convicted of child abuse?
5. Should schools administer corporal punishment to children?
6. Should welfare agencies interview friends and neighbors of a family suspected of child abuse before it has been proven?
7. Is Sweden's law forbidding all corporal punishment a proper use of government power?
8. Should the government be involved in family discipline? How?
9. Since people abused as children are prone to become child abusers, should they be forbidden to have children?
10. Do you believe that corporal punishment has any long-term negative effects? Any long-term positive ones?
11. Do we need more or less corporal punishment?

## For Further Study

Erlanger, Howard. "Social Class and Corporal Punishment in Childrearing: A Reassessment." *American Sociological Review* 39 (1974): 68–85.

Greven, Philip. *Spare the Child: The Religious Roots of Physical Punishment and the Psychological Impact of Physical Abuse.* New York: Knopf, 1990.

Hewlett, Sylvia Ann. *When the Bough Breaks: The Cost of Neglecting Our Children.* New York: Basic Books, 1991.

Pfohl, Steven J. "The Discovery of Child Abuse." *Social Problems* 24 (1977): 310–323.

"Violence Toward Youth in Families" (special issue). *Journal of Social Issues* 35 (1979): 1–176.

Straus, Murray A., and Denise A. Donnelly. *Beating the Devil Out of Them: Corporal Punishment in American Families.* San Francisco: Lexington Books/Jossey-Bass, 1994.

Straus, Murray A., Richard J. Gelles, and Suzanne K. Steinmetz. *Behind Closed Doors: Violence in the American Family.* New York: Doubleday, 1980.

## Notes and References

1.  Iona Opie and Peter Opie, *The Lore and Language of Schoolchildren* (London: Oxford University Press, 1959), p. 2.
2.  Jean Piaget, *The Origins of Intelligence in Children* (New York: International Universities Press, 1952).
3.  Charles Horton Cooley, *Human Nature and Social Order* (New York: Schocken, 1964), p. 184.
4.  George Herbert Mead, *Mind, Self, and Society* (Chicago: University of Chicago Press, 1934), pp. 150–152.
5.  *Ibid.*, pp. 152–163.
6.  Erving Goffman, *Presentation of Self in Everyday Life* (New York: Anchor, 1959), pp. 208–237.
7.  Murray A. Straus quoted these survey results, from 1999, in a letter to the *Wall Street Journal*, dated June 11, 2000. See also Gallup Organization, *Disciplining Children in America: A Gallup Poll Report* (survey #765) (Princeton, NJ: Author).
8.  The figure of 90 percent is referred to in Murray A. Straus, *Beating the Devil Out of Them*, p. 199. Data on spanking through the adolescent years is cited from Murray A. Straus and Julie H. Stewart, "Corporal Punishment by American Parents: National Data on Prevalence, Chronicity, Severity, and Duration, in Relation to Child and Family Characteristics," *Clinical Child and Family Psychology Review*, Vol. 2, No. 2, 1999, p. 55.
9.  Barbara Carson, "Parents Who Don't Spank: Deviation in the Legitimation of Physical Force," Ph.D. Dissertation (Sociology), University of New Hampshire, 1986.
10.  Straus and Donnelly, *Beating the Devil Out of Them*, p. 439.
11.  Ed Magnuson, "Child Abuse: The Ultimate Betrayal," *Time* (September 5, 1983): 20.
12.  U.S. Department of Health and Human Services, "HHS Reports New Child Abuse and Neglect Statistics," *HHS NEWS*, published April 10, 2001.
13.  Ibid.
14.  Howard Erlanger, "Social Class and Corporal Punishment in Childrearing," pp. 68–85; Richard J. Gelles, "Violence in the Family: A Review of Research in the Seventies," *Journal of Marriage and the Family* 42 (November, 1980): 878–879.
15.  Herbert Costner, *The Changing Folkways of Parenthood: A Content Analysis* (New York: Arno Press, 1980); Peter Stearns, "The Problem of Change in Emotions Research: New Standards for Anger in Twentieth-Century American Childrearing," *Symbolic Interaction* 10 (1987): pp. 85–99.
16.  Magnuson, "Child Abuse," p. 22.
17.  Cited in Lynn Rossellini, "When to Spank," *U.S. News and World Report* (April 13, 1998): p. 55. See also Diana Baumrind, "A Blanket Injunction against Disciplinary Use of Spanking Is Not Warranted by the Data," *Pediatrics* (October 1996): 828; David Benatar, "Corporal Punishment," *Social Theory and Practice* 24 (Summer 1998): 237–260; and Daniel Costello, "Spanking Makes a Comeback," *Wall Street Journal* (June 9, 2000): W1.

18. Amelia Adamo, "New Rights for Children and Parents in Sweden," *Children Today* (November–December, 1981): 15.

19. Irene Barth, "Bruising a Parent's Image to Protect a Battered Child," *Minneapolis Star and Tribune* (September 13, 1983): 13A.

20. "U.S. Seems Powerless on Child Abuse," *Atlanta Journal/Constitution* (September 15, 1991): A20.

21. Lois G. Foner, "For Children's Sake, Bring Back the Orphanage," *Star/Tribune* (Minneapolis), (November 21, 1988): 9A.

22. John Vinocur, "Swedes Shun Norse Adage, Ban Spanking," *New York Times* (April 4, 1979): A7.

23. Similar laws have been passed in Austria, Finland, Norway, and Denmark. See Claire Sanders, "Smack Habits," *New Statesman* (July 14, 1989): 25.

24. Jim Klobuchar, "Will Kindergarten Kids Caucus?" *Minneapolis Star Tribune* (April 11, 1979): 1B.

25. Bob Greene, "The Lessons That Must Be Learned from the Horror," *Chicago Tribune* (March 31, 1999).

26. D. Newell, "A Holy Family—Parental Government and Discipline," *Christian Family Magazine* (1842): 123–124.

27. "Family Discipline, Intimacy, and Children Rights," *Center Magazine* (November/December, 1981): 36–37.

28. William F. Buckley, "The Child Beaters and Their Critics," *National Review* (April 16, 1982): 449.

29. "Family Discipline, Intimacy, and Children's Rights," p. 39.

30. Walter E. Williams, "Making a Case for Corporal Punishment," *Insight on the News* (September 13, 1994): 46.

31. Frances Kendall, *Super Parents, Super Children* (Johannesburg: Delta, 1983): 20.

32. Bernice Weissbourd, "A Good Spanking: A Bad Idea," *Parents* (September 1981): 100.

33. Lillian G. Katz, "Spank or Speak?" *Parents* (February 1980): 84.

34. "Family Discipline, Intimacy, and Children's Rights," p. 39.

35. Allan C. Carlson, "Family Abuse," *Reason* (May 1986): 34.

36. Ellen L. Hopkins, "Abuse the Rights of Parents," *Newsweek* (October 18, 1993): 26.

37. Straus and Donnelly, *Beating the Devil Out of Them*, p. 4.

38. Ibid., p. 202.

39. Ibid., pp. 199–200.

40. Ibid., p. 165.

# CHAPTER THREE

# Deviance and Social Control: Should Drug Use Be Legalized?

■ Who is more sensitive to rules than a teenager? When a teenager tests the limits of what he or she can say, wear, drink, smoke, watch, or hear, an age-old sociological issue comes into focus—the minuet between forces of social control and forces that attempt to evade that control. Whatever is ordered, some resist. Indeed, the enforcement of norms and values appears necessary because many of the actions that are controlled are the ones people might wish to choose. If we did not desire to engage in such behavior, control would be unnecessary.

Possibly no arena of social life has been as closely examined by sociologists as the relationship between deviance and social control. Sociological studies date back well into the nineteenth century, including Emile Durkheim's classic empirical study *Suicide* (1897). The question of why deviance occurs is as central to the discipline as is the question of how social order is possible—the two questions demand each other. Social order does not come out of thin air—it is produced. In orderly societies, human beings establish institutions to enforce social control. Exploring how the social order is constructed requires examining how and why people deviate and our responses to those who break the rules.

Simply put, *deviance* is behavior that is thought to be improper by large numbers of people in a society—behavior that violates their social expectations. Deviance involves not only behaving in a manner distinct from most people (becoming a surgeon would qualify under that criterion), but also behaving in a way that is negatively valued. Few behaviors are inherently deviant; what is considered deviant differs from one culture to another.

Social control is designed to prevent or limit deviant behavior. Some social scientists distinguish between ideological social control and direct social control. *Ideological social control* refers to attempts to shape people's perceptions so that they are willing to accept the status quo and the legitimacy of social institutions. The family, the church, one's peer group, the schools one attends, and the mass media each contribute to the belief that the dominant view of the world is the correct one. Of course, these institutions are not in complete agreement, nor do they work sufficiently well to enforce a total ideology; yet, most people adopt the worldview these institutions offer. People may disobey or question some values, such as religious prohibitions on abortion and premarital sex, yet few people reject (at least publicly) religious institutions or belief in God altogether. It takes either a person with a very strong (or perverse) sense of self or a person in a strong subculture to reject a dominant view of how life should be lived.

In order to deal with major acts of deviance, societies maintain a collection of formal institutions to force people into appropriate patterns of behavior or to remove them from society. The main elements of this direct social control are the police force, the courts, the prison system, and mental hospitals. Direct social control centers on attempts to punish, change, or geographically isolate those who deviate or do not "fit in," including the mentally ill, criminals, and political dissidents. Even those institutions that on their face have a humanitarian goal of serving others actively enforce social control. Police officers can arrest and detain individual citizens without their consent and physically overpower them if they resist an officer's orders; mental institutions are legally permitted to retain custody of patients against their will until institutional authorities pronounce them "cured."

Although it would be nice to believe that institutions of direct social control treat all individuals who come before them equitably and without regard to class or race, many sociological research studies reveal that, sadly, such is not the case. Blacks and the poor, in particular, receive fewer leniencies than other groups. For example, while a majority of citizens may perceive police officers as protecting and serving them, some African Americans and other minorities who live in large urban cities view the police as an "occupying army." They may also be subject to "racial profiling" (sometimes labeled DWB—"driving while black"!) and to disproportionately severe sentencing within the criminal justice system. Rich white kids, of course, do sometimes get into trouble, but a greater presumption exists that their "crimes" are just a phase, rather than the start of a career of crime. This may be right, since other forms of social control are more inclined to push them into moral lives, and their youthful sins never label them permanently.[1] Still, that is little comfort for those not afforded similar mercy.

Many sociological approaches attempt to explain deviant behavior. Some focus on individual characteristics of deviant actors, and others examine the influence of environmental factors. *Social pathologists* examine the physiological characteristics of people who break the rules, arguing, for example, that violent criminals differ physically from "normal" people. They have, perhaps, a genetic anomaly (an extra male chromosome), special physiques, brain malfunctions, or hereditary factors based on race or ethnicity. Such biologically driven theories have not been shown to be valid. To be taken seriously, they will have to be more sophisticated and complex than they currently are.

Others examine the psychological characteristics of deviant actors, suggesting they lacked affection in childhood, had psychosexual traumas, or never developed proper attachment to adults or other children. In theory, it should be possible to predict that these children will "get in trouble," and then to give them appropriate conditioning or training to prevent this outcome. Yet, at our current stage of knowledge, the science behind making these predictions is imperfect and in any event, making such individual predictions and following up on them raises civil liberties questions.

Some researchers claim that psychological and social features of living in urban environments, such as overcrowding, produce deviant behaviors.[2] A second environmental argument is that the sort of people a person associates with determines that person's subsequent behavior: Deviants associate with individuals different from those with whom nondeviants associate. This approach is termed *differential association*.[3] People learn both attitudes that approve of deviant behaviors and ways to ignore moral prohibitions against them from their associates. Current arguments along this line attempt to explain the behavior of the "underclass" by virtue of their isolation from those with more socially approved lifestyles. In studies focusing on the distinctive subculture of the lower class—the so-called *culture of poverty*—many values of this group run directly counter to the culture of the larger society and are more congruent with deviant behavior.[4] Again, social isolation and de facto segregation help to reinforce these values. A third view examines the goals and values of potential criminals and argues that they do not follow socially approved means to achieve socially desired ends, often because approved means are closed to them.[5] In such cases, people innovate new means and turn to crime to acquire otherwise inaccessible ends. There is little agreement among social scientists as to which, if any, of these approaches best explains deviant behavior.

Other sociologists do not examine the deviants themselves but rather the society they feel makes them deviant. According to these theorists, society "blames the victim."[6] The leading approach of this type is *labeling theory*. According to this interactionist argument, almost everyone has acted deviantly, but not everyone gets labeled deviant. Whether a person gets labeled depends on who he or she is and whether he or she has been fortunate enough to avoid an official stigma. In the case of drugs, since a large portion of young adults have tried marijuana, much of the youthful population could be labeled as drug offenders, yet relatively few have had this misfortune. Once labeled, people find themselves treated conspicuously—their behavior is now evaluated differently (and with closer scrutiny), and there is less tolerance for additional offenses. Because of these constraints *secondary deviance* occurs, that is, individuals now have an increasingly deviant identity as a result of their label. Being shunned by those not labeled encourages further deviant behavior. Other deviants may now be the only friends someone labeled deviant can make; the underground economy may become the only job market. From this interactionist perspective, how a person is labeled is a direct consequence of their relations with others.

As in most things, functionalists and conflict theorists disagree about the significance of deviant behavior. The functionalist sees deviance as ultimately caused by the failure of a social system to socialize its members properly. The functionalist believes deviance is illegitimate but has some positive effects. The labeling of some people as deviant brings nondeviant members of society together and emphasizes their similarities in contrast to the behavior of deviants. Social order is reinforced through such affirmations. Conflict theorists, on the other hand, stress the social and political components of deviance. For conflict theorists, deviant behavior exposes social injustices. Blocked opportunities, economic and cultural disenfranchisement, and institutional discrimination breed crime, deviant labels, and the brutal enforcement of social control, particularly against minorities and the poor. For example, John Hagan and his coauthors, in a recent study of crime and homelessness among urban youth, argued that cities with more social welfare programs to benefit youth have lower youth crime rates than cities without them.[7] To eliminate deviance, people must radically restructure the social system, altering the social conditions that cause deviance and the class system that permits some people the luxury to define others as deviant.

## ■ Question:

### Should drug use be legalized?

Almost forty years ago, Bob Dylan sang, "Everybody must get stoned."[8] Considering the double meaning of stoned, this lyric has great resonance for the continuing drug debate in U.S. society. If we include alcohol and nicotine among drugs, almost everyone has gotten "stoned," yet relatively few are "stoned" by the legal system.

The National Commission on Marijuana and Drug Abuse defines a drug as any chemical that affects the structure or function of a living organism.[9] Such a definition covers a lot—marijuana, cocaine, heroin, LSD, alcohol, nicotine, caffeine, and perhaps salt, sugar, and beef fat. Nevertheless, most people agree on what is meant by "chemical abuse," "substance abuse," or "drug abuse." Alcohol, which by all reasonable definitions, is a "drug," and a potentially harmful one at that, is legal (though regulated), whereas marijuana, which seems to be harmful when used continually, but less clearly so than alcohol, is not legal in the United States.[10] Tobacco, more deadly than either marijuana or alcohol, is not typically discussed in terms of drug abuse, and so will not be examined here.

Alcohol is the drug of preference for most Americans, due to its easy availability and relatively mild (and sometimes beneficial) consequences when used in moderation. According to the National Institute on Drug Abuse, about half of all Americans ages twelve and older (51.7 percent) report being current drinkers of alcohol, which translates into 105 million people. Among youths twelve to seventeen, an estimated 18.6 percent used alcohol in the last month. Of college students eighteen to twenty-two years old, 63.2 percent reported drinking within the last month, with roughly half (31.7 percent) falling into a category of "binge drinking," meaning they consumed more than five drinks at one sitting. Of persons eighteen to twenty-five, 16.4 percent reported using marijuana or hashish within the last month. The figures for other drugs are lower, but there are hundreds of thousands of new drug users every year—1998 saw 934,000 new cocaine users and 1,245,000 new hallucinogen users.[11] Despite legal constraints, many Americans are willing to pay the price for using a wide variety of mind-altering substances.

Much of the discussion about legalizing drugs deals with how harmful they are. This is a complicated area about which we are learning more each year. It is fair to say that drugs are not harmless, but neither are they as deadly as a bullet from a revolver. Yet, the amount of damage they do is not crucial to the issues we describe. After all, knowing the evidence about cigarette smoking has not caused our society to outlaw cigarettes, and until recently some high schools even provided rooms in which students could smoke. The first federal law aimed at controlling the use of drugs was the 1914 Harrison Act, which was designed to regulate, license, and tax the distribution of narcotic drugs. Perhaps unexpectedly, the Narcotics Division of the Treasury Department, given the responsibility to enforce the law, criminalized the use of these drugs, turning users into "criminals." The first law regulating marijuana was the 1937 Marijuana Tax Act, which provided severe penalties for use of the drug—and as much as twenty years imprisonment for possession. Some state laws were even tougher, providing for life imprisonment. Louisiana and Missouri permitted the death penalty for drug sales to minors.

By the late 1960s and 1970s, sentiment slowly began to change toward control of marijuana, a consequence of the drug's widespread popularity, perhaps even because the children of leading politicians were using those drugs. Although no state has legalized marijuana, eleven states, from Mississippi to Minnesota, Maine to Oregon, decriminalized the use of small amounts. In 1970, the federal government sharply reduced the penalties for "crimes" involving marijuana. During this period, politicians from Barry Goldwater to Jimmy Carter supported its decriminalization. From 1969 to 1977, the percentage of Americans who supported the legalization of marijuana increased from 12 to 28 percent. Predictions were made that marijuana would be legalized in a decade.[12] Since 1978, however, no new states have decriminalized marijuana, and some, such as Alaska, recriminalized its use. By the late 1980s and into the twenty-first century, there was a greater concern among parents and politicians about the use of all drugs (with only 14 percent supporting drug legalization).[13] Evidence of the health risks of various drugs also may have affected people's attitudes; by 1988, there were approximately 6,000 deaths from illegal drugs—about half of these from cocaine.[14] Ten years later, in 1998, 4,587 cocaine deaths alone were reported in the United States.[15]

While varying both by time and by drug, drug use recently seems to be decreasing, although in some communities it is still a major problem. It now appears that no public policy changes are likely. Attitudes toward "drugs" changed dramatically with marijuana being almost forgotten in the process of making cocaine "a folk devil." Although a few brave politicians, like New Mexico governor Gary Johnson and former secretary of state George Shultz, called for legalization or decriminalization of some drugs, most politicians wish to increase penalties for those caught using and, especially, selling cocaine and its potent form, crack. "Just Say No!" may be the most symptomatic phrase of the late twentieth century; the "war on drugs" was a particularly revealing metaphor of our period. Former president Clinton with his countercultural past and dubious claim to have tried marijuana, but not to have inhaled, was in no position to advocate legalizing drugs, and he quickly distanced himself from Dr. Jocelyn Elders, his surgeon general, who suggested that legalization might deserve study. However, by the end of the 1990s, in the case of marijuana, the tide began shifting slowly toward a less punitive policy. Several states, including Alaska, Colorado, Hawaii, Maine, Nevada,

Oregon, Washington, and most importantly, California, passed statewide referendums in which a majority approved the legalization of marijuana for medical use. Contrary to these statewide referendums, marijuana remains illegal under federal law, placing law enforcement officials in those states that decline to prosecute marijuana use for medical purposes at odds with their federal counterparts.[16]

The seesawing debate over legalizing marijuana and other drugs is critically important because of the tremendous profits associated with selling illicit drugs and the staggering human and financial costs of drug enforcement policies. In 1988, the retail value of the marijuana grown in the United States was approximately $33 billion, making it, according to one source, the largest cash crop grown in this country.[17] Overall, illegal drugs today represent a significant segment of the U.S. economy, estimated at about a $150 billion market. It has been estimated that drug use costs over $75 billion per year of public money, is responsible for nearly 50 percent of the million Americans who are today in jail, and takes the time of 400,000 police officers.[18] In the words of former secretary of labor Robert Reich: "Narcotics is one of America's major industries, right up there with consumer electronics, automobiles and steel."[19]

## The Conservative Point of View

Most, though not all, conservatives oppose legalizing drugs, and public opinion clearly supports them, with the exception of public approval for legalizing marijuana for medical use. Drugs, with their mind-altering properties, give people pleasure, and this private pleasure separates them from those social institutions that should be most important; they separate the individual from the community, and they reflect and cause the rejection of social mores, a major threat to order. This view is reflected in the extreme rhetoric of California's former state superintendent of public instruction, Max Rafferty. "What to do about the dope syndrome, Mom and Pop?" asked Rafferty. "First, recognize it for what it is. Just one more symptom of the nation's unraveling moral fiber. A sign of our times. Then resolve to combat it in your own family, mercilessly, with no holds barred. Remember that souls are the things actually at stake in the war you're declaring, and fight accordingly."[20] Former President Reagan claimed that drug sellers are "killing America and terrorizing it with slow but sure chemical destruction."[21] One New York City councilman responded to the threat of drugs by suggesting that we chain addicts to trees so that people could spit on them.[22] Some claim that drug users display an "amotivational syndrome" that deprives the society of these citizens' work in its behalf. In other words, they remove themselves from the community from which they should be contributing. Consider the remarks of columnist Carl Rowan:

> As surely as if they were nuclear bombs from a dreaded enemy, the tons of heroin from Asia, the mountains of cocaine from Bolivia and Peru, the endless supply of marijuana, Quaaludes and other illicit drugs from Columbia—and from American farms and laboratories—are wrecking this society. . . . Illegal drugs are playing havoc with our business communities, with sales of marijuana, heroin and cocaine commonplace on

Wall Street. Drug abuse has become the scourge of professional athletics, the curse of our entertainment world from Hollywood to Broadway, a shame of Congress. It is a tragedy that touches every type of family in this land.[23]

The real threat of drugs for the conservative is the danger they pose to social order. In particular, conservatives are concerned about the effects of drug use on children. If children are not properly socialized, the continuation of an orderly society is hopeless. The fact that the young are likely to indulge makes drugs a particular menace for the conservative. Richard Vigilante, an editorial writer for the *Charleston Daily Mail,* recognized this, commenting, "The special dangers for young users and the prospect of 10 to 15 percent of the adolescent population being too doped up to mature normally or get an education certainly justify, in theory, state intervention."[24] As former drug czar William Bennett noted pungently, "Why, in God's name, should we foster the use of a drug that makes you stupid?"[25]

While conservatives do not like government interference, they do believe that government action is necessary when there is a substantial danger to the fabric or structure of society. Conservatives accept the basic right of government to intervene to protect "core values." Ultimately, it is harm to people that justifies action, even though there might be a reduction in drug-related crime if drugs were widely available. Judianne Densen-Gerber, founder of Odyssey House, an experimental program for young drug abusers, is concerned that

> the major value question brought into focus is whether society values its property more than its people. The legalization of all narcotic substances, particularly heroin, would lessen the amount of crime, especially crimes against property. But such legalization would increase the number of the afflicted and the severity of the disease in each individual addict. As an example, during Prohibition, although millions of people violated the law by drinking, the number of alcoholics markedly decreased.[26]

The Swiss city of Zurich attempted to handle their drug problem by setting aside a park in which drugs were decriminalized. Health care was available and clean syringes supplied. Within a few years, the experiment was halted as the park was filled with litter and soaked with urine. Worse, the cheap availability of drugs increased the number of young users.[27]

The conservative contends that taking drugs is not a "victimless crime." The drug user does not live in isolation but is part of a family, a church, a community, and a society, and society has an obligation to uphold moral standards. As political scientist James Q. Wilson noted:

> Society is not and could never be a collection of autonomous individuals. We all have a stake in ensuring that each of us displays a minimal level of dignity, responsibility, and empathy. We cannot, of course, coerce people into goodness, but we can and should insist that some standards must be met if society itself—on which the very existence of the human personality depends—is to persist. Drawing the line that defines those standards is difficult and contentious, but if crack and heroin use do not fall below it, what does?[28]

Taking drugs signals that one refuses to take responsibilities as a citizen. In this way, drugs are a threat to the continuation of social order.

## The Libertarian Point of View

The 2000 Libertarian Party platform advocated the repeal of all laws that prohibit the production, sale, possession, or use of drugs. For the libertarian, drug use is a personal matter in which the State has no business. The radical psychiatrist, Thomas Szasz, stated this position eloquently. Szasz wrote, "Every individual is capable of injuring or killing himself. This potentiality is a fundamental expression of human freedom. . . . I believe that just as we regard freedom of speech and religion as fundamental rights, so we should also regard freedom of self-medication as a fundamental right."[29] Szasz, like most libertarians, believed strongly in free will. The choice of the individual to do well or do ill is ultimately a personal choice. Szasz even argued that drugs are like ideas. "Although I recognize that some drugs—notably heroin, the amphetamines, and LSD, among those now in vogue—may have undesirable or dangerous consequences, I favor free trade in drugs for the same reason the Founding Fathers favored free trade in ideas. In an open society, it is none of the government's business what idea a man puts into his mind; likewise it should be none of the government's business what drug he puts into his body."[30]

This right to control one's body parallels the argument that pro-choice activists make about the right to abortion. Szasz made an interesting point in generalizing his argument by noting that most medicines are available only with a doctor's prescription. If you wish to give yourself insulin or penicillin, you need a doctor's signature (and you pay the doctor for that signature), rather than just purchasing it yourself. Szasz saw this control as being as wrong as restrictive drug laws.

For some libertarians, the issue is the right to privacy; for others, it is the right to freedom of choice; and for still others, it is the right to pursue happiness. H. L. Mencken once derided Puritanism as a lurking fear that someone somewhere may be happy, and after all, according to Michael Aldrich, drug use is enjoyable: "Marijuana should be legalized because it's fun. Social use of *cannabis* [marijuana] depends primarily on the fact that altering one's perception is pleasurable; if the mental changes produced by smoking, eating, or drinking marijuana are not pleasurable, use will not normally be continued."[31] Of course, this position assumes that the drug does not control the individual and that the individual has sufficient will power to make his or her own decisions about drug use. We strongly enjoy consuming and do, in fact, consume regularly many things, even against our better judgment (for example, coffee or chocolate), but does this mean that we are physiologically addicted? There is no single definition of "addiction." Just as we learn to use alcohol, we can learn to use drugs. Just as our society (imperfectly) socializes people to the use of alcohol and regulates its use, so libertarians suggest we can do with drugs.

Critics of current policy believe laws create the "drug problem," rather than the drugs themselves.[32] Prohibition turns otherwise honest citizens into criminals. Further, making drugs illegal may increase drug impurities and make drugs stronger.[33] Consider the increased potency of "crack cocaine" and the decreased potency of "lite beer." The libertarian disputes the conservative's contention that drug use is not a victimless crime, saying that although some may be indirectly hurt or offended by drug use, and relationships may change, coercion is not involved. Indeed, laws against drug use cost taxpayers enormous sums in law enforcement (estimates are as high as $17 billion per year) and thousands of lives in drug-sale related murders and crimes committed to get money for drugs, priced artificially high because of the additional costs involved in distributing an illegal product.

Libertarians also perceive a grave and urgent problem in those laws giving the government additional powers of intervention and control. Drug laws give the police extensive powers to search cars, people, and property—powers libertarians feel are far more deadly than an occasional toke or snort of cocaine. Drug laws, accompanied and supported by a frightening fervor, permit government intervention far beyond any acceptable level. Sociologist Erich Goode described this win-at-all-costs fervency:

> What counts is crushing the monster of drug abuse. Pragmatism enters only through the backdoor. What we have here is a kind of holy war, a struggle of good against evil—and winning it can represent an end, a goal, and a good in itself. There can be no compromise with evil. It is assumed that harsher penalties translate into less use but it is not especially important if it does not. What counts is being on the right side and being tough and uncompromising against the enemy.[34]

As theologian Walter Wink noted, arguing for legalization: "When we oppose evil with the same weapons that evil employs, we commit the same atrocities, violate the same civil liberties and break the same laws as do those whom we oppose. We become what we hate."[35] From this perspective, the war on drugs has us as casualties.

## The Social Democratic Point of View

Social democrats are of several minds about regulating drug use. They realize that drugs often harm the most vulnerable groups in society—minorities and the young; yet, they also recognize that drug enforcement has typically come down hardest on these same groups. The social democrat points out that for most of our history, drugs have not been regulated. Why did this change? The answer: racial and ethnic prejudice. David Richards, in his book *Sex, Drugs, Death, and the Law,* wrote that "the use of liquor in the United States was identified with the Catholic immigrants and their subversive (non-Protestant) values; when heroin came under attack, it was identified with Chinese influences from which America, it was said, must be protected; marijuana was associated with undesirable Hispanic influences on American values, and cocaine with black influences."[36] President William Howard Taft, for example, linked cocaine to rape by Southern blacks.[37] More recently, the attack on drugs has been seen by some to be an attack on young people. Significantly, one of the states with the most liberal drug laws is Utah, a state with a homogeneous population.[38]

Class bias is evident in who gets arrested for drug abuse and who does not. Drug laws do not affect most middle-class citizens, whereas the poor, the young, and non-whites receive the brunt of enforcement. For some on the Left, such as Michael Rossman, a San Francisco political activist, this presents a cruel paradox—while the government attacks the young, it ignores other "criminal elements":

> As for the government, I think it should keep its bloody hands off the young and its sacraments . . . and turn its attention towards cleansing our society of its dreadful ugliness and violence, instead of helping industry turn the sky black for a buck, exploit man as badly as nature, and play at genocide here and there.[39]

Ultimately the drug problem becomes, for social democrats, an economic problem, connected to societal racism. Ira Glasser, the executive director of the American Civil Liberties Union, noted that drug dealing occurs because of a lack of economic justice: "Drug dealing is the major economic opportunity this country provides ghetto youth. How do we tell kids with no realistic economic opportunity, 'just say no' to $300 or more a day? The money, not the drug, attracts many ambitious young people into a life of violence."[40] Pushing drugs is one of the few means of escaping poverty. The former police chief of Kansas City, Joseph McNamara, noted the futility of drug enforcement efforts given the lucrative nature of the drug trade: "About $500 worth of heroin or cocaine in a source country will bring in about $100,000 on the streets of an American city. All the cops, armies, prisons, and executions in the world cannot impede a market with that kind of tax free profit margin."[41]

Social democrats are not calling for government inaction, but, rather, for government action in other areas, such as fighting discrimination and pollution. With regard to drug use, social democrats do not call for a free market in drugs, as do libertarians; they want a regulated market. Some, such as *Consumer Reports*, speak of drugs (especially marijuana) as a hazardous product, which should be regulated. Implicit in the social democrat's view is extensive government regulation of the quality of drugs. This would require the Food and Drug Administration or the Consumer Product Safety Commission to ensure the purity and quality of the drugs, and tax or even sell them. Columnist Charles Krauthammer satirized where this might lead:

> You come in and browse at a government-run store that prices and sells the stuff. After checking out competing brands of hashish, heroin, crack, and PCP, you pay for what you want and take the lot home. But . . . you are not permitted to buy a lethal dose unless you have a doctor's prescription. . . . *The Economist* . . . weighs in with the helpful suggestion that it should be distributed by the . . . "post office, which has perfected the art of driving customers away."[42]

Ultimately, this social democratic approach makes the "problem" of drug "abuse" a medical problem, rather than a legal one.

Yet to more radical social democrats, the real purpose of the drug war has been to divert attention from poverty, urban decay, unemployment, and an unjust distribution of social resources by blaming all social problems on the "chemical bogeyman"—a premise that also attempts to persuade people that drug problems reflect character flaws and not an outcome of structural inequality.[43] This scapegoating has led to the implementation of increasingly severe criminal sentences for drug offenders, leading the United States to have one of the highest incarceration rates in the Western world, disproportionately incarcerating minorities and the poor. Radical social democrats also side with libertarians in perceiving the war on drugs as having had a corrupting influence on law enforcement. They cite multiple cases of police officers "testi-lying" about how they obtained evidence of drug offenses, implying a significant encroachment on civil liberties.

There is, however, another side to the social democratic argument—a position that is not as lenient toward legalizing drug use. Social democrats opposed to drug legalization are concerned about the effects of legalization on blacks, Hispanics, and the white underclass. In 1970, the board of trustees of the American Civil Liberties Union refused to support a proposal to allow the freedom to use and purchase heroin because of what it might do to minorities.[44] Since social democrats believe in a benevolently parental government, such thinking makes sense. Their approach criticizes the "ideology of tolerance." Ronald Bayer, an expert on attitudes toward heroin, described heroin decriminalization as repressive.

> The ideology of tolerance, present as a critical force in the service of freeing those caught in the web of contemporary social control, actually tends to serve a profoundly repressive function. . . . Instead of assisting in the struggle against human misery those concepts provide the justification for choosing human misery. Because the ideology of tolerance tends to conceal the extent to which certain forms of deviance are reactions to deprivations rooted in the social order—indeed, can be considered as determined by that order—and because it seeks to integrate behavior that should serve as the starting point for a critique of society, it serves to neutralize the possibility of opposition.[45]

This view denies some of the drug user's autonomy, but it does so because the proponents believe these individuals do not understand the structural reasons for their drug habit. These users do not recognize that drug use prevents them from asserting their rights and gaining economic and social justice. Physical addiction and a profit-driven economic system reinforce each other in destroying the human potential of these young people. Such an understanding puts decision making where, some suggest, it rightfully belongs—in the hands of the sociologist.

# Marijuana and Social Research

For many students, marijuana seems almost as much a part of college life as multiple-choice tests. It was not always so. Prior to the mid-1960s, "blowing smoke" or "sipping tea" was something that "good" people did not do. Marijuana was found in various deviant subcultures—jazz musicians, beat poets, and prostitutes. It was partly for this reason that Howard S. Becker's article "Becoming a Marijuana User" had such a dramatic impact when it was published in the prestigious *American Journal of Sociology* in

1953.[46] Not only did Becker present the thoughts and actions of marijuana users in their own words, but also he did not treat them as criminals! He did not ask where these people went wrong.

The problem for Becker, a prominent symbolic interactionist, was How does a person learn to smoke marijuana properly? How does he or she define the effects of the drug, and how does he or she decide these effects are pleasurable? In order to answer these questions, Becker (and his colleagues Harold Finestone and Solomon Kobrin) conducted in-depth interviews with fifty marijuana users to learn about their experiences with the drug—how they became socialized to marijuana use.

Unlike many in-depth interview studies, Becker was not particularly concerned with the *people* he interviewed but with unraveling the *process* of becoming a marijuana user and the *natural history* of drug use. Becker did not agree with those who suggest that marijuana use is related to some trait in the individual user—a point of view that we can now largely discard since a large segment of American youths have tried the drug. Instead, Becker asked What must someone *do* to construct the social experience of "getting high"?

Choosing to rely on in-depth interviews, Becker was, in some sense, at the mercy of the users for his information and, thus, had to rely on their perceptions. By treating a "deviant" as a normal person, this research technique leaned toward the libertarian attitude of refusing to condemn behavior on the basis of societal attitudes. To accept the informants' accounts as accurate implies (although it does not insist) someone must see this behavior as an acceptable choice of rational, reasonable people—or why else trust them? While conducting the interviews, Becker moonlighted as a professional jazz musician, so we might suppose that he had some familiarity with this subculture. This permitted him to check his interview findings with information gained elsewhere.

Have you smoked marijuana? If you have, recall the first time you tried it. Did you try to smoke the reefer as if it were a cigarette? Did you wonder, as the young noninhaling Bill Clinton might have wondered, what the fuss was all about? One of Becker's conclusions is that knowing how to smoke dope does not come naturally. Just as we must learn our multiplication tables, so we must learn how to inhale—deeply and long. If you do not draw marijuana smoke into your lungs, nothing much happens. Without learning the proper technique to get high—often taught by a friend—you are not likely to continue to smoke.

Becker also suggested that people must learn what being high feels like. Specifically, you must feel the effects caused by marijuana and then must connect them with the use of the drug. At first, you may not be sure how you will react, and you search for clues. You get high "with a little help from [your] friends." One user explained, "I heard little remarks that were made by other people. Somebody said, 'My legs are rubbery,' and I can't remember all the remarks that were made because I was very attentively listening for all these cues for what I was supposed to feel like."[47] Becker argued that it is crucial to label feelings in such a way that you know you are high. Because the user is focusing so hard on what he or she is feeling, possibly part of being "high" the first time is simply becoming aware of those things that are always present but are never noticed.

Finally, to continue to use marijuana you must decide that the feelings are pleasant. For some people (usually former users), the experience may be decidedly unpleasant. You could, for example, feel like you are losing your mind. A distortion of spatial relationships and sounds, and feeling violent hunger, thirst, and panic are not anyone's idea of a good time. Unless you can label your physical reactions as enjoyable, marijuana use will stop. Thus, Becker placed great emphasis on the definitions that users have of their experience and on the fact that these experiences are not only chemical but also social. Your fellow smokers have a large impact in determining the nature of your experiences, but ultimately it is a personal decision whether to continue to smoke:

> It is quite common for experienced users suddenly to have an unpleasant or frightening experience, which they cannot define as pleasurable, either because they have used a larger amount of marijuana than usual or because it turns out to be a higher-quality marijuana than they expected. . . . [He] may make this the occasion for a rethinking of his attitude toward the drug and decide that it no longer can give him pleasure. When this occurs and is not followed by a redefinition of the drug as capable of producing pleasure, use will cease.[48]

Becker discussed drug use as a voluntary decision of the user. People have free will in their marijuana consumption. Since marijuana is not overtly harmful and does not harm others, Becker's conclusions are consistent with the libertarian approach to social order. Why should society prevent rational, reasonable people from doing what they wish? If some people do not find marijuana pleasant, they are not forced to smoke. Like the libertarian, Becker, accepting the word of those he interviewed, appears to advocate personal decision making, rather than government control of citizens. Marijuana is a "recreational" drug, so this line of reasoning goes, and it would be a highly intrusive government that would limit personal recreation.

# Social Control, Deviance, and Drug Use

What should the role of the state be in dealing with deviance? How tolerant should we be in dealing with behavior that we may disagree with and that is different from our own? No one wishes to live in a society in which everyone must march in lock step, but how much diversity is too much? Libertarians have the simplest answer. If it feels good, do it—just as long as it does not physically coerce others. They see the ability to be deviant as a sign that freedom exists. Perhaps the most frightening aspect of George Orwell's *1984* is not the various tortures and murders practiced by the government but the horrifying sameness of the people, the drabness of their lives and world. For the libertarian, youthful rebellion is not something to be feared but is simply the attempt of the new generation to demonstrate that they are free. Only to the extent that young people choose to behave like their peers is there danger of deviance actually being subcultural conformity.

The social democrat sees each act of deviance in its own context. Who is doing what to whom, and how does it conform to the ideals of equality and justice? Painting swastikas on Jewish synagogues is deviant, but it is not the sort of deviance that a government should tolerate. On the other hand, dress styles that express ethnic or subcultural values might be seen by the social democrat as an indication of a healthy multicultural state. A critical issue for the social democrat is the structural conditions of society that gave impetus to the deviant display. Some deviance, crime, for example, is due as much (or more) to the social condition in which the criminal finds him or herself, than it is to any free will of the criminal. For the social democrat, who generally accepts conflict theory, deviance indicates structural inequalities that need to be corrected by changing the priorities of society. What the powerful do is often considered "normal," but similar behaviors by the powerless are labeled criminal or mentally ill. The powerful have greater access to the means of defining behavior and more control over those who enforce that behavior. Drugs favored by the rich are legal, or not too illegal, whereas the drug preferences of the poor have long prison terms attached to them.

The conservative, of course, sees the issue of deviance in quite a different light. An absolute moral order exists within society; as a result, we should not tolerate behavior that attacks the core values of that order. Drugs, pornography, homosexuality, and abortion fly in the face of what most American conservatives believe is morally proper behavior. These behaviors undermine family and personal responsibility. If we permit behavior that undercuts fundamental institutions, little will hold us together as a society. Although conservatives do not wish to enforce a rigid uniformity, they are much more willing to draw lines beyond which we must not pass under penalty of law. Because conservatives value order and, thus, a stable functional interrelationship within social systems, the less diversity we have on important questions of value, the stronger a society we will be. Drug *use* poses the same bogeyman for the conservative that drug *laws* pose for the libertarian.

## Questions

1. Should marijuana be legalized? If it is legalized, should the government regulate it?

2. Should cocaine be legalized? If it is legalized, should the government regulate it?

3. Should marijuana possession be decriminalized?

4. Are certain drugs still illegal because of the characteristics of their users?

5. Should there be a free market in drugs?

6. Does drug use undermine the "fabric" of society?

7. Should young people under eighteen be allowed to use drugs if they wish? If so, under what conditions?

8. Why do people use drugs? Are they weak individuals on a psychological or physiological level? People who simply want to have a good time? People who succumb to peer pressure? People who because of their circumstances must numb their pain?

9. Should society tolerate most deviance or try to outlaw it? Is diversity healthy for society or divisive?

10. Should there still be a "war on drugs," or are the costs of that war too high?

11. How would you react to your children using drugs?

## For Further Study

Adler, Patricia. *Wheeling and Dealing: An Ethnography of an Upper-Level Drug Dealing and Smuggling Community*. New York: Columbia University Press, 1985.

Benjamin, Daniel, and Roger Leroy Miller. *Undoing Drugs: Beyond Legalization*. New York: Basic Books, 1992.

Becker, Howard. *Outsiders*. New York: Free Press, 1963. (This work includes "Becoming a Marijuana User.")

Galliher, John F. *Morals Legislation Without Morality: The Case of Nevada*. New Brunswick, NJ: Rutgers University Press, 1983.

Goode, Erich. *Between Politics and Reason: The Drug Legalization Debate*. New York: St. Martins Press, 1997.

Hagan, John, and Bill McCarthy with Patricia Parker and Jo-Ann Climenhage. *Mean Streets: Youth Crime and Homelessness*. New York: Cambridge University Press, 1997.

Jackall, Robert. *Wild Cowboys: Urban Marauders & the Forces of Order*. Cambridge: Harvard University Press, 1997.

Katz, Jack. *Seductions of Crime: Moral and Sensual Attractions in Doing Evil*. New York: Basic Books, 1988.

Pfohl, Stephen. *Images of Deviance and Social Control*. New York: McGraw-Hill, 1994.

Szasz, Thomas. *Ceremonial Chemistry: The Ritual Persecution of Drugs, Addicts, and Pushers*. New York: Anchor, 1975.

Wilson, James Q. "Against the Legalization of Drugs." *Commentary* 89 (February 1990): 21–28.

## Notes and References

1. William J. Chambliss, "The Saints and the Roughnecks," *Society* 11 (November–December 1973): 24–31. See also Donna Gaines, *Teenage Wasteland* (Chicago: University of Chicago Press, 1998).

2. Louis Wirth, "Urbanism as a Way of Life," *American Journal of Sociology* 44 (July 1983): 1–24.

3. Edwin H. Sutherland and Donald R. Cressey, *Principles of Criminology*, 7th ed. (Philadelphia: J.B. Lippincott, 1966), pp. 81–82.

4. Walter B. Miller, "Lower Class Culture as a Generating Milieu of Gang Delinquency," *Journal of Social Issues* 14:3 (1958): 5–19.

5. Robert K. Merton, *Social Theory and Social Structure*, enlarged ed. (New York: Free Press, 1968), pp. 185–214.

6. William Ryan, *Blaming the Victim* (New York: Vintage, 1972).

7. John Hagan, and Bill McCarthy with Patricia Parker and Jo-Ann Climenhage, *Mean Streets: Youth Crime and Homelessness* (New York: Cambridge University Press, 1997).

8. Bob Dylan, "Rainy Day Woman #12 and 35," *Blonde on Blonde*, Columbia Records, 1966.

9. National Commission on Marijuana and Drug Abuse, *Drug Use in America: Problem in Perspective* (Washington, DC: Government Printing Office, 1973), p. 9.

10. Lester Grinspoon, *Marijuana Reconsidered* (Cambridge: Harvard University Press, 1977).

11. For current usage statistics: Substance Abuse and Mental Illness Health Services, Office of Applied Studies, National Household Survey on Drug Abuse, 1994-1999 PAPI. These statistics are available online at http://www.samhsa.gov/oas/NHSDA/1999/Chapter 4.htm, pp. 10–11. For statistics on new users, please see the same source, p. 3.

12. Jacob Sullum, "The Pitfalls of Marijuana Reform," *Reason* (June 1993): 21.

13. Gallup Poll, December 4–7, 1990, Survey #GO 922001.

14. Walter Wink, "Biting the Bullet: The Case for Legalizing Drugs," *Christian Century* 107 (August 8–15, 1990): 738.

15. Cited in http://www.samhsa.gov/oas/DAWN/98me_annual.pdf (p. 68).

16. Congressional testimony by Laura Nagel, of the Drug Enforcement Administration, before the House Committee on Government Reform: Subcommittee on Criminal Justice, Drug Policy and Human Resources, March 27, 2001.

17. Marvin C. Miller, "Why Prohibition Has Failed," *High Times* (January 1989): 33.

18. These figures are cited in "The War on Drugs Is Lost," Editorial in the *National Review* (February 12, 1996): V. 48, p. 12.

19. Rae Corelli, "A New War of Words," *Maclean's* (January 22, 1990): 39.

20. Max Rafferty, in Harold H. Hart (ed.), *Drugs: For & Against* (New York: Hart, 1970), p. 28.

21. Tom Morganthau, "Drug Fever in Washington," *Newsweek* 108 (September 22, 1986): 39.

22. Wink, "Biting the Bullet," p. 736.

23. Carl T. Rowan, "The Drug Scourge Must Be Stopped," *Readers' Digest* (August 1983): 135.

24. Richard Vigilante, "Pot-talk: Is Decriminalization Advisable: No," *National Review* (April 29, 1983): 489.

25. William J. Bennett, "Drug Policy and the Intellectuals," *The Police Chief* (May 1990): 31.

26. Judianne Densen-Gerber, in Harold H. Hart, *Drugs: For & Against* (New York: Hart, 1970), p. 113.

27. Gerald W. Lynch and Roberta Blotner, "Legalizing Drugs Is Not the Solution," *America* 168 (February 13, 1993): 8–9.

28. James Q. Wilson, "Against the Legalization of Drugs," *Commentary* 89 (February 1990): 24.

29. Thomas S. Szasz, "The Ethics of Addiction," *Harper's* (April 1972): 75, 77.

30. Ibid., p. 75.

31. Michael Aldrich, in Harold H. Hart, *Drugs: For & Against* (New York: Hart, 1970), p. 77.

32. William F. Buckley, "Reefer Madness at the Bar," *National Review* (October 24, 1994): 79.

33. David Boas, "The Corner Drugstore," *Reason* (October 1988): 23; Michael Aldrich, "Legalize the Lesser to Minimize the Greater: Modern Applications of Ancient Wisdom," *Journal of Drug Issues* 20(4) (1990): 543.

34. Erich Goode, "Strange Bedfellows: Ideology, Politics, and Drug Legalization. *Society* (May–June 1998): 20.

35. Wink, "Biting the Bullet," p. 736.

36. David A. J. Richards, *Sex, Drugs, Death and the Law* (Totowa, NJ: Rowman and Littlefield, 1982), p. 179.

37. Michael C. Monson, "The Dirty Little Secret Behind Our Drug Laws," *Reason* (November 1980): 49.

38. John F. Galliher and Linda Basilick, "Utah's Liberal Drug Laws: Structural Foundations and Triggering Events," *Social Problems* 26 (1979): 284–297.
39. Michael Rossman, in Harold H. Hart, *Drugs: For & Against* (New York: Hart, 1970), p. 180.
40. Ira Glasser, "Now for a Drug Policy That Doesn't Do Harm," *New York Times* (December 18, 1990): A24.
41. Quoted in "The War on Drugs Is Lost," p. 44.
42. Charles Krauthammer, "Mistakes of the Legalizers . . ." *The Washington Post* (April 13, 1990): A25.
43. Erich Goode, "Strange Bedfellows: Ideology, Politics, and Drug Legalization. *Society* (May–June 1998).
44. Ronald Bayer, "Heroin Decriminalization and the Ideology of Tolerance: A Critical View," *Law and Society* 12 (1978): 307.
45. Ibid., p. 314.
46. Howard S. Becker, "Becoming a Marijuana User," *American Journal of Sociology* 59 (1953): 235–242.
47. Ibid., p. 238.
48. Ibid., p. 241.

# CHAPTER FOUR

# Human Sexuality: Is Adultery Wrong?

■ If controversy is what you seek, try talking about sex in public. Between politically correct radicals, anything-goes libertarians, angry feminists, unrepentant chauvinists, and outraged conservatives, you should expect a firestorm. Yet, no behavior is more central to society than sex. From a social science standpoint, suppressing a serious discussion of sexual behaviors keeps us ignorant about a fundamental societal arrangement. Human reproduction, legal rights, marriage, cultural values, and issues of personal freedom are all affected by the societal norms governing sex-related behaviors. The age of consent, what form of sex education occurs in schools, or whether you can purchase pornography, identify yourself publicly as a homosexual, solicit a prostitute, obtain contraceptive devices or an abortion—all represent sex-related behaviors that are not simply a matter of individual discretion. They are subject to cultural influences and institutional social control and are regulated differently around the world.

Human sexuality is socially organized. All nations regulate educational and media depictions of sexual activity. Every society has some cultural or legal prohibitions on sexual contact across different ages, ethnic, familial, racial, and religious lines. Functionalist theorists argue that all societies attempt to regulate with whom and when people can have sex in order to prioritize the family unit and ensure effective reproduction. Bans on incest and premarital and extramarital sex as well as classification of "legitimate" and "illegitimate" children create a stronger family unit. Extramarital sex, for example, threatens the social order, because having sex with someone other than your marital partner imperils marriage and raising children. The widespread availability of contraceptive technologies has led to a reduced emphasis on controlling premarital sex, because sex can now be more easily separated from reproduction. Functional social control aimed at preserving existing family units, such as the taboo on incest and general condemnation of extramarital sex, still remains strong.

Over the last forty years, American culture has become increasingly sexualized. The 1960s and 1970s saw the "sexual revolution," the era of "free love," and the emergence of the gay liberation movement enter the public consciousness. Some traditional beliefs about sex have fallen from favor. The traditional *double standard* that required different sexual behaviors from men and women, and suggested that women could not enjoy or pursue sex has diminished. Similarly, the moral outrage that many people at one time reserved for homosexuals is declining, although it is certainly far from eliminated entirely. For example, it would have been unthinkable a few decades ago to have television programs depict the lives of openly gay characters or even to suggest, much less pass, a law prohibiting discrimination against homosexuals or a law permitting same-sex marriages. Following a "sex sells" strategy, mainstream mass media and advertisers now increasingly rely on sexual themes to attract audiences, whether through MTV videos, scantily clad models in Abercrombie and Fitch clothing catalogs, steamy soap operas, T&A television programs, or cinematic fare such as "American Pie." Television movies gain large ratings by dealing with topics such as incest, prostitution, and adultery—words that could not even be mentioned on the airwaves a few decades ago, much less depicted as existing realities. Although sexual depictions have always existed in popular culture, they have never been as openly available, explicit, and omnipresent as today.

Cultural and technological changes have also enabled a wider distribution of sex-related products in the global marketplace. Consider pornography. The Internet, subverting its initial scientific goals, is now the main medium for the worldwide consumption and distribution of pornography. Although porncity.net (the most visited pornographic web site) lacks the scientific minutiae of www.nasa.gov or the establishment legitimacy of amazon.com, selling "e-porn" actually makes money, with adult web sites drawing more "hits" than any other kind. Providing virtual worlds of sex that can cater to every imaginable sexual fetish (sexfarm.com or eagergrannies.com) is one of the rare dot-com businesses that turns a profit. Sex-related industries, such as "adult" videotapes, cable channels, phone sex operations, and strip clubs, have also grown tremendously. In the 1970s, a federal study found that the retail value of hard-core pornography was between $5 and $10 million. In 2001, overall annual expenditures on pornography are estimated at being somewhere between *$10 to 14 billion,*[1] which makes pornography one of the major unacknowledged industries in the United States. While pornographic magazines were once mailed in plain brown wrappers and only available at adult bookstores in run-down neighborhoods, X-rated films are now available in almost every hotel room and cable broadcast system in the United States. The modern cultural availability of sexual depictions and dialogue—from "lesbian dial-a-date" being broadcast on Howard Stern's radio show, to the ubiquity of "e-porn"—is one of the most dramatic cultural sea changes of the last fifty years.

In general, American attitudes toward sex have become increasingly liberalized to conform to more liberal behavior. Of course, not everyone has welcomed greater sexual freedom, or depending on your view, sexual decadence. There are concerns across the political spectrum that today's greater sexual freedoms bring with them increased rates of abortion, unwanted pregnancies, promotion of "homosexual lifestyles," promiscuity, sexually transmitted diseases, rape, the degradation of women, and greater pressures for adolescents to engage in premarital sex. Sexual activity can be problematic, sometimes in ways that everyone agrees are devastating (rape, sexually transmitted diseases), others in ways that vary depending on people's individual views (homosexuality, promiscuity). The construction of sexual activity, as symbolic interactionists note, is a matter of cultural divergence, including identification of what counts as adultery.

Cross-cultural studies of sexual behavior have demonstrated a wide variation in what people consider acceptable sexual behavior. Homosexuality, for example, is treated quite differently among cultures—from being required in men to being punished by death.[2] The positions in which men and women practice sexual intercourse vary widely, revealing how incredibly plastic the human body can be. Even the use of the "missionary position," (common in the West), is far from universal—much sexual satisfaction occurs from other angles.

Even though there are biological components of human sexuality, the form that sexual behavior takes is learned, rather than innate. In a diverse society such as ours, we should expect some differences in sexual ideology.[3] Men and women are socialized to their places in the sexual order. Ira Reiss, a prominent sex researcher, described two major ideologies toward sex that he claimed characterize U.S. society. The first he defined as the *traditional-romantic ideology* and characterized it by the following tenets:

> 1. Gender roles should be distinct and interdependent, with the male gender role as dominant. . . . 2. Body-centered sexuality is to be avoided by females. . . . 3. Sexuality is a very powerful emotion and one that should be particularly feared by females. . . . 4. The major goal of sexuality is heterosexual coitus and that is where the man's focus should be placed. . . . 5. Love redeems sexuality from its guilt, particularly for females.[4]

This perspective sharply contrasts with the *modern-naturalistic* perspective, which is presently dominant. Its tenets consist of the following:

> 1. Gender roles should be similar for males and females and should promote equalitarian participation in the society. 2. Body-centered sexuality is of less worth than person-centered sexuality, but it still has a positive value for both genders. 3. One's sexual emotions are strong but manageable, by both males and females, in the same way as other basic emotions. 4. The major goals of sexuality are physical pleasure and psychological intimacy in a variety of sexual acts and this is so [for] both genders. 5. A wide range of sexuality should be accepted without guilt by both genders providing it does not involve force or fraud.[5]

Of course, it is altogether possible to accept a stance that merges these two perspectives. An egalitarian view of sexuality might be coupled with certain traditional themes, such as the importance of love and marriage. Reiss's two ideologies stress two different functional properties of sexuality: procreation and intimacy. Since each gender typically holds a different perspective, conflict is not only ideological, but social as well (for instance, religious people versus nonreligious people or less-educated Americans versus those with more schooling).

Research on people's actual sexual behaviors has not had a long history, partially as a result of our Puritan or Victorian belief (until recently) that it was not a fit subject for study. Around fifty years ago, Alfred Kinsey and his colleagues at the Institute for Sex Research at Indiana University undertook the first major studies of human sexuality. Kinsey, a zoologist by training, published lengthy volumes on male and female sexual behavior (in 1948 and 1953, respectively).[6] These volumes, based on large, if biased, samples, demonstrated that a much greater variety of sexual behavior existed in the United States than many people had imagined. For example, Kinsey uncovered that nearly 40 percent of all adult males had engaged in homosexual behavior, nearly 70 percent had visited a prostitute, 60 percent had practiced oral sex, about 25 percent of married women had committed adultery, and so forth. Based on his figures, Kinsey could claim, "a call for a cleanup of sex offenders in the community is, in effect, a proposal that 5 percent of the population should support the other 95 percent in penal institutions."[7] While Kinsey's exact figures cannot be trusted because of the difficulties in obtaining honest responses, his data do demonstrate that there is considerable diversity of sexual behavior in the U.S. population. The results of recent studies have partially overcome Kinsey's problem of validity. Later in this chapter, we examine the findings of the most comprehensive recent research on sexual practices and attitudes in the United States.[8]

Sexuality is a major battleground in today's "Culture Wars." Approaches to sexuality are based on attitudes toward human nature (Is it good or is it tainted by selfishness or original sin?) and toward social order (Should it be open to a wide range of possible behaviors or does it need to be controlled by social institutions?). Nowhere is the societal influence on human sexuality more evident than in reactions to adultery.

## ■ Question:

*Is adultery wrong?*

> *When two people are under the influence of the most violent, most*
> *insane, most delusive, and most transient of passions, they are*
> *required to swear that they will remain in that excited, abnormal,*
> *and exhausting condition continuously until death do them part.*
> —George Bernard Shaw, Preface to *Getting Married*

Pick up a novel, go to a film or play, listen to a popular song, and the chances are high that it will deal with adultery.[9] What the unlikely company of *Madame Bovary,* *The Scarlet Letter, The Great Gatsby,* Jerry Springer, soap operas, and the media frenzy surrounding the affairs of famous people (Prince Charles and Princess Di, New York Mayor Rudolph Giuliani, and Former President Clinton) have in common is that they demonstrate our artistic and cultural preoccupation with adultery. The theme of marital infidelity strikes a common chord. The ideal of romantic love in marriage is a precious, valued, and sought-after commodity; fear of betrayal is universal, and the illicit sexual liaisons of others are titillating and voyeuristically satisfying and make for easy criticism and scorn. Although adultery is pervasive in popular culture and makes for compelling public drama, how much extramarital sexual activity actually occurs?

Adultery occurs when a married man or a married woman engages in sexual acts with someone who is not at that time his or her spouse.[10] Roughly a quarter of all married men and 10 percent of all married women have cheated in their marriages.[11] Research into the factors associated with infidelity indicates that differences in religious affiliation and education have no significant impact on the odds that someone will cheat in their marriage.[12] Extramarital sex is also unrelated to the size of the community in which married people live.[13] Predictors for infidelity include having had many sex partners prior to marriage, having been divorced prior to the present marriage, and having frequent sexual thoughts and dissatisfaction with one's present marriage. Researchers have also found several consistent gender differences. Men cheat more often than women do. Younger women have more affairs than older women, while male infidelity increases with age. Married men report straying for purely sexual reasons more than women do. Men also report less emotional attachment to their extramarital partners—they are four times more likely than women to report feeling no, or only a slight, emotional attachment to an extramarital partner.[14]

Interestingly, most surveys only ask respondents about whether they have had extramarital sexual partners, but they don't explore *who* those partners are. This omission is surprising because the type of partner one has is of great sociological significance. Whether an extramarital partner is a one-night stand or a long-term mistress seems relevant; so is whether a married man or woman is having extramarital sex with a single person or another married person, or even with someone of his or her own gender. Adulterous relationships can occur in several ways—those that are "recreational" with little emotional attachment, such as one-night stands; those that are officially condoned, such as "tolerated" affairs; those that are long-term engagements with a mistress or male equivalent that parallels the companionship associated with a formal marriage.[15] These situations all represent a different social organization and qualitative complexity to adultery. The moral calculus surrounding these differences is also relevant to how wrong adultery is perceived to be. For example, having a "one-night stand" when drunk may be considered "better" than cheating in a long-term arrangement with someone who is also married, which expands betrayal to two relationships rather than confining it to one.

The symbolic interactionist emphasizes that what sex means has to be defined in particular circumstances and would urge researchers to analyze the social construction of adultery. Who is one's partner? What is the nature of their sexual contact? For example, identifying someone as an adulterer is often limited to their having "actual sex" [what a concept!]; yet, as noted, people are now involved in online affairs that involve sexual communication without physical contact.[16] Is cyber-adultery possible? Are exchanging torrid e-mail messages with strangers, flirting at a party, having a candlelight dinner, even fantasizing sexually about other people, infidelity? Does oral sex "not count" as Bill and Monica alleged? "Open marriages," in which both partners agree to "see" other people, pose still a further complication—if extramarital sex takes place with the consent of both partners, is it really still "wrong"? In a recent survey, more than half of married men and women felt that kissing someone else and having a sexually explicit conversation on the Internet or phone constituted cheating. Nearly 40 percent of married men and 43 percent of married women felt that fantasizing about having sex with someone else was a form of cheating in marriage.[17] Former President Jimmy Carter once commented on how he committed lust in his heart. For many married people, adultery is an emotional betrayal, one that can occur without actual physical sexual contact. What, then, is the threshold for policing or even feeling that adultery is in progress—fantasy, emotional detachment, flirting, physical sex? Where should people draw the line in the marital sand?

If you believe that sexual exclusivity with one partner should be the norm in human society, the current statistics on adultery reveal a troubling amount of deviance; 25 percent of men and 10 percent of women may not seem like overwhelmingly large percentages but they represent a reality in which millions of married people have extramarital sex. Should we be shocked that so many married people stray? There is no escaping the fact that a substantial minority of married men and women do cheat. Perhaps your parents do, and perhaps you see nothing wrong with it. On the other hand, we might also ask whether we ought to be *surprised* that so many more married people remain monogamous. Monogamy has never been normative in human societies. For example, 1,000 out of the 1,154 human societies that anthropologists have studied have been polygamous (meaning that males were allowed to have multiple wives).[18] Viewed in this historical context, one can argue that current statistics on adultery show a surprising loyalty to sexual fidelity and the strength of monogamous marriage as a social institution, since a majority of Americans (75 percent of men and 90 percent of women) claim to remain faithful.

The present level of sexual fidelity is all the more striking given that evolutionary biologists believe that humans, like most animals, are not monogamous "by nature." As Daniel Barash noted, "monogamy is definitely under siege, not by government, not by declining morals . . . but by our evolutionary biology."[19] The natural instinct of many animals is to seek out multiple sex partners. In general, males are instinctually programmed to be "easily stimulated, not terribly discriminating as to sexual partners, and generally willing—indeed eager—to fertilize as many eggs as possible." Through "mating with males who are especially fit and/or who possess secondary sexual traits that are particularly appealing to other females, would-be mothers apparently can increase the fitness as well as sexual attractiveness of their offspring." A bird's social father, as an example, is sometimes not his or her biological father—up to *40 percent* of a bird's nestlings are sometimes attributable to "extra-pair copulations."[20] Males who spread their seed around increase their chances of extending their lineage. Females who have sex with different and more attractive males enhance their own prospects and those of their offspring. From a biological perspective, adultery makes functional sense; it helps to ensure the successful reproduction of the species.

What about the difficulty of maintaining a marriage? The popular, romantic ideal is that people should find a permanent love story in their marriages. A spouse should represent a perfect mix of companionship, sharing of responsibilities, attraction, and sexual fulfillment all rolled into one. If the reality of marriage falls short of these goals, what should spouses do? One answer may be to "work at one's marriage" or to perceive some shortfalls as inevitable and to be tolerated. Marriage is, after all, "for better or worse . . . 'til death do us part." An alternative strategy, though, is to "subcontract out" those missing elements to an alternative person. Consider this assessment of the motivations behind a person's affair:

> We come together for the good things in life: great sex, passion, attention, desire, intellectual confrontations, interesting trips, pleasure. We have our spouses for sharing the responsibilities of paying the bills, raising the children, dividing up the salaries. . . . We attempt to provide equal love to all the people we care about, it's just a different kind of love. . . . We have come to realize that there is not one person in the world who can totally satisfy all the needs of another. There is nobody to blame for this and nobody should expect it. Affairs are immoral, but necessary in our cold and hypocritical society. It is something to make a person feel young, wanted and loved. An affair can greatly improve life and self-esteem as long as the people involved do not lose their heads.[21]

One reaction to this view is to assert that spouses also deserve to share some of the "good things in life." Yet, this speaker also argued that if it is impossible for one person to satisfy all of someone's needs, then "subcontracting" them out to other people makes cold logical sense (albeit an exploitative one, if the partner does not do the same). For example, if a spouse does not perform certain sexual acts, then a husband can easily rationalize patronizing a prostitute to do so. Even if such cheating is "immoral" or unfair to one's partner in marriage, the emotional or sexual subcontracting motivation for adultery is a powerful one. Why struggle when one can find an easier solution? Of course, this alternative depends on evading detection and mitigating any feelings of guilt.

Unlike other animals, humans *can* redirect or repress their sexual desires in the name of social order. Overcoming instinctual drives is an inherent part of socialization. What many people object to about adultery is that they perceive participants as lacking the inner strength of character to suppress their urges, particularly when they know that giving free reign to their desires can have harmful consequences. Among the attacks on former president Clinton was that he knew in advance that he risked his political aspirations and presidency by having repeated affairs—and he still gave in to temptation. Self-control is a form of social commitment. However, the struggle to repress the sexual temptation of adultery is not simply a private psychological battle (a "sexual addiction")—it has also historically been a public one.

Though some today define adultery as a "personal or private matter," it is important to remember that infidelity has always had a public significance that encouraged prohibitive social controls. Historically, adultery has never been treated simply as a personal or private matter. Marriage is a social institution involving a legal and public contract, the maintenance of an agreed upon bloodline, and a public alliance between a man, woman, and their respective families—these are not simply private and individual concerns. Adultery is a breach of a religious, symbolic, and legal contract. As a significant familial and financial partnership, marriages were often planned in advance and are still commonly arranged around the world, with parents and "matchmakers" striving to create good unions. Adultery threatens the financial and religious goals that are secured through obtaining a suitable marriage partner. Consider how adultery could affect inheritance. Having out-of-wedlock children both complicates and dilutes bloodlines, threatening fixed pathways for inheriting wealth and other social resources, like land and title. Illegitimate children have always suffered for this reason, although they are less stigmatized today than historically.

Although most people claim that adultery is wrong, there are pervasive disagreements over why adultery is wrong and about what sort of penalties, if any, to attach to it. For example, in some nations, adultery warrants the death penalty or other severe forms of physical punishment. Americans, in the wake of former president Clinton's serial philandering, have undergone a public debate over whether adulterers should be stigmatized to the extent of having their employment terminated. Is adultery sufficiently immoral to discredit the whole person? How far should the stigma of adultery go? Should extramarital sexual activity really be considered a private issue to manage within the family? Or is adultery a violation of the highest magnitude, one that violates God's word and rips the social order asunder, warranting serious punishment? As with many morally stigmatized behaviors, there are different views about what counts as deviant and about what social control is appropriate in the case of adultery. Adultery offers a venue for considering different general visions of how sexual behaviors, law, religiosity, marriage, politics, and gender should intersect.

## The Conservative Point of View

The conservative has sometimes been pictured as the Scrooge of the Bedroom. It is not so much that conservatives do not enjoy sex, but they are more concerned about its effects on society. For the conservative, sexual behavior is potentially dangerous because if left unchecked it, could subvert the social order. It needs to be explicitly regulated. David Carlin, Jr. writing in *Commonweal* magazine explained the tie between sex and the social order:

> Though sexual activity might be *performed* in private, it was not really a private act. Others—family, friends, neighbors, potential spouses, and society generally—felt that they had interests that might be jeopardized by one's sexual activity; hence social regulation of that activity was warranted. The traditional rule that sex should be confined within marriage meant that one was not free to act sexually in one's capacity as a mere private or natural individual; instead, one acted in virtue of a kind of public office— husband or wife—that society had artificially created and inducted one into.[22]

The conservative's opposition to adultery in particular is not based in some "old-fashioned" prudishness about sex acts. Today, there are even marriage manuals for devout, evangelical Christians suggesting sexual intercourse (inside marriage, of course) can be fun and not simply for procreation. Sex within marriage is a divine blessing. However, as a microcosm of the social order, marriage is a legal and public contract limiting sexual activity to one's spouse. The marital vows create the familial bedrock on which the social order rests. Marriage is a social expression of faithfulness, of an obligation to honor and obey and to forsake all others to make a family. Adultery betrays a vow made under God and to one's partner, as well as to the community. Broken vows lead to a broken community. The fallout from adultery then includes children who lose the benefits of two-parent homes, diluted inheritance, and alienation of affection, all of which threaten social order.

Adultery is also a veritable grab bag of sins, incorporating lying, infidelity, lust, greed, envy, and covetousness all wrapped in one. Though the path to living a virtuous life is difficult, trying to do so is the morally worthwhile existential struggle that religious and social ideals set before us. Adultery violates those ideals at the most basic level. Who is more of a cheat and liar than a person having an affair? Errant spouses deceive the most important people around them—in doing so, they degrade themselves. Both adulterers and their spouses cite the deceit involved as one of the most disturbing aspects of adultery. Some adulterers confess to their spouses simply because they can no longer take the guilt of hiding their actions. Adulterers cause no end of pain to their spouses by casting aside trust, that most essential ingredient of social life. As one embittered spouse asserted:

> During the past ten years, I have gone through mental and physical hell. I am still unable to come to terms with the fact that for eighteen years of our then thirty years' marriage, my husband lived a lie to me, that is, a fifteen-year affair. . . . For years I could hardly bear to exist after he told me. It is impossible to describe the mental and physical pain.[23]

Why should society make itself more vulnerable to such harm by lessening prohibitions against adultery? Adultery should be illegal and lead to social shunning and punishment. Many conservatives favor severe legal and social prohibitions against adultery as an expression of an appropriate collective conscience.[24] As Rebecca Hagelin observed: "If these laws [against adultery] had been enforced with regularity in this country, then a lot more people would think twice about participating in sexually immoral acts."[25]

Further alarming conservatives is their fear that the United States has entered into a new era of moral relativism that has relaxed moral standards to a point of meaninglessness. Conservative commentators cite the indifference of Americans to former president Clinton's adultery as a case in point. William Bennett wrote, "If a nation of free people can no longer make clear pronouncements on fundamental matters of right and wrong—for example, that a married, 50-year-old commander-in-chief ought not to have sexual relations with a young intern in his office and then lie about it—it has lost its way."[26] For the conservative, adultery indicates a lack of trustworthiness that is all encompassing, a sin that is even worse when a public figure magnifies the example. Yet, many Americans felt that former president Clinton's deception about not having "sexual relations with that woman" did not discredit his ability to do his job well. The community seemed to have spoken—with a giggle and a smirk.

How should we judge the adultery of public figures? They are role models, constituting mirrors onto which we can see our own morals in reflection. Many famous athletes, musicians, politicians, and religious figures have cheated—should their accomplishments be denigrated because of their public exposure as adulterers? In reality, sticking to such condemnation consistently is difficult. We tend to divorce shameful personal qualities from the evaluation of those public figures that we like and to decry them in those we do not, which certainly occurred in the Clinton case. A reward of elevated status is also access to more casual sex. It is a male fantasy to imagine being a rock star or athlete with access to willing groupies. Women are also attracted to fame and power, finding successful public figures sexually exciting—accomplished men, married or not, do not lack for available sexual partners. The language of status can translate into the power to transgress conventional morality, which is one reason why many are more accepting of powerful men (but not women) having multiple liaisons outside of marriage. Thus, sexual infidelity in powerful public figures may be considered a moral flaw; it also may traditionally be viewed as a perk of power, something one has earned as a result of professional accomplishments and skills.

For conservatives, progress does not always bring blessings, just more problems for traditional values to overcome. The moral compass is swinging toward a more relative view of adultery, which conservatives fear, and has been accompanied by greater sexual freedoms that can also contribute to infidelity. The temptation to stray can only increase in a more sexualized popular culture and permissive social environment. That many agreed with former president Clinton's tortured legal distinction that oral sex did not "count" as sex disturbs and surprises many conservatives. Our moral status is ever precarious—conservatives believe in making every effort to maintain the sanctity and value of marriage, both by law and reputational sanctions.

## The Social Democratic Point of View

The social democrat has a pragmatic attitude toward sexuality; so long as it does not disrupt the social fabric, it should be left alone. To the extent it causes a social problem, it should be dealt with as a health and welfare problem, not a moral issue. Since primary social institutions, such as the family and the church, do not have special standing in the eyes of the social democrat, enforcing the chosen morality of these institutions is not a governmental requirement. Instead, the support of "traditional morality" in the conservative's sense may well direct us away from considering social problems that perpetuate inequality and injustice. For example, embracing the ideal that a "woman's place is in the home" can lead to overlooking gender inequities in the workplace. It is important to remember, though, that social institutions are stakeholders in sexual activities. A teenage couple's raging hormones may produce children that government must support, sexually transmitted diseases are public health problems as well as individual ones, and coerced sex or prostitution may involve law enforcement. The social democrat does recognize a government responsibility to address these problems, but not one to legally enforce "traditional" morality.

How societies respond to adultery often reflects how they view the gender relations between men and women. The history of human sexuality is fraught with men extending control over female sexuality. Women were expected to remain chaste and to avoid any suggestion of being accessible sexually outside of or before marriage. Adultery was historically perceived as a theft of a man's property: "Thus the married woman was not merely her husband's possession—his "anything"; she was his inferior and subordinate, one who could be chastised and beaten at will and who owed him conjugal rights . . . as the act of the wife, adultery is a revolt against the husband's property rights."[27]

The double standard of sex has always seen men in an advantaged position relative to women. Married men are subject to urges brought out by "temptresses." There is no gendered word for men that is pejorative regarding their sexual promiscuity—to be called a "stud" is as positive as a woman being called a "slut" is negative. With regard to marital sexuality, women historically have had scant legal freedom or protection from abuse by their husbands. The social democrat, sensitive to social inequality, sees government as having an important function in eliminating this discrimination. Married women in the West today have many more rights in marriage than they did historically. These include property rights and the capacity to initiate divorce and have physical abuse and marital rape prosecuted.

Control over female sexuality, however, rather than being a historical anachronism, continues most viscerally in the form of "honor killings." In strongly patriarchic societies, typically those falling under Islamic law, such as in Pakistan, women who are rumored to be, or who actually have been, sexually active outside of marriage must be killed to prevent their families from being shamed. As Ahmar Mustikhan reported,

> The right of life of women in Pakistan is conditional on their obeying social norms and traditions. A female stands condemned to instant death upon mere suspicion or allegation that she has had, or was about to have extramarital sex. . . . Perceived as the embodiment of the honour of their family; women must guard their virginity and chastity. By entering an adulterous relationship, a woman subverts the order of things, undermines the ownership rights of others to her body and indirectly challenges the social order as a whole. . . . A woman's physical chastity is of uppermost importance and she loses her inherent value as an object worthy of possession—and therefore her right to life—at the merest hint of sexual interest.[28]

To the social democrat, adultery should never warrant the death penalty. If a man or woman commits adultery, the social democrat does not believe that one gender should be punished more heavily than the other. Social democrats weigh into the adultery debate, in part, by serving as a check on gender inequity.

In Western societies, although historical data indicate that more men cheat than women, a recent study has shown that women's rates of cheating have now caught up to men's—there is no difference in lifetime incidence of adultery between married men and married women under forty.[29] Women, who have entered the workplace in greater numbers recently, and who have been encouraged to act more assertively sexually as part of feminism, are behaving more like men in unanticipated ways, such as in being more aggressive sexually and cheating more themselves. A greater presence in the workplace has provided women with greater access to more attractive, potential sexual partners. Some women may also pursue an affair because they long for an "old-fashioned" gender relationship, as this "other woman" testifies:

> I hadn't realized how powerful a force he would be in my life because I hadn't realized how much I needed a safe harbor. A place where I didn't have to know everything and make all the decisions. Me needing someone to look after me took me by surprise. That's what swept me off my feet.[30]

While political correctness often dampens thinking about any unintended adverse consequences of progressive social movements like feminism, all social movements, conservative or radical, have such consequences. One associated with feminism may be an increased likelihood of married women having affairs. The last fifty years have seen an escalation in women's rights. Part of changing gender roles, for the social democrat, is mitigating gender inequity. This advancement can have unintended consequences, such as a greater involvement in adultery, as women increasingly pursue the autonomy to cheat as men do.

# The Libertarian Point of View

Libertarians are likely to be more permissive—laid back—about sexual activity than either conservatives or social democrats. As long as the act is between two responsible individuals, then the government should not be involved. Although most Americans know that adultery is prohibited by many religions, fewer Americans may be aware that adultery is also against the law in many U.S. states. Although hardly ever enforced, these laws are difficult to repeal, since few politicians see their election prospects as boosted by coming out in "favor of adultery." Unlike the conservative, the libertarian does not see society as having a vested interest in the private behaviors two consenting adults engage in with each other.

The problem of sex is not sex itself, but laws and repressive values related to it. This attitude of "do your own thing, providing it doesn't hurt others" is sometimes called the playboy philosophy after a series of articles written by *Playboy* editor, Hugh Hefner from 1962 to 1965, well before the era of AIDS. In these articles, Hefner proclaimed that "sex can be one of the most profound and rewarding elements in the adventure of living; if we recognize it as not necessarily limited to procreation then we should also acknowledge openly that it is not necessarily limited to love either. Sex exists—with and without love—and in both forms it does far more good than harm. The attempts at its suppression, however, are almost universally harmful, both to the individuals involved and to society as a whole."[31] Libertarians define sexual freedom as equally important as political freedom. State control is offensive whether it is in the boardroom or in the bedroom, and in this they sharply disagree with both conservatives and social democrats. Libertarians are not necessarily arguing for promiscuity, "free sex," or adultery. Instead, they suggest that these are personal issues on which reasonable people have the right to exercise different views.

One person's adultery also may not be another's—there is no need to give power to any government to establish and police standards for sexual fidelity. If an individual couple, which marries of their own free will, is happy with an open marriage or swinging, so be it. If one person is cheating and the other person is displeased, then they can handle that situation individually. The rights of individuals are paramount; with this freedom comes the responsibility to manage problems. People who marry assume risks in their relationship; these are their responsibility. While adultery is not to be celebrated, the greater problem with adultery as a public issue is that it can distract attention from more serious problems. For libertarians, the whole Clinton adultery scandal was irrelevant—they didn't care. What mattered was what the government was doing, not the former president's sexual antics. As Steve Dasbach, Libertarian Party Chairman, noted:

> We Libertarians know that allegations come and go; sleazy politicians come and go; special prosecutors come and go. The problem is that the growth of government continues onward—no matter what scandal is titillating the media that particular day. And such scandals simply distract us from the important question: What is the proper role of government in a free society?[32]

Marriage is a contract freely entered into by consenting adults. People must accept the responsibility to manage adultery as their own problem, either as a victim or a perpetrator. Nor should they open the door to having government legislate wrongdoing. If a husband feels that cheating does not harm his relationship, he can do so. If his wife disagrees, she is free to end her relationship with that man. Whatever steps they take in the meantime are their business, not the government's. Adultery is wrong only by personal fiat. Handling its fallout and management is the responsibility of the involved individuals.

## Sexuality and Social Research

Sex is a topic, like religion, where there is an abundance of opinions, but a minimum of hard facts. In response to a lack of objective and valid knowledge about sexual practices, Edward O. Laumann, John H. Gagnon, Robert T. Michael, and Stuart Michaels completed a comprehensive survey of sexual practices in the United States.[33] They surveyed 3,432 respondents between the ages of 18 and 59 about the range and frequency of their sexual practices.

In the past, social scientists avoided using random surveys of the population to research people's sexual activities. They felt that potential respondents would be uncomfortable with questions addressing their sexual activities and would lie about them to avoid embarrassment. Put yourself in the social scientist's place. Imagine asking strangers about their sexual habits, such as whether they are faithful, gay, have multiple sexual partners or kinky fetishes. If your respondents even answered you, do you think that they would be honest? Laumann and his research team adopted several strategies to combat this problem. They stressed the importance of research on sexual behaviors in the era of AIDS, informing subjects that obtaining accurate information about sexual activity could help save lives. They also reassured respondents that their answers were confidential and would remain anonymous. The researchers also backed up these claims by destroying identifying information after recording a respondent's answers, distributing sensitive questions in ways that prevented the interviewer from seeing a respondent's answers, and by phrasing questions sensitively to avoid any appearance of making moral judgments about respondents. While there is no guarantee that these precautions led to unimpeachable data, and researchers cautioned readers that the data might still underreport some sexual activities, they believe they effectively minimized this danger.

Research on sensitive behaviors also confronts political concerns. By choosing an activity, in this case sex, that is typically considered outside the bounds of "decent society" and treating those involved in an objective and nonjudgmental way, such research investigations are read by some as implicitly legitimating that behavior, and for this reason many conservatives object to research on sexual attitudes and behaviors. The federal government, in part because of objections that conservative Senator Jesse Helms (R-North Carolina) raised about the subject matter, refused to allow federal funds to be used to help support this research. This outcome raises an important question: What conditions, if any, justify supporting research on "sensitive" subjects?

Laumann and his coauthors summarized the opposition to research on sexual practices and their own motivations for pursuing the subject as follows:

> Inquiry about sexual behavior is controversial for at least three reasons. First, there are those on both sides of the political spectrum who oppose one or another sexual practice and contend that reporting incidence may legitimate and even encourage certain behaviors. Others have strong opinions about the right to engage in certain sexual practices and wish to increase public tolerance of those practices. They contend that if only a small percentage of people are reported to engage in those practices such information might encourage efforts to forbid those practices or to ostracize those people involved in them. We contend that orchestrated ignorance about basic human behavior has never been wise public policy. Anti-intellectualism and fear are not convincing arguments against inquiry and knowledge. . . . The case to be made in favor of inquiry into sexual behavior includes the following points. First an informed citizenry is essential in a democratic society, and while sex is essentially private, it has many public aspects as well. These require us as a democracy to make judgments and reach agreements about the rules by which we all will live—rules about the treatment of homosexuals, about the legality and availability of paying for abortions, about public nudity, about sexual harassment, rape and gender discrimination, about contraceptives, about sexually transmitted infections, and on and on and on. Information is imperative if we are to make wise collective judgments.[34]

Many social scientists see little sense in ignoring "dirty data"—disturbing knowledge may be too critically important to neglect. As an example, to understand patterns of HIV infection requires both acknowledging and reporting the reality of gay men's sexual activities. Conservatives may object to this research for fear of condoning homosexuality; liberals might reject this research because it could reveal unflattering information about gay men's promiscuity and thus spawn increasingly negative attitudes toward homosexuals. Yet, failing to gather data on patterns of HIV transmission through male sexual activity limits our knowledge of how AIDS spreads in the population. Political, moral, and scientific considerations are always potential sources of conflict in research on sensitive topics. As a result of these conflicts, some knowledge will be produced and other knowledge abandoned. Sensitive topics are especially difficult to fund, as well as to conduct, because subjects may misrepresent their attitudes and behaviors. The picture of sex in the United States that Laumann and his coauthors presented was nowhere near as decadent as conservatives feared. Contrary to people's assumptions of "what other people must be doing," Americans "do not have a secret life of abundant sex." Instead, Americans report that they hew to a fairly traditional model of sexual behavior:

> Those having the most partnered sex and enjoying it most are married people. The young single people who flit from partner to partner and seem to be having a sex life that is satisfying beyond most people's dreams are, it seems, mostly a media creation. In real life, the unheralded, seldom discussed world of married sex is actually the one that satisfies people the most.[35]

Laumann and his coauthors discovered that about a third of all people claim to have sex twice a week, a third have sex with a partner twice a month, and the rest have sex only a few times a year, if at all. Married people make up the majority of people who have frequent sex. Regarding sexual practices, the researchers found that for the most part, sexual behavior conforms to the tried and true—the vast majority of men and women find vaginal sex most appealing, followed by watching their partner undress, followed by oral sex. Few men or women find the idea of group sex or anal sex appealing. Both men and women would rather receive than give oral sex, with a higher percentage of men being willing to do either.

People usually attribute sexual behaviors to our untamed biological instincts and impulses. Laumann and his coauthors argued instead that society shapes people's sexual behaviors. For these authors, the key sociological inquiry into sex is to examine how our collective understandings, incentives, and social networks combine to produce our sexual behaviors. Laumann and his coauthors found that we usually have sex with people who tend to be like us—whites with whites, blacks with blacks, and so forth, with people who have close to the same level of education and who are close to our own social class. The social networks that we inhabit set up a pool of available sexual partners. The crucial point to understand here is the influence of social structure on the most seemingly private of behaviors—how and with whom we choose to couple. Society shapes what seem like these personal choices. For example, married people have the most sex because married people cohabitate, are already attracted to one another, are accessible, and because marital sex is the most socially legitimate category for having sex.

Laumann and his coauthors also explored the distribution of sexually transmitted diseases (STDs). Regarding STDs other than HIV and AIDS, the greatest risk factor is having unprotected sex with many partners; it doesn't matter if those partners are

Asian, black, white, Hispanic, rich, or poor. The authors also concluded that the risk of being infected by HIV is not at epidemic proportions in the United States. Those likely to be infected are people who have unprotected sex with intravenous drug users who share needles and with men who engage repeatedly in unprotected anal sex. Many gay men, realizing the risks of unprotected sex, have lessened their involvement in that form of sexual activity or taken better precautions when doing so. Few in the population are vulnerable to infection, which confines the risk of contraction to a small pool of Americans, insufficient to produce an epidemic. This finding is controversial because many groups believe that large sums of money should go to support AIDS prevention to avoid a widespread epidemic in the United States. The authors believe that given their evidence, money currently devoted to preventing the spread of AIDS through sexual activity would be better spent helping those who already suffer from the disease.

These authors took the unusual step of writing two books simultaneously to describe their research findings. One book, *Sex in America,* was intended for a general public audience. The second book, *The Social Organization of Sexuality,* was written for academics, public policy officials, and professionals who work in therapeutic fields. Their writing two books begs the question of how research findings are filtered depending on their audience. *Sex in America* is a jargon-free book that states findings very plainly, offering a rudimentary description of the methodological design of the research and hardly any mention of pertinent social theories. *Social Organization* is a more densely written book that makes full and detailed reference to existing theoretical debates and methodological and statistical procedures and develops the theory of social networks to which these authors, in particular Edward Laumann, are notably attached.

There is an increasing gulf between public audiences and social science scholarship. Social scientists are sometimes guilty of failing to communicate their ideas and findings clearly, and so they usually do not find any audience other than fellow academicians. Sometimes this outcome results from arrogance; at other times, social scientists find it too difficult to communicate all the complexities of the ideas and methods involved in sophisticated research projects to persons who lack the professional background to appreciate them. Further at issue is that laypersons may be disinterested (although sex will draw an audience of these laypersons), and social scientists are unwilling to work to "sell" the importance of their work to a popular audience. This gap is troubling. Social scientists often work on subjects that shed light on how social forces affect people in everyday life. Laumann and his coauthors, by writing two books, highlighted the estrangement between an audience of professional researchers and the popular audience. Simultaneously, Laumann and his coauthors acted on this gap by trying to reach both audiences. A firmer bridge is clearly needed to connect the public with the latest important research findings that bear on them.

# Human Sexuality, Adultery, and Society

Human nature is sexual nature. Our conception of human nature, whether it is essentially good or evil, colors our opinion about how people should behave sexually. The libertarian, who believes in the potential of rational behavior, sees little danger in the grand emotion of sexuality, provided that biological dangers are heeded. Sexuality is merely pleasurable and has little effect on social intercourse. Sex is a *natural* function that connects human beings with their primate forebears. No laws should govern sexual conduct other than the right of individuals to do what they will. Far more important is that an intrusive government not be allowed to legislate morality and regulate nonforcible sexual acts between consenting adults. Legislation against adultery, like that for other moral issues that the left and right try to legislate against, such as prostitution or pornography, should be opposed for reducing individual autonomy and for encouraging government control over personal behavior. As individuals, libertarians are not "for" adultery. What libertarians are for is providing people with the freedom to make their own decisions, including their own mistakes, such as trusting an errant husband or wife. People should also be free to decide whether they care if their spouse cheats or not.

The conservatives see sexual passion bubbling beneath human behavior, and while love is good, unrestrained passion may be destructive. People are continually struggling against their baser, animal instincts; adultery provides a case in which people's most troubling instincts win. Marriage, the only legitimate realm for sexuality, must be protected with whatever support deemed necessary from the government. The state should exercise its influence to maintain the family as the bastion of morality and as one of the primary institutions of society. Adultery is the worst kind of surrender. At a personal level, it gives in to sin; at a social level, it leads the social order of the family to collapse. Adultery is not only shameful, but also a crime against God and society.

With adultery, the social democrat feels less strongly about the sex act per se and more strongly about discrimination resulting from adulterous acts or the perception of them. Adultery may be a wrong, but vicious punishment in retaliation, typically disproportionately toward women, is a worse wrong. In the case of honor killings, for example, the wrong of an alleged sexual activity is far less than that of murdering women and certainly never warrants the death penalty. The casualties of adultery also typically include weaker figures in society—women and sometimes children who become damaged economically and psychologically in subsequent marital fallout. The problem that social democrats have with adultery is that reactions to it are worse than the act itself.

## Questions

1. Is sex a purely private act, or does it affect society?

2. Do you plan to commit adultery? If you answer this publicly, are you lying?

3. How would you (or did you) feel if you learned that a parent was having an affair?

4. What behaviors should count as "adultery"? Are torrid e-mail exchanges with a stranger adultery?

5. Do the current statistics on the incidence of adultery show the strength or weakness of marriage today?

6. Are people instinctually programmed for infidelity?

7. Is adultery always wrong?

8. Is adultery different for men than it is for women? Why are women now cheating at rates comparable to men?

9. What penalties, if any, should be attached to adultery? Why?

10. Should Bill Clinton's sexual behaviors have affected our opinion of his performance as president?

11. Can you believe surveys of human sexual behavior?


## For Further Study

Bailey, Beth. *Sex in the Heartland.* Cambridge: Harvard University Press, 1999.

Barash, David P., and Judith Eve Lipton. *The Myth of Monogamy: Fidelity and Infidelity in Animals and People.* New York: W. H. Freeman, 2001.

Davis, Murray S. *Smut: Erotic Reality/Obscene Ideology.* Chicago: University of Chicago Press, 1983.

Gregor, Thomas. *Anxious Pleasures: The Sexual Lives of an Amazonian People.* Chicago: University of Chicago Press, 1985.

Laumann, Edward O. et al. *The Social Organization of Sexuality: Sexual Practices in the United States.* Chicago: University of Chicago Press, 1994.

Lawson, Annette. *Adultery: An Analysis of Love and Betrayal.* New York: Basic Books, 1988.

Michael, Robert T., et al. *Sex in America: A Definitive Survey.* New York: Little, Brown and Company, 1994.

Reiss, Ira L. "Some Observations on Ideology and Sexuality in America." *Journal of Marriage and the Family* 43 (1981): 271–283.

Richardson, Laurel. *The New Other Woman: Contemporary Single Women in Affairs with Married Men.* New York: Free Press, 1985.

## Notes and References

1. Frank Rich, "Naked Capitalists," *The New York Times Magazine* (May 20, 2001): 50–57, 80–81, 92.

2. David Greenberg, *The Construction of Homosexuality* (Chicago: University of Chicago Press, 1988).

3. Murray Davis divided sexual ideologies into three categories: the Jehovanist (traditional), the Naturalist (the modern Playboy philosophy), and the Gnostic (a la Marquis de Sade). See Murray Davis, *Smut: Erotic Reality/Obscene Ideology* (Chicago: University of Chicago Press, 1983).

4. Ira Reiss, "Some Observations on Ideology and Sexuality in America,"pp. 279–280.

5. Ibid., p. 280.

6. Alfred Kinsey et al., *Sexual Behavior in the Human Male* (Philadelphia: W.B. Saunders, 1948); Alfred Kinsey et al., *Sexual Behavior in the Human Female* (Philadelphia: W.B. Saunders, 1953).

7. Ian Robertson, *Sociology,* 2nd ed. (New York: Worth, 1981), p. 215.

8. Edward O. Laumann et al., *The Social Organization of Sexuality*.

9. Annette Lawson, *Adultery*, p. 17.

10. Ibid., *Adultery*, p. 37.

11. See Michael W. Wiederman, "Extramarital Sex: Prevalence and Correlates in a National Survey," *Journal of Sex Research* (Spring 1997): 167; Robert T. Michael et al., *Sex in America*. Wiederman's figures are 22.6 percent men, 11.6 percent women; Michael et al.'s figures are 25 percent men and 10 percent women.

12. I. Olenick, "Odds of Spousal Infidelity Are Influenced by Social and Demographic Variables," *Family Planning Perspectives* (May 2000): 148.

13. Michael Wiederman, "Extramarital Affairs: An Exaggerated Myth," *USA Today Magazine*, July 1999.

14. These factors are cited in Olenick, "Odds"; Lawson, *Adultery*, p. 147; Wiederman, "Extramarital Sex"; and Wiederman, "Extramarital Affairs," p. 74.

15. See Annette Lawson, *Adultery*, for a further elaboration of these categories.

16. Anastasia Toufexis, "Romancing the Computer: The First Cyber-Adultery Suit Shows the Risks of Looking for Love Online," *Time*, Feb. 19, 1996, p. 53.

17. Bruce Handy, "How We Really Feel About Fidelity," *Time*, August 31, 1998, p. 53.

18. Robert Wright, "Our Changing Hearts," *Time*, August 15, 1994, pp. 44–53.

19. Daniel P. Barash, "Deflating the Myth of Monogamy," *Chronicle of Higher Education*, April 20, 2001, p. B17; see also David P. Barash and Judith Eve Lipton, *The Myth of Monogamy: Fidelity and Infidelity in Animals and People* (New York: W. H. Freeman, 2001).

20. The preceding quotes and this statistic are cited from Barash, "Deflating the Myth of Monogamy," pp. B16–17.

21. Cheryl Lavin, "Tales from the Front," *Chicago Tribune*, May 27, 2001, Section 7, p. 14.

22. David Carlin, Jr., "The 'Squeal Rule' and 'Lolita Rights,'" *Commonweal*, September 9, 1983, pp. 465–466.

23. Lawson, *Adultery*, p. 222.

24. Andrea Sachs, "Handing Out Scarlet Letters: Antiquated Sex Laws Turn into a Bludgeon for Divorcing Spouses," *Time*, Oct. 1, 1990, p. 98.

25. Sachs, "Handing Out," p. 98.

26. William J. Bennett, "Why It Matters," Op-Ed, *Wall Street Journal*, March 6, 1998.

27. Lawson, *Adultery*, p. 44.

28. Ahmar Mustikhan, "Honour Killings," *Canadian Dimension*, February 2000, pp. 29–30.

29. Wiederman, "Extramarital Sex: Prevalence and Correlates in a National Survey," p. 167.

30. Laurel Richardson, *The New Other Woman* (New York: Free Press, 1985).

31. Hugh Hefner, "The Playboy Philosophy," *Playboy*, July 1963, p. 48.

32. "Libertarian Party takes a novel approach to Clinton's latest sex scandal: We don't care." *Libertarian Party Press Release*, January 22, 1998.

33. Laumann et al., *The Social Organization of Sexuality*.

34. Laumann et al., *The Social Organization of Sexuality*, pp. xxviii–xxix.

35. Robert T. Michael et al., *Sex in America: A Definitive Survey*, p. 131.

# CHAPTER FIVE

# Economy and Stratification: Is Global Free Trade Harmful?

■ What does the future hold for America? Throughout the twentieth century, Americans were convinced that they were destined to be the most prosperous people that the world had ever known. Because of U.S. economic growth and military strength, the last century was labeled "The American Century," and it ended with the United States as the dominant cultural, economic, and military power on earth. Confronted now with increased economic competition from the European Union and Pacific Rim nations, a downturn in some important U.S. industries, and the potential for massive development in Eastern European and Third World economies, it is uncertain whether the twenty-first century will see the United States retain its present standing. The crucial question now facing U.S. businesses, government officials, workers, and the public is how to best advance U.S. interests and prosperity in today's global economy. Should the United States embrace increased global free trade, our government's present course? Or should the United States follow the lead of the World Trade Organization protests in Seattle—a protest of both the left and the right—and reject global free trade as a pathway to ruin? Examining how sociologists view the economy as a social institution and determinant of individual quality of life provides a useful background for considering this debate.

When sociologists speak of "the economy," they refer to a social institution that organizes the production and exchange of goods and services. Goods are items like clothing, food, and shelter; services are functions that people perform for one another, such as education, defense, labor, and health care. To ensure individual and collective survival, societies must develop institutions that meet people's basic needs for goods and services. Nations must make products, create an infrastructure for distributing them, and develop a division of labor that enables economic functions to take place. Modern economies consist of hundreds of thousands of subsidiary organizations; businesses, industries, markets, labor unions, government agencies, educational facilities, and consumers, in concert, make today's mass production and distribution of goods and services possible. Today's consumers can acquire almost any good or service they can afford: Belgian chocolates sent overnight to a Manhattan party, out-of-print books bought over the Internet, 24-hour access to money at automated teller machines, retail stores fully stocked with goods in every U.S. city, and satellite dishes that broadcast any sporting event of choice to any family's home. The organizational infrastructure and technology making all this possible represents the pinnacle in economic progress, or so it seems.

Some view understanding the economy solely as a matter of memorizing statistical formulas and immutable "laws," such as that of "supply and demand." Yet, economic activities are profoundly sociological phenomena, because all economic transactions are embedded in social relations that determine how goods and services are produced, distributed, and consumed. Social life and personal relations affect economic transactions. Economic activities are based on more than rational decision making. Regulatory activities, the social networks within which business transactions occur, the labor market, and social inequality all influence the numbers reflected in measures of economic activity. For example, advertisers attempt to manipulate norms to label some products "hot" or "essential," creating markets and demand for those products among consumers. Think about your clothing choices—or your deodorant. Accounting and credit rating operations employ a process of translating qualitatively complex social characteristics, like trustworthiness, into numbers, a seemingly "objective" transformation that suggests that some social characteristics are more important that others.[1] As an example, consider *redlining*. This refers to a now illegal practice in which banks and insurers drew an imaginary red line through poor or minority neighborhoods on maps, rejecting loan applications from individuals in those areas because their neighborhoods and zip codes (and skin color) labeled them "risks." Yes, there are some objective features of the neighborhoods that raise concerns about profit, but the practice doesn't consider the circumstance of the individual applicant, but only the group stereotype. Likewise, child labor laws are based on social expectations about the age at which a child should properly work or the locations in which that work is to take place. Different societies or the same society at different points of history can have very different views of this matter.

People have different visions of how a society should organize economic activities. The major distinction between them is in the amount of control ceded to government. On one side is the libertarian ideal of completely free markets and private enterprise in which the economy consists of a set of private and individual decisions; on the other, some accept the socialist argument for centralized planning, in which the government takes control over economic institutions in the name of its citizens.

The dissolution of the Soviet Union and the failure of the nations of Eastern Europe have led many to doubt the effectiveness of totally government-controlled economies that fail to take consumer demand and entrepreneurial enterprise into account. This source of failure is ironic, as communist nations strived, as an ideal, to organize their national economies to address the basic needs of all individual citizens, with the hope of providing everyone with benefits. They attempted to eliminate historical class distinctions and claimed to provide for everyone according to need. Educational institutions, medical services, housing, and other basic necessities were all heavily subsidized and cost little or were free. Imagine receiving a college education, an apartment, or surgery practically free; being guaranteed a job; and paying only pennies for heavily subsidized consumer goods, such as bread and milk.

This option sounds ideal *if* you had the right to choose the specific goods and services you wished and *if* the ones you wanted were available and of high quality. Alternatively, imagine that to reap such benefits, you pay almost every cent of your income to the government and have basically no choice in the quality of goods and services provided. Under this system, citizens were often not free to decide where they lived or what job they could have (unless in some cases, they had the resources to bribe appropriate officials). People did not have the authority to compete for themselves, such as owning their own restaurant or retail store. Under the socialist system, the state provided goods and services regardless of need but with minimal concern for choice, quality, or customer service. Choice, quality, and service often depend on competition in which numerous producers and sellers strive to meet the needs of customers. The tradeoff in this economic system was guaranteed security. Both failure and success were eliminated.

To American thinking, the absence of individual ownership or free enterprise would be disastrous. Americans are socialized into valuing an individualistic economic orientation, one prioritizing the right of individuals to pursue and accumulate as much affluence as possible, either to sink or swim, but with little public intervention if they sink. Capitalist economies operate on the fundamental assumption that the "market" is self-regulating and that massive government involvement is unnecessary and undesirable, even though the "business cycle" may produce severe swings from prosperity to depression. Individuals are free to act as entrepreneurs, to have private ownership of property, and to compete with one another as best as they can to attain economic success. While a few individuals will succeed beyond their wildest dreams and some will attain middle-class status, many will fail. Indeed, one justification for a free enterprise economic system is that it distributes resources *unequally,* and people are therefore motivated to work harder to acquire what they want. A society without a "work ethic" is unlikely to be productive, or at least not very affluent.

Most Western nations now fall somewhere between a true free market, capitalist economy and a planned, socialist one. They represent what are called "mixed economies." Such systems include some measure of a "welfare state" mentality in which the government is expected to play a significant role in protecting people from the "excesses" of the free market. Scandinavian nations are often put forward as representing how this model should work. Social democrats support this approach—one that is generally accepted by moderate conservatives as well—as a means of providing an extensive safety net that lessens the divide between the haves and the have-nots.

The American system of rewards depends not only on hard work, but also on the "accident of birth." Former president Jimmy Carter once reminded us: "Life is not fair." In this, he recognized a profound sociological truth. People are not treated equally, and how they are treated is not entirely a result of their own actions. Being born into wealth offers more advantages than being born into poverty. In this sense, everyone begins life with a particular economic identity or set of *life chances* that influence—although they do not wholly determine—their eventual economic outcomes. *Ascribed status* refers to forms of social status that result from a category over which you have no control, usually social characteristics attributed to you at birth, like gender, race, or family wealth. For example, you didn't choose to be female, Latino, or nineteen years old, nor did you select your parents because they were wealthy; those identities "chose" you. By contrast, *achieved status* refers to positions achieved at least partially by your own efforts, such as your occupation or athletic achievements.

*Social stratification* is the term sociologists use to describe hierarchical inequality. Some inequality relates to the reality that groups near the top of the hierarchy have greater access to rewards than those toward the bottom. Levels of stratification differ in kind and degree from society to society. In the most extreme case, a society is officially divided into castes based on race, religion, or ethnicity. In this system, as was once true of India and the Republic of South Africa, status (or socially defined position) is given at birth, with little later opportunity for social mobility or for intermarriage among the castes.

The United States is stratified by a class system. In a class system, individuals are ranked hierarchically, but this position is a function of their economic rank. Even though a person's family affects his or her class position, there is opportunity for mobility between classes, and marriage is not heavily restricted. People can earn graduate degrees, be great athletes or entertainers, marry wealth or otherwise climb up the class ladder. The dimensions of the class system also can be conceptualized in several ways. Two of the most widely used are those postulated by Karl Marx and by Max Weber. Marx believed that economic factors alone were decisive in determining status. Those who own and control the means of production are the dominant class. Those who are employed by those who own the means of production are the proletariat or working class. For Weber determining status was not as simple. He divided the idea of class into three closely related factors: power, wealth, and prestige. While these factors often go hand-in-hand, some people have power without wealth (some politicians), others have wealth without prestige (certain nouveau riche millionaires), and others have prestige but little power (clergymen, for example).

Access to economic resources continues to divide Americans. For better or worse, we do not have complete equality of opportunity and certainly not equality of outcome. Any observant person will recognize that the United States is a stratified society. We do not have the excesses of wealth of Saudi Arabia nor the depths of poverty of India, but we do have many millionaires and many more poor people. Even if few people starve, many fall beneath the "poverty line." In a society in which all individuals were nearly equal, we would expect the 20 percent with the least income to make nearly as much as the 20 percent who make the most. As of 1999, the lowest 20 percent made only 3.6 percent of America's total income, whereas the top 20 percent made 49.4 percent.[2] These percentages have not changed much in the past quarter century, which suggests that U.S. society is becoming neither more nor less stratified, but remaining unequal. If we examine wealth—that is, assets, including property, stocks, savings, and other capital—we find it is distributed even less equally. The top 5 percent percent of all Americans own 21.4 percent percent of all the wealth, whereas the bottom 20 percent own only 0.2 percent of the wealth.[3]

The American dream, as it pertains to economics, consists of obtaining a good job and accumulating wealth and financial security. How do we best maintain the possibility of realizing this dream? There are some threats on the horizon. Many formerly important industries, such as steel, automobiles, clothing, and electronics are no longer dominated by U.S. firms, resulting in the loss of hundreds of thousands of well-paying, skilled "blue collar" jobs in the manufacturing sector of the U.S. economy. Referred to as the *deindustrialization of America*, this change has contributed to the growth of an urban underclass, the need for dual-career families, the weakening of labor unions, and a decline in middle- and working-class standards of living.[4] There is also an ongoing epidemic of downsizing, producing economic insecurity for millions of people in the United States, rich and poor alike. To combat these problems, some argue for more government intervention in the economy, in the form of protectionist legislation, whereby the government would subsidize U.S. products or tax foreign products that compete with U.S. industries through tariffs. Others argue for nationalizing certain critical industries. Still others, like libertarians, argue that market forces ought to be left alone to take whatever course they will, permitting consumers and businesses to purchase the best products at the lowest prices, no matter where the products are made. These contrasting agendas represent the different capitalist, socialist, and mixed visions of organizing economy and society. They also set the stage for considering the question of whether global free trade is harmful or helpful—a goal to pursue or one to reject.

# ▪ Question:

## *Is global free trade harmful?*

A classic theme in science fiction is how human interaction with alien civilizations might unfold. In imagining what these relations might be like, such stories often depict wondrous technology, terrifying dangers, and exotic cultural traditions. Remember the scene in the trading post bar in Star Wars in which aliens of all shapes and sizes were drinking together. These fictional exercises have their true-life counterparts in the historical expeditions of European explorers, who voyaged across vast distances to make contact with civilizations that were previously unknown—at least to them. These brave souls encountered organized groups of humans, who appeared different physically, wore strange garb, carried unusual equipment, had domesticated odd animals, spoke an unknown language, and exhibited unfamiliar customs. The question of how the world's different civilizations develop and maintain a wide range of social relations with one another—from aggressive to cooperative, exploitative to isolationist—emerged from early historical contacts to become the substantive issue of *globalization.*

Global free trade is a subset of large-scale processes of globalization. More than ever, people in distant countries are connected to one another. Globalization has produced an "intensification of worldwide social relations which link distant localities in such a way that local happenings are shaped by events occurring many miles away and vice versa."[5] Globalization references the increasing exchange, trade, and distribution of products, information, natural resources, traditions, and social policies (i.e., the "spread of democracy" or the "free market") across national borders. Being able to find a McDonald's in almost every large city in the world is a dramatic instance of globalization—as is the acceptance of English into a common, quasi-planetary language; finding Mongolian teenagers wearing Michael Jordan T-shirts; or worrying about Ebola virus or hoof-and-mouth disease spreading across the world. Sociologists are particularly interested in researching the consequences globalization has on specific cultures and understanding what evolving social arrangements connect different societies. In what ways is globalization a boon, bane, or mixed blessing?

Global free trade, as part of globalization, is a complex phenomenon. Global free trade in *what*—Hollywood entertainment, international students, the ideology of gender equality, manufactured goods, illegal drugs, technology, viruses? Even though we consider different types of exchange in examining global free trade, a necessary first step is to outline the structures that influence how global exchanges occur.

The designations "first" and "third world countries" are terms that distinguish between groups of modern, developed nations and underdeveloped, poorer ones (the communist world used to be the "second" world, in Western eyes). Immanuel Wallerstein originated *world systems theory* to analyze the interdependent, embedded sets of relations among different nations.[6] Wallerstein argued that nations fall into an overall global structure of *core, semi-periphery,* and *periphery.* Core nations, such as the Western powers (the United States, Germany, or Japan), have preeminent economic status in the world and can structure advantageous economic exchanges with periphery states, which are weaker and are dependent on the core. Semi-periphery states (Turkey, Thailand, or Chile) have some economic power but are weaker than the core states. Periphery nations constitute the "Third" or "Fourth" World (Belize, Bangladesh, or Benin). The conflict theorist analyzes globalization as a system of social arrangements that powerful nations establish to maintain the unequal distribution of resources, with devastating consequences for the periphery and great benefits for the core.

The last three centuries often involved a chronicle of wars fought by colonies seeking independence from core nations that completely dominated their economies, natural resources, and peoples. In this historic sense, global trade has not always meant "free" trade, but unfair trade, as colonial powers imposed exploitative terms of trade on peripheral nations. According to conflict theorists, periphery countries today are weakened by their prior colonial statuses, drained of resources, and unable to modernize on their own. *Modernization* refers to achieving self-sufficient economic production and agricultural development; building an efficient industrial infrastructure; achieving low infant mortality and high life expectancy; and creating resilient and stable public institutions and a good quality of life for citizens.

Nations on the periphery remain involuntarily dependent on core nations for help in modernizing and are vulnerable to core nations imposing economic policies in exchange for aid. Conflict theorists focus their criticism on global economic institutions, such as the World Bank, which core countries finance to loan money to periphery countries. Borrowing countries are forced to agree to difficult conditions and penalties in order to secure large loans that they may not be able to pay back. The conditions of these loans often involve restrictions on government spending on public programs (referred to as austerity programs), which from one perspective prevent pervasive corruption and waste, but from another, cause tremendous harm to the poor and to efforts to attain economic self-sufficiency. These measures either force the recipient nation to budget properly and develop systems of financial control, focusing the aid where it is most needed, or, by constraining budgetary choices, delay the periphery nation's efforts at modernization, leaving it structurally vulnerable to continued, future exploitation. Both perspectives may be right in part. Surely, it is understandable that Americans wouldn't want their tax dollars wasted, but it is also understandable that what U.S. politicians and bankers desire may not always be in the best interest of the poor of other nations. Cheap labor and abundant natural resources are the main assets that developed countries desire from periphery nations. The comparative advantages of developed countries—technology, capital, management and marketing skills, an educated citizenry, political stability, and an established consumer base—enable their economic domination of the world system.

Globalization also raises the question of how existing societal arrangements (such as ideas about how people should dress, work, live, worship, use technology, and so forth) are affected when the global spread of fresh ideas and innovations provides alternatives. For functionalists, globalization presents the difficult challenge of organizing social relations with other cultures to realize one's own benefits and continued survival. The "trade" in global free trade is not just in manufactured goods and technology, but also in ideas and cultural practices, which must be measured in terms of how they help an existing civilization to thrive. Like conservatives, functionalists are loath to change existing values and traditions, and fear their "contamination" by alien traditions and cultural practices. For example, the Japanese fear changes in the traditional veneration of the elderly, and Americans fear that our prized "melting pot" culture might be replaced by balkanized cultures. Hence the ongoing battles across the world in which countries attempt to exclude what they label as "undesirable influences" on their culture, say by banning books, practices of gender equality, religious diversity, guns, or a free press. Indeed, students of Slavic descent and others from the Balkans might notice and reject the pejorative and stereotyped use of the term "balkanized" to refer to the undesirable inability to make cultural compromises.

Embedded in the functionalist position is a potential *isolationism,* by which nations seek to protect themselves against the influences of other nations, rejecting a more cooperative and developmental stance, unless forced otherwise, or only when viewing helping other countries as being in the national interest. Consider the complexity of the moral decision making that is required here. Should the United States seek to prosper in Darwin's world, where the strong survive and the weak rightfully wither away? Or is the goal to help all societies to function as well as modern ones? Are these goals compatible? Or is improving the position of other countries ultimately in the national interest of the United States—expanding peace, stability, and prosperity?

As college students, you often encounter political activists who demand that U.S. consumers boycott companies who exploit sweatshop labor. Do you want to pay more for your Nikes? Others allege that U.S. intelligence and military agencies act covertly around the world to support U.S. commercial interests. Would you rather that gas prices jump? The hard question looming behind both the conflict and functionalist approach here is, Should Americans pursue economic advantages at the expense of weaker nations? While some are outraged at U.S. intervention around the world in support of U.S.

companies, others see such exercises as exactly what the United States should be doing—protecting and advancing U.S. interests whenever possible.

Symbolic interactionism, the third major theoretical approach in sociology, is less overtly political than the other two. Interactionism focuses on the relations among individuals and the meanings these relations have for participants. Globalization is a vast territory of *meaning construction:* the activities one culture takes for granted as "how things are done" often have different interpretations and organization elsewhere in the world. Whereas Americans reject arranged marriages, other countries rely on them. Why does American popular culture hold such sway around the world? What explains the power of "McDonaldization"? The symbolic interactionist is always oriented to understanding how some cultural and social practices vary around the world in both their meanings and consequences and how others are remarkably constant.

A larger question of concern to symbolic interactionists is whether globalization is leading to a "monoculture"; a global culture based on Western ideals and cultural products that overcome and supplant traditional and diverse local cultural practices.[7] Is the world truly undergoing McDonaldization, or is this picture extreme, since even McDonalds adjusts its menu to suit a country's local tastes?[8] Asking whether globalization leads to monoculture essentially means asking whether an increasing global trade in information, new products, and ways of doing things enhances diversity or heightens the pressure toward a globally homogenous culture. Nationalism and tribalization, as embedded in local cultural values, stand in opposition to an overpowering consumer culture presently based on U.S. cultural marketing (Hollywood entertainment and U.S. multinationals). Globalization heightens the tension between these forces, an effect Benjamin Barber described as "Jihad versus McWorld."[9]

Globalization is immutably tied to technological advances, which make today's rapid exchanges of goods and information possible. Air travel, advances in shipping, and sophisticated telecommunications have been crucial in connecting the world. Although technology makes globalization possible, eliminating protectionism allows globalization and global free trade to take place. *Protectionism* refers to "protecting" a country's domestic industries and producers from foreign competition by imposing onerous regulations and significant tariffs on any goods manufactured outside national borders. Tariffs prevent foreign products from competing effectively because the regulatory requirements and taxes levied on them increase their prices beyond what consumers will usually choose to pay.

As a hypothetical example, say that a Japanese tariff on selling U.S. beef in Japan causes the price of that product to be $16.00 a pound (instead of, say, $6.00 a pound), compared to beef sold by a Japanese producer who can sell it for $11.00 a pound. This tariff protects the Japanese producer from having to compete with U.S. producers in the domestic market for meat in Japan. This tariff makes Japanese beef producers happy, but Japanese consumers must pay an artificially high price for meat, because without the tariff, competition with U.S. producers would exert downward pressures on prices. The Japanese beef producers are protected, but at the expense of their consumers and the American cattlemen.

Global free trade allows producers to sell their products in markets around the world without being disadvantaged by tariffs and other regulations that protect domestic industries. The U.S. government has pursued a policy of expanding free trade and free markets, as have many other nations, usually in agreements between nations within a common geographic region, such as the European Union or North America. Their goal is to minimize the tariffs and barriers each nation will face when trading with member nations. The North American Free Trade Agreement (NAFTA) began on January 1, 1994 after a contentious domestic battle in the United States (and in Canada) to pass this legislation. NAFTA regulates investments and reduces nontariff barriers and tariffs on trade across the U.S., Canadian, and Mexican borders. As a result, the total trade between the United States, Canada, and Mexico surpassed $752 billion in 1998, a large increase from pre-NAFTA levels.[10] More recently, most of the nations of the world entered into GATT (General Agreement on Tariffs and Trade) negotiations, which will slowly take effect over the next few decades.

The debate over whether global free trade is harmful or beneficial is one of the most contentious global issues. Is opening the door to trading partners a Pandora's box that lets destructive forces wreak havoc on a nation's culture, economy, environment, and workforce? Or is extending free trade the key to global growth and prosperity, with free markets bringing unprecedented affordable goods, modernization, unity, and security? Libertarians, social democrats, and conservatives all have drastically different views of globalization's effects, and their disagreements—as recent protests have demonstrated—are increasing in rancor and intensity.

## The Libertarian Point of View

Global free trade (the permanent establishment of free markets) is embraced with religious fervor by libertarians. Free markets offset government controls, allow for rational management of resources according to laws of supply and demand, and increase individual autonomy. The economy should operate by the rational decisions of free people. This requires a free market, not one under an artificial control, as occurs when governments interfere with the market by subsidizing domestic industries or imposing tariffs. The libertarian position is that open markets represent the best opportunity to attain economic growth and individual freedom. Michael Tanner of the Libertarian Party explained the principles behind the libertarian policy on trade:

> Free trade is firmly rooted in the American tradition of free enterprise and limited government. The Founding Fathers understood the danger of trade restrictions. Benjamin Franklin said, "No nation is ever ruined by free trade." Indeed opponents of free trade are in the position of arguing that government should pick and choose losers amongst various types of businesses and impose itself between the buyer and seller of various goods and services, an idea completely contrary to the American ideal of individual liberty and free enterprise. The right to engage in voluntary exchange transcends national boundaries.[11]

Libertarians not only support NAFTA and GATT, which encourage trade by restricting tariffs, but they also believe that the United States should unilaterally reduce or eliminate any tariffs, quotas, or other barriers to foreign goods without exception.

Yet, it seems that opposition to global free trade is presently in vogue. As Peruvian economist Mario Vargas Llosa wrote scornfully of the opponents of trade:

> Brainy professors . . . pull their hair out trying to show that free markets do little more than make the rich richer and the poor poorer. They tell us that internationalization and globalization only benefit the giant multinationals, allowing them to squeeze developing countries to the point of asphyxiation and to devastate entirely the planetary ecology.[12]

Libertarians believe that empirical data supports their romance with trade. The libertarian points to free trade as the primary explanation for the most successful recent cases of rapid economic growth, such as Hong Kong and Singapore. Global free trade spurs faster economic growth, reduces poverty, provides investment in infrastructure and logistics worldwide, and raises standards of living. For libertarians, free markets offer the best hope for all individuals to succeed economically and for poorer nations to be developed. Companies, for example, who want to build plants in Mexico or Vietnam, invest capital there in order to build their facilities, benefiting local citizens who might perish otherwise. Consumers can select inexpensive goods, and impoverished nations can build industries. Libertarians argue that global free trade increases investment in underdeveloped countries. This, in addition to providing jobs and financial capital, also ends up transferring modern technologies and management skills, updating infrastructure (new highways and airports), and reducing government overregulation. Perhaps at first these nations will seem exploited, but the next generation will have the capital to compete directly with the core nations. Free trade leads to modernization and prosperity; tariffs imperil these goals.

Consumers benefit from global free trade because competition in a market exerts downward pressures on the prices of consumer goods. For libertarians, tariffs are simply taxes on consumers by a different name. If a consumer wishes to purchase foreign goods, tariffs raise the prices of those goods artificially (costing consumers an extra $70 billion a year—or $752.00 per household), with a haphazard logic that sees mink coats be duty-free while imported baby sweaters are taxed at 34.6 percent.[13] High tariffs are often linked to political pressures and deal making, a good example of how corporate contributions to politicians lead to mischievous ends.

For the libertarian, global free trade leads not only to more freedom for consumers, but also to more open and freer societies. Ideals of freedom and autonomy flow over national borders along with goods, as do new living options and individual choices. Libertarians suggest, for example, that the real losers of the decision to award the 2008 Olympics to Beijing will ultimately be the autocratic leaders of that nation, who cannot hope to keep out ideas of freedom and consumerism. How can you keep them down on the communal farm once they have seen Bebe? A libertarian does not insist that people be forced to maintain traditions, but that they be free to be exposed to new ways to live and to choose their own paths. A Western "monoculture" that influences and alters the lifestyles of other societies does not disturb the libertarian, as long as people are free to choose whether to embrace this "monoculture," traditional ways, or some mix of the two. For the libertarian, the ideas, technologies, and cultural practices that spread with globalization have great potential to ennoble the individual.

From a libertarian perspective, cultural choices are an individual right. The social democrat finds the idea of native groups maintaining their lifestyle, and being forced to maintain that lifestyle by being kept isolated, an appealing example of cultural diversity that is potentially sacrificed to globalization. Is the romantic imagery of being a "noble savage," who lives in harmony with nature, realistic or even desirable? Ronald Bailey wrote about the reality:

> Even during "good times" if one looks at the level of material existence, many traditional peoples lived in unimaginable squalor and filth and were assaulted by disease, insects, and violence. They were embedded in rigid kin hierarchies and subject to enormous rates of infant mortality and death in childbirth. Their intellectual lives were restricted to their immediate landscapes, families and neighbors.[14]

The problem for libertarians is that elites are deciding for tribal peoples what is best for them. To be sure, modernization may be a genie that cannot be returned to the bottle, but still protecting people from their choices is not a suitable role of government. What if rainforest peoples would prefer to be city dwellers with porcelain toilets, factory jobs, television, Western clothing, fast food, and cellular phones? Libertarians believe social democrats insist on perpetrating their own form of cultural domination, which keeps native peoples handcuffed to ancient customs and ways of life (except for ones that offend liberal sensibilities, like genital mutilation or clubbing baby seals!). A mass migration of native peoples to crowded cities and tight living conditions might not be in their best interests, but that is for them to decide. Libertarians believe in free choice in all things and do not believe that bossy elites have the right to dictate what forms of modernization should be withheld from native peoples.

Global free trade is about making unrestrained economic choices available to individuals—without government interference. A brave new world can result from the increased growth these economic policies would produce. Granted some jobs will be lost due to changes in the market, but those jobs will be offset by new and different jobs. Further, artificially propping up inefficient industries that cannot compete is unreasonable and wasteful. The buggy whip industry is no more. Libertarians recognize that environmental sacrifices must be made in order for periphery nations to develop, but they also believe that with development and eventual private ownership, environmental progress will ensue. Environmental concern is a concern of prosperous peoples. Libertarians note that the most developed economic nations have some of the most pristine and best-preserved environments. Global free trade will, in the end, only have an upside for us all.

## The Social Democratic Point of View

The libertarian's enthusiasm for free trade contrasts with the social democrat's suspicion. Certainly many prominent Democrats, notably Bill Clinton and Al Gore, were enthusiastic supporters of free trade, but as a theoretical matter, unfettered global free trade is a source of social democratic concern. Where the libertarian sees consumers freed from paying higher prices under free trade, which, in effect, raises the value of their wages, the social democrat sees the disappearance of "living wages" under global free trade. The social democrat's problem with free trade is not what prices a consumer pays, but how free trade enables capitalists and businesses to be unrestrained from any obligation to labor, the environment, the community, or the state. For social democrats, global free trade ends up centralizing and expanding corporate power at the expense of individuals and nations. The globalization social democrats fear is that of undaunted corporate monoliths acting only in pursuit of profit, causing enormous harm.

The social democrat fears the nightmare vision of capitalism without restraint, in which surplus production leads to falling prices, declining rates of return on capital, and a rising global army of the unemployed.[15] Although Michael Kinsley supports free trade, he (ironically) summarized the appeal of social democrats' main arguments against free trade:

> If a factory shuts down because of a flood of cheap foreign products, how is that good? If middle-class Americans find themselves competing with foreigners being paid practically nothing and living in squalor, how can this send American's standard of living up and not down? If another nation is willing to pollute its air and water in order to produce goods for sale in the global economy, how can America join that economy and still hope to keep its air and water clean?[16]

The social democrat views global free trade as more than a mechanism through which corporations can sell goods around the world. What globalization and global free trade enable is a corporation's ability to manufacture and produce goods around the world, or what is referred to as *transnational production*. The social democrat fears that corporations will move capital to foreign countries, where wages are lower, simply manufacturing goods in that nation and then selling them back in the United States. Global free trade thus translates into a corporation's ability to maintain its domestic market without having to pay living wages, while escaping taxes and environmental and labor laws that protect the public interest.

Social democrats fear that as a result of global free trade, the world system will be transformed into an apparent system of global job auctions between countries and multinational corporations for low-paying manufacturing jobs. As William Greider put it, "The country willing to tolerate the lowest wages and most 'flexible' regulation and social control, the greatest concessions from the public domain, to benefit multinationals, will get awarded a share of production. . . . The result is a 'race to the bottom,' with the winner getting lower wages, lower taxes and lower accountability."[17] Unions are naturally actively opposed to this frightening scenario and publicize the numbers of jobs that are lost to free trade to garner support for enacting more protectionist measures and government limits on corporate power. Many people who are appalled at what they believe are exploitative working conditions abroad also join labor unions in a united opposition to unfettered global free trade.

Consider some examples that flame the social democrat's passions:

> Ever wonder how U.S. companies shed their U.S. workforce to go offshore, where they pay 51 cent an hour wages, yet their prices stay the same? Take Lee Apparel Company,

for example, which makes pants in the Caribbean and ships them to the U.S. at a total cost of $6.62 and then sells them at a 514 percent markup for $34.00. . . . In the Dominican Republic, Abbott Labs pays its employees a little over $2000.00 a year, and then gouges the U.S. public with 300 to 500 percent mark-ups on intravenous sets assembled there and exported to the U.S. duty free. . . . At this moment, an American Tourister plant is shutting down in Rhode Island. American Tourister can assemble its garment bag in the Dominican Republic for a total labor cost of $1.53 and sell the bag for $259.00 in the U.S.[18]

As of May 2001, more than 343,103 workers have been certified, under a special government NAFTA unemployment program, as having lost their jobs due to NAFTA. According to labor unions and activists, these figures are only a fraction of the total U.S. jobs lost to NAFTA.[19]

While unions often cite lost U.S. jobs and exploitative working conditions worldwide, the thrust of the social democrat's opposition to global free trade is in opposing the strength of corporate capital as opposed to the power of the state. Can a government of the people compete with growing corporate power? For the social democrat, a strong state is desirable in a way that it is not for libertarians. William Greider pointed out that "of the top 100 economies in the world, 51 are not countries but businesses, and that the 500 most powerful companies alone represent 70 percent of world commerce."[20] If corporate actions are unrestrained by the only other actor powerful enough to oppose them, the state, then individual freedom and quality of life will be threatened. Is the state becoming weaker in the face of those companies, making concessions to them, such as many states and cities do now, in offering to cut taxes and regulations to entice them to provide jobs in a locality?

The issue is not just the loss of wages, threats to the environment, and undermining of unions, but also the beggaring of the public realm by reducing the tax base and public obligations of the multinationals. With global free trade, out goes public power and in comes multinational power. To the social democrat, global free trade allows corporations to violate laws that protect labor, human rights, and the environment, either by finding ways to force host countries to thwart enforcement of them or by escaping their jurisdiction. Social democrats fret that countries will allow companies to engage in environmentally destructive actions, to crush unionization, or to avoid taxes. Together, this will make achieving social equality and social justice impossible. Government can control capitalism with two weapons: the power to raise revenues for social purposes and the power to regulate.[21] Diminish these powers and the world will see an unparalleled increase in exploitation and suffering.

# The Conservative Point of View

Conservatives are nationalists; patriots, they like to think of themselves. If the state is not central to the conservative, the sanctity of the nation certainly is. As a result, conservatives have often embraced cultural and political isolationism—sometimes to xenophobic extremes—*while* also embracing the free market. Remember that conservatives believe in tradition, and globalization threatens the traditions of a nation. These twin sentiments make global free trade a particularly complex and thorny issue for conservatives, because conservatives both reject attempts to shackle global business growth and free markets, yet they oppose any activities that could harm national culture and sovereignty. Reconciling the implications of believing that businesses should be free to expand, but mistrusting foreign influences, as well as immigration, is difficult. The idea that "international organizations" might limit national sovereignty is very troubling to conservatives. The conservative's economic and cultural stances seem to conflict, and, as a result, conservatives may take different sides—as occurred when conservative presidential candidate Pat Buchanan opposed NAFTA and other free trade initiatives from a populist position, while conservative leaders, more attuned to business needs, in general supported it.

As in most things economic, conservatives and libertarians are allied in opposition to social democrats, in that both support the idea of an unfettered economy. Free trade seems to promote innovation, lessens government control, heightens economic growth, disseminates democratic values, and fosters economic freedom.[22] Conservatives also believe that economic claims against free trade are not compelling enough to outweigh the advantages of the economic gains free trade produces. For example, conservatives interpret the economic boom in the U.S. economy following NAFTA as a consequence of that trade negotiation.

Although conservatives acknowledge the job losses associated with free trade (Ross Perot spoke of this as the "giant sucking sound" of U.S. jobs heading to Mexico), many point to free trade bringing employment benefits, such as the creation of well-paying jobs in export industries. Recent statistics show that "export jobs pay 15% more than the average wages, such firms expand employment 20% faster than non-exporting firms and are 10% less likely to fail. Small and medium-sized exporters do even better than large ones and account for 70% of all sales abroad."[23] Rather than view U.S. job losses emanating from global free trade as being too severe, conservatives believe that most recent job losses in U.S. industry originate from domestic competition and technological innovations. Although global free trade is at times a villain in job loss, it is far from the primary one explaining the bulk of contemporary downsizing and layoffs.

Free trade also benefits U.S. producers through allowing them to purchase foreign goods that help their own production and profits. A tariff that protects one domestic industry thus places financial burden on others, such as companies that might want to purchase a product that is subject to high tariffs. Protectionism also penalizes other U.S. industries, when other countries retaliate against U.S. tariffs and duties by slapping their own tariffs and duties onto U.S. goods. Conservatives, in general, like libertarians, have no quarrel with the economic benefits of free trade, which they see as reducing government controls, allowing rational competition, and benefiting both industry and consumers.

However, conservatives do prize national economic and cultural sovereignty, tendencies that run counter to the homogenizing pressure associated with globalization. There are two forms of this type of nationalist sentiment. One is resentment and fear of a "global" government, such as the United Nations (UN) and the World Trade

Organization (WTO), coming to exert control over the nation. The conservative recoils at this possibility and advocates taking forceful steps to prioritize U.S. sovereignty. Pat Buchanan made this point with rhetorical vigor:

> My friends, this to me is one of the great issues, now that the cold war is over, and it is whether America is going to remain forever independent and free, with liberty and justice in this country, as determined by us, Americans. Or whether this decision-making authority is going to go back to the United Nations and leave this country, and that is where a number of elitists want to take us. Let me tell you what I would do if I were elected president. I will get the United States out of the World Trade Organization. I will get the United States out of the International Monetary Fund, and I will tell Kofi Annan, up at the U.N.: "Sir, your lease on Turtle Bay has run out. We want the United Nations out of the United States by year's end. And if you're having trouble leaving, we'll send up 10,000 marines to help you pack."[24]

Bad enough having one's life run by American bureaucrats, but by bureaucrats from Belgium, Bolivia, or Botswana?

The WTO's ostensible purpose is to administrate common rules of trade among participating nations. If member nations have a dispute over trade policies, the exclusion of one good or another from tariffs, or a claim that another country is neglecting their obligations, the WTO's job is to manage and decide these disputes. The conservative shudders at the prospect of the WTO attempting to limit autonomy, much as conservatives mistrust the United Nations for perceived anti-American bias. How can there even be "united" nations, when each nation should properly have its own traditions? The conservative welcomes free trade if there is no global governing agency. But for foreigners with their own interests to impinge on U.S. autonomy and possibly act against U.S. interests is a truly scary thought. Did we fight the British only to give up our independence to technocrats?

The second basis of the conservative rejection of globalization is concern about foreign cultural influences as threats—almost akin to an alien virus that could make the nation sick. One of the ironies of the debate over globalization is that populist conservatives find themselves with some strange bedfellows. For the populist right of Patrick Buchanan to be aligned with unwashed Marxist radicals is no small achievement. But both worry about the loss of national culture and sovereignty in the face of external controls and corporate homogenization (Big Macs for everyone!). Opposition groups in many nations mistrust what then-president George Bush, Sr. termed the "New World Order."[25] Former presidential candidate Ross Perot even titled his book against passing NAFTA, *Save Your Job, Save Your Country!* Pat Buchanan expressed much of this conservative sentiment when he stated, "loyalty to the New World Order is disloyalty to the Republic. In nation after nation, the struggle between patriotism and globalism is under way."[26]

Some of the most feverish opposition to "McWorld" culture comes from countries that wish to protect themselves from an onslaught of American culture. While American conservatives do not object to American values being dominant in the world, other countries do, perhaps none more so than the French. In the words of Francois

Mitterand, the former president of France, "no single country should be allowed to control the images of the whole world. What is at stake is the identity of our nations, the right of each people to its own culture."[27] As with many other issues, conservatives see the globalization battle as being about what cultural ideas, values, and expectations will shape younger generations. In such battles, conservatives embrace tried and true national cultural traditions.

## Global Free Trade and Social Research

What is it like to work in a *maquiladora*, one of the new transnational export-processing facilities that, as a result of global free trade, was built in Northern Mexico? Can you put yourself in the shoes (or sandals) of these workers? Examining the reality of how global free trade translates into actual working conditions helps us understand the human impacts of globalization. How are individuals affected by the social world in which they live and work? Global free trade has produced many factories in free trade zones across the world. How are these facilities run? Describing the experience of work at a maquiladora puts a human face into the abstract debates over global free trade.

Ever since Kathy Lee Gifford's weepy disavowal of exploiting child labor in Central America to manufacture her clothing line, the press has focused on the use of "sweatshops" and child labor in global industries. Do you know where—and how—your collegiate sweatshirt was made? The outrage over exploiting child labor is emotionally powerful, and now great pressure is being applied to curb child labor, both by regulators and by consumer opinion—a movement that some suggest is forcing Western values on other nations. Are there any objective criteria for at what age and how hard children should work?

As a result of this publicity, many may assume that child laborers constitute the majority of transnational production workers. Fewer people may know that most transnational production facilities actually target another demographic group to work (legally) for them: teenage girls. Aside from the accident of birth, it could be you—if you are female. Why do transnational producers tend to target young women as workers, to the extent that many companies will *only* hire females and will go to great extents to find them?

To address the lived experience of women working in a maquiladora, Leslie Salzinger studied the shop floor relations in a Mexican export-processing plant.[28] Salzinger spent eighteen months doing participant observation in a plant owned by "Panoptimex" (a pseudonym). Her research method, participant observation (or ethnography), requires the social scientist to completely immerse herself into the social context of her informants. Salzinger engaged in the same labor that other maquiladora workers did, working the same nine and one-half hour days, to experience as much as possible the social activities of these young women.

Of course, Salzinger was not a "normal" worker—her neighbors and the plant management were well-aware she was an outsider. These plants do not receive many employment applications from American academics. Her special status meant that the people might have treated her differently than they would another worker, potentially making her experiences atypical. However, the great advantage of intensive participant observation is the complexity of detail and depth the researcher can capture. A researcher actually witnesses the social processes unfolding, rather than learning of them solely from secondhand information. This complexity comes at a cost: Participant observation is grueling and time-consuming. Salzinger worked for 18 months at the maquiladora, and it took her additional years to publish her analysis. Ethnography involves taking painstaking notes daily, not to mention being vulnerable in the field.

Why do transnational factories hire young women? Salzinger noted, "Young women have become the paradigmatic workers for a transnational political economy in which a highly sexualized form of femininity has become a standard 'factor of production.'"[29] Her explanation for this pattern of hiring is that gender stereotypes and sexuality are a key part of maintaining control and productivity on the shopfloor. Transnational producers often seek women as workers because they will take less attractive manufacturing jobs in developing countries than men will, and women are more "docile." Yet, what are the dynamics on a shopfloor that heighten the ability to have greater social control over women in these production facilities? This was the puzzle Salzinger wished to solve.

Social control is crucial in the maquiladora, and the physical design of the plant supports this control, as Salzinger described:

> The visual idiom of control is most clearly embodied in the physical structure of the shopfloor. Clean, light, spacious and orderly—the production area is the very image of a "well-run" factory. . . . The factory floor is not only easy on the eye however; it is organized for visibility—a fish bowl in which everything is marked. . . . Ringing the top of the production floor is a wall of windows, a manager behind every one. They sit in the semi-privacy of the reflected glare, watching at will . . . it's common knowledge on the shopfloor that there are still cameras embedded in the ceilings for this purpose. They've set it up so that even the walls have eyes.[30]

Workers are watched continuously. How is gender relevant to this social control? Female workers are paid $40 a week, are typically aged between 18 and 20, and most often live with their parents, since their wages are insufficient to allow them to live independently. Promotions are rare, and their pay is so little that it would not be enough to motivate higher production among workers. As a result, Salzinger argued that at Panoptimex, "sexuality is an integral part of the fabric of production, an essential aspect of the process through which labor is transformed into labor power and women into the docile and dexterous workers of transnational repute."[31] The older male supervisors use surveillance and the sexual self-consciousness of the young teenage women who work in the maquiladora to control them. Salzinger explained:

> Supervisors not only use their position in production for sexual access, they also use a highly sexualized discourse around workers as a means of labor control. It is striking to watch them wandering their lines, monitoring efficiency and legs simultaneously— their gaze focused sometimes on fingers at work, sometimes on the nail polish that

adorns them. . . . Their approval marks "good worker" and "desirable woman" in a single gesture. Each supervisor has a few workers he hangs around with, laughing and gossiping throughout the day. It is not lost on their coworkers that these favorites eventually emerge elsewhere, in slightly higher positions on the line as well as among those with the self-confidence to enter the plant beauty contest. Through each day, managers and supervisors frame women workers as sexual beings, and sexual objects. In this process, women workers become vulnerable to personal, as well as work-based, evaluations.[32]

Male workers on the line are also subject to control using gender, as managers threaten them with being placed among female workers, thus shaming them, if they fall behind or slip up in their work.

Transnational employers desire female employees because they are easier to control. This control combines gender stereotypes and male dominance, using the sexual treatment of female workers as a powerful tool of managerial control. Salzinger's ideas bring a fresh eye to the traditional view that sexual harassment is an *individual* phenomenon where a "bad apple" inappropriately imposes his sexual desires on female employees. Instead, Salzinger saw transnational production in the maquiladora as integrating sexual harassment into the ongoing act of managerial control. There is social pressure on women to be found "desirable," heightening their vulnerability to sexual advances and control, a characteristic of the experience of working in a maquiladora.

While many hold out hope that globalization might spread ideas of social equality and democracy around the world, the sad truth of Salzinger's article is that, in the early stages of the process, the reverse can be true. Corporations, in the case of this maquiladora, race eagerly to locations where they can violate ideals of gender equality with impunity and take advantage of rampant sexism to exploit and control women. They use gender discrimination to improve productivity and profit in processing facilities. You, the consumer, and you, the stockholders, benefit from this system. Globalization presents us with a dilemma of profit and lower costs versus gender equity and higher wages. Of course, without some form of globalization, there would be no jobs for these women; their gender oppression would come from other sources. For many, the image of corporations taking advantage of gender equality is not pretty, but the profits reaped from doing so, which pass on lower prices to consumers and make shareholders wealthy, are. When you look at the labels on your clothing or electronics, think of the choices that such purchases involve. How much extra would you pay for those new jeans?

## Global Free Trade and the Economy

Globalization and global free trade present the best and worst cases for economic development. What should our global society look like? On one side, the free market's relentless pursuit of profits leads to exploitation of people and the environment, to the diminishing of local culture and national sovereignty, and to increasing the gap between rich and poor. On the other, global free trade presents an unprecedented opportunity to spread modern technologies, goods, cultural diversity, and greater freedom around the world, eventually permitting all peoples to participate in global affluence. Remember that at one time, economically powerful countries, such as Taiwan and South Korea, Chile and Spain, were mired in deep poverty.

These broad positive and negative consequences of globalization are occurring simultaneously and are not mutually exclusive. Given the inevitability of globalization, which consequences will emerge as most salient? Can adverse consequences be mitigated? If exploitation leads to profit and profit is desirable, can you reconcile these opposing values? If new ideas and culture are threatening but also innovative and desirable, how do you reconcile them? If low prices are good for consumers, but bad for workers, what choices should be made? And who should decide—the market, individual nations, or global organizations? If environmental degradation is useful in effecting modernization in the Third World, and modernizing is good, how you do reconcile them—the desire to protect the environment with the desire to increase job opportunities in the Third World? Should rain forest residents be forced to gather nuts and berries? Globalization presents multiple, morally complex issues.

The choices that we make about our lifestyle and our responsibility to other humans are choices that affect our economy. Libertarians believe that by leaving decisions to the "market," in time all will be well. At first, there may be exploitation, but gradually the exploited (or their children) will gain the skills to succeed. The economy, when left alone, will produce what people want and what they deserve. Globalization also permits greater freedom for individuals to choose to live as they will, opening up possibilities that are shut by isolationism. In the largest sense, the libertarian view of globalization assumes that individual freedom to choose will produce optimal outcomes. Government control will be sharply curtailed, and people will be freer than ever before. Unfortunately, critics suggest that global society may be too complex for libertarian fantasies. Individual freedom may permit some people to become very wealthy, and others, through no fault of their own, to be impoverished. Is there to be no control over these doleful effects?

The social democrat is more concerned about providing for those less fortunate—of preventing globalization's casualties. The social democrat typically focuses on constraints on large, transnational industry. If there is any economic dislocation for poor workers, the government can provide unemployment compensation, welfare, and job retraining, and even enact protectionist legislation and more regulatory safeguards. In other words, whatever pain globalization causes, the government can solve. That is the mission of a good and moral government. The social democrat is less concerned by the fact that unfettered global free trade may be a means by which some citizens are able to better themselves and change their class status. The fact that some individuals lose freedom as a result and that others are taxed to pay for this aid is simply not a concern for the social democrat.

Conservatives are more than a little disturbed by the antibusiness rhetoric of the social democrats' opposition to free trade and their willingness to allow international organizations to control national politics, but they are also disturbed by the blithe disregard of the libertarian who seems unconcerned about national tradition. The problem is to attain a truly free trade so that global regulatory agencies do not come to control U.S. interests. Conservatives object to the decay of traditional national values, since they may spell an end to traditional beliefs that help society to coalesce. A global economy is desirable, a global culture is not. For the conservative, the integration of new ideas and lifestyles and ultimately the presence of different people in one's culture is a slippery slope—one that threatens to unleash tremendous conflict around the world

Ultimately, the debate over globalization and free trade serves to remind us just how complex and interconnected the global economy is today. We surely have a world system, but how to organize and control it is no easy task. What should the role of nations be in such an economy? Should there be nations at all, or a global government? The reality is that the economy that you are facing is vastly different from the one that your parents faced at your age. The question is whether your children or your grandchildren will find themselves competing with Pakistanis, Peruvians, and Nigerians for jobs, and whether, by that time they will consider themselves as Americans or as Globals.

## *Questions*

1. Is the market the best model to organize the economy or should the government play a major role?

2. Is economic success in the United States more attributable to "accident of birth" or to an individual's hard work and merit?

3. Should U.S. economic success be more important for our government than Third World development?

4. Should corporations relocate their manufacturing operations abroad if they can realize greater profits by doing so, given the cost to current employees? Is a company that does not maximize shareholder profit acting immorally?

5. Do you believe that the world is edging closer to a "monoculture"? Is that desirable? Why or why not?

6. Should global agencies, like the UN and the WTO, be able to control the actions of individual nations?

7. Should America protect domestic industries from extinction through tariffs and trade restrictions? How should one choose which industries to protect? What, if anything, should the government do for workers who lose their jobs as a result of foreign competition?

8. Is globalization inevitable? Can protectionism prevent globalization?

9. Do you support free trade?

10. Do the overall economic benefits of global free trade to consumers justify the weakening of labor unions or the existence of poor working conditions?

# For Further Study

Abu-Lughod, Janet. *Before European Hegemony: The World System A.D. 1250–1350.* New York: Oxford University Press, 1989.

Barber, Benjamin. *Jihad versus McWorld.* New York: Ballantine Books, 1995.

Carruthers, Bruce, and Sarah Babb. *Economy and Society.* Thousand Oaks, CA: Pine Forge Press, 2000.

Featherstone, Michael. *Global Culture: Nationalism, Globalization, Modernity.* London: Sage, 1994.

Friedman, Thomas. *The Lexus and the Olive Tree.* New York: Farrar, Straus, and Giroux, 1999.

Greider, William. *One World: Ready or Not: The Manic Logic of Global Capitalism.* New York: Simon & Schuster, 1997.

Lechner, Frank J., and John Boli. *The Globalization Reader.* Malden, MA: Blackwell, 2000.

Ritzer, George. *The McDonaldization of Society,* 2nd Edition. Thousand Oaks, CA: Pine Forge Press, 2000.

Sassen, Saskia. *The Global City: New York, London, Tokyo,* 2nd Edition. Princeton, NJ: Princeton University Press, 2001.

Wallerstein, Immanuel. *The Modern World System I.* San Diego: Academic Press, 1974.

# Notes and References

1. For further discussion of the social embeddedness of the economy and of commensuration, see Bruce Carruthers and Sarah Babb, *Economy and Society;* Wendy Espeland, *The Struggle for Water* (Chicago: University of Chicago, 1998); Mark Granovetter, "Economic Action and Social Structure: The Problem of Embeddedness," *American Journal of Sociology* 91 (1985): 481–510.

2. U.S. Bureau of the Census, Current Population Reports, series P-60, reported in U.S. Department of Commerce, *Statistical Abstracts of the United States 2001.* (Washington, DC: Department of Commerce, 2001), p. xviii.

3. U.S. Bureau of the Census, Changing Shape of Nation's Income Distribution, reported in U.S. Department of Commerce, *Statistical Abstracts of the United States 2001.* (Washington, DC: Department of Commerce, 2001), Table 2.

4. Barry Bluestone and Bennett Harrison, *The Deindustrialization of America* (New York: Basic Books, 1982).

5. Anthony Giddens, *The Consequences of Modernity* (Cambridge, UK: Polity, 1990), p. 60.

6. Immanuel Wallerstein, *The Modern World System I.*

7. A term used in Ronald Bailey, "Rage against the Machine," *Reason* (July 2001): 26–35.

8. Frank J. Lechner and John Boli, *The Globalization Reader* (Malden, MA: Blackwell, 2000), p. 2.

9. Benjamin Barber, *Jihad versus McWorld.*

10. "What Is NAFTA," Canadian Department of Foreign Affairs and International Trade.

11. Michael Tanner, "Libertarian Foreign Policy: Why Free Trade Equals Prosperity," *Libertarian Party: Issues and Positions.* Cited from the Libertarian Party web site at www.lp.org/issues/trade/html.

12. Mario Vargas Llosa, "Global Village or Global Pillage," *Reason* (July 2001): 42.

13. Statistics cited in Michael Tanner, "Libertarian Foreign Policy: Why Free Trade Equals Prosperity," *Libertarian Party: Issues and Positions.* Cited from the Libertarian Party web site at www.lp.org/issues/trade/html.

14. Bailey, "Rage against the Machine," p. 32.

15. See Lester Thurow, "The Revolution upon Us," *Atlantic Monthly* 279, no. 3 (March 1997): 97–100.

16. Michael Kinsley, "The Mystical Power of Free Trade: Some People Find it Hard to Believe It Really Works, But It Does," *Time* (December 13, 1999): 124.

17. William Greider, *One World: Ready or Not.*

18. Examples quoted in the National Labor Committee Report, "Free Trade's Hidden Secrets: Why We Are Losing Our Shirts," available at www.nclnet.org/ftdrep.htm.

19. Public Citizen, Global Trade Watch, "A Sampling of NAFTA Related Job Loss," posted on the Public Citizen web site at www.tradewatch.org/taa.

20. William Greider, *One World: Ready or Not.*

21. Robert Kuttner, "The End of Citizenship?" *The American Prospect* (December 20, 1999): 4.

22. Denise Froning, "The Benefits of Free Trade: A Guide for Policymakers," *Center for International Trade and Economics.* Washington, DC: Heritage Foundation, August 25, 2000.

23. Quoted from C. Fred Bergsten, "Globalizing Free Trade," *Foreign Affairs* (May–June 1996): 105–121.

24. Speech, Bob Jones University, Greenville, SC, September 18, 2000.

25. "Dueling Globalizations: Opposing Views of Globalization," *Foreign Policy* (Fall 1999).

26. Associated Press, "Attack World Government," January 6, 2000.

27. David Ellwood, "French Anti-Americanism and McDonalds," *History Today* (February 2001): 38.

28. Leslie Salzinger "Manufacturing Sexual Subjects: Harassment, Desire and Discipline on a Maquiladora Shopfloor," *Ethnography* 1 (2000): 67–92.

29. Ibid., p. 68.

30. Ibid., pp. 73–74.

31. Ibid., p. 68.

32. Ibid., p. 80.

# CHAPTER SIX

# Gender Roles and Sexual Stratification: Is Marriage Detrimental to Women?

■ Suppose parents were encouraged to choose the sex of their children: Would you have a boy or a girl? Or would you let "biological chance" make your decision for you? If you decided to choose, a range of social assumptions about gender might influence your decision. Do you think, for example, that girls have nicer dispositions, making them easier to parent than boys? Do you have a son or a daughter already, and wish to "complete your collection"? Or, would you prefer to have your child have a same-sex playmate? Is having a male heir important to carry on the family name? Would you prefer to dress a girl? Do the people around you value male children more than female ones? For some, the stakes in having a boy or a girl can be so high that some expectant parents use various strategies to increase the likelihood of getting their desired child, or more darkly, rely upon illegal sex-based abortion to deal with "mistakes." Under China's national "one-child" policy, some parents aborted female children to ensure that their one child was male. Before we know our children as individual human beings, their biological sex acts as a social template that shapes how we think of, treat, and value them—and in the most extreme case, even determines whether they will survive.

Human societies organize themselves using biological sex to make social distinctions. In U.S. society, as elsewhere, men and women have different expectations. How could it be otherwise? Expectations must capitulate to biology. Anatomy is destiny—so said Sigmund Freud. Only women can become mothers, although both sexes can "mother." Sociologists define *sex* as a biological category and *gender* as a set of social distinctions based on one's sex. The weight of scholarly evidence is that most gender-linked behavior typical of men and women is socially, rather than biologically, determined. Although this conclusion may change as we learn more about the subtle effect of genes and hormones, most sociologists feel that the social distinctions of gender are not simply nature's default settings—numerous institutions direct individuals into what their society considers proper gender roles. Nothing innate makes curtsying "female" or liking the Three Stooges "male."

Families, the mass media, peers, schools, and religion socialize men and women into their gender roles. *Gender ideology* refers to ingrained and socially reinforced ideas about the proper social roles of men and women. *Gender strategies* refer to the strategies that men and women use to fit prevailing gender ideology. Symbolic interactionists often study what actions constitute appropriate displays of one's gender. To the symbolic interactionist, one's gender is a recognizable social performance, a series of acts that signify "doing" gender. As an example, consider some distinctive ways that men and women behave in class. Women are likely to cross their legs under their desks, to wear make-up, and to carry their books next to their chests. Men will stick their legs straight out, take fewer pains with their facial appearance, and carry their books held close to their sides. Such "gendered" behaviors simply become "natural" to people, an unconscious part of identifiably demonstrating femininity or masculinity. Familiar admonishments, like "tomboy," "unladylike," "sissy," or "throwing like a girl," remind children that one's gender constitutes a standard to which they should aspire. Men and women learn to conform to norms of masculinity and femininity and to incorporate them into daily life in countless, unconscious ways.

Recognizing the boundaries of physique and hormonal equipment, the potential range of human action is broad. Both sexes can carry out the activities necessary to make a living, yet, in most societies, a sexual division of labor remains, with some tasks defined as "female" and others as "male." Some tasks that are predominantly male in one culture are predominantly female in another.[1] However, a division of labor based on *physical* prowess seems no longer necessary, particularly in Western societies, where work is becoming increasingly technological and women have freedom from pregnancy through birth control measures.

Is a traditional division of gender roles functional for society? Sociologists differ on this point. Functionalists argue that a traditional division of labor between the sexes makes sense (or did once) because men are physically stronger—better able to be providers in a competitive and harsh world. Women bear children and are thus better suited to child rearing and family nurturance. These differences lead to the traditional belief that society is organized most effectively when men work outside the home and women work in it. The man should have the "instrumental" role in the family and focus on dealing with the external world and obtaining resources. The woman should carry out an "expressive" role and focus on relationships within the family, keeping the family functioning smoothly by distributing support and love.[2] While these roles blur in practice, the traditional sensibility is that men and women each cleave primarily to an instrumental or expressive role in family life.

Conflict theorists see these gender roles in a different light. For conflict theorists, rather than being functional for all of society, traditional gender roles benefit some (men) while exploiting others (women). Men, because of their status advantages, can dominate women economically, confining them to the home or making them work at low-paying, demeaning jobs. Women are, in this view, similar to every other oppressed minority group and must revolt to become free, a sentiment sparking much of the feminist revolution of the 1960s and 1970s. Today, women still earn considerably lower wages than men and are also less likely to attain high-level career mobility—the so-called glass ceiling.

Yet, despite women's lower wages, one cannot deny, that over the last thirty years, women have made large advances in the occupational, social, political, and economic mainstream of the United States. There is, for example, greater tolerance for seeing women in a wide variety of jobs; indeed, by 1998, 94 percent of all Americans claim to be willing to vote for a woman for President.[3] Today, teenagers barely question the reality of female airline pilots, corporate lawyers, managers, police officers, professors, and athletes. Sociologists Andrew Cherlin and Pamela Walters have found relatively few differences between males and females in their attitudes toward gender equality.[4] Clearly a sea change has taken place in U.S. society in terms of women's occupational and political rights, even though it will take longer to gauge its full effects, and some forms of discrimination still exist.

Today, masculinity no longer represents a standard by which all humankind is to be judged. Yet, gender still constitutes a distinct social boundary. Most people still feel more comfortable in a world where men and women are brought up and act differently. A world of people, rather than one of men and women, would be shocking to anyone who has grown up in this one. Men and women still often socialize in primary same-sex friendship groups, consume separate "male" and "female" products, and establish gender-segregated social enclaves, such as "ladies night out" and time with "the boys." Shows, such as Comedy Central's *The Man Show*, satirically play off this stereotype, as, in their way, do female-oriented cable channels, such as *We, Lifetime,* and *Oxygen.* As gender equality advances, much voluntary—and at times involuntary—segregation by gender remains. The grounds on which men and women relate—work, school, family, culture—involve tension in managing interacting on equal terms in some spheres with a disinclination to do so in others. Should a man still hold the door open for a "lady"? Should a woman initiate and pay for a date? Is a man complimenting a woman's appearance at work sexual harassment or evidence of being a pleasant colleague? Should a man teach women's studies courses? What role should women play on the battlefield?

The social side of the "women's revolution" remains difficult to evaluate. For example, what roles women should seek in this new era are hotly disputed. Some argue that women should have the characteristics of men, others that women should remain distinctively feminine, and still others propose a form of social androgyny for both sexes, that is, having some characteristics of both men and women.[5] Contemporary feminism itself is wracked by this debate. Some argue that academic feminists should empower women by prioritizing how an oppressive male social structure allows tremendous levels of violence, sexual predation, and discrimination to victimize them, from claims of an epidemic "date rape" culture to educational discrimination. Other feminists argue that this approach reflects an exaggerated and overwrought politically correct orthodoxy, based on biased research and data that are damaging the cause of gender equity, making women seem weak and helpless.[6]

The debate over appropriate gender roles in the twenty-first century has affected traditional social institutions like marriage that formalize relationships between men and women. As divorce rates rose in the 1970s and remain high, along with increasing rates of cohabitation and births outside of marriage, many Americans worry today that the institution of marriage and the traditional nuclear family are disintegrating. Although these trends have different causes, including economic factors and changes in laws, they have also been facilitated (whether for good or ill) by some of the same changes in values that encouraged the women's movement. There are now contrasting views of what the roles of "husband" and "wife" should be in contemporary marriages and of their attached benefits and costs. Some view the institution of marriage as exploitative, an arrangement that benefits one sex over the other. From this perspective, a decline in marriage is all for the better, signifying women choosing welcome new paths of greater independence and autonomy in living their lives. Others see marriage as an effective and rewarding partnership between men and women, a key to attaining social stability and personal happiness. From this perspective, any decline in marriage is a disaster for both men and women.

## ■ Question

*Is marriage detrimental to women?*

> *Americans have not come to grips with the gap between the families we live with and the symbolic families we live by.*
> —John Gillis

Michel de Montaigne once quipped that "a perfect marriage would involve a blind wife and a deaf husband." Popular magazines and books, ranging from *Maxim* to *Cosmopolitan* to *Men are from Mars, Women are from Venus*, promise, in their different ways, to offer readers tips for managing relations with the "opposite sex." Sigmund Freud once asked, somewhat plaintively perhaps, "What does a woman want?"[7] Women might ask, with equal trepidation, "What makes a man happy?" These two questions haunt many of us. Men and women are both very different from and very similar to each other. It is this similarity but difference that makes living with each other so challenging, and, for some, so fulfilling.

Sociologists view marriage as a voluntary and legally sanctioned relationship between a man and woman, who form a partnership that encompasses economic cooperation, companionship, sexual activity, and child rearing. Most Americans view marriage as an individual choice premised on an overpowering attraction to a prospective mate. Yet, whom we marry is more socially determined than our culture's romantic imagery indicates. Cupid's arrow may hit a mysterious stranger, but the *kind* of mysterious stranger that Cupid's arrow strikes is much more predictable than is generally thought. Americans tend to marry others who are very close to them in social status. Almost all U.S. marriages, for example, join people who are no more than one socioeconomic class apart.[8] We usually, although not always, marry within the same race, religion, social class, and educational level.

Americans marry along lines of *homogamy*—we tend to meet and seek affiliations with those like ourselves, which helps explain why fellow college students, co-workers, and congregants all marry one another. Homogamy has its uses. We may be attracted to and most compatible with a partner who shares some of our social characteristics. We also do not want to move downward in social status through marriage, for the simple reason that partnership with a weaker marital partner (in terms of their resources) seems to operate against one's self-interest. If social life is a competition over resources, an individual is better off allying with a person of means. Some dating services even specialize in exquisitely matched homogamy, offering to match single Ivy League graduates with other single Ivy League graduates. In much of the rest of the world, the invisible hand of social determination is readily apparent in the choice of marriage partners. Parents and elders in many cultures arrange the marriages of their children, because in their view, marriage is too important a decision to leave to chance and youthful hormones. Would you find the idea of your mother and father picking your spouse comforting or horrifying? Would marriages be better off if America's parents did the matching?

However Americans arrive at their match, mysterious stranger or not, they remain committed to the ideal of marriage. Survey data show that the vast majority of American men and women prize getting married and living happily ever. Ninety-two percent of Americans report that having a successful marriage is very important to them. Only 8 percent consider "marriage an outdated institution."[9] Yet, Americans are increasingly willing to divorce, to live together as unmarried couples, and to postpone marriage. According to data from the 2000 U.S. Census, the number of unmarried couples that live together has increased tenfold since 1960. Seventy-three percent of women and 84 percent of men between the ages of 20 and 24 have never married, double the amount from 1970. In 2000, 68 percent of women of prime marital age (25–55) were married; in 1960, 85 percent of them were. The average age for women to marry was 20 in 1970; in 2000 it was 25.[10] Six out of every ten new marriages now end in divorce.[11] Married-couple households with children now constitute only 24 percent of all U.S. households. Although the romantic ideal of marriage remains strong, current statistics indicate that finding a partner and staying happily married is an uncertain proposition.

Leaving aside whether a decline in marriage is for good or ill, what explains these trends? Causes include a variety of economic, educational, political, and technological changes in the American landscape over the last fifty years. The disappearance of many high-paying manufacturing jobs has left young men who lack college degrees less able to tackle the financial obligations associated with marriage. The social movements of the 1960s and 1970s led young women to postpone marriage in order to pursue educational and work opportunities. The advent of birth control pills and greater social acceptance of premarital sex also had an effect. By making sexual activity outside marriage less risky and more socially acceptable, men and women did not need to marry to obtain legitimate and regular sexual activity. In 1971, California was the first state to pass "no fault" divorce legislation, which allowed divorce purely on the grounds of irreconcilable differences, rather than desertion, adultery, or "extreme cruelty," which were the prior historical requirements. Other states also began to lessen the necessary requirements for obtaining a divorce—changes in the legal structure that made marriages easier to dissolve.

A change in attitudes about the importance of self-fulfillment in marriage also reduced the stigma of divorce. The 1970s saw a growing expectation that a successful marriage should include a high degree of personal fulfillment and satisfaction. An unhappy marriage was no longer to be suffered, in the "for better or worse" sense, as one's social duty. Instead, the new consciousness was that marriage should involve taking stock of whether one is happy and fulfilled, over and above an obligation to stay married at all costs. Betty Friedan's *The Feminine Mystique* captured some of this sea change in attitudes in its descriptions of the predicament of suburban wives mired silently in unfulfilling marital roles:

> Each suburban wife struggled with it alone. As she made the bed, shopped for groceries, matched slipcover material, ate peanut butter sandwiches with her children, chauffeured Cub Scouts and Brownies, lay beside her husband at night—she was afraid to ask even of herself the silent question—"is this all?" . . . If the fundamental human drive is not the urge for pleasure or the satisfaction of biological needs, but the need to grow and to realize one's full potential . . . comfortable, empty, purposeless days are indeed cause for a nameless terror.[12]

At the same time, some men began to reassess their own understanding of marital obligations, increasingly divorcing and seeking a "flight from commitment," a relief from the demanding role of breadwinner and provider. Men began to ask themselves, if women were going to work, why did men have to commit their own earnings to supporting their wives, instead of to support a more independent, sometimes hedonistic, lifestyle for themselves?[13] Both men and women could now feel that divorce was an increasingly legitimate option for avoiding the suffocating trappings associated with an unfulfilling breadwinner or housewife role.

In many ways, the contemporary increase in cohabitation represents a modern compromise on marriage. For some, such as homosexual couples, cohabitation is their only option for living together—marriage, with rare exceptions, is a legal status that is only available to heterosexual couples. Cohabitation also allows men and women to attempt to gain the benefits of living together without the binding legal and economic entanglements of marital status. Many people also now view living together as a form of trial marriage, in which both parties experiment with taking a pseudo marital relation for a "test drive." Alternatively, lacking the legal and economic entanglements of marriage is exactly what many criticize about cohabitation, since cohabitation can lack the social structure, personal commitment, and moral responsibility that marriage provides for handling finances and children. Although living together is now more socially acceptable (no doubt contributing to its increase), 75 percent of cohabitating couples still expect to marry their current partner.[14] The institutional and individual hold of marriage is so powerful that most people view its alternative, cohabitation, as mainly a transition to marriage rather than a permanent substitution for it.

Marriage is a social institution joining men and women together into a voluntary, public, and legal social relationship. When marriage fails, either because men and women cannot find a suitable partner or because the partnership breaks down, is this a failure of the institution of marriage itself, the involved individuals, or both? Social institutions bestow particular statuses on people, with attendant rights and obligations. Is the institutional arrangement and social structure constituting marriage so difficult that individuals should properly choose to exit? Should women, confronted with expectations of diminished autonomy in such a social structure, act to reject marriage? Or are individuals to blame for being unable to forge an enduring, committed bond within the institution of marriage? People make marriages, but does entering a social "status" enable the status itself to be blamed for individual behaviors? We all know people who seem to be terrible marital prospects under any circumstances: Are they to be single and isolated? Is there a proper partner for every adult?

Some sociologists believe that the institution of marriage itself is blameworthy, and that women now have a welcome new freedom to exit social structures that work to their detriment. Others see marriage as an essential social institution, and as a social institution, it can be strengthened to serve both men and women better, through enhancing the benefits of marriage to both and by making marriages harder to exit. The conservative, libertarian, and social democratic perspectives each offer a different view on this question, from what the distinct role of the state should be in preserving or weakening marriage to disagreements over the impact marriage has on each gender.

# The Social Democratic Point of View

The heart of the social democratic critique of marriage lies in Jessie Bernard's famous conclusion that "every marriage actually contains two marriages: 'his' and 'hers'—and 'his' seems to be the better deal." [15] Social democrats prize gender equality and view the traditional institution of marriage as structured to benefit men at women's expense. Historically, marriage enshrined male privilege into law; a "wife" was a husband's "property" (in part because the husband was to support the wife financially), which enabled some husbands to act violently and to force nonconsensual sex on their wives without breaking the law.

A wife's legal rights have improved with respect to legislation against domestic violence and marital rape; law enforcement now provides women with greater protection against such abuses. There is also now a greater public consciousness in the United States that domestic violence and coerced sex should be labeled social problems and not justifiable male privilege. Of course, the issue of male violence toward women transcends a simple equation of marriage as the primary generator of such violence—cohabitating men and women act violently, as do gay and lesbian couples. What made the institution of marriage so distinctly detrimental in the social democrat's eyes is that marriage constituted a social status that historically permitted husbands to victimize their wives with legal impunity. Some politicians today believe marital relations have such potential for violence toward women that marriage licenses should have warning labels printed on them, in order to warn young women about marriage's "hazards." Margarita Prentice, a state senator from Washington, commented: "The origin of the wedding ring represents part of a chain binding the wife to her master. I would say simply, 'Beware. Stop, look, listen and be cautious.'"[16] Certainly the symbolism of marriage, with the male father giving away the bride to a new male figure does little to staunch the sense that marriage cements patriarchy.

Social democrats also object to the potential for adverse consequences in the economic dependence wives traditionally had on their husbands. When husbands are sole providers, divorce has worse economic consequences for wives than for husbands. Should a wife who forsakes college and work experience be divorced or seek a divorce, she would lack effective credentials and work experience for acquiring a good job. Her children may also not receive child support from their father. Men had an economic monopoly in marriage that ensured that power remained in the hands of men, which restricted a wife's independence. Today, there is more individual discretion in agreeing to a relationship in which men work outside the home and women within it. Historically, there was less discretion to do so when women faced social pressure to stay home and discrimination when seeking work outside the home.

Today many married women work, and as a result, gain greater economic independence. The national economy has changed, in many cases requiring both husbands and wives to enter the workforce in order to make ends meet. Yet greater economic power has not ended marital inequality. In many cases, having two-earner families expanded a different form of inequality in the household economy. Arlie Hochschild and Anne Machung wrote of a *stalled revolution,* referring to the idea that while workplaces have opened their doors to greater gender equality, the overall distribution of work for women *in the home* has not changed to reflect the new reality of women in the workplace.[17] So, in effect, a problem with advancing the feminist revolution and the status of women in the United States is that women have to balance work and home obligations in more demanding ways than men do. Wives, who now work outside the home in greater numbers, have been unable to convince their male partners to shoulder a corresponding increase in the "second shift" of household work, from cleaning to childcare tasks. Can you legislate that men wash the dishes and diaper their toddlers as much as their wives, or even that they should? Women spend 15.6 hours on housework a week and men 9.5.[18] The result is a disproportionate burden on wives, who, in Hochschild's words, "talk about sleep like starving people talk about food."

Is "his marriage" really a better deal, beyond simply getting out of doing the dishes and diapering the baby? There are a variety of statistical indicators that suggest married men derive a great many more benefits from marriage than married women do, although there is a great amount of controversy about the legitimacy of these indicators. According to some research, marriage incurs penalties on women's health, income, and education. Health statistics indicate that marriage benefits men's health more, since men get sick less and experience fewer emotional problems. Three times as many married women as single women show signs of anxiety, depression, and emotional distress.[19] Twenty-eight percent of women in unmarried households are more educated than their partners; 21 percent of married women are. Sixty-five percent of unmarried couples had both partners working, compared to 54 percent in married couples. Twenty-two percent of women in unmarried partner households earned at least $5,000 more than their partners. Only 15 percent of married women did.[20] The simple independence of unmarried status is also attractive, as this "happily unmarried" woman tells a reporter: "I don't have to negotiate with somebody else where I spend my time or where I spend my money or how I set my priorities."[21] Data from the *1998 Survey of Families and Households* reported that wives were less satisfied with their marriages then men, lending "some support to feminist assertions about the adverse aspects of marriage for women."[22]

Modern times are changing women's expectations of marriage. As Gloria Steinem once remarked, "some of us are becoming the men we wanted to marry," giving voice to the sentiment that today's women can assume the economic and occupational status of a previous era's Mr. Right. Ms. Steinem, who also once famously said that "a woman needs marriage like a fish needs a bicycle," recently got married herself, implying that while marriage has its pitfalls for women, even for older feminists the right man has his charms as does a formal commitment to him. Steven Nock took this point further:

> Research confirms that most women who marry today desire marriages that differ importantly from those of their grandmothers because women's' lives have changed in so many other ways in recent decades. However, though the options available to women have expanded in other respects, the basic pattern of marriage is pretty much the same as it has been for decades. The revolution in gender has not yet touched women's marriages. . . . Quite simply, marriage must reflect the gender equality found everywhere else, or women will not marry.[23]

Social democrats are not against the idea of marriage per se; they are against a structure of marriage that perpetuates male advantage and female disadvantages. Marriage's detriments to women include working more than men do, and compared to unmarried women, higher rates of depression, lower income, worse health, and less independence. Of course, the social democrat's vision does not take into account a range of individual discretion, including women who report happiness in marriage and in voluntary assumption of "unequal" obligations within marriage. Arlie Hochschild, for example, found wives who sought to prevent their husbands from doing more in the home or tried to avoid publicizing male contributions to the second shift, because they feared appearing to violate expectations about what a wife versus a husband should do in the home.

If the structure of marriage is or becomes unequal to women, then social democrats favor government intervention, through legislation on divorce, support of gay marriage, and tightening of enforcement on child support and legislation against domestic abuses. In an ironic way, many social democrats seek government power to insist on maintaining the implicit promise of traditional gender roles, such as ensuring that husbands maintain financial support to ex-wives and children. Social democrats believe in intervening in the inequalities of marriage, so as to make marriage less detrimental to women, including forcing men to make good on their traditional role as providers. As a consequence of the gender revolution, women should also have autonomy and independence, including a full right to avoid marriage.

Gender ideologies and strategies die hard. Social democrats believe that marriage remains a place where men can duplicate what they consider outdated modes of "doing gender." For example, sociologist Julie Brines reported that the more a husband depends on his wife for income, the less housework he is likely to do.[24] It is common to hear unmarried, harried, professional women say that "they could use a wife," a pejorative assessment of a "wife" as an all-purpose maid, valet, and martyr. Let us clone Martha Stewart. Of course, this picture is highly selective, but its implications do drive social democratic reaction to marriage as detrimental to women. Social democrats also generally prioritize more tolerance of diversity, and accept cohabitation, remaining single, or being unmarried as reasonable alternatives to marriage. Social democrats feel that if Rosie O'Donnell or Jodie Foster want to be unmarried mothers, so be it; their rights as independent women to make that choice should be accepted, not denigrated. As long as marriage constitutes a social structure that disadvantages women, social democrats will argue for the acceptability of reconstituting marriage in new ways, using governmental means, and for destigmatizing what they perceive as more female-friendly alternatives to marriage.

## The Conservative Point of View

A hallmark of conservative politics and social philosophy is "family values," a catchphrase referencing the veneration and preservation of the nuclear family through marriage. Conservatives view marriage and the family as the locus of socializing children into traditional values, the primary site of modeling civility, love, and order for future generations. For some conservatives, a fervent belief in marriage emanates from deep-seated religious convictions. Their faith dictates that marriage is a divinely inspired solution so that man does not live life alone, as cited in Genesis (2:24): "Therefore a man leaves his father and mother and clings to his wife, and they become one flesh." Conservatives also believe that divorce, illegitimacy, and single-parent families are the roots of major national problems of crime and poverty. Broken families expose a decline in individual morals and herald disaster for social order, as children of divorce and unmarried mothers are perceived disproportionately to turn to crime and to fall into poverty for lack of available models of discipline, responsibility, and commitment at home. If a solid marriage is not modeled in childhood, the prospects of children themselves marrying successfully diminishes, thus perpetuating a dangerous cycle, threatening the institution of family life.

Where social democrats readily point out inequalities in marital arrangements that work to the detriment of women, conservatives advocate the many disadvantages of being unmarried, a single mother, or divorced for both men and women. Conservatives frequently point to economic consequences affecting children of divorce as evidence of the need to preserve marriage, noting that girls and boys are damaged when their parents' marriages fail:

Only 28 out of every hundred children conceived in the United States will reach age 18 having the marriage of the biological father and mother intact . . . despite our rhetoric of concern for children we have so far refused to give them that which they most desire and want: the love of their parents for each other. It is time to redress this disastrous cultural drift. Not only the welfare of the nation needs it, the welfare of children cries out for it.[25]

Conservatives view illegitimate children and children of divorce as being deprived of important socialization that would help them prosper and cite social science research supporting this conclusion. Children of divorce and single mothers tend to have worse health, to be poorer, to engage in crime and drug abuse disproportionately, to engage in premarital sex more often, to be more likely to divorce, and to handle social relations less adequately.[26] Social democrats question some of these conclusions and also do not believe that marriage necessarily produces positive alternative outcomes.

Conservatives noted other social trends—such as open homosexuality, increased premarital cohabitation, the decline of religion, and rising abortion rates—emerging at about the same time as the growth of women's rights. Conservatives feel that traditional values have remained under siege, and conservative activists have initiated social movements that seek to restore traditional gender roles to the family, with the aim of strengthening marriage. Bill McCartney's *Promisekeepers* organization, for example, asked millions of men, in rallies held in overflowing stadiums, to renew a commitment to be responsible family men who, as heads of their households, should continually strive to honor their parental obligations to their wives and children. Laura Doyle, founder of the "surrendered wife" movement, asked women to reembrace a traditional role as a wife, ceding control and responsibility to the man, rather than seeking a more equal or dominant decision-making role in marriage. Gender equality may be crucial for the workplace, said Doyle, but not for attaining a happier marriage and home for women:

> Feminism addresses what I want at work but says little about what to do in my marriage; about the romantic, intimate relationship I want. With John I am softer and more flexible, a feminine spirit who delights in being attended to. The minute you start to surrender in your marriage, people tell me they can see a pretty dramatic change . . . you start to see, all of a sudden the husband seems more considerate, there's more romance, less tension, sex improves.[27]

Where a social democrat may advocate gender equality as an absolutely universal need, with an unequal marriage being a bane for today's women, conservatives argue that diminishing traditional gender roles in marriage may also work to disadvantage women, if the institution of marriage collapses in their absence. Danielle Crittenden wrote:

> Traditional structure is not so readily reconciled with modern convenience, and yet modern convenience is something few people today will go without. So we may pledge to love each other until death do us part—but we blanch at the first hint of sacrifice. We may express strong views on the sanctity of marriage—but we would not impose

social sanctions on those who betray their vows or even upon couples who refuse to take those vows in the first place . . . we certainly won't take sole charge of the housekeeping and will snap at our husbands if for a moment they expect otherwise. Many of these changes, like the advent of refrigeration and modern plumbing seem progressive: Why should anyone stay in a marriage that is unhappy? Why should women compromise their ambitions to raise children? But like the drywall and plywood of modern houses, these attitudes have made our institutions much flimsier, and over time they endure less well. . . . Rather than believe in a utopian vision of equality, based upon the sexes being not just equal but the same—whether it's in the jobs they take on or the roles within marriage—we perhaps should accept that women now have achieved equality in every important way—politically, legally and within the workforce. Our new goal should be happiness.[28]

Conservatives believe that government should have an important role in preserving marriage. Many conservatives think that government policies easing the process of obtaining a divorce and penalizing marriage with higher taxes harmed the institution of marriage. These policies should be immediately reversed, along with enacting new policies that bolster marriage. Such legislative efforts include repealing or revising no-fault divorce and changing tax codes to create financial incentives to get and remain married. Other government actions includes the 1996 *Defense of Marriage Act,* which defined marriage as exclusively between men and women, thus preventing, in the conservative view, a subversion of the institution to promote homosexual marriage. Conservatives also have sponsored other, more cultural initiatives to defend marriage, such as suggesting that illegitimate births be restigmatized and that traditional gender roles in the home no longer be denigrated within popular culture. During the 1990s, former vice-president Dan Quayle's famous attack on the fictional television character Murphy Brown choosing to become a single mother was a clarion call for many conservatives who saw the culture's moral standards slipping away.

While some critics of such policies believe divorce and alternate family arrangements are private decisions, conservatives respond that broken marriages and their results are a public issue. Governor Frank Keating of Oklahoma commented: "When people ask what's a political guy doing getting involved in what are really private decisions, I say yes, they're private decisions, but to the extent that these are issues that impoverish a society, we need to debate them and come up with whatever solution is appropriate."[29]

An option under increasing consideration is establishing covenant marriage licenses, which make divorce more difficult and require classes on marital relations prior to receiving a license. Louisiana has passed an option for obtaining a covenant marriage, for example, that requires couples to have premarital counseling and prior to getting a divorce, two years of living apart, plus marital therapy. Behind the covenant movement is the belief that marriage should not be easily exited with divorce, even if the state has to step in to ensure that marriages stick. The "easily available" remedy of divorce can lead to an attitude of simply giving marriage a trial run, rather than making a deep commitment. Covenant marriages are finding their adherents in couples seeking to retain a renewed commitment to marriage that has, in their view, been lost and abandoned by their parents' generation. "With a covenant marriage, you eliminate the option of walking out from a mind-set point of view, explains Mike Johnson of Baton Rouge. . . . We're saying, 'let's not do marriage-lite . . . it's marriage-heavy.'"[30]

## The Libertarian Point of View

The libertarian's view of whether marriage is detrimental to women identifies this question as an issue for each individual woman to decide. One-size governmental prescriptions of what role a woman should have in marriage are exactly what libertarians oppose, viewing them as restraints on an individual's autonomy. For libertarians, marriage is not so much an institution, connected to a state system, but rather a contract between two free individuals. Libertarians oppose restricting individual freedom and personal arrangements. If a woman chooses to use her body as a commodity, for example, and works as a prostitute, that is her decision, and she should not be stopped from doing so by government or anyone else.

Brian Micklethwait summarized the libertarian position on marriage:

> This bad idea is, *that the government ought to decide what marriage means.* Against that idea, I say that the meaning of any particular 'marriage' should be decided by those who are taking part in the arrangement. I want to see the principle of consent applied not just to some marriages . . . , but to all marriages. As with all such libertarian suggestions, it is necessary to repeat (for it cannot be repeated too often) that to allow something is not the same as recommending it. The government now allows sex between consenting adult gays in the privacy of their own homes, and quite right too, but this does not mean that the government is recommending such behaviour, nor should it. Allowing everything that people consent to, but nothing that they don't consent to, will "open the floodgates" only to a civilisation more civilised than any the world has ever seen before.[31]

If a woman seeks a same-sex marriage, or a marriage where she is the "little woman," or even a polygamous marriage, she should have the full right to seek those arrangements, or to avoid them as she sees fit. Most paramount is the right of participants to choose or not choose a particular type of marital arrangement. People should be able to make a consensual contract regarding marriage, choose a suitable partner, and exit the partnership should they have, in retrospect, made a poor choice. The only role for a third party in this process is to allow the freest range of choices and to guarantee that individual freedom from violence within the home is secure. Otherwise, libertarians view marriage as an individual option, with each individual to decide whether a particular marital arrangement is detrimental.

Libertarians have strongly opposed state interventions in deciding the number and type of people who can or should get married. For example, if women wish to participate in a polygamous relationship, that is not a matter for prosecutors and courts. Elizabeth Joseph, for example writes in defense of polygamy, "It's helpful to think of polygamy in terms of a free-market approach to marriage. Why shouldn't you or your daughters have the opportunity to marry the best man available, regardless of his marital status?"[32] This arrangement would eliminate the problem of "all the good ones being taken." In fact, knowing that a man has remained in a stable marriage could serve as a prequalification of his value.

Such arguments resonate with libertarian sensibility, in that currently legal forms of marriage present a market that is unnecessarily closed if only one man and one woman can enter into the arrangement. Suppose one were to catalog a hypothetical set of advantages associated with polygamy that are lost under current government controls. Under polygamy, children in the marriage would potentially have several adults available at home, allowing some women to work and some to stay home. There would also be less worry that adultery would end a marriage (for the man), as multiple acceptable sexual partners would be available to him (for the women, the story is obviously more complicated). There would be several adults who could hypothetically contribute to the household's income. Of course, it is up to women and men to decide whether they are disadvantaged or advantaged in a polygamous arrangement. The libertarian has no problem with women deciding against or for a polygamous relation—their ire is more that this decision is taken out of their hands and made for them without their consent.

Libertarians also object to rules about which *kind* of people can get married or whether marriage should be encouraged. The Libertarian Party issued a formal rejection of the passing of the 1996 *Defense of Marriage Act:*

> The government should get out of the business of deciding who can fall in love and get married—and should eliminate all laws that prohibit same-sex marriages. If two adults want to legally say I do, the government shouldn't have the right to say, "No you don't." Marriage should be a private contract between two consenting adults and their church. Intolerant laws shouldn't be part of the picture.[33]

Libertarians also opposed the Bush's administration's recent suggestion to offer each poor single mother a $5,000.00 "marriage incentive" of taxpayer money to marry the father of her child:

> Shame on George W. Bush for even considering the idea of bribing Americans to get married. Marriage is a decision to be made by two adults—not two adults and the federal government. Politicians have no business encouraging, discouraging, or otherwise interfering with that choice.[34]

Libertarians do recognize a role for the state as the protector of abused and victimized individuals. There are circumstances in which the state apparatus can serve individual liberty, either through criminal laws or permitting civil suits. In addition to protecting victims, the state can also serve as a means of enforcing a range of marital contracts. However, for the most part, a libertarian marriage is an individual decision in which the state should have no business. Let people have the freedom to select the nature of the social structures that they join consensually, along with the responsibility to judge and manage the effects of that decision.

# Marriage and Social Research

Marriages are both public and private arrangements. Individuals receive marriage licenses; the state sets age limits determining when people can marry and how marital status affects their finances. If marriages dissolve, a judge determines who gains custody of any children, who supports whom financially and in what amounts, and who gets what distribution of property. In these circumstances, marriage allows for a public determination of private issues, such as parenting and personal wealth. In sum, a marriage is an established and enduring form of voluntary association, which the state and community view as an organization that men and women form to address life's challenges, obligations, and pleasures.

A marriage provides a collective face to the world—people are a couple socially, a family socializing children, and a pair to be advertised to and managed economically as a household. Marriage is a social institution, a form of established social relations that on its own warrants sociological assessment. What impact does marriage have on society, on the men and women who enroll in that status, and as a public phenomenon? Should people encourage, decry, or reshape marriage? Men and women stand today in a new era where the most traditional form society uses to organize gender relations—marriage—is in decline. What is the case for or against marriage as a social institution? Is marriage simply one of a range of possible options for men and women to pursue adult life together—or should people view marriage as the socially preferable option to all other alternatives, with government acting in support of this view?

The very title of Linda Waite and Maggie Gallagher's book, *The Case for Marriage: Why Married People Are Happier, Healthier and Better Off Financially,* eliminates the element of surprise—readers know instantly that Waite, a prominent sociologist, and Gallagher, a journalist, strongly advocate marital status as a remedy for assorted social problems.[35] Because advocacy research has the potential to minimize opposing evidence, you need to think critically about alternative readings of arguments and data when assessing such work. Nonetheless, it is also important to consider what responsibility social scientists should have to make pronouncements about what actions are good or bad for society. If medical researchers pronounce the harm of alcohol and tobacco use, based on having done research, shouldn't social scientists also advocate what is or isn't good for us, based on their research? Must objectivity yield when taking a pointed stand on an issue? Yet, caution is always warranted to ensure that one's moral fervor does not overtake one's objectivity.

Whether marriage is detrimental to women, men, or children is a battle fought in fiery rhetoric and divergent interpretations of statistics. Waite and Gallagher inventoried data from several national surveys of Americans' health, income, education, sexual behavior, divorce, and children. For example, they use data from *The Social Organization of Sexuality,* profiled in Chapter Four, to discuss sexual satisfaction in marriage. Other data sets include the *National Crime Victimization Survey* and the *National Survey of Families and Households.* Waite and Gallagher argued that data from these different surveys aggregate into forceful evidence that marriage provides important social benefits.

Waite and Gallagher summarized the evidence as follows:

Both men and women get health and earnings benefits from marriage, but men benefit more in physical health and earnings. Both men and women are safer, more sexually satisfied, and wealthier, if married, but women benefit more on sexual satisfaction, financial well-being, and protection from domestic violence, and they benefit about equally on emotional well-being. If you are keeping a gender scorecard, you'd have to call contemporary marriage a pretty good deal for both sexes—both men and women benefit in important ways, sometimes in different amounts. But in most areas of life, marriage makes both men and women better off.[36]

However, Waite and Gallagher's secondary analysis of survey data findings on men and women's income, safety, and health, for example, do not mean that their explanations of why those statistics emerge as they do are accurate. For example, Waite and Gallagher explained in part married men's statistical health benefits from marriage as "summed up in a single phrase: fewer stupid bachelor tricks." How are stupid bachelor tricks curtailed? Nagging, at least according to Waite and Gallagher's use of anecdotal evidence from undetailed interviews. For example, "Marriage didn't make Albert a teetotaler, but under consistent prodding from Lisa he has cut back considerably." Lisa: "I just told him something has to be done."[37] Maybe nagging does explain health benefits for men, such as cutting down drinking, telling a husband to go to the doctor, and so forth. Yet, how is one to attribute causal power to nagging as a taken-for-granted advantage of marriage? Perhaps being nagged also contributes to high stress and other maladies. In sum, Waite and Gallagher may be right in identifying benefits of marriage statistically, but their explanation of exactly how marriage is responsible for these benefits is more speculative, relying often on a casual anecdote from a single couple's lives. For example, the causal power of nagging emerges anecdotally, as if "Albert" might be everyman, to show "how" nagging produces health benefits.

However, we should not deny the common sense behind many of Waite and Gallagher's inferences about why marriage benefits both men and women. Married people pool resources. They offer each other a partner who can care for the other and provide emotional support and trust; a man can help a woman economically with more resources like health insurance and a high salary; and a woman can restrain a man's bad impulses and so forth. Also, divorce does harm a woman financially and often devastates children. Simply being socially integrated, being loved and loving, and being tied in and important to another is a blessing. Yet, marriage may simply not cause all the effects Waite and Gallagher attributed to it—there is room for considering what kind of marriage produces the Waite and Gallagher benefits, rather than assuming simply that the institution of marriage as such does, irrespective of the individuals involved in that institution.

So, if marriage is so great, why is marriage in trouble as a social institution? According to Waite and Gallagher:

We want marriage but we are afraid to discourage divorce or unwed childbearing. The marriage vow thus receives less support from families, society, experts, government, and the law. Important changes in sex roles have challenged married couples to make new adjustments at the very time the social prestige of marriage as a uniquely favored union has declined, and divorce as a solution to emotional difficulties is more widely approved than ever before. Marriage is more often described as just one of an array of personal lifestyles, no one of which is intrinsically preferable to any other.[38]

The solutions Waite and Gallagher preferred resemble those conservatives recommend: greater promotion of marriage, tougher actions to stem unwed pregnancies, and making divorce more difficult, particularly unilateral divorces. Unlike some conservatives, Waite and Gallagher did not demand a return to a traditional division of gender roles in marriage. Instead, they argued that greater awareness of the benefits men derive from marriage would encourage them to be more supportive of an egalitarian household, though they did not explain exactly why or how this transformation would occur.

Waite and Gallagher's general prescription is that marriage is a benefit for all life's ills. Alternatively, what is good for everyone might not be good for any particular individual. In this dilemma lies an important question about what social science findings mean for individuals in making decisions about how to live their everyday lives.

Social science, like other social forces, often tells us what is good for us, from how to think about race and marriage, to whether welfare-to-work policies are oppressive, to criticizing the police. Expectations can form their own tyranny in our lives, as we question why the reality around us does not resemble the smooth predictions of social scientists and other advocates. The best social science gathers good information about the world—whether in surveys or interviews, observations or experiments, content analysis or focus groups—and interprets this evidence. However, in this study—and others—the researchers are at the mercy of their data, some of which is better and more relevant than others. Secondary analysis of data has this problem: One uses whatever is available, however imperfect it might be. From this, social scientists attempt to provide social prescriptions about how to organize the world and our lives. Yet, given the complexity of our lives and the many possible variations of social phenomena like marriage and the family, what is good for everyone may not be good for the individual. Be informed about the evidence and perspectives social scientists bring to the table, but also reflect critically on them.

# Gender Roles and Marriage

The debate among conservatives, libertarians, and social democrats on gender is a central one for understanding the relations between men and women in U.S. society. Over the past forty years, since the publication of Betty Friedan's *The Feminine Mystique* in 1962, the position of women in U.S. society has changed dramatically and attitudes toward women have changed as well. Many of the once taken-for-granted aspects of gender-role behavior are now openly questioned. All this social change has produced confusion—what are gender roles becoming? What should they be? Imagine writing an extensive marriage contract to communicate your expectations of a husband or wife. Would you want an egalitarian pairing with your partner? Would you want a traditional pairing? Would you want a covenant marriage or the ability to divorce without contestation?

To a conservative, marriage is the best means to achieve social order and to provide all of society's benefits—trust, a division of labor, love—to small groups of adult individuals and children. Gender is a distinct biological and social identity, a blessing from a higher power, and marriage is the ideal realization of gender's distinction. To abandon marriage is to a conservative to embrace selfishness over the social good, further evidence of men and women slipping into chaos by letting traditional bonds weaken. What happened to commitment, to sacrifice, to battling out tough times, and to forming family? What happened to "for better or worse"? To give up commitment to one another and traditional gender roles in marriage is, writ small, evidence of a willingness to forgo commitment writ large—taking care of children and providing for one another in society. Conservatives argue vehemently that men and women are worse off without making a sanctioned public commitment to one another. A decline in marriage is a decline in society large and small.

The libertarian celebrates individual autonomy and the freedom of any man or woman to find the gender role he or she feels is most suitable. This sentiment is in keeping with the women's revolution. However, insisting on freedom of choice does mean in some sense declining to enforce social practices, such as marriage, that may benefit men and women. If marriage does provide benefits to individuals and they make that choice, the state does have a role in helping men and women attain that choice since marriage is sanctioned by the state. The libertarian's reluctance to embrace a public sphere can ironically weaken the power of marriage to be a forceful individual good.

The social democrat views contemporary marriage with skepticism. Marriage is one of a variety of options, but one that thankfully gender equality has made less oppressive. An embrace of traditional gender roles is too easily structured into oppressive patriarchy. Weakening the hold of marriage enhances gender equality. Yet, the freedom to escape marriage may be a freedom leading to social inequality and isolation for both genders. A fundamental question for the future is to understand how society's ongoing debate over gender will continue to transform our most established means of organizing gender relations, marriage.

## Questions

1. Is a traditional division of gender roles functional for society?

2. How are men and women different?

3. Should men and women split household chores equally?

4. Would you want your parents to arrange your marriage? Why or why not?

5. Is marriage is detrimental to women? Why or why not?

6. Should government act to preserve marriage, for example, by making a divorce more difficult to obtain, as through covenant marriages?

7. Should the government make polygamy illegal?

8. Does everyone need "a wife"?

9. Are the "surrendered wife" and *Promisekeepers* movements fundamentally sexist?

10. Should same-sex marriages be legal?

## For Further Study

Bernard, Jessie. *The Future of Marriage*. New Haven: Yale University Press, 1982.

Ehrenreich, Barbara. *The Hearts of Men: American Dreams and the Flight from Commitment.* New York: Anchor, 1983

Friedan, Betty. *The Feminine Mystique*. New York: W.W. Norton, 1963.

Hochschild, Arlie Russell, and Anne Machung. *The Second Shift*. New York: Avon, 1989.

Kimmel, Michael. *Manhood in America: A Cultural History*. New York: Free Press, 1996.

Klatch, Rebecca. *Women of the New Right*. Philadelphia: Temple University Press, 1989.

Schwalbe, Michael. *Unlocking the Iron Cage: The Men's Movement, Gender Politics, and American Culture*. New York: Oxford University Press, 1996.

Tannen, Deborah. *You Just Don't Understand: Women and Men in Conversation*. New York: Ballantine, 1990.

Waite, Linda J., and Maggie Gallagher. *The Case for Marriage: Why Married People Are Happier, Healthier and Better Off Financially*. New York: Doubleday, 2000.

## Notes and References

1. George P. Murdock and Caterina Provost, "Factors in the Division of Labor by Sex: A Cross-Cultural Analysis," *Ethnology* 12 (April 1973): 207.

2. Talcott Parsons et al., *Family, Socialization and Interaction Process* (New York: Free Press, 1955), pp. 3–9.

3. *General Social Surveys, 1972–1990: Cumulative Codebook* (Chicago: National Opinion Research Center, University of Chicago, 1990), p. 247.

4. Andrew Cherlin and Pamela B. Walters, "Trends in United States Men's and Women's Sex-Role Attitudes: 1972 to 1978," *American Sociological Review* 46 (August 1981): 453–460.

5. Gayle Graham Yates, *What Women Want: The Ideas of the Movement* (Cambridge, MA: Harvard University Press, 1975).

6. See Carol Gilligan, *In a Different Voice: Psychological Theory and Women's Development* (Cambridge MA: Harvard University Press, 1982); Catherine MacKinnon, *Only Words* (Cambridge MA: Harvard University Press, 1993); Christina Hoff Sommers, *Who Stole Feminism: How Women Have Betrayed Women* (New York: Simon and Schuster, 1994); Christina Hoff Sommers, *The War Against Boys: How Misguided Feminism Is Harming Our Young Men* (New York: Simon and Schuster, 2000).

7. Ernest Jones, *The Life and Work of Sigmund Freud*, vol. 2, *1909–1919: Years of Maturity* (New York: Basic Books, 1955), p. 421.

8. See Michael Hout, "The Association between Husbands and Wives' Occupations in Two-Earner Families," *American Journal of Sociology* 88 (1982): 397–409.

9. Roper Center Data Review, "The Family: Marriage Highly Valued," *The Public Perspective* 9(8) (February/March 1998): 17.

10. Taken from Jason Fields and Lynne M. Casper. "America's Families and Living Arrangements: March 2000," *Current Population Reports.* P20-537 (Washington, DC: U.S. Census Bureau, June 2001).

11. Quoted in Kathryn Edin, "Few Good Men," *The American Prospect* vol. 11 no. 4 (January 3, 2000).

12. Betty Friedan, *The Feminine Mystique*, p. 63.

13. Barbara Ehrenreich, *The Hearts of Men: American Dreams and the Flight from Commitment.*

14. Pamela Smock, "Cohabitation in the United States," *Annual Review of Sociology* (2000).

15. Jessie Bernard, *The Future of Marriage.*

16. "Warning: Marriage Could Be Hazardous," *New York Times*, February 19, 1995, Section 1, 40.

17. Arlie Russell Hochschild and Anne Machung, *The Second Shift* (New York: Avon).

18. Cited in Helene Stapinksi, "Let's Talk Dirty," *American Demographics* 20 (1998): 50–56.

19. J. Carr, *Crisis in Intimacy* (Pacific Grove, CA: Brooks/Cole, 1998).

20. Taken from Jason Fields and Lynne M. Casper. "America's Families and Living Arrangements: March 2000."

21. Barbara Brotman, "Happily Unmarried," *Chicago Tribune*, Wednesday, December 20, 2000. Section 8, p. 1.

22. Walter R. Schumm, Farrell J. Webb, and Stephan R. Bollman, "Gender and Marital Satisfaction: Data from the National Survey of Families and Households," *Psychological Reports* 83 (1998): 319.

23. Steven Nock, "The Problem with Marriage," *Society* (July 1999), p. 21.

24. Julie Brines, "Economic Dependency, Gender, and the Division of Labor at Home," *American Journal of Sociology* 100 (1994): 652–688.

25. Patrick F. Fagan, "The Federal and State Governments, Welfare and Marriage Issues." Testimony before the United States House of Representatives, May 22, 2001. Text available at www.heritage.org/library/testimony/test052201.htm.

26. Fagan, "The Federal and State Governments, Welfare and Marriage Issues."

27. Julia Duin, "Sweet Surrender: Laura Doyle on Marriage," *Insight on the News*, March 5, 2001, p. 34.

28. Danielle Crittenden, "Is Early Marriage the Best Choice for American Women?" *Insight on the News*, February 22, 1999, p. 25.

29. Frank Keating, "Making Marriage Matter," Speech given September 27, 2000.

30. Francine Russo, "Bridal Vows Revisited," *Time*, July 24, 2000, p. G1.

31. Brian Micklethwait, "People—Not the Government—Should Decide What Marriage Means," *Political Notes* No. 129, The Libertarian Party.

32. Elizabeth Joseph, "Polygamy: The Ultimate Feminist Lifestyle," from her speech, "Creating a Dialogue: Women Talking to Women," a conference organized by the Utah chapter of the National Organization for Women, May 1997. Available online at www.polygamy.com/practical/ultimate.htm.

33. "Reject Defense of Marriage Act," Libertarian Party Press Release, July 1996.

34. "Government wants to give $5000 to bribe poor into getting married," Libertarian Party Press Release, May 23, 2001.

35. Linda J. Waite and Maggie Gallagher, *The Case for Marriage: Why Married People Are Happier, Healthier and Better Off Financially.*

36. Waite and Gallagher, *The Case for Marriage*, p. 171.

37. Waite and Gallagher, *The Case for Marriage*, p. 53.

38. Waite and Gallagher, *The Case for Marriage*, p. 185.

# CHAPTER SEVEN

# Race and Ethnicity: Should Minorities Be Given Preferential Treatment in Admission to Higher Education and Hiring?

■ Would you wish to be black in America? Chinese? Hispanic? Arab? white? We pose this question not to reflect on the moral character of these groups, but to consider how belonging to any one of them means confronting prejudice and discrimination. Consider your own views toward any of these groups or the popular vocabulary of stereotypical assumptions that exist about them. Black men are dangerous, white men are all privileged racists, Asian American women are meek and servile, Hispanics are all "illegals," Arab-Americans are terrorists. Even in a nation characterized by economic prosperity and the legal enforcement of civil rights, people may act toward others on the basis of their ethnic, racial, religious, and national identities. Many people today try to avoid discriminating against others, believing sincerely that prejudice on the basis of race, color, or creed is morally objectionable. Yet, this ideal does not describe historical or contemporary behavior accurately. The moral belief some people hold—that no group is inherently better than any other—is extremely rare historically and uncommon today. Being tolerant to "outsiders" is swimming against the tide of human history.

Few societies have avoided systematic ethnic or racial prejudice. Many societies enshrined discriminatory policies into law, such as the former apartheid government of South Africa, which legally guaranteed a privileged position to white citizens in educational, employment, and housing opportunities, and set up special categories for "Asian" and "colored" citizens, separate from the black majority. In addition to discriminating against subordinate groups within their own borders, nations also discriminated against peoples elsewhere whom they viewed as inferiors. Western nations labeled peoples in the New World, Africa, and Asia as "savages" and "uncivilized"; Germans declared themselves the "master race"; and Chinese and Japanese societies closed themselves off to outsiders. Even African and Native American tribes revealed hostility toward outsider groups, often engaging in warfare against these enemies. Killings in the name of race and ethnicity still occur frequently today in Rwanda, Sri Lanka, Chechnya, and elsewhere.

The contemporary Western ideal of racial and ethnic equality notwithstanding, prejudice is very hard to erase. Equality is easy to mouth but difficult to maintain. Unless you are a white, male, Episcopalian, from Vermont, of English descent (on both sides of the family), you have probably experienced some form of prejudice or discrimination. Almost everyone has encountered at least some prejudice, from schoolyard taunts to workplace jokes. Even if you fit the facetious description above, your mother or sister has likely faced discrimination. (Consider the discussion on gender roles in Chapter Six.) Most white Americans belong to ethnic groups that were historical targets of intense prejudice and discrimination. For example, Irish and Italian immigrants encountered "No Irish, Italians need apply" signs hanging from employers' doors, and Eastern European immigrants confronted "No dogs or Jews" postings in residential neighborhoods. Today, some claim, because of political correctness and affirmative action, that white males in the United States face increasing discrimination and prejudice in seeking higher education and employment opportunities. However, some groups have suffered more than others. African Americans, Armenians, Jews, and American Indians, for instance, have been victims of slavery, brutality, or genocidal state policies. Japanese Americans were unfairly placed in internment camps during World War II, and Turkish immigrants today confront violence in Germany and elsewhere.

The term *race* in these contexts refers to genetic differences between individuals and groups that are typically related to skin color and other anatomical characteristics, such as the shape of facial features. *Ethnicity* refers more directly to a cultural distinction. An ethnic group shares a culture and perceives itself as a cultural group. When members of such groups regularly marry within their own group, they may have common genetic traits (such as some hereditary diseases), but typically the genetic component of ethnic groups is less salient than their cultural unity. In some cases, ethnicity does not easily map onto race: What "race" are Hispanics or Arab Americans? This question could have been raised a century ago about the Irish (the Celtic "race") or Jews. Sometimes race can be transformed into ethnicity, or the reverse.

Many people assume that genetics account for differences between racial and ethnic groups, particularly in variations in IQ scores. However, we still know too little about genetic features related to race, particularly cognition and intelligence, to make any definitive statements about how exactly genetics, if at all, contribute to differences in social outcomes between races. For example, although African Americans on average regularly score lower on some standard intelligence (IQ) tests than white Americans, the reasons for this difference are hotly disputed, with test biases and environmental factors advanced as plausible alternatives to a genetic explanation. Until definitive proof of genetic differences in cognition and behavior emerges, it is best to assume that "racial" differences in test scores are attributable to environmental factors and are therefore subject to change.[1]

Sociologists distinguish between *prejudice* and *discrimination*. Prejudice is a set of attitudes, feelings, and beliefs toward a particular group. Prejudices have emotional weight behind them, are not readily altered by reason or experience, and produce a predisposition to act toward a group in a negative or positive way. Where prejudice reflects attitudes, discrimination refers to *actions* directed against a group or its members, such as refusing to provide opportunities or rewards, including loans, employment, and housing, to members of a particular group. Most Americans do recognize that some prejudice and discrimination still exist against many racial and ethnic groups. Although the extent of prejudice and discrimination has definitely declined in the United States over the past few decades, both remain ingrained in segments of our society.

Sociologist W. E. B. DuBois used the term *double-consciousness* to refer to people's awareness of how others perceive them because of their race, in contrast to how a person sees him- or herself as an individual.[2] Double-consciousness reminds us that race and ethnicity project public identities for a whole group onto many different types of persons, forcing affected individuals to confront labels and discrimination that have no bearing on their individual behavior. Obviously characteristics that typify a group do not apply to all or even most group members (e.g., blacks having "rhythm," the French being arrogant, Chinese people being martial arts experts, Italians being Mafiosi, and the English keeping a stiff upper lip).

Difficulty in ethnic and race relations can occur on several levels. Prejudice and discrimination are often viewed as individual-level concepts; that is, they are things individuals feel and do because of personal traits (for example, an authoritarian personality) or experience (such as never having had contact with a member of a minority group). Some forms of racism are overt, growing from individual prejudice. When Los Angeles policeman Mark Fuhrman, during the O. J. Simpson trial, revealed that he treated black and white motorists differently and could always find a reason to arrest blacks, this represented discrimination emanating from individual prejudice. Joe Feagin and Melvin Sikes have documented affronts that African Americans routinely face in public places.[3]

However, individual discrimination does not occur in a social vacuum. Media attention often focuses on individuals as racists without examining the larger social context that can allow discrimination to take place. For example, Mark Fuhrman could depend on societal fear of black criminality—and what some view as a discriminatory criminal justice system—to carry out his actions without getting caught. What is defined as racism, prejudice, or discrimination is a social construction. People fight over the right to legitimately judge what actions can be constituted as "racist." For example, a vigorous debate, particularly in universities, is ongoing as to whether blacks can even be racist toward whites, or whether only oppressors can be racist. The ability to condemn others for racism creates a socially privileged position of moral entrepreneurship in society, a position that disadvantages other groups by diminishing contrary views as illegitimate. Reverend Jesse Jackson, for example, has become an arbiter of whether various corporations in the United States are "doing enough" to hire African Americans. He has promoted his legitimacy as both a diagnostician and eradicator of racism.

Sometimes these are complex issues. Consider the vigorous debate over the legitimacy of "racial profiling," a police technique that would often target African Americans drivers who happened to be traveling on known drug routes. It is understandable that black males became upset by seemingly being accused of "DWB" [Driving While Black], while others could travel unhindered. Police for their part sometimes argued that with limited resources, they needed to stop those who had the highest likelihood of committing crimes. Just as racial profiling was being controlled, Arab terrorists hijacked four commercial airliners and crashed them into the Pentagon, World Trade Center towers, and Pennsylvania countryside, causing massive death and destruction. Increased airline security went into effect, but against whom? Should African Americans passengers, highly unlikely to be terrorists, be targeted as frequently as Arab Americans? If DWB is oppressive, FWB [Flying While Black] might save aggravation. Should Anglo-Americans, Asian Americans, and Hispanics have to bear the burden that a few Middle Eastern extremists imposed? Such additional searches would likely provide little in the way of security. Yet, surely one can understand that loyal and lawful Arab Americans would be as upset with discriminatory treatment as were black drivers—treatment that related only to perceptions of their group and not to their own actions as individuals.

Sociologists believe that discrimination's widest effects, however, are not attributable to prejudiced individuals: stereotypical malevolent rednecks with two teeth, no education, and an appetite for violence. Racial or ethnic groups may be harmed without any individual deliberately seeking that end. The term, *institutional racism*, or *institutional discrimination*, refers to organizational and institutional actions of a broad scope that disproportionately disadvantage minorities. For example, many minorities are channeled into low-paying, dead-end jobs because of poor schools, which leave them unable to move to better neighborhoods. No one person has forced them to take lower-paying jobs; ostensibly it was their own choice, but their social circumstances or environment made it difficult to improve their lot.

Institutional discrimination also has helped produce residential segregation. Residential segregation in turn produces more discriminatory effects on minority neighborhoods. In the hardest hit urban areas, some of these neighborhoods have scant employment opportunities, inadequate municipal services, a plethora of bad role models, and unhealthy living conditions, from higher crime rates to greater environmental hazards. These aftereffects of institutional discrimination end up producing a truly disadvantaged group.[4] How is this outcome possible without an army of prejudiced individuals? Imagine a grocery chain that avoids placing stores in embattled neighborhoods for security concerns. Or an employer who believes that white candidates from suburban schools are better prepared for work than minority graduates of inner-city schools. As individual businesspersons, these company decision makers may be acting completely without any hatred toward a particular group. The result of their collective business decisions, however, is discrimination against minorities through limiting their access to goods, services, and employment.

Most Americans recognize that contemporary race relations are troubled. The response to the O. J. Simpson verdict demonstrated this divide dramatically. Distrust and rumors have permeated race relations. For example, many African Americans refused to have their children vaccinated, fearful that the vaccine was intended to infect their children with diseases, such as AIDS, rather than to protect them. Whites, for their part, were alarmed by false rumors that inner-city gangs initiate new members by having them rape a white woman. While these fears are groundless, they and other rumors have the power to pollute race relations and have fueled racial tensions throughout history.[5] The history of racism in the United States is powerful and clouds trust between the races. Whites worry that minorities will perceive all of their actions as racist, while minorities fret about being paranoid and always looking over their shoulders. Whites may perceive minorities as refusing to acknowledge the removal of historical discriminatory barriers, preferring instead to blame any problems on racist whites. Minorities, in turn, can be outraged at white reluctance to recognize what minorities perceive as everyday race-based advantages for whites, such as freedom from overt police scrutiny. How can honest dialogue occur under such circumstances of suspicion and recrimination?

Some functional theorists argue that racial and ethnic segmentation, unpleasant as we might find it, has a hidden or latent benefit for society as a whole, in that it provides for a division of labor. Someone must do the physically demanding, low-paying dirty jobs; by categorizing some people as second-class citizens, society has a supply of cheap labor. Sociologists refer to this difference in labor costs between racial or ethnic groups as a "dual-labor market," an orienting concept that distinguishes between characteristics of high-paying, professional work and lower-paying, service-oriented work. Other forms of racism result from belief in scientifically discredited theories that argue that some races are genetically superior to others. Racial and ethnic segmentation also provides scapegoats for social problems and a basis, particularly during wartime, for reinforcing social solidarity by casting other races and ethnic groups as enemies. Consider the animus that was evident against "Arabs" in the aftermath of the terrorist attacks on the Pentagon and World Trade Center towers in 2001.

Conflict theorists attribute racism in complex ways. On one hand, racism may result from competition among races for economic opportunities, a situation that often generates fear of one group's taking jobs from another (a familiar refrain against immigration). A different conflict-based explanation is that racism emanates from economic injustice, with some groups hoping to exploit other groups for their material gain, as occurred in expropriating Native American land and, most perniciously in the United States, in the institution of slavery. Open conflict between groups may be needed to increase the standing of subjugated groups, hence the appearance of race-based social movements seeking social change through both nonviolent and violent means.

Although neither functionalists nor conflict theorists welcome racism and prejudice, they approach the problem from different angles. They also have different responses to one of contemporary U.S. society's most contentious questions—whether minorities should receive preferential treatment in admission to higher education and hiring. Do various types of affirmative action remedy the effects of historical and contemporary racial discrimination? Or does preferential treatment substitute a different odious discrimination in its place?

# ▪ Question

*Should minorities be given preferential treatment in admission to higher education and hiring?*

You are a white applicant for undergraduate admission to your state university. The university rejects you while admitting black and Hispanic applicants with significantly lower grade point averages and scores almost 800 points lower on their SATs. You are a female athlete, of any color, who benefits from Title IX, which expands your opportunities in college and university athletics, while your nonathletic boyfriend has no such benefits. You are a black applicant for employment in the oil industry. The Texaco Corporation has just settled a discrimination lawsuit for $115 million dollars. Does this settlement encourage you to believe that blacks receive fair treatment in hiring decisions in the oil industry? If not, how can minorities confront widespread discrimination against them in hiring? We can state the debate over *affirmative action* in simple terms as a sociological problem. Affirmative action policies are guidelines that help determine the access that members of different groups will have to the opportunities that employers, government, and higher education offer. At issue in affirmative action is deciding under what conditions, if any, guidelines should exist that allow some groups of people, and not others, to receive privileged access to these opportunities.

Affirmative action has become a prominent part of the cultural, legal, and political landscape over the past three decades. Consider the famous and visceral political advertisement for North Carolina Senator Jesse Helms, in which a white hand crumples a letter of rejection for a job that was given to a black. In 1996, California residents passed Proposition 209 (the California Civil Rights Initiative) by a 54.6 percent to 45.4 percent margin, adding to the state constitution a new directive: "Government shall not discriminate against, or grant preferential treatment to, any individual or group on the basis of race, sex, color, ethnicity or national origin in the operation of public employment, public education or public contracting." White comedians crack jokes about identifying themselves as black, Hispanic, Native American, or handicapped women to get into good colleges—for example, "Did that say Roger? I'm Rahima."

Americans recognize that certain groups are underrepresented in some jobs and overrepresented in others. Blacks and Hispanics represent about one-quarter of the U.S. population, but are 25 percent of doctors and lawyers black or hispanic? Are 25 percent of bankers or astronauts black or Hispanic? Are 25 percent of all cleaning women, farm laborers, and dishwashers black or Hispanic? The issue is not whether over- and underrepresentation of minorities in given jobs exists, but about whether our society should enact affirmative action to remedy these disparities.

The list of statistics demonstrating that blacks are disadvantaged is almost endless. For example, the median black family income was 62 percent that of whites in 1998, a figure that had changed little during the previous two decades.[6] Black levels of unemployment are approximately twice those of whites. A smaller percentage of blacks than whites attend college. Experimental studies in which similarly qualified blacks and whites visit employment agencies find that whites are more likely to be offered positions. Blacks are even quoted higher prices than whites are when they shop for cars![7] Despite these inequalities, most overt discrimination has vanished. Employers no longer tell black applicants that they have been rejected *because* they are black. Nevertheless, it is understandable why many black Americans, after listening to this list of statistics, feel that discrimination is in the minds of many white Americans, if not on their tongues.

Since we can assume that the reason there are fewer white Americans, proportionately, among farm laborers or menial workers is not because they are discriminated against, the real question is what can be done to increase the number of minority professionals, white-collar workers, and skilled craftsmen. To see this as a *problem,* we must make two important assumptions: The first assumption is that minority members wish to hold these positions—that is, they are in the labor pool but are not being hired. The second assumption is that enough minority applicants have the *minimum* qualifications necessary for employment. Although specific job classes may not meet these assumptions, we shall assume for our discussion that these two assumptions have been met.

Affirmative action programs were instituted in order to correct the absence of minorities in employment and higher education. The term *affirmative action* is tricky to define precisely. The term's meaning has changed with time and with circumstances, as an examination of the use of affirmative action in hiring illustrates. The first formal government action on the subject of racial discrimination was Executive Order 8801, issued by President Franklin Roosevelt on June 25, 1941. This order barred discrimination in defense industries and government because of race, creed, color, or national origin, and stated that "it is the duty of employees and of labor organizations . . . to provide for the full and equitable participation of all workers in defense industries."[8] It was not until 1961 that the government used the phrase *affirmative action.* President Kennedy, in requiring government contractors to recruit workers on a nondiscriminatory basis, wrote, "The Contractor will take affirmative action to ensure that applicants are employed, without regard to their race, creed, color, or national origin."[9] No longer was it enough for employers to refrain from discrimination, they now had to *actively recruit* applicants who belonged to minority groups.

During the mid-1960s, people went further and assumed that *hiring* should be "without regard to race and ethnicity." By the late 1960s and through the 1970s, this "race-blind" view took another turn. It was not enough for employers merely to recruit minority workers openly. Increasingly, employers were expected, or even required, to balance the number of minorities in their workforce. By 1971, under the Nixon administration, federal orders demanded the establishment of goals and timetables for increasing minority employment. For some, these phrases and how they were implemented smacked of quotas and "reverse discrimination" against groups like Jews, Italian Americans, Polish Americans, and, in some circumstances, Asian Americans, who were increasingly defined as part of the "majority." If the workforce is not integrated according to the estimated racial composition of the pool of workers, the employer has the burden of proof to demonstrate that discrimination does not exist. The angry debate over the 1991 Civil Rights bill, eventually passed by Congress and signed by former president George Bush, consisted of how large a burden of proof businesses had in such situations and whether this might lead to informal "quotas" to avoid possible lawsuits.

The 1978 Supreme Court ruling in the *Bakke* case (*Regents of the University of California* v. *Allan Bakke*) was a blow to affirmative action. The court found that the University of California, Davis Medical School, could not exclude nonminorities by reserving a precise number of places for minority applicants—a fixed quota, (although this decision still allowed the university to use race as a factor in admissions decisions). Most Supreme Court decisions since then have supported programs with targets and goals. During the 1990s, the Supreme Court has increasingly held that remedies must be narrowly tailored to make up for past discrimination, and increasingly the court is overturning broad affirmative action solutions, such as set-asides for minority businesses.

When California voters passed Proposition 209, they were persuaded that state government should dismantle preferential treatment of some groups over others in admissions to public educational institutions and for public employment. Proponents of affirmative action feared that the passing of Proposition 209 would lead to a groundswell of similar legislation across the country. Their concern has been somewhat unwarranted. Despite vocal proponents, Houston voters rejected a similar proposition, and many state institutions have fought lawsuits against affirmative action policies tooth and nail, and have done so successfully. Numerous state agencies have also done their best to ignore implementing the requirements of Proposition 209. Even the University of California regents recently repealed their ban on affirmative action in admissions.[10]

This difference between quotas and goals is, according to critics, one of semantics rather than substance. In a world with limited resources, the fact that one person or group is hired, promoted, or admitted to college means that other people or groups are not. One study by Alfred Blumrosen found that five million minority workers have better jobs today than they would have had without preferences and anti-discrimination laws (and possibly another five million majority workers have worse jobs).[11] On an individual level, most decisions have "winners" or "losers," although taking a broader perspective, we may all benefit from an integrated, diverse society. The question is Should people who belong to a minority group be given preference in hiring if they are equally or slightly less qualified—provided that they meet the minimum requirements necessary for the job? Should "preferential treatment" also be a matter of government policy?

Throughout the last few pages we have used the terms *majority* and *minority*, but it is not always clear who comprises these groups and who should benefit from preferential hiring programs. To the extent that women as a group are victims of discrimination, they can be considered a *minority* even though they are a numerical majority. In other words, women constitute a majority with a minority of power. Other groups covered previously by affirmative action plans have changed somewhat over the years and for particular purposes. The 1977 Public Works Employment Act requires that 10 percent of all federal public works contracts be reserved for "minority-owned" construction firms. Minority, in 1977, was defined as black, Spanish-speaking, American

Indian, Eskimo, Aleut,[12] and Asian. One might ask why a language group was included since speaking Spanish implies neither race nor ethnicity. Today, Pacific Islanders, such as Samoans, would be included.

With intermarriage increasing, we also wonder how to treat mixed race individuals. Is a person with a black father and a white, Jewish mother, black or Jewish, both or neither? The label may affect a person's life chances. Furthermore, the inclusion of Asians might strike one as unusual if the concern is to help the disadvantaged. Although Chinese Americans and Japanese Americans have both suffered discrimination, as have Jews and Finns, they have higher incomes than many ethnic groups not included, such as German, Irish, Italian, or Polish Americans.[13] Should the child of a black doctor be favored over the child of a white plumber? Clearly such a criterion is based primarily on skin color, and not entirely on being disadvantaged. Thus, it is not surprising that Jews, Italian Americans, Polish Americans, and other "non-minority" groups with histories of discrimination and current economic problems should feel resentment toward a system that rewards others and ignores their troubles. Deciding which groups deserve special treatment is complicated and grounded in politics as well as in economic circumstance. The contrasting views that social democrats, libertarians, and conservatives have toward preferential treatment in higher education and hiring illustrate these nuances.

## The Social Democratic Point of View

Preferential hiring, even that which is government mandated, poses little problem for the social democrat. From the social democratic perspective, government at its most moral should intervene to ensure that no group is systematically denied justice and equal treatment, which also includes remedying past discrimination and inequality. Jesse Jackson presented the social democratic case when he said, "a special responsibility rests with those who hold effective power. It is their moral obligation to share power . . . to the point that it is used to bind up the wounds of the nation caused by racial injustice."[14] Even if some people who belong to the majority group are denied jobs, society must help disadvantaged people compete, and in the process break down class boundaries that are tied to group membership. Equal opportunity, alone, ignores the heavy weight of history and oppression. Lyndon Johnson expressed this sentiment in his famous address at Howard University:

> Freedom is not enough. You do not wipe out scars of centuries by saying "now you're free to go where you want and do as you desire." You do not take a person who for years has been hobbled by chains and liberate him, bringing him up to the starting line of a race and then say, "you're free to compete" and justly believe that you have been completely fair. All of our citizens must have the ability to walk through those gates; and this is the next and most profound stage of the battle for civil rights.[15]

The social democrat recognizes that historical injustice has affected groups negatively. Regardless of whether injustice is equally applicable to everyone within a group (for example, the injustice may be less for the son of two black doctors than for the son of an unemployed single mother living in a slum), group justice is central. This justice will benefit society as a whole, in that it produces a "truly open" society in which all groups can participate equally. The *Philadelphia Evening Bulletin* editorialized on the value of preferential admission to medical schools:

> Some people argue that to provide special consideration for black students is to discriminate against whites. The sad fact is that if the effects of years of discrimination against minorities are to be undone, for a while some individuals in the majority are going to suffer deprivation. That isn't pretty, but it is a fact. . . . Until effective equal opportunity programs have made it possible for minorities to catch up with the rest of society—and that will take decades—minority people must receive some special consideration. That way the ideal of a truly open society will be brought closer to reality.[16]

Likewise, supporters of affirmative action tell white students the following:

> You have benefited in countless ways from racism, from its notions of beauty [and] its exclusion of minorities in jobs and schools. For most of this country's history, the nation's top universities practiced the most effective form of affirmative action ever: the quota was for 100 percent white males.[17]

Some people also argue that without meaningful affirmative action programs, we court disaster. It is in the interest of society to protect itself by insuring justice for everyone. George McAlmon, a director of the Fund for the Republic, observed that millions of Americans, the chronically unemployed and the propertyless, could actually do better under communism. Why, then, should they be committed to free enterprise and private ownership? What morality prevents these citizens from engaging in violent and destructive behavior?[18]

Supporters of preferential hiring point out that hiring criteria may systematically discriminate against minorities because the measuring stick used for hiring favors the majority. Scores on standardized tests, past work histories, or attendance at prestigious schools are only some criteria that can predict success. Moreover, supporters of preferential hiring note that not all hiring and admissions are based on criteria that predict success.[19] The admission of the Kennedys to Harvard was not based on their grade point averages. For example, some schools give preference to in-state residents and to children of wealthy alumni and athletes. "Connections" can always produce unstated forms of affirmative action in terms of preferential treatment for the children of families with social capital.[20] Some unions make it impossible for anyone but relatives of members to join. Some organizations give special weight to veterans. Some employers prefer individuals who are married or who dress in a particular style. Thus, consideration on the basis of race is not unique, but is only one means by which employers hire or universities accept.

The use of "seniority" is another indication that ability is not the only criterion for employment. In many companies when employees must be laid off, those who were last hired are the first fired. This flies in the face of the belief in merit as the sole means of judging people. Why not lay off those workers who are least qualified? Such a process, however, would be offensive to many unions; the seniority system assumes that there is a level of competency above which ability does not really matter. Once people have met this level of acceptability, termination should be on the basis of years with the company. Without seniority, companies might choose to hire only young, cheap workers and just replace them as soon as they age and become more expensive.

Social democrats see the controversy over preferential hiring as an issue that involves the rights of groups, rather than those of individuals. The question for them is how we can insure equitable representation for disadvantaged groups, rather than how *individuals* can be treated fairly. Frequently, the major concern is insuring "equal representation." Although some writers claim that this need not derogate individual rights since other factors are involved in hiring,[21] other writers vigorously criticize this position,[22] suggesting that invidious discrimination is inevitable. Surely, in some cases, whites are being denied rewards that would otherwise be theirs if there were no programs of preferential hiring. The social democrat's concern, then, is with equalizing the positions of groups and lessening class differences, rather than insuring that individuals are treated equitably. Former Supreme Court justice Harry Blackmun stated this effectively in his dissent in the *Bakke* case: "In order to get beyond racism, we must first take account of race. There is no other way."[23]

## The Libertarian Point of View

The 1998 Libertarian Party platform clearly and emphatically stated the party's position on preferential treatment:

> Discrimination imposed by the government has brought disruption in normal relations of people, set neighbor against neighbor, created gross injustices, and diminished human potential. Anti-discrimination enforced by the government is the reverse side of the coin and will for the same reasons create the same problems. Consequently, we oppose any government attempts to regulate private discrimination, including discrimination in employment, housing, and privately owned so-called public accommodations. The right to trade includes the right not to trade—for any reasons whatsoever.[24]

For libertarians, individual rights are paramount. This includes property rights and the right to trade. Thus, libertarians assent to what seems to be a paradoxical position: Individuals have the right to ignore the "equal rights" of others. This position, however, is only paradoxical until one considers the libertarian concept of freedom. People have freedom to do what they wish providing it does not coerce others; they do not have the freedom to make others act toward them in any particular way.[25] This is based on the view that each individual has the freedom to acquire as much power and wealth as he wishes—a philosophy perhaps more applicable in the ideal world in which all are created equal, than in the real world in which some are born with social handicaps. Ending all discrimination appears to offer a premise of equal opportunity to trade as one would choose. Yet, cumulative advantages and disadvantages between the races still imperil a free market in such trade, with the effects of past discrimination potentially "fixing" the market for trading partners and isolating minorities from inclusion.

Government attempts to intervene in human relations also incense libertarians. Most libertarians personally reject discrimination; yet, they don't see discrimination by its nature as coercive. In this sense, the libertarian believes voluntary preferential treatment plans are acceptable, although not desirable. If white employers choose to hire all whites (or, for that matter, all blacks), this would not require any kind of government intervention because employers are exercising their own rights to use resources as they see fit. If implementing affirmative action were an employer's voluntary decision, not the result of government coercion, libertarians would not prevent it.

A controversial court case, *Kaiser Aluminum & Chemical Corporation v. Brian F. Weber et al.*, illustrates the conflict private decisions versus government interference pose for libertarians. In 1974 Kaiser Aluminum & Chemical Corporation and the United Steelworkers of America agreed together to set up skilled-craft training programs at fifteen Kaiser plants around the country. Half of the positions in the programs were set aside for minorities and women. Seniority (who worked in the plant longest) determined which whites could enter the program, while the minorities and female participants were selected from a separate seniority list. This program was easily justified because of very low representation of women and minorities in these mostly all-white male jobs. When Brian Weber, a white male laboratory analyst, applied to this training program, he was rejected because he lacked enough seniority. He then learned that several of the minority applicants accepted from the other seniority list had less seniority than he did. He subsequently charged racial discrimination under the 1964 Civil Rights Act.

When the case finally wound its way to the Supreme Court, the court decided, by a vote of 5 to 2, that the Kaiser plan was legal under the 1964 Civil Rights Act, even though the act appeared to outlaw discrimination on the basis of race or ethnicity. Weber contended that if he were black, he would have been trained, a point that was uncontested. The Supreme Court majority brushed aside the surface reading of the law and pointed to its intent—to reduce discrimination in employment. Pertinent to libertarian theory was that ostensibly this was a private decision that government did not directly dictate. Kaiser could, if it wished, train and hire whatever percentage of minorities they chose, provided they did not discriminate against minorities, which all agreed was illegal under the Civil Rights Act. Government intervention was not totally absent. Executive Order 8801 did call for federal contractors to take affirmative action to insure that minorities were represented in the workforce by telling companies they could lose their federal contracts, although this coercion was indirect.

Still, it is ironic that the supporters of civil rights were now taking a similar position to those, such as Senator Barry Goldwater who, speaking against the Civil Rights Act, said employers should have the *freedom* to take race or ethnicity into account in hiring.[26] A business should choose the best person for the job *regardless of race*, or it will suffer by having a less qualified workforce than its competitors. Interestingly, most large corporations have fully incorporated affirmative action into their hiring decisions,

believing that a diverse workforce benefits both their business and their customer relations with a diverse consumer market. Even if government didn't pressure companies
to maintain affirmative action goals, many would continue their current practices as
good business.[27]

A second part of the libertarian attitude toward preferential hiring finds affirmative action practices abhorrent. The libertarian philosophy is based on the individual's moral stature. Libertarians believe that every person should succeed or fail by
virtue of his or her own abilities. Preferential hiring violates this belief by promoting
some citizens simply because they are of a particular race or ethnic group, over others
who are "objectively" more qualified. While libertarians would acknowledge that other
nonability-based criteria are used in judging hiring, these are equally as questionable as
using race or ethnicity as a means for making hiring decisions. Libertarians agree with
Supreme Court justice John M. Harlan who said that "the Constitution is color-blind
and neither knows nor tolerates classes among citizens."[28] Furthermore, preferential
treatment is akin to punishing the children for the sins of the fathers. Brian Weber did
not discriminate against minorities; previous generations of Americans did. Yet Brian
Weber carried the burden for these past acts, as do others who will now pay for acts that
other people perpetrated. Many libertarians see this as unfair, even if the end result is
satisfactory. In this case, the ends truly do not justify the means. For libertarians, two
wrongs do not make a right.

## The Conservative Point of View

It is ironic that some who at one time felt blacks were inferior and not deserving of any
but the most menial jobs are now in the forefront of those who call for scrupulously
equal treatment. In our current political debate, white males, in an ironic, if cruel, twist
appropriate the language of victimization to prevent the gains of those who had been
oppressed.[29] Perhaps they should receive the benefit of the doubt just as we give the
benefit of the doubt to the social democrats who once spoke out in support of the Civil
Rights Act by saying that it would not produce special treatment for minorities.

Consider as an example of conservative thought, the blunt comments of the late
William Loeb, the ultraconservative editor of the *Manchester (N.H.) Union Leader,* on
preferential admission to graduate school:

> It makes no sense to try to make up for the wrong of discrimination against blacks in
> the past by now discriminating against whites. What we are trying to do in this
> country—at least what this newspaper thought we were trying to do in this country—is
> to find the ablest people in our society and give them the best possible education so
> that they can then best serve the nation. . . . If we are going to lower the standards and
> say to incompetent black students, "You may not have any brains, but we will let you
> in college anyway because years ago we discriminated against blacks," at the same
> time we would be saying to many white students, "You are more qualified, by the
> proven level of your intelligence and your entrance examinations, to become a lawyer
> or doctor or architect, etc., but we're sorry, old boy or old girl, you will have to step

aside and let this less qualified black take your place because we are discriminating now in favor of blacks."[30]

Increasingly, it is not only old-line white conservatives who question the principles of affirmative action, but also conservative black intellectuals, who wonder whether the effects of these proposals do not create self-doubt and public misgivings about equal treatment. One of the leaders of the movement to pass Proposition 209 was a black businessman and regent of the University of California, Ward Connerly. Connerly, not one to mince words, remarked, "Liberals need to believe that Rosa Parks is still stuck in the back of the bus, even though we live in a time when Oprah is on a billboard on the side of the bus." Connerly believed affirmative action represents cynicism about African Americans:

> The defenders of preferences don't want any good news. They don't want to believe that the American dream is realizable for black people. It contradicts their whole value system. Their arguments rest on the notion that Americans are bad, that white people cannot be trusted, that you have to have a gun to their heads to make them do the right thing, and that black people need this system to navigate the daily transactions of American life. That we can't make it without it—not because we're not talented, but because we won't get a fair deal.[31]

The number of black conservatives is growing, just as the numbers of black professionals, many of whom were helped through affirmative action programs, also increases.

Although libertarians and conservatives share distaste for programs of preferential hiring for minorities, they dislike them for somewhat different reasons. The libertarian focuses on the unfairness to the individual, while the conservative suggests that the new system is unfair to the majority group and perhaps in the long run to the minority group who will end up questioning their own abilities. Of course, many who argue against preferential hiring use both arguments and may not even distinguish between them, but the bases of the arguments are different. The conservative dislikes the radical change preferential hiring brings in relations between employers and workers, and the government-sponsored changes that affect racial and ethnic relations. The conservative believes that all citizens increasingly believe that race should not be a factor in hiring, and so they do not like the government attempting to alter public values, instituting in their place sanctioned discrimination against unprotected groups (whites).

Black economist Thomas Sowell, a vocal conservative critic of preferential hiring, noted that by including women under the banner of affirmative action, "discrimination is legally authorized against one third of the U.S. population (Jewish, Italian, Irish [males])—and for government contractors and subcontractors, it is not merely authorized but required."[32] Leonard Walentynowicz, executive director of the Polish American Congress emphasized this point: "If America's job opportunities and money are to be parceled out to groups, we are a definable group, and we want our share."[33] If preferential treatment is extended to every group that is underrepresented in the upper-levels of the workforce, what will the effect be on overrepresented groups? Jewish leaders, for example, worry that a strong and large-scale program of preferential hiring would be anti-Semitism in disguise.

Conservatives also point out that despite continuing steps made toward affirmative action and preferential hiring, many political leaders and most Americans—white and black—oppose it. The policy changes during the growth of affirmative action demonstrate the clout of an unelected bureaucracy, which runs the day-to-day operation of government, not the clout of a majority of citizens. Thus, conservative economists Peter Brimelow and Leslie Spencer spoke of affirmative action as "American neosocialism, putting politics (and lawyers) in command of its workplace."[34] Thomas Sowell offered some concrete support for this argument:

> The insulation of administrative processes from political control is illustrated by the fact that (1) administrative agencies went beyond what was authorized by the two Democrats (Kennedy and Johnson) in the White House who first authorized "affirmative action" in a sense limited to decisions *without regard* to group identity, and (2) continue to do so despite the two Republican Presidents (Nixon and Ford) who followed, who were positively opposed to the trends in agencies formally under their control as parts of the Executive branch of government.[35]

Surveys about affirmative action are equivocal, depending on how the question is asked. A 1994 Gallup Poll revealed that Americans favored strengthening affirmative action laws by a 49 to 43 percent plurality. Yet, a 1995 *Newsweek* poll found that by a 79 to 14 percent majority whites oppose racial preferences in employment and college admissions (blacks support them by a thin 50 to 46 percent margin).[36] Presumably "affirmative action" sounds more acceptable than "racial preferences." The conservative believes that regardless of whether white Americans discriminate against black Americans, people should hire the best person for the job. Conservative North Carolina senator Jesse Helms spoke of a "merit-based society."[37] The leading conservative journal, *National Review*, suggested, perhaps sarcastically, that it would be simpler if Congress passed a "Black Reparations Act"—a point of view with which some social democrats might sincerely agree, in spirit, if not in name. Social democrats suggested reparations during the turbulent 1960s and an increasing number of African American activists seek them today.

# Race, Public Policy, and Social Research

Affirmative action is meant to remedy the effects of past and present discrimination against minorities, particularly African Americans. Is affirmative action in education and occupations the best policy step to take to achieve this end? Addressing this question requires examining the causes of inequality between the races. Scholars debate whether differences in social class produce economic inequalities more than present-day racial discrimination in higher education and hiring do. The significance of this question is ultimately in considering whether affirmative action policies would be better based on social class rather than on race.

Sociologist Dalton Conley argued that a group's net worth, their social class, better explains inequality between the races than race itself does.[38] In his influential book, *Being Black, Living in the Red: Race, Wealth and Social Policy in America,* Conley explored the significance of the wealth gap between African Americans and whites. In 1994, the median white family held assets worth more than seven times those of the median nonwhite family.[39] Wealth, in fact, may be more significant than income in determining social position. What difference does such a pronounced gap in wealth make in explaining racial differences in education, work, and earnings? In a controversial and famous argument, sociologist William Julius Wilson argued that civil rights legislation led to a decline in racial discrimination; the result was that economic class overtook race in explaining the life chances of African Americans. Many African Americans and liberals rejected the argument that racism is no longer as significant as economic factors. Conley's goal was to add to this debate by further delineating the interaction between race and class in explaining inequality.

Dalton Conley used net worth and overall economic assets to examine the impact of class in the economic outcomes of whites and blacks. He argued that prior research neglected net worth and inheritance by adopting less comprehensive measures of position, such as income alone. Conley used statistical data from the *Panel Study of Income Dynamics* (PSID), which measures the assets and liabilities of families (as well as traditional data on income, occupations, residence, and so forth) every five years. The PSID data allow Conley to conduct a longitudinal study of how children born since 1962 in these sampled families fared economically as adults in the 1990s. Conley could thus examine the impact of inheritance—the intergenerational transmission of wealth through family structure—to see what impact parental wealth had on the economic outcomes of the children of both black and white families. Since prior research had not taken detailed information about overall wealth (owning a home, stocks, and so forth) into account, Conley's data offered a fresh contribution to this debate.

The type of methodology that Conley used is known as secondary data analysis. That is, researchers analyze data others originally collected for different, but related purposes. Such a methodology, of course, is much less costly than collecting the equivalent research data from scratch. It is common for social scientists to use large amounts of data that were originally collected for different purposes. In many cases, only the federal government has the resources to engage in this kind of data collection—a point with which the libertarian would groan in agreement. A weakness of secondary data analyses is that someone else collects the data; the original research may omit certain crucial questions. Particularly when using government data, there may be an establishment bent to the research in that the questions asked are those that the government wishes to know the answers to and that the powerful consider important. Symbolic interactionists also fault massive data collection for typically providing little of the detailed information about people that permits us to understand how people think about their decisions and outcomes.

Conley found that "in almost all instances . . . socioeconomic variables have a much greater impact in predicting outcomes than does skin color or racial identity for this recent cohort (young adults who have grown up since the landmark civil rights legislation of the 1960s)."[40] Conley's data show that, on average, "whites and blacks without homes or savings act the same, just as those with many assets, a great deal of education, and so on tend to behave in a similar manner."[41] In other words, when blacks and whites have the same economic background, their outcomes tend to be the same, whether in education or occupational attainments, with wealthy blacks even showing some advantages in high school graduation rates, college completion, and sometimes in wages. Conley concluded that parental assets have the greatest effect in shaping people's economic future as adults.

Of course, there is intuitive logic to this claim. Wealthy parents can provide advantages to their children in terms of everything from buying computers, owning a home, having higher expectations for their completing college, to being able to provide support as their children complete their studies and look for work. What is significant is that with equal wealth, racial identity does not appear to push down the economic outcomes of blacks.

What are the implications for affirmative action policies? Conley argued that

> Wealth, not occupation or education, is the realm in which the greatest degree of racial inequality lies in contemporary America. The implications of this finding for social policy are twofold. The first possibility involves shifting race-based affirmative action policy from the areas of education and occupation to a focus on asset inequality. The second argues for a shift to a class-based affirmative action policy—that is, implementing educational, hiring and contracting preferences that are based on class and not skin color; such a policy must, however, include net worth in its definition of class if we are to avoid worsening black-white inequities.[42]

What are we to make of this suggestion? If blacks and whites of equal wealth fare the same, then favoring blacks over whites appears to be a questionable choice. The problem, for Conley, was more that asset-poor groups need resources first and foremost, not necessarily solutions based on jobs and education. In other words, we can do more to advance a child's future if we buy their parents a house than if we get them into affirmative action summer jobs. Race's effect on prior generations of African Americans decreased their wealth to the point of producing the class differences that strike African Americans so much harder than whites. This fact suggests to Conley that a race-based asset policy is necessary, not affirmative action in education and employment by race. Of course, how much this policy is vulnerable to producing reverse discrimination is also open to question. Are establishing preferences by class, but with a careful eye on race-based asset differences, simply the emperor's new clothes? Of course, a critical question is whether the political will exists (or should exist) to produce a substantial investment in a new set of class-based affirmative action policies.

# Race and Affirmative Action

The question of preferential hiring, affirmative action (as supporters call it), or reverse discrimination (as opponents call it) will not disappear until all groups in our society are integrated into the workforce in proportions equivalent to their numbers in the population. As much as any issue discussed in this book, this is a highly personal one because it will affect your success in this world. It is easy for those who already have it made to support affirmative action; it won't hurt them. It is equally easy for those who are racially prejudiced to use opposition to reverse discrimination to disguise their own bigotry. But it is you who will apply for jobs and potentially to graduate school, and you who these policies will help or hinder. Despite the fact that some individuals are affected, we should remember that we are dealing with relatively small numbers; most affirmative action goals will not dramatically limit the opportunity for young white males to advance, nor will they permit minorities to enter into the economic mainstream overnight. They represent a commitment by our society to do better than we have in the past in insuring equitable participation by all. Whether this is the proper means to reach this goal depends on which social policy perspective you find most appealing.

The three views offer different answers to the legitimacy of preferential hiring and admission based on race. The libertarian, who believes in freedom and individual action, suggests that individuals have the right to hire whomever they choose, including hiring only blacks. Yet, the idea of hiring by race suggests that the supporter of affirmative action wishes that all groups had an equality of outcome. Most libertarians reject this notion as inequitable and suggest that it will ultimately weaken motivation to succeed. Why work hard as an individual if your group membership will gain those same rewards?

The social democrat supports preferential hiring and state-managed equality in order to narrow group differences between blacks and whites. The social democrat argues that the differences between blacks and whites are not due to innate differences in ability but to barriers of discrimination that are difficult to overcome without assistance. Fairness demands that people should not be denied the fruits of society simply because of being born into a certain group.

Although conservatives find discrimination against minorities to be pernicious and immoral, they do not object to the existence of social classes. Conservatives believe in class mobility, but they do not equate wealth with happiness and goodness, as the other philosophies appear to do. Conservatives suggest there is no reason why a working-class family cannot be as happy as a rich one—a comforting belief if you happen to be rich and oppose change, or if you are poor and doubt the possibility of change. If we can evolve into a society that judges only by ability, everyone will have an opportunity to succeed. A well-adjusted society for the conservative is a stable and orderly one. Seen in this light, conservative social theory has a close resemblance to functional theory in its emphasis on social equilibrium.

Consider one final, difficult question. Why should we not discriminate? What is wrong with wanting to be with people like ourselves and giving them what rewards we can offer? Today most people reject discrimination, without considering why they should. Why is racial discrimination wrong? Have we created a society in which we have no loyalty to our own kind? Numerous social organizations are devoted to promoting narrow racial and ethnic interests. Are these racist? The answer ultimately comes down to a question of how we choose to define "our kind" and whether other people suffer unfairly because of that choice. As interactionist theory tells us, meaning is not inevitable. Skin color is one very salient way in which people differ, but then so is height, hair color, and regional accent. A person is not "black" or "white," "redheaded" or "blond," but a particular shade. Also, we must select which categories are most important. Are we "brunettes" or "whites"? Are Chinese Americans and Japanese Americans both Asian Americans, or are they two distinct ethnic groups? What about Vietnamese and Cambodian immigrants? What about Spaniards and Columbians? Are Floridians and Georgians both southerners, or should they be distinguished? We not only label our own kind; we also label other "kinds." Do we act violently or mistreat others as a secondary consequence of that labeling?

It is not our intention to end this chapter with a syrupy plea for tolerance; we only suggest that the group you identify with is not carved in stone but is a social decision. Whatever group you see yourself as belonging to, some will resent and dislike that group. Others also may choose to place you into groups that may categorize you to your disadvantage. While group loyalty and solidarity have positive aspects, they also carry with them the sense that outsiders do not deserve equal treatment.

## Questions

1. What does affirmative action mean? What should it mean?

2. Is reverse discrimination ever justified? Does the end justify the means?

3. If there is little or no discrimination today, should we use preferential hiring to address past discrimination?

4. What groups, if any, should be eligible for affirmative action?

5. How much weight should one's race carry in admission to college?

6. What is diversity? Should it justify preferential treatment of minorities in admissions to higher education?

7. Should government insure affirmative action in hiring or should companies handle it voluntarily?

8. Would you support Proposition 209? Why or why not?

9. Should affirmative action be based on class, rather than race?

10. Is racial or ethnic prejudice and discrimination ever justified?

## For Further Study

Bowen, William G., and Derek Bok. *The Shape of the River: Long-Term Consequences of Considering Race in College and University Admissions*. Princeton, NJ: Princeton University Press, 1999.

Conley, Dalton. *Being Black, Living in the Red: Race, Wealth and Social Policy in America*. Berkeley, CA: University of California Press, 1999.

Connerly, Ward. *Creating Equal: My Fight Against Racial Preferences.* San Francisco: Encounter Books, 2000.

Cose, Ellis. *The Rage of a Privileged Class.* New York: HarperCollins, 1993.

Feagin, Joseph, and Melvin Sikes. *Living with Racism.* Boston: Beacon, 1994.

Fine, Gary Alan, and Patricia Turner. *Whispers on the Color Line: Rumor and Race in America.* Berkeley, CA: University of California Press, 2001.

Hacker, Andrew. *Two Nations: Black and White, Separate, Hostile, Unequal.* New York: Random House, 1992.

Lynch, Frederick R. *Invisible Victims: White Males and the Crisis of Affirmative Action.* New York: Praeger, 1991.

Massey, Douglas, and Nancy Denton. *American Apartheid.* Cambridge. MA: Harvard University Press, 1993.

Sowell, Thomas. *Preferential Policies.* New York: William Morrow, 1990.

## Notes and References

1. See Richard J. Herrnstein, Charles Murray. *The Bell Curve: Intelligence and Class Structure in American Life* (New York: Free Press, 1994); Claude S. Fischer et al., *Inequality by Design: Cracking the Bell Curve Myth* (Princeton, NJ: Princeton University Press, 1996).

2. W.E.B. DuBois, *The Souls of Black Folk* (New York, NY: Knopf, 1993). (First published in 1903.)

3. Joe Feagin and Melvin Sikes, *Living with Racism* (Boston: Beacon Press, 1994).

4. William Julius Wilson, *The Truly Disadvantaged: The Inner City, The Underclass and Public Policy* (Chicago: University of Chicago Press, 1987).

5. Gary Alan Fine and Patricia Turner, *Whispers on the Color Line: Rumor and Race in America.*

6. U.S. Census Bureau, *Money Income in the United States* (Washington, DC: Government Printing Office, 1999).

7. Ian Ayres and Peter Siegelman. "Race and gender discrimination in bargaining for a new car," *American Economic Review* 85: 304–322, 1995.

8. Nijole V. Benokraitis and Joe R. Feagin, *Affirmative Action and Equal Opportunity: Action, Inaction, Reaction* (Boulder: Westview Press, 1978), p. 7, quoting *Federal Register* 6, no. 3109, 1941.

9. Ibid., p. 10, quoting *Federal Register* 26, no. 1977, 3 C.F.R., 1959–63, comp. 448, pt. 3, 301(1).

10. Pamela Burdman, "In Symbolic Gesture, UC Regents Repeal Ban on Affirmative Action," *Black Issues in Higher Education,* June 7, 2001.

11. "Rethinking the Dream," *Newsweek,* June 26, 1995, p. 20.

12. The Aleuts are a small group (population of 2,000) who inhabit the Aleutian Islands, which stretch out to the southwest of Alaska. They have a distinctive language, culture, and racial composition.

13. Thomas Sowell, "A Dissenting Opinion about Affirmative Action," *Across the Board* 18 (January 1981): 66.

14. Jesse L. Jackson, "Race and Racism in America," *National Forum Spring 2000,* p. 9.

15. D. Stanley Eitzen, *In Conflict and Order: Understanding Society,* 2nd ed. (Boston: Allyn & Bacon, 1982), p. 332.

16. Editorial, *Philadelphia Evening Bulletin,* September 25, 1977.
17. Randall Kennedy and R. Richard Banks, quoted in Stephen L. Carter, *Reflections of an Affirmative Action Baby* (New York: Basic Books, 1991), p. 19.
18. George A. McAlmon, "A Critical Look at Affirmative Action," *The Center Magazine* 11 (March 1978): 45–56.
19. Derek Bok, "The Case for Racial Preferences: Admitting Success," *The New Republic* (February 4, 1985): 15.
20. Cited in Wilbert Jenkins, "Why we must retain affirmative action," *USA Today Magazine,* September 1999, p. 60.
21. Ronald Dworkin, *Taking Rights Seriously* (Cambridge: Harvard University Press, 1977).
22. Ronald Simon, "Individual Rights and 'Benign' Discrimination," *Ethics* 90 (October 1979): 88–97.
23. J. S. Fuerst and Roy Petty, "In Defense of Managed Integration," *Commonweal* 113 (February 14, 1986): 77.
24. 1998 Libertarian Party Platform.
25. Scott Bixler, "The Right to Discriminate," *Freeman* 30 (1980): 358–376.
26. William F. Buckley, "Double Thought," *National Review* 31 (August 3, 1979): 990.
27. Stan Crook, "A Thunderous Impact on Equal Opportunity," *Business Week* (June 26, 1995), p. 37; Rich Lowry, "Quitting Quotas" *National Review* (March 20, 1995), p. 26.
28. In Harlan's famous dissenting opinion to the case of *Plessy* v. *Ferguson* in which the court majority legalized "separate but equal" treatment for blacks.
29. Michael Eric Dyson, "Deaffirmation," *The Nation* 249 (July 3, 1989), p. 4.
30. William Loeb, editorial, *Manchester (N.H.) Union Leader,* November 22, 1977.
31. Michael W. Lynch, "Racial Preferences Are Dead," *Reason* 29 (1998): 35.
32. Sowell, "A Dissenting Opinion about Affirmative Action," p. 66.
33. "What the Weber Ruling Does," *Time* 114 (July 9, 1979): 49.
34. Peter Brimelow and Leslie Spencer, "When Quotas Replace Merit, Everybody Suffers." *Forbes* (Feb. 15, 1993), p. 80.
35. Sowell, "A Dissenting Opinion about Affirmative Action," p. 67.
36. Howard Fineman, "Race and Rage," *Newsweek,* April 3, 1995, p. 25.
37. Ellis Cose, "The Myth of Meritocracy," *Newsweek,* April 3, 1995, p. 34.
38. Dalton Conley, *Being Black, Living in the Red: Race, Wealth and Social Policy in America.* (Berkeley, CA: University of California Press, 1999).
39. Conley, *Being Black,* p. 1.
40. Conley, *Being Black,* p. 134.
41. Conley, *Being Black,* p. 23.
42. Conley, *Being Black,* p. 152.

# CHAPTER EIGHT

# Family: Who Should Be Allowed to Adopt?

■ When politicians scramble for votes, they stress their love for family—their own and others—and they speak of America as being "one big family." The family is one of the grand rhetorical images in the arsenal of public speakers. Our family background, of course, does influence us sometimes more than we know in our socialization, culture, education, income, and class position. Most of us have the experience of growing up in a family. Whatever we might think of that experience, we cannot deny being affected by it. And most of us (96 percent) will choose to marry at least once in our lifetime.

The family is a central building block of society. But what is a family? To sociologists, a *family* is a long-term social arrangement in which people related through marriage, birth, or adoption reside together as a social and economic unit and raise children. Societies around the world organize family structures differently. There are polygamous families, extended families, single mothers raising children, and newly blended families with combined stepchildren. There are families where everyone, from grandchildren to cousins, lives in a patriarch or matriarch's home; there are also nuclear families with a mom, a dad, a boy, and a girl.

Sociologists distinguish between a person's *family of origin* or *orientation* (the unit he or she was born into) and a person's *family of procreation* (the unit which he or she creates to produce and rear offspring). Because of its role in propagating and socializing our species, the family is the most basic of all social institutions—in fact, functionalists view the family as a convincing example of the necessity of social institutions. Social order would not exist without *some* institution to perform the tasks that we expect of families.

Families provide the following important social functions in most societies:

1. They regulate and control sexual behavior—determining who will mate with whom. Intercourse often involves an intense social and emotional relationship, which changes the relations of the two people involved and their subsequent relations with others in society. No society can permit totally free and open sexual behavior. Totally free sexuality would produce severe and changing lines of stress because sexual relationships might never be stabilized to particular

partners. The institution of family can provide a legitimate and functional organization of sexual relations.

2. The family provides for the stable replacement of the population. No society can exist for long if the death rate remains higher than the birthrate.
3. Along with the birth of new members, the family provides an efficient means for teaching individuals the rules and values of a culture. The family is the first, and perhaps most important, mechanism of socializing new members of society.
4. The family is a means of fitting children into social structure. Some families are wealthy and powerful ("the elite," "the bluebloods," "the Four Hundred"), while other families are stigmatized as poor, homeless, or uneducated. Children arrive in the world bearing the ascribed status and class position of their parents.
5. The family distributes goods. It is a micro-social welfare agency that provides food, shelter, and interaction, ideally meeting the overall economic and social needs of new members of society.

The functional services that families provide are only part of the picture. The conflict theorist, while acknowledging that the family may meet certain important societal goals, also sees a darker side. Like other forms of social organization, families can be rife with conflict and inequality. Most societies are patriarchal. That is, men (or fathers) dominate decision making. Despite the joke that some chauvinists once made that "the only way for women to gain equality is for them to come down off their pedestal," the husband has historically made most of the important decisions in the traditional family. He decides where the family will live (the right of domicile), controls the family's money, and, in large measure, what the wife shall do (whether she can or must work outside the home). Although this pattern has changed substantially in the last half century (see Chapter Six), husbands still have more power than wives in many marriages. This structure indicates that the family system can still oppress women.

Friedrich Engels, Karl Marx's co-author of the *Communist Manifesto,* argued that the family system represented the first instance of repression in history and that the relationship between husband and wife is the model on which other types of economic oppression are based.[1] Marx and Engels suggest that a wife is in essence a prostitute—both provide sexual favors in return for money and goods.[2] The domination of the male over the family is also evident in violence against children and wives, which historically was not only legal, but in some measure valued as a means for men as authority figures to cultivate "appropriate" behavior and deference in their charges. Today, while the image of the family in our society is of a loving "team," this team is often racked by disputes and sometimes, even bloodshed, and is often split by divorce or desertion.

Sociologists distinguish between *nuclear families* and *extended families.* The former refers to the kinship unit that is composed of parents and children, whereas the latter includes other relatives, especially "grown children" and grandparents. Nuclear families are particularly characteristic of highly mobile societies in which each adult generation has sufficient resources to live independently. Some argue that the Social Security system, with its payments to senior citizens is, in part, responsible for the decline in extended families. An increasing number of families fall into neither category.

These are "families" with a single head of household, usually a single mother. According to 2000 Census figures, only 69 percent of all children live with both parents (26 percent with mothers alone). In the African American community, the numbers are more striking: 65 percent of African American mothers are unmarried.[3] These families pose many challenges to the traditional sociological explanations of family life, in terms of how single-parent families, in contrast to two-parent families, manage the socialization of children.

As we have discussed, whom we marry is based largely on *homogamy*—that is, we are attracted to and likely to marry partners with similar social backgrounds. The greater the similarity of social experiences, values, beliefs, and expectations, the more likely we are to celebrate a marriage and then to raise a family. But should what holds true for marriage also always hold true for adoption? If a family wishes to adopt a child, should the prospective parents and child be allowed to form a family only if they match on as many social characteristics as possible?

Family life can run a spectrum between ideal nurturing and nightmare. Symbolic interactionists argue that defining good parenting and a child's best interests often involve competing efforts to label behavior. An action is either detrimental or in a child's best interests. For example, in Chapter Two we reviewed arguments over whether corporal punishment is in a child's best interest. The debate over who should be allowed to adopt involves battles over defining which parents are in a child's best interests.

## ■ Question:

*Who should be allowed to adopt?*

"Compared with childbirth, adoption is a civilized business. The preliminaries involve more red tape than passion. The delivery of the child occurs in an office rather than a hospital. It is free of panic, agony, and danger."[4] Yet, adoption is not free of emotion—joy, and, if the birth mother is present, sadness. Few images are as sad as a child who is unwanted, who has no home. Every child deserves a family—a happy, loving family. Once the primary purpose of adoption was to fill a family need; today adoption is supposed to be for the child, and adoption procedures are to be in the child's "best interests." But we do not always know what these are; nor do we know for sure what kind of home provides the best upbringing.

In American marriages, where people consciously or unconsciously use homogamy to find a spouse, there is some individual autonomy involved in deciding on a suitable partner. In adoption, alternatively, there is much more direct regulation and external oversight over the child's proposed family. Prospective parents must meet social criteria, in the form of government or organizational regulations, in order to be allowed to adopt. The struggle over regulating proposed families, particularly over what characteristics of parents are in the best interest of children, reveals conflicting social preferences and ideal values about what a family should be. These ideals are particularly striking for being pursued so vigorously among adoptive families as opposed to biological ones. Prospective adoptive parents confront much more social control over their suitability than prospective birth parents do; the latter can add children with no oversight, regardless of their social circumstances and resources, as long as they are physically capable of procreating.

Adoption has had a long history, going back beyond the time when Pharaoh's daughter discovered young Moses in the bulrushes. Romulus and Remus, the founders of Rome, were supposedly adopted by a she-wolf and suckled by her. Oedipus was adopted so as to make the murder of his "true" father and marriage to his "true" mother inevitable. The great legal code of Hammurabi contained a detailed treatment of adoption in ancient Babylonia. The longevity of adoption is but one testimony to its success. Many studies of adoption indicate that children so placed are quite happy and healthy, even compared to children who are raised in their birth family.[5] Since the adopting families often have more social status and wealth than birth families, this outcome suggests both the power of environment and the flexibility of children in overcoming difficult circumstances.

The present adoption situation demonstrates the effects of rapid social change. Thirty years ago, the adoption problem was the reverse of what it is today. At that time, there were too many babies and not enough adoptive parents. Today we have a "baby shortage." There is far more demand for certain types of infants in the United States than there are infants to meet the need. According to the Bureau of the Census, by the mid-1990s only about 60,000 babies were adopted, compared to 89,000 in 1970.[6]

Why has there been such dramatic change? Several factors are involved. With the change in sexual morality and tolerance for different lifestyles, it is more acceptable for a single mother to keep her child. In the late 1960s, it was estimated that 80 percent of single mothers gave up their children for adoption; a decade later 80 percent were keeping their children.[7] Schools have made special provisions so that pregnant teenagers do not have to drop out. Second, a greater knowledge and distribution of new methods of birth control have decreased the proportion of "accidents." Third, there are now more government programs to aid poor, unmarried mothers. Having a child out of wedlock is less of an economic hardship now than it was without such programs. Finally, the Supreme Court decided in January 1973, in *Roe* v. *Wade,* to legalize most abortions. Among the unintended consequences of this controversial decision was a decrease in the number of babies available for adoption. Why would a woman wish to deliver a baby she knew she would not keep? Only ethical considerations would lead to that decision, but that has not been enough in many cases.

As the supply of babies has dwindled, people have struggled to adopt; now it is virtually impossible to adopt a healthy white infant unless you pass rigorous screening and can prove you are infertile—and even then your chances are uncertain. This has given social workers enormous power in determining who is fit to raise the small number of children available. It has also given rise to the development of alternatives: surrogate motherhood and (more commonly) transnational adoptions—adoptions of infants from other countries, such as Korea, China, and the nations of the former Soviet Union. From 1981 to 1987, the number of foreign adoptions nearly doubled to over 10,000 each year.[8] In 1999, Americans adopted 16,396 children from abroad, the large majority coming from those three locations.[9] We maintain a substantial "trade deficit" in babies.

Putting aside surrogate mother contracts, there are three types of nonkin adoptions—agency adoptions (the white market), independent adoptions (the gray market), and baby selling (the black market). Approximately half of the adoptions in the country are through agencies, and half are independent. Needless to say, no records are kept of black market adoptions. In an agency adoption, the mother (and increasingly the father as well) signs away rights to the child to a social welfare agency (either public or private), and the agency's social workers find suitable parents (with court approval). In independent adoptions, which are legal in most states, adoptive parents and mothers who choose not to keep their children find each other (often through middlemen, such as friends or lawyers) and arrange to have the child transferred. Under this system, money is not supposed to change hands other than for the mother's medical expenses and a reasonable lawyer's fee—an approach that some states are using for surrogate motherhood. Black market adoption is identical to independent adoption except that the money paid is considerably higher, and the transaction amounts to "purchasing" the child. We shall discuss this further in considering the libertarian perspective.

Considering the reality of the baby shortage, it is significant that as of 1999, there were 581,000 children in foster care ("temporary" homes paid for by the state).[10] Obviously these children are not included in discussing the baby shortage, despite their lack of homes. These children are racial minorities, older children, the handicapped, the chronically or fatally ill, and the troubled. Our society treats these children as "damaged goods." If many whites consider the matter honestly, they long for the healthy, blue-eyed, blond cherub and consider the other children less attractive alternatives. The baby shortage has forced potential parents to consider these "hard-to-place" children. Even though these children may not be their first choices, they can still love and be loved.

Simultaneously, there has been pressure to broaden the definition of who can adopt a child. In particular, single women (and some men) have argued for rights to adopt, noting that millions of children under eighteen live with only one of their natural parents. Adoption by single parents through adoption agencies is a fairly recent phenomenon. Even though there is little evidence that having a single parent harms a child, it was not until the mid-1960s that adoption agencies agreed to consider single men and women as suitable adoptive parents. Homosexual couples who wish to adopt face an even tougher challenge than single parents. The stigma against gay and lesbian parents extends also to transnational adoptions. The *Intercountry Adoption Act of 2000*, which former president Bill Clinton signed into law in October of 2000, requires agencies to state the sexual orientation, religion, and race of prospective parents. China, for example, makes all adopting parents sign an affidavit declaring that they are not homosexuals.[11]

Another controversial issue in broadening the definition of who can adopt concerns transracial adoptions. The first recorded case in the United States occurred in Minneapolis in 1948 when a white family adopted an impossible-to-place black child. By 1971, 35 percent of all black adopted children were placed in white homes. While this percentage has decreased dramatically because of objections from the black community, transracial adoptions do continue (particularly of foreign children), and a recent court ruling has said that race cannot be the sole criteria for foster care placement. In 1994, Congress passed the Multiethnic Placement Act (MEPA), which prevented race from being the primary factor in placing children for adoption. A subsequent law, the Interethnic Adoption Provisions, amended MEPA, further forbidding agencies from denying or delaying placement of a child for adoption solely on the basis of race or national origin. By the mid-1970s, it was estimated that 15,000 African American children lived in white homes.[12] In 1998, 5,400 of the 36,000 children who were adopted from the public welfare system were adopted transracially.[13] Such figures have been interpreted as a hopeful sign of our developing a truly multiracial society, and, conversely, as an example of "cultural genocide."

Who can adopt? How should adoption be regulated, if at all? There is an unmistakable quality of social engineering in adoption. Adoption represents an ongoing social experiment in planned parenting, as standards of who can and cannot adopt change over time. Agencies label prospective parents as acceptable or unsuitable for a range of reasons. Government can also encourage or slow the number of adoptions through lowering or raising financial and legal barriers. Adoption also represents a societal acknowledgement that a biological relation is not the only acceptable basis for parenting. Yet, what social prescriptions should replace a biological connection as a satisfactory basis for forming an appropriate family? Heterosexuality? Racial background? IQ? Health? Money? A stay-at-home mother? What recipe should society use to create families?

## The Libertarian Point of View

What would a system of adoption with minimal state involvement look like? According to some libertarians, it would be a "stork market." In a provocative article, two libertarians, Lawrence Alexander and Lyla O'Driscoll, argued that people should be allowed to sell their rights and duties as parents. A mother who did not wish to keep her child could visit an adoption market and sell her interest in her child for whatever the market would bear.[14] Note that parents would not sell their children (children are not property, even for the libertarian) but rather would sell their parental rights and duties.

Alexander and O'Driscoll contended that our current system also constitutes a market, but is simply not recognized as such. In independent adoption, for example, prospective parents are permitted to pay for the medical expenses of the mother, and we are not upset by this payment. Surely this is not all that a woman loses by being pregnant. Pregnancy is not a wholly pleasant experience, and a pregnant woman may lose many opportunities, economic and otherwise. The libertarian believes that it is only reasonable for a mother to be compensated for those opportunity costs. Rather than have cash paid under the table, the system should be open, avoiding the fraud and blackmail that now occur in the black market. For the libertarian, the major problem with the black market is that it is illegal and so attracts criminals, leading to illegal behaviors, and stigmatizes "honest" citizens. James Edwards made the libertarian case regarding the "stork market" when he stated that: "all that is necessary is to remove the existing state coercion that is acting to prevent and preclude the mutual gains available, between those having babies they do not want and those wanting babies they do not have."[15]

Critics might ask whether a couple can truly love a child that they have purchased. What would their motives be for such a transaction? Although there is no direct evidence on this point, Alexander and O'Driscoll used the analogy of buying a pet:

> In transactions regarding pet animals, people do not . . . seem to believe . . . that those who *buy* pets are likely to have motives or expectations different from—or less suitable than—the motives or expectations of those who pay no cash price. Nor do they seem to think them less likely to love and care for the pet once they have it, or that their having paid cash (as opposed to some other or no medium of exchange) is itself likely to corrupt their attitude toward the pet. Indeed, some who have young animals to distribute prefer to charge at least a nominal cash price rather than to give the animal away; they apparently believe that, other things being equal, the purchaser's willingness to make an explicit sacrifice is a sign that the pet is "really wanted" and will be given good care.[16]

Libertarians assert that under our current system money is involved in all the adoption markets. Adoption agencies routinely consider the financial status and the "cultural atmosphere" of the applicants; the amount of income one has contributes to the likelihood of being able to adopt. Even though being rich does not guarantee that someone will be a good parent, and being poor does not mean that he or she will be a poor parent, most people would probably entrust a child to the family with more wealth, status, and education because care and love are difficult, if not impossible, to measure. Baby selling, while not without flaws, insures that the purchased child will be wanted and that the family will have the resources to care for it.[17] If you had to choose adoptive parents, not knowing their capacity for love, what factors would you look for? Having money is an acceptable proxy in conditions of uncertainty about the quality of future parenting. The quality of life a child will have is simply likely to be higher with money than without it.

Further linking adoption to the market is the recognition that "advertising" a hard-to-place, older, adoptable child is effective. William Hamm, chief of Washington, D.C.'s Adoption and Placement Resources Branch, noted, "when you advertise the children, it works."[18] Newspapers, for example, often feature a weekly profile of a hard-to-place child, appealing to the heartstrings of readers. Perhaps someday the Home Shopping Network will have a segment for adoptable children!

Recently, the discussion of baby selling has taken a controversial turn with the publicity attached to surrogate motherhood. In the past, there have been instances (in the "black market") of couples paying pregnant women to carry a baby to term. Infertile spouses contract with women who are willing to be impregnated with the husband's sperm or the couple's impregnated egg. Medical technology has made this option possible, even routine. But morally this choice raises numerous questions. While some surrogacy contracts work well, in others the surrogate objects to giving up the child.[19]

Consider the famous "Baby M" case. Despite a seemingly legal "contract" with Elizabeth and William Stern, Mary Beth Whitehead, the surrogate mother, decided that she wished to keep "her" child. After a bitter trial and appeal, the New Jersey Supreme Court ruled that the contract violated New Jersey's adoption laws. The court revoked the adoption of the child by Elizabeth Stern, restored visitation rights to Mary Beth Whitehead, but left the biological father, William Stern, with custody of "Baby M."

Despite the presence of intricate and legalistic contracts, courts have also found that laws against "black market babies" cover surrogacy. Different states have handled the problem differently; where one resides determines the possibility of surrogacy. Michigan forbids commercial surrogacy; whereas Nevada exempts surrogate contracts from the ban on payments connected with adoption.[20] While recognizing certain special problems inherent in these contracts, libertarians believe that such contracts should be legal, although the all too frequent regrets of the surrogate mother surely cast a pall over the whole enterprise. No matter how "rational" we wish to be, the lure of a child one has been carrying for nine months is difficult to resist. But so is the hope of infertile couples being able to obtain a child who is "genetically" their own.

Critics raise numerous questions about these contracts. Should there be any control on costs, about determining what happens in the event of a miscarriage, and about who can enter into such contracts (only infertile, heterosexual couples)? What counseling and informed consent are necessary? Does the contract become null and void if the fetus is discovered to have a birth defect? The questions and the moral problems that ensue seem endless, but so is the potential joy.

The libertarian is always troubled by the state intruding into people's lives. Some resent the "home visits" that adoption agencies make to the homes of prospective clients, suggesting that it would be logically consistent for state welfare officers to pay the same "home visits" to prospective parents before licensing them to have children—an image consistent with George Orwell's *1984*. Libertarians believe, within broad guidelines (for example, preventing extreme child abuse), that parents should be allowed to raise children as they wish. Just as the state should not tell biological parents how many children they should have and how to raise them, the state should keep its hands off the adoption process.

## The Conservative Point of View

For the conservative, the family is the cornerstone of society. Organized society cannot exist without the family—it is a sacred institution. Conservatives have none of the cold, rational calculation of the libertarians when it comes to buying and selling babies. A conservative feels that such a practice is ghastly. Perhaps it is the mixing of "filthy" money with "pure" love that is so grotesque. Conservatives look upon adoption as a beautiful and important relationship. By adopting a homeless child, a family can socialize the child properly. Many conservatives also feel that adoption is the only moral alternative to "unwanted" pregnancies and abortion—why abort children when so many prospective parents are seeking to adopt them?

But what is a family to a conservative? For many, it is the "Walt Disney model of daddy coming home to mommy in the house with a white picket fence and the boy, the girl and the dog running out to greet [him]."[21] Single parents, handicapped parents, homosexual parents, older parents, and ill parents run families, and they often do so well. But such families are not likely to receive a healthy adopted child, particularly from a conservative's vantage point. Joyce Ladner, in her study of transracial adoption, learned that most adoption agencies had a fairly restrictive list of criteria, given the shortage of babies. These requirements include the following:

1. Both parents have publicly declared a religious faith.
2. Both parents have the same religious faith.
3. They have good physical and mental health.
4. The husband is employed.
5. The wife is a housewife and not otherwise employed.
6. They have a middle-class income and lifestyle, including a separate room for a child.
7. They cannot be too old or too young (they must be the age they would have been had the wife given birth).
8. They should not be too intense about their desire for a child nor appear too uncaring.

If your parents wished to adopt you, given all these requirements, would they have been allowed to? Ours wouldn't have been. Ladner suggested that these criteria have the effect of "screening out" parents, rather than "screening them in."[22]

When one adds to this the high cost of adoption, even with support from employers and government subsidies, few potential parents qualify, especially in cases where people work with independent agencies, where costs range from $8,000 to $50,000, depending on a child's distinct characteristics.[23] Inevitably, the social worker plays God, choosing among well-heeled applicants. One can argue for each of these criteria (which have been liberalized to some extent in the quarter-century since Ladner's study), but taken together they exclude many good parents and may cause some couples to shade the truth and present themselves in the best possible light. Given the shortage of babies, do these requirements make for the best possible adoptive parents and serve the best interests of children?

Ultimately the conservative's goal is to place each child in a warm, welcoming, stable family. Joseph Goldstein, Anna Freud, and Albert Solnit, writing from a psychoanalytic perspective, described the goal of child placement (with the exception of violent juveniles):

> [The goal] is to assure for each child, membership in a family with at least one partner who wants him. It is to assure for each child and his parents an opportunity to maintain, establish, or reestablish psychological ties to each other free of further interruption by the state. . . . The intact family offers the child a rare and continuing combination of elements to further his growth: reciprocal affection between the child and two, or at

least one, caretaking adult; the feeling of being wanted and therefore valued; and the stimulation of inborn capacities.[24]

Where the libertarian values the freedom of the individual actor, the conservative points to the necessary stability of a family; even a bad family might be better than a good, temporary foster home. The conservative, like the libertarian, objects to state intervention except under the greatest provocation. Because government agencies receive more funding when they have more children in the system, conservatives believe that public welfare agencies choose policies that keep children in foster care over ones that release them more easily for adoption.[25]

Conservatives believe that adoption decisions should be streamlined, the custodial rights of abusive and neglectful parents should be terminated more easily, greater tax breaks should be offered to subsidize adoption costs, and barriers to transracial adoptions should be eliminated. Conservatives also view more adopted children as a solution for several social problems, ultimately reducing abortions and the amount of public money spent on foster care and welfare (as the expenses associated with children are essentially privatized under adoption). Conservatives also view suitably adopted children are less likely to incur later costs in the criminal justice system, as a stable two-parent family is more likely to instill positive values than a foster care or institutional environment.

The debate over adoption is particularly intense in debating whether a single person can adopt a child. Where the libertarian has few qualms about allowing a wider range of prospective parents (as long as they can pay market prices), conservatives favor more restraints on who should be allowed to adopt. Is a two-parent home preferable to a single-parent home? Conservatives would say yes, and this appears to be the sentiment of most Americans, despite considerable evidence that a single-parent home does not necessarily disadvantage a child.[26]

In 1969, over thirty years ago, *Good Housekeeping* magazine conducted a survey of their readers, asking, Should a single person adopt a child? Of those responding, 73 percent favored the idea, while 23 percent opposed it. However, even those who supported the idea did not believe that a single-parent home was as good a setting for bringing up a child as one with two parents present.[27] Even today, while more people might approve of a single person being able to adopt, it is likely that people would still favor the option of having two parents present. This sentiment generally suggests that "one parent is better than none," just as it is better to have one eye than to be blind. Howard Stein, the executive director of Family Service of Westchester, however, did not completely agree that a single-parent household is acceptable. He wrote that "a child really needs both parents—the parent of the same sex to identify with and of the opposite sex as a love object to fix on. A boy brought up only by a woman faces serious psychological hazards; a girl without a father may be also be shortchanged. Any child growing up in a one-sided household is deprived of an important life experience and may be poorly prepared for his or her own marriage and parenthood."[28]

While Stein's view may be somewhat exaggerated today, few people would claim that a single-parent home is the best of all possible worlds. Sometimes single parents without huge financial resources who wish to adopt children must settle for less desired children, such as children with special needs. Such a situation is ironic. Children with special needs are precisely those for whom two parents are particularly desirable, but they are rarely the first choice of "first-choice" parents. Conservatives prioritize the importance of families, but the question of what should constitute a family is something of a puzzle.

## The Social Democratic Point of View

The social democrat does not see anything inherently wrong with state agencies intervening in family life if the welfare of a child is at stake. The question is What should the government do? What image of the family should it encourage? What is the best upbringing for a child? Social democrats are particularly concerned with equality of opportunity in society and with protecting the rights of minorities. Sometimes resolving the question of who should be allowed to adopt brings these values into conflict. A particularly thorny question that has dominated the social democratic discourse on adoption is whether transracial adoptions are morally justified or whether they reflect a form of discrimination against minorities. This question is difficult for the social democrat to resolve, because their values may lead to opposite answers.

The first transracial adoption occurred in the late 1940s, but it was not until the late 1960s that many white families began to adopt black children. By this time, the number of healthy white infants available for adoption was decreasing, as was the overt racial discrimination that had characterized U.S. society. By the early 1970s, over one-third of all adopted black children were adopted by white parents. In 1972, a federal court struck down a Louisiana law that prohibited such adoptions. Ironically, this same year the National Association of Black Social Workers went on record as being "in vehement opposition to placing black children in white homes."[29] At the same time that the battle had been won against white racists in the South, black professionals began to advance arguments similar to those of segregationists. These arguments pitted the image of a society in which there would be no race consciousness against one in which all racial groups would retain their own identity. Social democrats were caught in the middle.

Those who argue in favor of transracial adoption contend that society's goal should be a multiracial society—a melting pot, a race-blind society. Race-mixing may even be desirable. The white mother of a black child and a Hispanic child expressed this view:

> In our experience the multicultural family has become something positive, something to celebrate. We tell our children that because we are a family, each of us can share in the cultural heritage of all the rest: "Thanks to Mark, we can all celebrate Martin Luther King Day, thanks to Adam we can all have birthday piñatas, thanks to Daddy we can all wear green for St. Patrick's Day, and thanks to Mommy we can all eat garlic bread." Although parenting a multicultural family is a challenge, it suggests practical ways to embody spiritual values in the daily life of the most intimate unit of society.[30]

Some supporters of transracial adoption point out that the policy now generally adhered to in the aftermath of the objections of black social workers is an instance of reverse discrimination. Although black parents adopt at the same rate as white parents (controlling for their income), there are not enough black parents to meet the demand. There are two major reasons for this: (1) there is a smaller *percentage* of black middle-class parents than whites, and (2) over 40 percent of the children put up for adoption are black. Welfare agencies have turned away white people who want to adopt black children, causing black children to wait much longer than whites to be placed.[31]

After a Connecticut court decision ruled that a white family could not adopt a black child whom it had raised from birth, civil rights leader Roy Wilkins commented that this policy

> has the effect of depriving otherwise-adoptable black children of a stable, loving family life. The state which permits such archaic considerations as the race of the prospective parents to bar an adoption bears a heavy responsibility for cruelty to children by sending them instead to institutions or passing them from one foster home to the next. . . . To render a black child "unadoptable" or label his white foster parents "unable" or unfit to adopt him on the grounds of racial incompatibility would be the advice of the segregationist.[32]

Yet, attitudes are changing. Social welfare agencies and courts are now more open to mixed-race adoptions than at any time in the past two decades. The 1994 Multiethnic Placement Act and subsequent Interethnic Adoption Provisions reflected attempts to permit more cross-race adoptions, and the federal Department of Health and Human Services has ruled that long searches to find same-race adoptive parents are illegal.[33] First Lady Hillary Rodham Clinton opined that "skin color [should] not outweigh the more important gift of love that adoptive parents want to offer."[34] What difference, after all, does race make?

For some, race does make quite a difference. Opponents of transracial adoptions say that the white demand for black babies did not begin until after whites learned they could no longer adopt healthy white babies. Blacks saw that in some cases whites who were given black babies did not qualify for white babies.[35] Just as the white parent may see a black baby as a second choice, the black adult may see the white parent as inferior. Blacks are now recommending that adoption agencies make an intense effort to find black parents to adopt black children, even if it means altering their criteria of income and home ownership and subsidizing some of these adoptions. Agencies responded by liberalizing standards for minorities.

Opponents of transracial adoption see adoption as a political issue with racial and class implications. Mary Benet noted that

> more recent doubts about adoption stem from today's controversies over inequality, imperialism, and the nature of the family itself. . . . Adoption has usually meant the transfer of a child from one social class to another slightly higher one. Today, as always, adopters tend to be richer than the natural parents of the children they adopt. They may also be members of a racial majority, adopting children of a minority; or citizens of a rich country, adopting children from a poor one.[36]

The contention is that the upper class use minority or third world children for their own satisfaction, sometimes wiping out the culture of those they adopt. One black man casts the issue in genocidal terms:

> Transracial adoption is one of the many conspiracies being waged against Black people. It is one of the white man's latest moves to wipe out the last vestiges of our culture if not us. He made progress in brainwashing us and our young with his churches, his schools, and birth control. And now he wishes to use his latest trick of mental genocide.[37]

This may be an extreme statement, but it captures the sensitivity of blacks toward preserving their heritage from being "whitened away." Such statements also resonate with social democrats who view this issue in terms of protecting a minority against the encroachment of a more powerful majority.

While caring white parents can certainly teach black history and literature, they cannot teach a child what it means to be black in the white-majority United States. Since the United States is likely to remain color conscious, some argue that a strong black identity is necessary. This may pose a particular problem once the black child has reached adolescence and must deal with white political institutions and also with his or her own sexuality in a largely white community. Racial and ethnic groups are the context from which definitions of the self and identity develop. Can members of a different group really socialize individuals into knowledge acquired from unique cultural experiences and histories that they have not had themselves?[38] While the testimony of many parents and children suggest that transracial adoptions are successful, the difficulties of such adoptions cannot be easily dismissed.[39]

Social democrats want to recognize both of these impulses: the desire for a color-blind society and the desire for a society in which all people can protect and be proud of their "roots." Racial matching was the norm, but racial matching policies are now fading. Of course, unofficial racial matching remains the de facto preference of many Americans, including those who go to Russia to find blonde, blue-eyed children.

## Adoption and Social Research

Children are "our greatest natural resource," "the future," and the "apples of our eyes." We feel love and affinity specific to our own children and, in the abstract, for all children. What does adoption represent if not an attempt to emphasize the well-being of children? Yet sociologists cannot overlook that advocacy identifying the "best interests" of children is often a means for promoting beliefs about the proper role of families, race relations, religion, gender, and work in daily life. The adoption process often fits children into larger formulations of the best interests of society and social institutions.

A historical analysis can clarify the interaction of adoption and social institutions. As an example, consider the "orphan trains." Created by the founder of the Children's Aid Society, Charles Loring Brace, "orphan trains" transported children from urban centers in the East to be adopted and raised by families in the rural Midwest and West.

Commencing in the late 1800s, by 1910 over 110,000 orphans had been placed in the West via "orphan trains."[40] The orphan trains removed children from what were viewed as detrimental institutional and urban environments. Many in cities were glad to see the orphans go, seeing the orphan trains as a de facto export and rehabilitation program for potential delinquents. In one fell swoop, the orphan trains, through the mechanism of adoption, ideally served several goals—children would be saved, delinquency or "ulcers of society" diminished, religious obligations toward fellow men and women met, families created, and needs for rural labor solved. The existence of orphan trains helps illustrate that adoption is about more than just placing children; it is also about how placing children affects the framing and operation of social institutions, such as the family, work, and religion.

A major change in sociological research over the past two decades has been an increasing interest and use of historical sources. Why should we limit ourselves to our own time and place for understanding human nature and social organization? Historical events offer researchers a bountiful array of social experiments to dissect. A case study offers sociological researchers the ability to explain the causes and consequences of events ranging from wars and riots, to the crafting of reputations and the development of social welfare policies. Of course, historical research also has limitations. Historical records can be incomplete. Once a document is destroyed, it is forever unavailable. Unlike interviews or ethnographic observation, for example, we cannot ask historical figures what they intended by their actions and words. If reliable documents cannot attest to deeds, motives, and feelings, researchers may substitute their own interpretations inaccurately, with some writers using historical events to support their cherished assumptions.

A compelling example of historical research, Linda Gordon's *The Great Arizona Orphan Abduction* presents a case study of how decisions about who should be allowed to adopt affect, and are influenced by, larger social institutions. Gordon explored these events to consider the intersection of race, religion, and adoption in historical context. Her account is based primarily on information from legal proceedings, newspaper articles, personal papers, and official records. She made every effort to document her claims with voluminous data and also acknowledged when she made inferences about people's views in the absence of documented evidence. In *The Great Arizona Orphan Abduction*, she described what happened when religious representatives of New York's Foundling Hospital brought forty Irish Catholic children on an "orphan train" to two Arizona mining communities in 1904.[41] The Irish children on the orphan train heading toward Morenci and Clifton, Arizona, had been matched originally on the basis of religion. Father Mandin, the new priest in Clifton, had corresponded with the New York Foundling Hospital to choose local Catholic homes for the orphans. The piety of many local Mexican residents of the town, most of whom formed his parish, led him to approve placing the children with them.[42]

The proposed transracial adoption of white children by Mexican families caused a great uproar among the town's Anglo population. They formed vigilante groups to remove the children from these families, an event that occurred on the same night the children arrived. The vigilantes who abducted these children then adopted many of them, an act applauded by public opinion of the time and upheld by the U.S. Supreme

Court, who ruled for the vigilantes when the Catholic Church sued to get the orphans back. According to Gordon, the vigilantes said later that

> Mandin did not understand "what the Mexicans were really like." They meant that he did not look upon the Mexicans as non-white, that is inferior and alien, and that he recognized significant social differences among them—class, cultural, religious differences. He distinguished among these differences to find what he considered moral, stable, superior homes for the orphans. His very individualization of the Mexicans, his apparent reluctance to think that they were all alike, was what the vigilantes blamed him for.[43]

According to Gordon's account, Father Mandin was an innocent in relation to Clifton's racial system. What was the predominant racial system? Mining interests dominated both towns; under this system, Anglos held better jobs and earned more money than Mexican residents did. A bitter strike in 1903 had pitted the local Anglos and Mexicans against one another, polarizing them. Gordon reported that following the strike, the town's Mexican population gained a reputation for being violent, dangerous, and immoral. Into this context of boiling racial tension came white children who Mexican families were to adopt. Their common religious background did not trump race. That event exploded into vigilantism, abduction of the children (occasionally at gunpoint), and the near lynching of Father Mandin and the nuns who arrived on the train with the orphans from the New York Foundling Hospital.

The Anglo townspeople were motivated to rescue white children "from becoming captives of dark people who would mistreat them." Justifications for their actions included accusing Mexican mothers of sexual immorality and calling them "bar prostitutes" and alleging that mothers were "feeding beers to the foundlings on their walk home." Mexicans were also accused of being "unwashed and infested with vermin" and having neither the money nor moral character to raise children.[44] A local doctor, A. M. Tuthill, "gave it as his opinion that half of the children would be dead in six months if they had been left with the Mexicans," and pleaded, "What ought these people [the vigilantes] to have done?"[45] An excerpt from a letter sent to the New York Foundling Hospital is typical, "demanding some reasonable explanation of your action to the people of Morenci, who at the present time are filled with disgust and loathing towards an institution that can so carelessly consign children by wholesale to a life of moral degeneracy."[46]

The motivation behind the initial adoption placements was a religious one, an effort to save the souls of Catholic children by placing them with Catholic families in the rural West. This religious imperative, however, clashed with the dominant socio-economic and racial climate of the town. Anglo children could not be adopted by Mexican families. Such a transracial adoption would constitute a subversion of an existing social order and would be detrimental not only to children, but also, in the eyes of local Anglo residents, to their local society. The Anglos felt that allowing these transracial adoptions would dilute the race of the white children, as well as the subordinate race of the adopting Mexican families. The eventual result would be to dilute the relative power of the local Anglo population, both economically and socially.

The great Arizona orphan abduction is just one of many historical cases where adoption involved racial social engineering. For example, during WWII, Germans developed adoption programs for blond Dutch and Polish youths in order to increase the population of "Aryans." White Australians implemented a public policy of taking light-skinned aborigines from their homes and placing them with white families. Adoption practices come with vested social interests and consequences. Enough adoptions from one group to another can shift balances of power between competing ethnic, racial, and religious groups. As we remain alert to the criteria by which we form families, we should also consider the social consequences of the family groupings that adoption can produce.

## Adoption and the Family

It is ironic that a healthy, white infant put up for adoption is likely to be placed in an "ideal American family," while babies reared in their families of procreation are often not so fortunate. Couples who cannot have their "perfect" children through procreation must compete with each other for a few children, sometimes paying tens of thousands of dollars to give "someone else's child" the upbringing their own biological child would have had. Because of this competition, adoption agencies can place children in families that meet the agencies' image of what a family should be. Even many children who are ill or "damaged"—but "perfect" in their love and humanity—are placed in permanent homes rather than being sent to foster homes and institutions.

How we treat children reveals a great deal about what we think about ourselves. First, the existence of the highly bureaucratic and careful adoption procedure suggests that we do not trust individuals to make personal arrangements for their children—perhaps a consequence of a large and complex social system. "Experts" have the power to make decisions about who should get which children. What agendas inform those decisions? Second, by placing the "most desirable" children with the "most desirable" parents, society underlines its support for the social elite. Yet, unlike some cultures, we do not let unwanted children die. We do not leave them out on the hillside in the middle of winter to fend for themselves—we place unwanted children with parents who will make a special effort to raise them.

One question involving how we maximize our human capital is that of whether we should match parents and children racially and culturally. There is a conventional belief that parental love knows no demographic qualifications; race, religious background, and ethnicity should not make any difference in how much a child will be loved and cared for. Why should a black child not be reared from birth by orthodox Jews, to later become a member of a Hasidic synagogue? Why not allow a Mexican American family to raise a Russian or Chinese baby? Some people reply that a person's roots are genetic and that religion, ethnicity, and race should not be lightly discarded. Furthermore, changes in a child's ethnicity or religion have political implications if duplicated often enough. Such a pattern of adoption might be enough to weaken a culture, a set of beliefs, or traditions of a group—a charge made by Catholics when it was their children who were put up for adoption to Protestant families. Of course, with race, parents and children can never escape public recognition and sometimes stigma. Americans are of two minds about what to do with matching children to parents. What we consider legitimate for race and, to some extent, for religion, would seem ludicrous if we extended it to political beliefs or leisure preferences.

Adoption reminds us that biology is not the only basis on which a family can be built. Just as husbands and wives can love each other even though they are not biologically related, people can love someone else's biological children. The social bonds that help form an adopted family appear as strong as any biological bond. The success rate of adoption gives testimony to the fact that, whatever our feelings about our own families of origin and procreation, the family remains a viable, attractive, and much needed social institution.

## Questions

1. Should the right to raise unwanted infants be bought and sold openly in a "stork market"?

2. Should the government offer subsidies to get parents to adopt certain types of "hard-to-place" children?

3. If you were to be adopted, what kind of parents would you want to have?

4. Should single parents be allowed to adopt children? Should they be allowed to adopt children only if no other suitable parents can be found?

5. Should white parents be allowed to adopt black children? Should they be allowed to adopt black children only if no suitable black parents can be found?

6. How important is money in adoption? How important should money be in evaluating a person's suitability for adopting a child?

7. Should parents be forbidden from pursuing international adoptions when American children are available and waiting for placement?

8. Should sexual orientation bar prospective gay and lesbian parents from adopting?

9. If white parents adopt Asian children, are the same cultural concerns warranted that exist when white parents adopt black children? If not, should they be?

10. If you learned that you and your spouse were infertile, would you attempt to adopt a child?

## For Further Study

Alexander, Lawrence A., and Lyla H. O'Driscoll. "Stork Markets: An Analysis of 'Baby-Selling.'" *Journal of Libertarian Studies* 4 (1980): 173–196.

Bartholet, Elizabeth. *Family Bonds: Adoption and the Politics of Parenting.* Boston: Houghton Mifflin, 1993.

Field, Martha A. *Surrogate Motherhood: The Legal and Human Issues.* Cambridge, MA: Harvard University Press, 1990.

Gordon, Linda. *The Great Arizona Orphan Abduction.* Cambridge, MA: Harvard University Press, 1999.

Hollingsworth, Leslie Doty. "Symbolic Interactionism, African-American Families and the Transracial Adoption Controversy." *Social Work* 44 (1999): 443–464.

Kane, Elizabeth. *Birth Mother: The Story of America's First Legal Surrogate Mother.* New York: Harcourt Brace Jovanovich, 1988.

Ladner, Joyce A. *Mixed Families: Adopting Across Racial Boundaries.* Garden City, NY: Anchor, 1977.

May, Elaine Tyler. *Barren in the Promised Land: Childless Americans and the Pursuit of Happiness.* New York: Basic Books, 1995.

Simon, Rita, and Howard Altstein. *Transracial Adopters and Their Families.* New York: Praeger, 1987.

# Notes and References

1. Friedrich Engels, *The Origin of the Family, Private Property, and the State* (New York: International Publishing, 1942, orig. 1884), pp. 59–60.

2. Karl Marx and Friedrich Engels, *The Communist Manifesto* (Arlington Heights, IL: AHM Publishing, 1955, orig. 1848), pp. 27–29.

3. Jason Fields and Lynne M. Casper, "America's Families and Living Arrangements, Population Characteristics," U.S. Bureau of the Census, Current Population Reports, June 2001.

4. David C. Anderson, *Children of Special Value* (New York: St. Martin's Press, 1971), p. 1.

5. Elizabeth Bartholet, "Blood Knots: Adoption, Reproduction, and the Politics of Family," *The American Prospect* (Fall 1993): p. 54.

6. U.S. Department of Commerce, Bureau of the Census, *Statistical Abstract of the United States, 1991.* Washington, DC: Government Printing Office, p. 376; Amey Stone, "Finding a Way Through the Adoption Maze," *Business Week* (June 12, 1995), p. 104.

7. Harold Kennedy, "As Adoptions Get More Difficult," *U.S. News and World Report*, June 25, 1984, p. 61.

8. U.S. Department of Commerce, Bureau of the Census, *Statistical Abstract of the United States, 1991*, p. 376

9. Taken from "Intercountry Adoption," National Adoption Information Clearinghouse, http://www.calib.com/naic

10. Adoption and Foster Care Analysis and Reporting System Data in "The AFCARS Report," U.S. Department of Health and Human Services, Administration for Children and Families, Administration on Children, Youth and Families, Children's Bureau, also online at www.acf.dhhs.gov/programs/cb/publications/afcars/june2001.htm

11. Stephanie Brill, "Overseas Adoptions: The Secret Everyone Is Talking About," *Curve*, May 2001, p. 32.

12. Joyce Ladner, *Mixed Families* (Garden City, NY: Anchor, 1977), p. 248.

13. Taken from "Transracial Adoption," National Adoption Information Clearinghouse, http://www.calib.com/naic

14. Lawrence A. Alexander and Lyla H. O'Driscoll, "Stork Markets: An Analysis of 'Baby-selling,'" *Journal of Libertarian Studies* 4 (1980): 174; see also Elizabeth M. Landes and Richard A. Posner, "The Economics of the Baby Shortage," *Journal of Legal Studies* 7 (1978): 323–348.

15. James Rolph Edwards, "A Market Solution to the Abortion and Adoption Problems," The Forum, *Libertarian Party News*, March 2001.

16. Alexander and O'Driscoll, "Stork Markets," p. 187.

17. Alexander and O'Driscoll (p. 196) suggest that a minimum age should exist above which a child could not be "sold." This age should be lower than the age at which the child becomes aware of the market. Otherwise, the child might worry that he or she could be sold to buy a new car—and rightly so.

18. Ellen Perlman, "The Failure of the Adoption Machine," *Governing* (July 1999): 32.

19. Elizabeth Kane, *Birth Mother: The Story of America's First Legal Surrogate Mother* (New York: Harcourt Brace Jovanovich, 1988).

20. "Birth Marketing," *Commonweal* 114 (December 4, 1987): 692; "Unnatural Acts," *Commonweal* 115 (October 21, 1988): 550.

21. Cynthia D. Martin, *Beating the Adoption Game* (La Jolla, CA: Oak Tree, 1980), p. 193.

22. Ladner, *Mixed Families*, pp. 218–219.

23. The first statistics are from Philip J. Hilts, "New Study Challenges Estimates on Odds of Adopting a Child," *The New York Times*, December 10, 1990, p. B10; Stone, "Finding a Way Through the Adoption Maze," p. 104; the second from Brill, "Overseas Adoption."

24. Joseph Goldstein, Anna Freud, and Albert J. Solnit, *Before the Best Interests of the Child* (New York: Free Press, 1979), pp. 5, 13.

25. Patrick Fagan, "Promoting Adoption Reform: Congress Can Give Children Another Chance," *Heritage Foundation Backgrounder No. 1080*, May 6, 1996.

26. Alfred Kadushin, "Single-Parent Adoptions: An Overview and Some Relevant Research," *Social Service Review* 44 (1970): 263–274.

27. "Should a Single Person Adopt a Child?" *Good Housekeeping*, August 1969, p. 12.

28. Ibid., p. 14.

29. Carole Klein, *The Single Parent Experience* (New York: Walker and Company, 1973), p. 96; in 1994, the NABSW softened its stance to make transracial adoption a third option behind strengthening the black family and finding black adults to adopt children.

30. Jane Zeni Flinn, "Many Cultures, One Family," *America*, October 21, 1981, p. 261

31. Jill Smolowe, "Adoption in Black and White," *Time*, August 14, 1995, p. 51.

32. Roy Wilkins, "What Color Is Love?" *OURS*, March/April 1980, p. 33.

33. "HHS Removes Race as Barrier to Adoptions of Minority Children," *Jet*, May 15, 1995, p. 4.

34. Smolowe, "Adoption in Black and White," p. 50.

35. Ladner, *Mixed Families*, p. 231.

36. Mary K. Benet, *The Politics of Adoption* (New York: Free Press, 1976), p. 12.

37. Ladner, *Mixed Families*, p. 88.

38. See Leslie Doty Hollingsworth, "Symbolic Interactionism, African-American Families and the Transracial Adoption Controversy, *Social Work* 44 (1999): 443–464.

39. Rita Simon and Howard Altstein, *Transracial Adoptees and Their Families* (New York: Praeger, 1987).

40. Linda Gordon, *The Great Arizona Orphan Abduction* (Cambridge, MA: Harvard University Press, 1999), p. 9.

41. Gordon, *The Great Arizona Orphan Abduction*.

42. Linda Gordon refers to the adoptive parents as "Mexicans" in her book. Because Gordon is referencing a particular historical context, she uses this term, rather than "Hispanic" or other more contemporary terms. We use the word *Mexican* here to keep in line with her usage.

43. Gordon, *The Great Arizona Orphan Abduction*, p. 105.

44. Gordon, *The Great Arizona Orphan Abduction*, p. 75.

45. Gordon, *The Great Arizona Orphan Abduction*, p. 282.

46. Gordon, *The Great Arizona Orphan Abduction*, p. 282.

# CHAPTER NINE

# Nation and State: Should the United States Have Open Borders?

■ The convulsive reactions to the September 11, 2001 terrorist attacks on New York City and Washington, D.C. illustrate the powerful symbolic meanings associated with being American. Many Americans immediately and publicly embraced a collective national identity as patriots; millions who had never owned American flags before rushed to purchase them to display on their cars, homes, and workplaces. Selfless acts of volunteering and giving blood, money, supplies, and for some, their lives were viewed as confirming a resilient and virtuous American national character. The attacks *also* revealed an alternative social construction of what being American means. Some around the world venerated the attackers for devastating Americans and American interests. Through their eyes, American policies deserved deadly violence aimed at its citizens. Terrorists and their supporters had a clear idea of what "being American" meant. These diverse reactions demonstrate how national identity can influence people to risk their lives to rescue, fight for, and kill other human beings. Why is national identity so compelling?

The idea of the nation has its roots in psychological and cultural principles. Anthony Smith noted, "A nation . . . may be defined as any social group with a common and distinctive history and culture, a definite territory, common sentiments of solidarity, a single economy and equal citizenship rights for all members."[1] To achieve a distinct national identity, most states create a complex symbol system, which includes customs, celebrations, artifacts, and a socially legitimated (and institutionally taught) history. Thus, most school systems in the United States require that students learn U.S. history (often in fifth, eighth, and eleventh grades) and then also that they learn the history of the individual locality where they reside. We learn *nationalism* in countless ways, becoming socialized to interpret an affiliation with a country as an important feature of our personal identities. To insult or threaten one's nation becomes interpreted as a personal affront. To burn a nation's flag becomes seen not as burning a rectangular cloth, but as committing symbolic violence toward a collective group. Through the agents of socialization, such as family and schools, patriots are made, not born.

Behind the concept of national identity stands the social structure of the state, which is "a political apparatus that claims or exerts absolute sovereignty over a given territory and its inhabitants."[2] Sociologists analyze the state as a social institution that functions to sustain a territory and its inhabitants, both materially and socially. States consist of huge organizations that administer bureaucratic functions, such as the nation's defense, international relations, law enforcement, and social welfare programs. One obligation of the modern state is to protect citizens against internal and external threats. As Max Weber noted, the state claims a monopoly on the legitimate use of physical force.³ The state has the "right" to use violence, but ordinary citizens with few exceptions (e.g., self-defense) lack that right. For the libertarian, it is precisely the state's capacity to use force "legitimately" that is so troubling.

Governments organize themselves in various ways. A traditional approach to governance is the monarchy, in which the power to rule is transferred from generation to generation, typically within a single family. A single individual has the authority to rule and represents the state. Just as we repeat, "God Bless America," the British recite, "God Save the Queen." The two phrases amount to the same thing. Some monarchs have had absolute power, although today most monarchs operate within a constitutional framework. Authoritarian rule, or totalitarianism, characterizes other states. Authoritarianism refers to a political system that denies popular participation in government. Under totalitarianism, the government goes further and attempts to direct many aspects of people's private lives. Absolute monarchies are authoritarian, while modern tyrannical dictatorships—Nazi Germany is the classic example, although some communist states, such as North Korea, also qualify—are totalitarian.

In the last decades of the twentieth century, democratic systems have increased in number. In a democratic system, the people exercise power, although often through their representatives in a representative democracy. United States citizens (some of them, at least) vote on Election Day, but have little control over the day-to-day operation of government. Some people call for experiments with "electronic democracy," but others wonder whether the people have the expertise and the maturity to make decisions about specific policies. Sociologist Nina Eliasoph has shown that while Americans may care deeply about political issues at an individual level, they do not engage in much public talk about political issues.⁴ Americans may use their freedoms to participate in political life or to avoid politics, but if they are interested in politics as individuals, why doesn't their interest emerge in public talk? For Eliasoph, failing to participate in politics reflects more than a lack of expertise and maturity; people also lack civic practices that would encourage more active public participation.

The state labels individuals with a legal and social identity as citizens. From a sociological standpoint, citizenship is an ascribed and achieved legal affiliation with a nation that carries rights, privileges, and restrictions. United States citizenship, for example, limits individuals from traveling to Cuba, guarantees their savings accounts; specifies a legal age for them to drive, drink, or vote; involuntarily taxes their earnings at a particular rate; and provides them with social security checks as they age. Citizenship, for better or worse, places the quality of people's lives in state hands. Because of this impact, the state acquires legitimate authority in controlling individual actions. Yet, acquiring power is not the same thing as gaining *moral legitimacy*. States require power and authority. That moral legitimacy does not always come easily helps to explain the brutality that states may show their "citizens" when they seek changes in government policies.

Citizenship is normally conferred upon birth. However, people also migrate—moving in and out of different territories—with many people hoping to become citizens of other nations through migrating there. Immigrants may leave their birth countries for many reasons, such as lack of economic opportunity, religious persecution, fear of political violence, or the wish to be reunited with relatives elsewhere. Immigration also does not occur in a social vacuum. People's immigration patterns also reflect existing historical and geographical ties between birth nations and destination countries. For example, citizens from former colonies often migrate to the nations that colonized them, such as Algerians moving to France or Indians and Pakistanis to Great Britain.

Acquiring citizenship in a developed country can carry tremendous benefits, affording people legal access to employment opportunities and social resources that do not exist in their homelands. The benefits that developed nations can offer are so compelling that many migrants will risk death to enter developed nations—Cubans on makeshift rafts brave dehydration, sharks, and storms to get to Florida; Chinese immigrants stow away in cargo holds to get to Canada; and Albanians risk their lives to enter Italy. Immigration patterns provide a judgment on the countries of the world, signifying the relative attractiveness of different nations. One of the great propaganda coups of the cold war, for example, was that communist countries had to build walls to keep their citizens in, while Western countries had people clamoring to enter them.

Because immigration represents a transfer of human and financial capital, as well as a potential drain on the resources of host nations, immigration is a complex, controversial, and global political issue. Some countries, for example, must fight to keep talented citizens within their borders, such as doctors, engineers and scientists; they must avoid a "brain drain" to other countries. Other nations must fight to keep people away. All nations have to develop immigration policies. How should outsiders be incorporated into a nation? Before September 11, 2001, President Bush suggested loosening restrictions on immigration. He even floated the idea of granting amnesty to millions of Mexican nationals currently living illegally within the United States. As a result of the September 11 attacks, however, the U.S. government has moved to tighten the nation's borders, with some people suggesting that these boundaries now become impermeable. As a consequence, future immigration policies may become even more controversial, and citizenship and nationhood further redefined. What should U.S. immigration policy be? How do sociological arguments inform this debate?

## ■ Question:

*Should the United States have open borders?*

> *Give me your tired, your poor, your huddled masses yearning to breathe free, the wretched refuse of your teeming shore. . . .*
> —Emma Lazarus, from the base of the Statue of Liberty

It has often been said that America is a nation of immigrants: Once we all were "huddled masses," tired and poor. Yet, this does not mean that we are of one mind about immigration policy. Your opinion of immigration ultimately revolves around what your national vision is, as columnist Michael Kinsley noted:

> It's almost a matter of faith. Your views on immigration depend on your sense of what makes America America. For some it's endless open spaces. For some it's a demographic image frozen in time. For some that stuff on the Statue of Liberty still plucks a chord. All these visions of America have a large component of fantasy.[5]

Even American Indians were originally migrants from Asia. In the 1600s and 1700s, voluntary migration was largely from England, with some other European nationals and not forgetting the vast number of Africans brought in chains from their homelands. The mid-nineteenth century witnessed waves of immigration from Ireland and Scandinavia. Later in the century, Southern and Eastern European immigrants passed through Ellis Island in New York harbor, enriching our nation, as did Chinese immigrants on the West Coast. Later migrants came from Puerto Rico. With changes in immigration laws in the 1960s, more migrants arrived from Southeast Asia, Central America, Samoa, the former Soviet Union, India, and the Middle East. Mexican nationals have long immigrated to the United States, although originally the incorporation of Mexicans into the U.S. was a consequence of United States expansion into previously Mexican territory. Surely the United States is a grand "melting pot." Our global economic, political, military, and cultural dominance has influenced citizens from around the globe to wish to reside in the United States. Some Americans thus believe that America's very dominance is now unleashing forces that threaten its future.[6] As with globalization, much of this debate revolves around whether people believe that outside influences, on balance, strengthen or weaken existing societies.

Americans, for centuries, have had several different minds about immigration. Often it seems that once one's own group has settled in America, that people then argue that immigration should be sharply limited. New immigrants seem different in kind—and in values and culture—from those here previously. Indeed, immigrants *do* change national culture in various unpredictable ways. By the mid-eighteenth century, for example, Benjamin Franklin was so concerned about the influx of German speakers into Pennsylvania that he wrote: "Why should [German] boors be suffered to swarm in our settlements and, by herding together, establish their language and manners to the exclusion of ours? Why should Pennsylvania, founded by the English, become a colony of *aliens*, who will shortly be so numerous as to Germanize us instead of our anglifying them?"[7] Yet, during the War of Independence, when the Continental Congress felt it necessary to seek support from German Americans, the Congress printed the articles of confederation in German.[8]

While sentiment toward immigrants varied during the nineteenth century, huge waves of immigration in the late nineteenth century and early twentieth century produced pressures that led Congress to pass the 1924 Quota Law that sharply limited immigration to 150,000 persons/year (in 1921 alone, 800,000 persons entered the United States). Each nationality was admitted in proportion to its share of the U.S. population in 1890, a decision that favored Western Europeans, limited openings for Southern and Eastern Europeans, and nearly barred immigration from Africa and Asia. American nativists then, just as today, felt that U.S. society and culture were changing too rapidly to allow open borders.

Not until 1965 did U.S. immigration policy change again—increasing the number of immigrants. Limited quotas for Third-World immigrants were also altered. Along with the magnitude of the new immigration, many Americans felt that these immigrants, especially Hispanic immigrants, were less willing than earlier generations to assimilate to "American culture." Spanish-speaking immigrants, for example, wished to retain their language and culture. President Theodore Roosevelt once argued that if Americans are to accept immigrants into our midst, the immigrants must willingly change their cultural traditions: "The greatness of this nation depends on the swift assimilation of the aliens she welcomes to her shores. Any force which attempts to retard that assimilative process is a force hostile to the highest interests of this country."[9]

The reluctance of some immigrant groups to assimilate has led to vigorous debates about bilingual education programs and attempts to enshrine English as our official language, as voters did in Florida, Colorado, and Arizona in 1988. The American fabric allows individual freedom, yet people also hope that immigrants alter their lives to integrate into U.S. culture. Otherwise, immigrant settlements simply become outposts of other cultures that happen to be located in the United States, rather than being *additions* to the United States.

While immigration to the United States is global, much of the debate over immigration policy concerns Hispanics[10] and is a particularly sensitive issue in states, especially California, where the Hispanic population is concentrated. The largest minority group in the United States is becoming Hispanic—Americans whose native language is not English but Spanish. Between 1986 and the year 2000, the Hispanic labor force was projected to have increased by 74 percent! The 2000 census listed 35 million Hispanics; that figure may reach 47 million by 2020. One out of every four Californians and half the population of Los Angeles is Latino. Because of their numbers and perceived unwillingness to give up their native culture and become "Americanized," many Hispanic immigrants are defined as posing special problems for U.S. society.

The problem of immigration is more than just debating who should be allowed in, but also of examining what happens once immigrants arrive. What effects does immigration have, not only on the life chances of those who arrive, but on the life chances of people who are already here? Most Americans believe that levels of immigration are too high—recent polls indicate that two-thirds of U.S. adults want immigration curtailed.[11] This sentiment reflects a pessimistic view of immigration's benefits. Many Americans see immigration as having negative effects on preexisting populations—half perceive that immigration's negative impact is strongest with respect to increasing crime, 40 percent believe the negative effect is on the quality of public schools, 46 percent on taxes, and 31 percent on job opportunities. Yet, the problem involves more than the million or so legal immigrants who arrive yearly. Estimates suggest that two to three times that number of illegal aliens (or, less pejoratively, undocumented immigrants) reach the United States, although not all remain here.

The most direct expression of concern over immigration policy of the last decade was the passage of Proposition 187—the "Save Our State" (SOS) Initiative—in

California in November 1994, by a 59 percent to 41 percent margin, with significant support (slightly under 25 percent) among Hispanic voters.[12] This proposition started with the rather simple premise that illegal aliens, largely Hispanic, are not entitled to state services, including education, welfare, and nonemergency medical services. Estimates at the time suggested that California, in which some 43 percent of America's illegal aliens resided, spent $2 to $4 billion each year on services to illegal aliens. Some 300,000 children of illegal aliens (who were illegal themselves) attended public school in California—10 percent of the students.[13] The passage of Proposition 187 was to send the message that illegal aliens should return to their homelands and that potential immigrants should stay home. In 1998, California judge Mariana Pfaelzer ruled that Proposition 187 was unconstitutional. In July 1999, California governor Gray Davis settled the legal case over whether Proposition 187 was constitutional. Davis's decision to settle effectively prevented the most controversial aspects of Proposition 187 from being implemented.

Disputes over immigration policy continue. The U.S. government has recently decided to extend the monitoring and restricting of citizens of Arab countries who wish to come to the United States. Illegal immigration also continues unabated. Does the desire to restrict entry and benefits to immigrants, illegal or otherwise, contradict the message of American inclusion and individual freedom that is at the heart of our national ideals? Or does excess immigration, both illegal and legal, harm U.S. interests, such that borders should be controlled? What are the societal benefits and disadvantages of immigration?

## The Conservative Point of View

Politically, the debate over immigration does not easily fall into conventional categories—some environmentalists, labor leaders, African Americans, and conservative nativists agree that immigration needs to be reduced because of threats, respectively, to the natural resources of the nation, working-class jobs and pay, inner-city communities, and changes to the culture. On the other side are believers in free markets, the American Civil Liberties Union, the National Rifle Association, and proponents of multiculturalism.[14]

Still, while the divisions are imperfect, conservatives are most likely to be skeptical of high levels of legal immigration, and they are more willing to endorse restrictions on illegal immigration. Part of the concern is cultural. To opponents, a fragmented and diverse nation is a weakened nation, particularly when immigrant groups seem intent on holding on to their own cultural traditions and languages. This can easily be caricatured as racist, and in some instances it surely is, but these advocates argue sincerely that nation-states survive by virtue of common belief and shared identity. Functionalists and conservatives share the understanding that a strong social order emerges from shared social values. Conservative activist Patrick Buchanan emphatically stated his argument:

I will stop illegal immigration cold, by putting a double-linked security fence along the border. I will bring our country together and make us one family, one people, one nation again. We need what we had from 1924 to 1965: a moratorium, a timeout on immigration, so we can assimilate and introduce the millions and millions who have come here to our history, our traditions, our language. We've got to become one country again.[15]

Whatever one might think about the idea of a security fence, Buchanan's imagery stresses the centrality of family and socialization into an American culture and identity.

Peter Skerry, a professor of political science at UCLA, argued that such concerns are not necessarily racist or xenophobic, but represent a legitimate anxiety when a way of life changes.[16] These ethnic divisions could, it is argued, lead to a balkanized America: Kosovo on the Potomac. Considering lower native birthrates (also a concern during previous waves of immigration), some see the United States becoming overrun by foreigners.[17] This influx may also produce political pressure to strengthen bilingual education or affirmative action. Add to this the problems of crime in low-income neighborhoods, and it is easy to feel, as does Daniel Stein of the Federation for American Immigration Reform that the immigrants depress the quality of life in many cities.[18] With regard to illegal immigration, these people are *criminals;* they are violating the law by entering and remaining in the United States illegally. To what other classes of criminals do we give benefits? These men and women are targets not because of their color, but because they are violating the law, while others from their nation are legally immigrating.

A second set of issues reflects economic concerns. Many recent immigrants—particularly those from Mexico, Central America, and the Caribbean—have few marketable skills, little education, limited facility in English, and no resources. While some economists have argued that, even so, the government gains more in taxes than they spend, others argue that states with large populations of illegal aliens, such as California, are hurt. It is widely believed, if difficult to demonstrate, that welfare, medical benefits, and education draw migrants, and that increasing support only increases the motivation of migrants to settle in the community. This suggests—within the limits of these economic assumptions—that undocumented immigrants are rational. Wouldn't you select your residence on the amenities offered to you? While others doubt that these benefits are the major draw for those who often work two or three backbreaking jobs, the argument has logic. These services increase taxes—a powerful concern. In addition, immigrants send billions of dollars of their wages back to their families at home, rather than purchasing goods and services here. Their willingness to work for low wages and few benefits undercuts the minimum wage, the eight-hour day, and pension plans.[19]

Paradoxically, given the concern with labor market participation, other conservatives argue that these illegals might add to the underclass, becoming dependant on welfare.[20] As Republican Florida congressman Clay Shaw noted, "Give me your poor, tired huddled masses," was "before welfare." Although some immigrants bring needed technical skills, many immigrants arrive without such skills. Tamar Jacoby noted that

Recent immigrants from some countries are highly skilled: over 60% of Indians, for example, have completed four years of college (compared to 25% of native-born Americans). But many other new arrivals come with little learning: According to one astounding count, in a full quarter of immigrant households, the most educated parent has completed less than 8 years of school. Many of these immigrants settle in harsh inner cities where jobs are scarce and schools are poor. Together, the combination of what social scientists call "weak human capital" and "structural conditions" can make it seem all but impossible for immigrant children to succeed.[21]

Given these characteristics of many immigrants, it is easy to fear that large groups of unskilled workers (and their children) may end up increasing the number of people in the underclass.

The conservative, while typically not opposed to all immigration, is vitally concerned with patterns of migration that seem out of control, bringing in waves of unskilled men and women. Legal immigration, says the conservative, should be kept within bounds and should emphasize those potential residents who have the skills to benefit the rest of us. Conservatives see illegal aliens as criminals, and if the punishments become sufficiently intense and the likelihood of capture sufficiently great, the probability of returning to the United States will be small. Conservatives argue that with vigorous law enforcement at the border and elsewhere, immigration problems can be solved.

## The Social Democratic Point of View

Excepting some environmentalists and labor leaders, social democrats support the incorporation of immigrants into our society as a matter of morality and justice. They are less prone to make economic arguments than are conservatives and libertarians. They emphasize that America is *by its nature* a nation of immigrants. President Franklin Roosevelt urged Americans to "remember always that they are descended from immigrants and revolutionists." Welcoming immigrants, and incorporating their culture, makes this nation special. Michael Kinsley argued that

> In other countries, concern about diluting the nation's ethnic stock even has certain validity. Such concerns have no validity in America. In fact, they are un-American. If applied in earlier times, when they were raised with equal passion, they would have excluded the ancestors of many who make the ethnic/cultural preservation argument today.[22]

Even political conservatives, such as William Bennett and Jack Kemp, worry that the panic over illegal aliens may lead to solutions at odds with our history. Bennett referred to California's Proposition 187, for example, as "poison in a democracy."[23] It is our nation's ability to transform outsiders to insiders—changing others to being us. In the words of Jacob Neusner: "When we lose faith in the power of this country and its unique social system to take the foreigner and make the stranger one of us—in our image, after our likeness—and make ourselves over too, we shall deny the power that has made us unique among other nations."[24] Indeed, although we have used the label "illegal alien" in this chapter, some argue that that is offensive and dehumanizing: Are these ambitious men and women, alien others? As one United Farm Workers poster put it, "No Human Being is Illegal."[25]

Given the sentiment behind Proposition 187, we must ask how far we are willing to go in the direction of monitoring and exclusion of immigrants. Do we want our doctors and teachers to be "snitches" to the Immigration and Naturalization Service, forced to report suspected illegal immigrants, leading some to engage in civil disobedience?[26] Such a stance might prevent people from receiving medical attention and preventive treatment, perhaps putting the public at risk or requiring that they later seek more expensive emergency care. Children not in school are often on the street, perhaps joining gangs, using drugs, or committing crimes.

As is often the case, social democrats frame the issue in light of children. In the debate over California's Proposition 187, opponents used horror stories about what did or might happen to children of migrants. These boys and girls are "innocent victims":

> Constantino and Rosa Ramirez say they feared for their 12-year old son, Julio Cano, two weeks ago [shortly after the passage of Proposition 187], when he developed shooting back pains and a deep cough. Yet they didn't dare take him to the hospital. "If it weren't for Proposition 187, the first day he felt sick we would have taken him to the hospital," [his father] told reporters. . . . When his condition worsened, the family called fire-department paramedics, but it was too late. Julio died on the way to the hospital.[27]

While no one wishes to see children die, conservatives would note that had the parents returned to Mexico or had they never left, this tragedy might have been averted.

While race is not the only reason that people wish to limit legal immigration and prevent illegal immigration, social democrats insist that race plays a role. White groups may simply not wish to cede any more space to nonwhites, and fears of more and more brown immigrants can play on prejudice. Edward Gaffney, Jr., the dean of the Valparaiso University School of Law, believes that "the vicious attacks on people of color mounted in TV and radio ads supporting the initiative (Proposition 187) were a raw assault on human dignity."[28] Mexican Americans worry whether immigrant bashing leads to brown-skinned people being seen as criminals. Especially in times of conflict and economic tension, it is easy for immigrants to become targets, whether for being potential financial threats or potential killers. In the wake of the September 11 attacks, any person appearing to be Arab American or Muslim became suspect, including Sikh citizens and immigrants, who were also singled out for suspicion—or worse—because of their skin tone and turbans.

Race also impacts assimilation. Conservatives, for example, may urge immigrants to merge into being "Americans," but social democrats note that racism affects whether immigrants *can* successfully integrate into the American mainstream. European immigrants and their descendents who were white had an easier time settling in;

blacks, Asians, and some darker-hued Hispanics may have less ability to skirt racial barriers than their white counterparts.[29] Yet, the perceived success of Asian immigrants (the model minority) complicates this theory.

Some critics of negative views of Hispanic immigrants insist that attacks on Hispanic character are especially unfair, as they are aimed against a community that has strong family and religious values and a deep work ethic. If American culture is breaking down, it seems hard to blame recent immigrants and illegal aliens alone; the roots of moral breakdown go back decades. Social democrats also oppose discrimination in most forms, so keeping people from pursuing a better life for themselves is repellent, particularly when opposition to immigration is perceived to be rooted in racial prejudice and economic self-interest.

## The Libertarian Point of View

Just as libertarians believe in the power of free trade—permitting goods to follow the market—they also believe in the freedom to migrate and the right of people to move freely. *The Wall Street Journal* proposed a constitutional amendment of just five words: "There shall be open borders."[30] Libertarians are, in general, suspicious of the power of nation-states, preferring the choices of private citizens. Of course, libertarians do not support providing illegal aliens with social services, but, then, they don't support providing *anyone* with those subsidies. Their support of self-sufficiency applies equally to all.

While we present conservatives as opposing completely open borders, many businessmen support loosening restrictions on immigration. Cheap, plentiful, and dedicated labor benefits capitalist enterprises. Nowhere is this truer than in the rich agricultural soil of California's San Joaquin Valley, where staunchly Republican agribusinessmen opposed Proposition 187. They noted that perhaps half of their laborers were, and are, illegal.[31] What would happen to their profits—and prices on our lettuce, raisins, cotton—if illegal aliens returned to Mexico? What would happen to the United States if tomorrow every undocumented worker suddenly and without warning disappeared? Grower Ray Lopez noted about anti-immigrant rhetoric: "It plays well as a political issue, but if the politicians get their way, we'll be in trouble. If you removed every illegal from this state tomorrow, you'll see the whole agricultural business start to crumble."[32] The result would be economic chaos, higher prices, lower tax revenues, and perhaps a depression.

America's dirty little secret is the importance of cheap labor. Farm owners need laborers, builders need construction workers, restaurateurs need pot washers, affluent housewives need gardeners, and intellectuals need nannies. Although California governor Pete Wilson is now an outspoken opponent of illegal immigration, during the 1980s, as senator from California, he sponsored the Seasonal Agricultural Worker program, permitting hundreds of thousands of laborers to enter the country as "guest workers" without complying with immigration laws.[33] Some economists argue that it is not only business which profits from the influx of migrants, but all of us. When an immigrant takes a job, the money spent in this country helps to create another job: a basic tenet of capitalist theory. Illegal immigrants are already ineligible for state welfare assistance or food stamps and use a small fraction (about 1 percent) of California's $57 billion medical services budget.[34]

While immigration may hurt some native workers, ultimately a vigorous stream of immigrants benefits everyone. Economist Julian Simon suggested that the economic benefits of immigration outweigh the costs, in the form of a higher standard of living, lower deficit, and greater international competitiveness.[35] One estimate suggests that each year legal and illegal immigrants generate a $25 to $30 billion surplus from the income and property taxes they pay.[36] In the words of Jonathan Alter:

> Immigration is the engine that drives national success. . . . For instance, over the last 20 years the middle class of New York City—made up of earlier generations of immigrant families—essentially moved to the suburbs. Without new immigrants, the city would have been composed of only the very rich and the very poor, with large sections of the outer boroughs depopulated and devastated. Some of the 854,000 who settled there during the 1980s became terrorists or tax cheats; others opened shops and watched their kids win high-school science prizes. Overall, they quite literally saved New York. . . . Whatever the early adjustment pains—for the aliens themselves and for the public services they burden—immigration eventually pays off big.[37]

Immigration will at first benefit elites, who do not compete for these jobs, whereas working-class men and women who do compete for these jobs may lose out. However, in the long run everyone benefits.

Libertarians also respect the entrepreneurial drive immigration represents. Individuals migrate to pursue their economic freedom and independence. Immigrants make new markets; as Joel Kotkin wrote, "immigrants are hungrier and more optimistic . . . their upward mobility is a form of energy."[38] The pursuit of freedom is dear to libertarians—restricting immigration operates against that belief; hence the Libertarian party platform advocates open borders and the end of the INS and U.S. Border Patrol.

Libertarians particularly object to one potential future aspect of immigration policy: having citizens carry a national ID card. That plastic wafer can be a stick of dynamite. As one libertarian put it, "For the land of liberty to flood prisons with identity-card violators seems an abomination."[39] It is because of this concern with government control that the National Rifle Association opposes many attempts to limit immigration. The possibility of involuntarily drafting teachers and doctors into amateur INS agents is no more comforting to libertarians than it is to social democrats. Immigration poses a challenge of socialization, but then for centuries it has.

# Immigration and Social Research

"When the last American leaves Miami, please take the flag." What sentiments lay behind this popular bumper sticker among Miami Anglos during the 1980s? When foreign-born populations settle in the United States, they are expected to assimilate quickly into the dominant mainstream culture, becoming first and foremost Americans, and only secondarily, members of their native ethnic groups. Sociologists use the term *acculturation* to describe the process by which immigrants adopt the norms, values, and lifestyle of the dominant culture. However, the impact of immigration operates in two dimensions; immigrants also transform their new environments. In *City on the Edge: The Transformation of Miami*, sociologists Alejandro Portes and Alex Stepick examined how waves of Cuban immigrants transformed the city of Miami.[40]

Portes and Stepick analyzed how immigrants adapted to life in Miami; in doing so, they showed that the settled African American and previously dominant Anglo communities in Miami were changed, both in voluntary and involuntary ways, from the impact of Cuban immigration. According to Portes and Stepick, Miami experienced "acculturation in reverse." This was a "process by which foreign customs, institutions and language were diffused within the native population."[41] Rather than Cuban immigrants becoming more like Anglos, the typical outcome of immigration suggested by theories of assimilation, Cuban Americans retained their language, customs, and political beliefs while becoming naturalized U.S. citizens.

Portes and Stepick used multiple methods to examine the history and impact of immigration on Miami. Alejandro Portes is a prominent quantitative sociologist and past president of the American Sociological Association; Alex Stepick is a sociologist who specializes in qualitative methodology. Their range of methodological expertise is reflected in their researching the transformation of Miami in a comprehensive fashion. They used surveys and secondary data analysis from the *U.S. Census* and local governmental records to identify demographic and economic changes in Miami among the three groups. They also performed a content analysis of decades of newspaper articles and editorials from the *Miami Herald* in order to document how Anglo, black, and Cuban American interests were portrayed over time. Portes and Stepick also interviewed members of the local Anglo, black and Cuban American communities as well as government officials, and they incorporated past research interviews with immigrants. Portes and Stepick developed both a qualitative and quantitative picture of Miami's history; they were able to document socioeconomic changes statistically, while presenting the immediacy of people's subjective experiences of immigration and urban change in Miami by means of interviews.

People normally view immigration in terms of "push" and "pull" factors; bad conditions push people out of their birth nations, while good conditions in destination countries attract them. However, immigration also reflects the existing social relations between destination countries and originating countries. To understand why Miami attracted Cuban immigrants is broader than stating simply that the United States had a more promising economy than did Cuba. The U.S. government, for example, welcomed unlimited Cuban immigrants because of their political opposition to communism in Cuba. Thus, the U.S. government's history of excluding many ethnic immigrants was reversed, and Cuban immigrants were welcomed to the United States with strong economic and political support. Miami and Cuba also had an entwined history, with many commercial relations between the cities existing prior to Castro's takeover and an existing Cuban community already living within Miami. Combined U.S. government support, economic and social connections between settled Cuban Americans and future immigrants, fervent and ironclad ideological opposition to Castro's Cuba, and ethnic and racial competition within the United States all allowed Cubans to keep their culture.

Portes and Stepick wrote

> The development of an ethnic economy of any substantial scale has three prerequisites: first, a stable market that small firms can control by offering to the immigrant community culturally defined goods and services not available on the outside; second, privileged access to a pool of cheap labor through networks within the community; and third, access to capital.[42]

Such is the formula Cuban Americans used to create a self-sufficient immigrant enclave. The first wave of Cuban immigrants who landed in Miami in the early 1960s after Castro's revolution were elites; businesspersons who knew that they would be unable and unwilling to stay in communist Cuba. This class of immigrants arrived in Miami with the capacity to provide capital to fund small businesses that cater to the existing immigrant community. Simultaneously, Cuban immigrants formed a moral community defined in opposition to Castro's Cuba.

Waiting to return to a "free" Cuba, the fierce anticommunist solidarity of Cuban Americans enabled them to produce a thriving ethnic economy:

> The consolidation of a moral community permeated imperceptibly the relationships between buyer and seller, lender and borrower, employer and worker in the ethnic enclave. A heightened sense of "we-ness" clarified the limits to which bounded solidarity would apply, while intensifying its hold. Cuban refugees bought from each other and sponsored each other's businesses to an extent seldom seen among Latin immigrant groups. Membership in this community defined, to a large extent, who was eligible for business loans and who was not . . . if the exile's political discourse had been more tolerant and less militant, it probably would not have been as effective in reinforcing the social capital on which their collective business advancement was cemented.[43]

Economic growth resulted. In 1967, Cuban exile enterprises numbered 919; in 1982, Cuban enterprises nationwide grew to 36,000, eventually growing to 61,500 in 1987. The 1987 aggregate receipts of Hispanic firms in Miami was $3.8 billion, over $400 million more than in Los Angeles and three times the receipts of those in New York, despite these cities having much larger Hispanic populations.[44]

The economic rise of the Cuban community frustrated the settled Anglo and African American communities. African Americans resented Cuban economic prosperity; Anglos objected to the threat Cubans posed to their cultural and economic dominance, as Spanish proliferated throughout Miami, and Cuban Americans' strong anticommunist political ideology started to affect Miami politics. The year 1980—with the Mariel boatlift of Cuban refugees, along with rioting by Miami blacks and the passage of an antibilingual ordinance—became a flash point for relations between the communities. African Americans who resented being eclipsed economically and thus being subordinated to both Cubans and Anglos exploded in violent protest. Anglos, who thought that passing an antibilingual referendum would send a message, "putting Cubans back in their place," awoke greater Cuban involvement in local politics.

Portes and Stepick explained:

> Obsessed with the dream of return, Cubans so far had had little time for local politics. When the unexpected and fierce hostility of Miami native Whites burst forth, the exiles were initially disoriented. It took time to fashion a response congruent with their past ideological stance. That response, when it finally came, stunned opponents both by its novelty and by its revolutionary implications. The *Miami Herald* and its supporters (those supporting the anti-bilingual referendum) had only wanted to restore normalcy to the city when they informed Cubans about how the political game was played in America and of their true position in the ethnic queue. The exiles responded by laying claim to the city.[45]

Cubans mobilized their sheer numbers, and, as naturalized citizens, voted Cuban candidates into political power, with successive legislative seats falling into their community during the 1980s and 1990s. During this period, Anglos began to move out of Miami. From 1980 to 1990, the share of Anglo residents fell from 47.7 percent to 30.3 percent, while the Cuban share of the population moved from 35 percent to 49.4 percent.[46] Signifying a great reversal, in 1991, the publisher of the *Miami Herald* newspaper that had once decried the growing influence of the Cuban population, urged his fellow Miamians to "enroll in a foreign language class," and to embrace "multicultural Miami as an example for the nation."[47]

Miami's transformation involves many features of the immigration experience in the United States—issues of assimilation and acculturation, nativist resentment of newcomers, ethnic solidarity, political conflict, and economic gains from immigration. All were essential in creating modern Miami. Thus Miami reflects *both* the uneasy and the most promising outcomes of immigration. The political and economic power of settled communities was displaced, but the economic promise of immigration was realized and the city of Miami was revitalized as an economic locus for the Caribbean.

The case of Miami raises the question of how American we should demand that our citizens be. Must an American speak English? Should an American dream only of a future here and not have their eyes fixed on a homeland abroad? A symbolic interactionist emphasizes the power of identity to fix reality. In Miami, acculturation shows the diverse stakes involved in fixing the identity of newcomers to our shores. A conflict theorist asks who wins and loses in the battle over fixing an identity; functionalist theorists extol the importance of retaining traditional values. The case of Miami demonstrates that there can be winners and losers in battles over what an immigrant identity should be, as well as the functional power of retaining ethnic solidarity in becoming economically self-sufficient.

# Nation and Immigration

The nation is a central institutional structure of human life. Individuals wish to think of themselves as members of a community, and then they build borders or barriers to keep others out and perhaps to keep themselves in. For most of us, being an American is not something trivial, not something that we just happen to be, but something that says much about who we are. We often attempt to specify what makes Americans different from others (sometimes called "American exceptionalism"), and we may even speculate on the existence of a national character.

Americans are not alone in this. The various wars and battles of nationalism—most recently evident in Bosnia, the Middle East, Somalia, and Northern Ireland suggest that who we are is tied to who will govern us. Even our peaceful northern neighbor, Canada, has recently gone through the wrenching processes of observing Quebecois deciding by the smallest of majorities to remain within Canada. No doubt this is an issue that will not pass. The convulsions in Germany in the Nazi era, and then in the unification of East and West in 1990, remind us that a sense of belonging and boundaries can have dramatic and dire consequences. Consider that more Americans died in the Civil War than in any other American war.

Despite the evident importance of nationalism, we live in a mobile world. Individuals can choose to travel anywhere they wish. Borders, relatively easy to patrol in the nineteenth century, are porous today. The problems that the United States is having today are mirrored throughout Europe, and nationalist parties have sprung up to object to the presence of foreigners—Algerians in France, Pakistanis in Britain, Turks in Germany, and so forth. Because industrial powers need cheap labor and also because they believe in tolerance, the debate is often heated. Once every nation is industrialized and wealthy (with consequences for those that have that status today), patterns of migration will surely change. Indeed, many migrants see themselves as temporary workers and often send money home to their impoverished families.

Libertarians are likely to stress that unfettered migration benefits everyone. Workers migrate voluntarily, the government receives a portion of the wages, and the host society receives cheap labor. Yet, some suggest that, as a consequence, some workers in the advanced state may be unemployed or forced to work for lower wages—no benefit to them. It is their land, too. Libertarians, worried about the potential power of government, object to proposals to have national identity cards or other forms of bureaucratic regimentation.

Most social democrats argue that the concept of nation should be inclusive. Nation is not equivalent to race, but is a voluntary relationship among people. The moral stance of social democrats is to appreciate a diverse, multicultural state—a state that welcomes those of color and those who are not as economically fortunate. Social democrats are likely to suggest that much of the debate over immigration is explicitly or implicitly racist, and this they reject. Once people reach our shores, we have an obligation to treat them with respect and humanity, including providing a range of social services.

For the conservative, the nation is one of the core social institutions that they admire—more so than the government per se. We are a people—a family—and this should mean something. Thus, many conservatives are willing to place strict limits on immigration to preserve the national culture and identity. Remember that conservatives object to rapid changes, which mass immigration seems to provoke. Illegal immigration is particularly troubling in that it seems to undercut the idea of the rule of law. If anyone has access to the benefits of American life simply by sneaking in and hiding out, what then is the value of being an American? Surely the privilege of being a citizen should stand for something.

Ultimately, sociologists recognize that the idea of a nation is a fundamental building block of social identity—socially constructed through the events of history and collective memory of those events, and enacted through the government of a state. While not all peoples have accepted the idea of a nation tied to a government, in almost every group a sense of who is an insider and who is an outsider exists. To be human involves not only kin, but also kith—the belonging to a social body beyond the ties of one's own blood.

## Questions

1. What is a nation? What does it mean to be a citizen?

2. How have the September 11 attacks changed what it means to be an American?

3. Should America permit open and unlimited immigration?

4. Is maintaining cultural homogeneity important for a nation? For example, would you support antibilingual referendums?

5. On balance, do immigrants (legal or illegal) benefit or damage the U.S. economy?

6. Should the United States develop a national identity card?

7. Does the government have the obligation to provide education for children of illegal aliens? What about medical care?

8. Should President Bush grant amnesty to illegal immigrants who already have established themselves in the United States?

9. Should the United States welcome all immigrants with advanced skills or favor accepting more immigrants who provide cheap labor?

10. Would you ever settle permanently in another country?

## For Further Study

Anderson, Benedict. *Imagined Communities* (rev. ed.). New York: Verso, 1991.

Brimelow, Peter. *Alien Nation: Common Sense about America's Immigrant Disaster*. New York: Random House, 1995.

Horowitz, Ruth. *Honor and the American Dream*. New Brunswick: Rutgers University Press, 1983.

Portes, Alejandro, and Ruben G. Rumbaut. *Immigrant America: A Portrait* (2nd ed.). Berkeley: University of California Press, 2001.

Portes, Alejandro, and Alex Stepick. *City on the Edge: The Transformation of Miami*. Berkeley: University of California Press, 1993.

Simon, Julian. *The Economic Consequences of Immigration*. New York: Blackwell, 1990.

Waters, Mary. *Ethnic Options: Choosing Identities in America*. Berkeley: University of California Press, 1990.

Wattenberg, Ben J. *The First Universal Nation*. New York: Free Press, 1991.

## Notes and References

1. Anthony D. Smith. *Nationalism in the Twentieth Century* (New York: New York University Press, 1979), p. 87.
2. Wilbur Zelinsky, *Nation into State: The Shifting Symbolic Foundations of American Nationalism* (Chapel Hill: University of North Carolina Press, 1988).
3. Cited in Hans Gerth and C. Wright Mills (eds.), *From Max Weber: Essays in Sociology* (New York: Oxford University Press, 1958), p. 78.
4. Nina Eliasoph, *Avoiding Politics: How Americans Produce Apathy in Everyday Life* (Cambridge: Cambridge University Press, 1998).
5. Michael Kinsley, "Gatecrashers," *The New Republic* (December 28, 1992): 6.
6. Tim Stafford, "Here Comes the World," *Christianity Today* (May 15, 1995): 20.
7. Stephen T. Wagner, "America's Non-English Heritage," *Society* (November–December 1981): 37.
8. Ibid., p. 41.
9. Ibid., p. 41.
10. Although there are a number of terms used to describe Spanish-speaking Americans, I will use the term *Hispanic* as the most general but least cumbersome term.
11. Cited in John Macionis, *Sociology*, 8th ed. (Upper Saddle River, NJ: Prentice-Hall, 2001), p. 377.
12. Polls in June actually showed that Hispanics supported Proposition 187. See John Zipperer, "Immigration Debate Divides Christians," *Christianity Today* (February 6, 1995): 43.
13. Nancy Gibbs, "Keep Out, You Tired, You Poor . . . ," *Time*, October 3, 1994, p. 47.
14. Steven A. Holmes, "The Strange Politics of Immigration," *The New York Times*, December 31, 1995, p. 3.
15. "Buchanan: In His Own Words," *The New York Times*, December 31, 1995, p. 10.
16. Peter Skerry, "Beware of Moderates Bearing Gifts," *National Review*, February 21, 1994, p. 45.
17. Peter Brimelow, "Time to Rethink Immigration?" *National Review*, June 22, 1992, p. 32.
18. John Zipperer, "Immigration Debate Divides Christians," *Christianity Today*, February 6, 1995, p. 42.
19. Robert Kuttner, "Illegal Immigration: Would a National ID Card Help?" *Business Week*, August 26, 1991, p. 14.
20. Skerry, "Beware of Moderates Bearing Gifts," p. 45.
21. Tamar Jacoby, "Second-Generation Question Mark," *The American Enterprise*, December 2000, p. 34.
22. Michael Kinsley, "Gatecrashers," *The New Republic* (December 28, 1992): 6.
23. Margaret Carlson, "Alienable Rights," *Time*, October 31, 1994, p. 39.
24. Stafford, "Here Comes the World," p. 25.
25. Hanna Rosin, "Raisin Hell," *The New Republic* (November 14, 1994): 15.

26. Carlson, "Alienable Rights." Of course, teachers and doctors are already government "snitches," when it comes to reporting child abuse to human service agencies. This rule dissuades some parents from taking their children to school or to the doctor. However, social democrats endorse this policy.
27. Geoffrey Cowley and Andrew Murr, "Good Politics, Bad Medicine," *Newsweek*, December 5, 1994, p. 34.
28. Edward McGlynn Gaffney, Jr., "Immigrant Bashing," *Christian Century*, (March 1, 1995): 229.
29. Alejandro Portes and Min Zhou, "Should Immigrants Assimilate?" *The Public Interest* (1994): 18–34.
30. Michael Lind, "Aliens Among Us," *The New Republic* (August 23 and 30, 1993).
31. Rosin, "Raisin Hell," p. 15.
32. Rosin, "Raisin Hell," p. 15.
33. Carlson, "Alienable Rights."
34. Ron K. Unz, "Sinking Our State," *Reason* (November 1994): 46.
35. Julian L. Simon, "Why Control the Borders?" *National Review*, February 1, 1993, p. 29.
36. Nancy Gibbs, "Keep Out, You Tired, You Poor . . . ." p. 47.
37. Jonathan Alter, "Elitism and the Immigration Backlash," *Newsweek*, July 26, 1993, p. 35.
38. Joel Kotkin, "Movers and Shakers: Immigrants Revive Dying Neighborhoods," *Reason* (December 2000).
39. Unz, "Sinking Our State," p. 46.
40. Alejandro Portes and Alex Stepick, *City on the Edge: The Transformation of Miami.*
41. Portes and Stepick, *City on the Edge,* p. 8.
42. Portes and Stepick, *City on the Edge,* p. 127.
43. Portes and Stepick, *City on the Edge,* p. 140.
44. Portes and Stepick, *City on the Edge,* p. 146.
45. Portes and Stepick, *City on the Edge,* p. 148.
46. Portes and Stepick, *City on the Edge,* p. 211.
47. Portes and Stepick, *City on the Edge,* p. 214.

# CHAPTER TEN

# Work and Organizations: Should Employers Investigate Their Employees' Private Lives?

■ Perhaps no other word in our lexicon provokes such ambivalent reactions as *work*. On the one hand, work can be ennobling and personally fulfilling. We search for the right *career*, signifying by that term, the hope that a single occupational choice will offer a lifetime of financial, social, and psychological sustenance. But there are times when we are not so rapturous about work's possibilities. Many people find that work does not express their "self," but is merely a means of earning what they need to express their "self" on Saturday nights. As Karl Marx recognized so forcefully, many workers are "alienated" from their work. They feel powerless, alienated, and psychologically separated from their tasks. Rather than satisfying their aspirations, they work, often in unpleasant conditions, to survive economically.

When most adults meet for the first time, they often ask each other, "What do you do?" This inquiry is more than politeness or routine; it is also an unvarnished scheme of social appraisal. We judge individuals by the tasks they do, gauging how prestigious or lucrative their work is and how other work (sometimes our own) compares. All work is not created equal. Some work is honored; other work is termed "dirty work"—work that is outside the bounds of proper society,[1] but which must be done in order for a social system to function. This includes jobs involving sanitation, cleaning or killing (persons and animals). Honored work receives high status and is rewarded either with an honorific title (such as doctor or reverend) or with large monetary rewards, like those that successful models, athletes, and bankers receive.

The divisions between types of work contribute mightily to the development of different social classes and status levels. Functionalist theorists argue that society is best organized when the brightest people do the most important work. Hence, occupations should be compensated unequally, with some paid more if their work is more important. Critics of this functionalist argument suggest that the rewards and status of jobs are unrelated to the actual importance of their work—otherwise firefighters, police officers, and teachers would receive more compensation than lobbyists or professional boxers do.

In some high-status occupations—those we label professions[2]—the workers themselves control (or attempt to control) the general conditions and rules of their work and what qualifications practitioners should have. While we expect factory workers to obey their immediate supervisors and to be monitored closely, we expect professionals, such as doctors, to have more autonomy to "govern" themselves. Of course, it is never that simple: No group is totally free, and outside forces can restrain professionals, through client control, bureaucracy, or governmental regulations.

Professionals, for example, must qualify for state licenses in order to work, a system that limits competition and entry into many professions. A professional license also constitutes a legal jurisdiction over specific tasks. For example, dentists are allowed to work on people's teeth, but not on other parts of the body, which prevents dentists and physicians from competing to carry out similar medical procedures.[3] Because a "professional" label has so much value, many occupations attempt to identify themselves as "professions." Nurses are professionals, but are tattoo artists or toll booth collectors? Who should get to call themselves "professionals"? Debates over which occupations merit professional status are contentious, because power and compensation are at stake.

Work is important not only to individuals' status and identity, but also the *nature and organization of work as a social institution* affects society. A great historical transformation has occurred in collective social life. Over time people have migrated from small, community-based group life to living in large, impersonal, complex societies. As societies became more complex, large organizations came to replace local, face-to-face groups (churches, farms, villages). In a small group, an individual is known personally and knows those who provide services. In a large organization, people are clients, and the people serving them are likely to be anonymous and impersonal. How is this shift reflected in social life? The French social theorist Emile Durkheim referred to this transition in terms of human organizations moving from *mechanical solidarity* to *organic solidarity*—from group life based on shared beliefs, strong social ties, and similarity, to a collective life based on differences between individuals and a common interdependence on an impersonal division of labor.[4]

We often imagine primitive society as a group in which all persons do every job. There are no specialists, but only tribespeople living together. However, the reality was not as egalitarian or simple as this image—there were gender and age differences in work, and ritual specialists (e.g., medicine men) and political specialists (e.g., chiefs). Still the "occupational" distinctions were not as extensive as the distinctions of modern, industrial societies. Sociologists speak of the "division of labor" to describe this specialization of work into distinct categories. Consider the range of modern occupations: there are actuaries, anesthesiologists, engineers, insurance agents, occupational therapists, punch-press operators, comedians, and web site developers.

Emile Durkheim thought that having an impersonal division of labor posed problems for social solidarity, in that different occupations give individuals different values and norms, undermining the consensus found in less complex societies. This fragmentation can lead to normlessness, or what has been called anomie and radical individualism. Still, complex societies provide *options* for behavior and *tolerance* for self-expression that may be unavailable in smaller and less complex social systems. A related feature of modern society is the tendency of persons to form groups or organizations to achieve some end. Although such groups occur in all spheres of human activity (consider Little League baseball teams or Mothers Against Drunk Driving), we focus here on organizations that are formed to structure particular kinds of work—companies or corporations. These organizations constitute the majority of people's present-day work environments.

Sociologists refer to large organizations as *formal organizations*. Formal organizations are often administered bureaucratically. These groups have detailed *organizational charts* showing how employees are connected to each other. These plans, in effect, describe the rights and responsibilities of members of the organization and suggest the proper patterns of communication among the different parts of the organization. These charts show in detail the "vertical" hierarchy (who supervises whom) and the "horizontal" divisions (the range of activities in which employees are engaged). In addition to establishing clear hierarchies, bureaucratic organizations (ideally) hire and promote employees based on merit; they maintain written records, associate power with organizational position rather than by an individual's charisma, and base organizational decision making on existing, rational rules.[5]

Rather than perceiving bureaucracy solely in terms of delay and "red tape," it is important to recognize the benefits that bureaucratic administration offers society. Bureaucracy, regardless of its frustrating impersonality, is the most efficient form of organization ever known. The quality of life in developed nations comes directly from bureaucratic efficiency—consider how successful the mass production and distribution of food, medicine, and consumer goods is in contemporary society. However, this efficiency has disadvantages. By extolling adherence to set routines and rules as the sole means of organizing work effectively, bureaucratic organization can produce a dehumanizing environment. Few Americans, for example, dream of landing permanent jobs where they will perform unskilled bureaucratic work; while we can appreciate McDonald's food as easily available and inexpensive, that doesn't mean we want to work there, or at other unskilled jobs, as our first career choices. Nor would we want a world in which McDonald's was our only eating option, despite its affordability and familiarity. We worry about what social theorist George Ritzer termed the "McDonaldization of society." Max Weber worried that bureaucratic administration would eventually "trap" people into the same routine, over and over, decreasing individual autonomy in and outside of work. Yet, what large organizations lose in granting individuals autonomy, they make up in efficiency and economy of scale.

Of course, few people at work follow the rules at all times. In fact, "orthodox" understandings of how people should work are often at odds with how people really do work. Interactionists correctly emphasize that organizational behavior rarely functions in exactly the manner specified in an organizational chart or procedural handbook. For example, diners enjoying a fine restaurant meal may never know that cooks inserted their fingers into their dishes to taste the outcome or to move the food so the plate looks prettier, part of the underside of work. Waiters and cooks know not to publicize this efficient but unappetizing procedure. In all workplaces, an informal structure exists among workers to gets things done through such agreements and tacit understandings. Interactionist sociologist Anselm Strauss referred to the informal ways that work is often accomplished as the *negotiated order.*[6]

While a job may not be "who" someone really is as a person, a person's line of work does imply a virtual social identity for him or her. College professors may insist that people refer to them as "Dr." Policemen may demand respect from those they question. In general, individuals identify themselves with attractive features of their occupation (how much they earn or honorific titles), while rejecting unattractive ones. How, in turn, do work organizations make claims on workers' identities?

At one level, all employees embody a "working personality," in which they display a demeanor that meets the role expectations of their particular job. Sociologists use the phrase *emotional labor* to describe how workers must express particular feelings and emotions as part of doing their job.[7] For example, flight attendants must display endless manufactured smiles to passengers, and salespersons, a dutiful deference to customers. Workplaces also make demands on identity through setting criteria for physical appearance. Actors and actresses, for example, are often picked by physical appearance; Disney workers cannot have visible tattoos; and flight attendants are fired if, in the view of airline management, they gain too much weight.

In addition to requiring some emotional and physical impression as part of performing a job, employers may make other demands on the private identities of workers. Does a private employer have the right to know whether a prospective or current employee is gay, genetically predisposed to chronic diseases, or has controversial political or racial beliefs? To what degree can employers scrutinize the private actions, history, and thoughts of their employees? Should employers be permitted to give their employees lie detector tests or to read and monitor employee e-mail without an employee's knowledge? When should employees' private lives be inaccessible to employers?

While workplaces can be repressive, unscrupulous, and exploitative, employees also can, and do, victimize both clients and employers. A perennial social conflict exists in balancing the desirability of social order versus protecting against potential excesses in exerting social controls. The technology involved in conducting investigations and surveillance into the private thoughts and lives of workers is becoming more sophisticated; surveillance technology is now making individual behavior more transparent. However, just because we can know more does not mean that we should.

## ■ Question:

*Should employers investigate their employees' private lives?*

When employers pay a wage, they contract for an employee's labor and time. But do they also buy access to a worker's private life? Surely an employer should be able to choose whom to hire, but what limits exist on that decision? If a person keeps private his or her sexual orientation, fondness for pornographic web sites, belief in racist theories, or prior prison record, is it any business of an employer? In some jobs, people assume that private identity can "contaminate" one's work—for example, the objections some people have to gay schoolteachers. At other times, people see personal character as unrelated to someone's fitness for their work. Two issues are paramount. The first is to determine what, if any, private aspects of identity reasonably disqualify someone from work. What character traits are so threatening that breaching individual privacy is warranted? The second issue is deciding what techniques employers should be allowed to use to investigate the individual character and veracity of employees. Should corporations be allowed to administer lie detector tests to employees during preemployment screening in order to disqualify undesirables?

Part of becoming an employee is entering into a contract, in which labor and time are exchanged for a set wage. Underlying this transaction is the agreement that employees accept some infringement of their privacy as a condition of seeking employment. For example, employees sign job application forms that allow employers to verify their qualifications. Did the applicant really go to college? Did she leave her old job for a better opportunity or was she fired? After hiring, employers also can scrutinize whether employees are performing their work satisfactorily, are stealing, or are taking drugs.

Employers have a right to protect themselves from the theft of their resources. In addition to these worries, more intangible goods, like e-mail networks, can be misappropriated. If people use the e-mail network at work to distribute salacious e-mail messages to coworkers, the employer may be liable for those actions. The oil company Chevron, for example, was required to pay plaintiffs $2.2 million when a list of jokes entitled "why beer is better than women," that was sent through e-mail to numerous employees, was viewed as a "smoking gun," as e-mail evidence of sexual harassment at Chevron.[8] Are an employee's e-mail communications an extension of personal privacy? Does an employer have to protect the employee's total privacy once the employee enters the workplace?

The answer is no—unlike an individual's telephone calls or personal mail, which are a private individual's personal property, employers "owned" the e-mail network and can set a policy of monitoring communications using their property—as long as they advise workers of their policy in advance. Employers argue for the most part that they are simply monitoring work where more and more work is taking place—electronically. According to the American Management Association, 63 percent of major U.S. companies monitor how long employees spend on the Internet and 47 percent store and read employee e-mail.[9]

But how far should employers go in the name of supervision and protecting themselves from liability? The key concern is the degree of control that employers have over workers. Generally, the closer an individual's private behavior is to being criminal (drug addiction, a history of violence), rather than being morally controversial (being a scientologist or being divorced), the more leeway employers have in investigating that individual. Critics worry that the pendulum of social control can swing too easily from commendable prevention to discriminatory repression. For these critics, the key concern is how worker autonomy, both in and outside of work, can be protected from the encroachment of managerial control.[10] For example, historically, expressing interest in joining a union or having political sympathies at odds with an employer's commercial interests, if exposed, were often offenses for which people could lose their jobs or even be physically beaten.

When and why an employer can scrutinize employees is often integrated into debates over the legality of *how* organizations seek to gather information about employees. When employers attempt to read workers' e-mail or to administer polygraphs or drug tests, justifications for how and when employers can pry into the actions of their employees emerge openly. For this reason, we explore issues of worker control primarily through examining one prominent historical debate over the social control of workplaces: whether organizations should be allowed to administer lie detector tests to employees. Employers used lie detector tests to examine the character and private thoughts of employees; in preemployment screening, in particular, lie detectors were sometimes used to scrutinize a prospective employee's personal life and traits. The debate over the polygraph raises several reasons why employers were considered to have the right to pry into the thoughts of employees, as well as the different objections to those attempts that led eventually to the strict regulation of polygraphs in preemployment screening.

Truth is a precious commodity. Sometimes it may also seem to be a rare commodity. Studies have indicated the difficulty of establishing whether a person is lying or telling the truth.[11] People have always attempted to create tests and to build devices that will reveal whether people are fibbing or can be trusted. Knowing "for sure" whether a person is lying is of considerable use in many spheres of life—from marriage to law enforcement to hiring situations. The polygraph, or lie detector test is a twentieth century American invention, used more widely in the United States than elsewhere, perhaps because of American faith in technology. Harvard Ph.D. (and the creator of the *Wonder Woman* comic strip) William M. Marston is credited with inventing the original machine and its label, "lie detector," during the first two decades of this century.[12] The original impetus for Marston's work was his interest in criminal apprehension and in counterespionage. In both areas, lie detectors remain in the arsenal of authorities.

The principle of lie detectors is simple, even when the machinery appears complex. The assumption is that when people lie, they are anxious, and the effects of anxiety can be measured physiologically: the pulse changes, hands sweat, and even the voice may sound different. The important, if obvious, point is that the machines do not measure *lying;* they measure bodily changes that are caused by anxiety, not by lying. In the past century, these machines have become more sophisticated, but the basic principle of measuring the physiological changes that anxiety produces has remained constant. Its success is aided enormously by a related factor that also creates anxiety—the examinee's belief that the machine works. As former president Richard Nixon noted, lie detectors "scare the hell out of people."[13]

An obvious weakness of the polygraph is that individuals can be anxious for many reasons, and some people can deceive without wavering. To cope with this problem, a lie detector operator doesn't merely ask the central, relevant questions and examine the measures based on your response; he or she compares responses to these questions to other, control questions. If you are investigated about a particular crime, you might be asked about whether you have ever lied, cheated on your taxes, or taken anything without permission. Many people lie in response to these questions, and this gives a base reading for your response when you feel secretly guilty. You might also be asked about a fictitious crime because a response that indicates dishonesty might simply be because you secretly believe that you are guilty of everything. The operator *compares* your answers with other answers that you have given.

While governmental agencies use lie detectors in criminal detection and in national security investigations, until recently they were widely used in another way: by companies as part of their hiring procedures and in determining whether workers should be fired. Significant differences exist between criminal and security investigations and employment tests. Some argue that national security is so important that even if innocent people are denied employment, every technique should be used to trap the guilty. In criminal investigations, detectives focus on whether a particular act did or did not occur. Polygraphs, on the other hand, do not predict whether an employee is "generally honest." Therefore, a person may be denied employment because of a history that is only marginally relevant—hence lie detectors are highly controversial in personnel testing and employee control.

During the 1980s, lie detection became increasingly popular in preemployment hiring decisions. Figures on the number of tests given vary, but estimates of tests in business ranged to over two million tests each year.[14] Three-quarters of those tests were used in preemployment screening, according to the American Polygraph Association,[15] often in an attempt to reduce internal thefts estimated to cost from $5 billion to $200 billion annually, with most estimates around $40 billion.[16] One recent study suggested that over 60 percent of all fast food workers confessed to stealing money or merchandise in the past six months.[17]

One wonders how accurate polygraphs are. This is not an easy question to answer. A lot depends on the qualifications of the tester, the type of machine, the kinds of questions asked, the conditions of stress, the amount of belief in the machines, and the proportion of truth tellers and liars being studied. One study indicates that most liars (about 80 percent) are caught by the machine, and some are not; most truth-tellers (about 60 percent) are exonerated, and some are not.[18] Is this good enough? It might be if you were an employer attempting to cut losses by avoiding taking risks in hiring; it might not be, if you were one of the honest 40 percent denied a job because of a machine. Is the lie detector a fire alarm that often goes off by mistake?

During the 1980s, reactions to lie detectors grew increasingly hostile, as their use by employers increased. In 1983, the Government's Office of Technology Assessment released a report that suggested that, while the polygraph was useful in criminal investigations, it was worthless for screening workers. By 1986, thirty-two states had laws restricting polygraph use.[19] Responding to this hostility, Congress, prodded by the unlikely coalition of conservative Utah senator Orrin Hatch and liberal Massachusetts senator Edward Kennedy, passed the 1988 Polygraph Protection Act. Former president Reagan signed this act, which sharply limited the use of lie detector tests in preemployment screening by employers involved in interstate commerce. As a consequence, the use of polygraphs for employment declined dramatically, although government employees and criminal suspects are still subject to them. Applicants no longer need fear these machines, but now need fear paper-and-pencil "honesty" tests, drug screening, and background checks. The use and decline of lie detectors among corporations offers a forum for considering some of the arguments used to justify or reject investigations into employees' private thoughts and actions in particular and exercises in workplace social control in general.

## The Libertarian Point of View

It would be nasty to suggest that libertarians like to lie, but something is profoundly liberating about lying. Lying is, after all, an act of free will—not letting facts, especially inconvenient ones, fetter you. One's own thoughts are, by rights, private, and that privacy should not be lightly invaded. The concern of employers should be whether a worker is good, diligent, and honest—we should judge behavior and not thoughts. Libertarians extol individual privacy as the key component of personal freedom. Any intrusions into privacy, particularly when government abetted, are to be opposed. The danger to individual privacy is evident in a set of questions that Coors Beer once asked their employees, including questions about their sexual behaviors ("Have you ever done anything with your wife that could be considered immoral?") and political attitudes ("Are you a Communist?"). Workers found these questions so objectionable that they went on strike.[20]

The libertarian believes deeply in a zone of personal privacy to which institutional forces should have no access. Even if this might mean that fewer "criminals" or dishonest people are caught, this would be worthwhile compared to imperiling an open society. The libertarian believes in the concept of "free minds." Institutional control is secondary to individual rights in the libertarian framework.

A second theme in the libertarian suspicion of polygraphs deserves note. These machines are "inhuman." Clearly, the machines are nonhuman, just as clearly the operator is "human." But is the process dehumanizing? Some writers think so and object to it, just as the Luddites in England in the early nineteenth century wished to destroy machines that threatened to change the nature of work. Law professor E. A. Jones put the argument dramatically:

> If the lie-detecting polygraph were indeed to be what it is *not*—a monument to technological infallibility—if it were a chrome-plated, flickery-lighted, superefficient computerized conduit of discovery, linked to the sweaty wrist and breath-gulping, heaving chest of an evasive, guilt-worried, fault-smothering, self-excusing human being, . . . I would still come down on the side of exclusion [from court evidence]. Each of us is too imperfect and fragile a creature to sustain such rigorous thrusts of suspicion and rejection into our being and yet maintain that sense of personal worth and higher purpose—and recurrent resolve to do better—which is indispensable to dignity and accomplishment. I think it is far preferable that a fellow human, concededly imperfect in the capacity to perceive calculated falsehood, be the assessor of credibility

than to achieve a mechanical perfection akin to Orwell's *1984* and Huxley's *Brave New World.*[21]

For Jones, and for those with a libertarian orientation, it may be preferable that the discovery of truth be an art, rather than a science. Certainty about truth implies total control over individuals.

Anecdotes about affronts to "honest" individuals are also part of this argument. Everyone can find someone who has been wrongly accused, and this adds piquancy to the attack on technology and corporate control. Consider the tragicomedy, sarcastically reported by attorney Irving Kaler of his son not being hired as a stockboy in the pet department in a local discount store:

> As a condition of his employment, Michael was subjected to a lie-detector test. After all, the pet department must be protected from unwittingly giving employment to a possible guppy snatcher or a goldfish filcher. But Michael, who is only 16 and who has never had any altercation with the law, became understandably agitated when asked questions such as how many times he had been married (none), and how many times he had been arrested. . . . Now, thanks to this incident, I almost feel as if I have joined the company of Ma Barker in the pantheon of wicked parents.[22]

In fairness, we should note that we have only Mr. Kaler's account of the sterling qualities of his son, and, further, a competent examiner would compare Michael's responses to questions about his marital status with questions that are more relevant, such as his treatment of his pets.

There is a dimension of personal responsibility that is also relevant here. When people agree to contracts in a free market for labor, they may agree knowingly to the monitoring conditions that they will experience. If, for example, people know in advance that their e-mail may be read without their knowledge, it is up to them to stay within the bounds of acceptable practices, or, if they object, to leave their employment. The libertarian objection is not to the right to apply polygraphs; their objection is to the potential abuse and involuntary application of such measures by social institutions. If people sign up willingly, as a condition of employment, to scrutiny of their private thoughts, they must reap what they sow. Similarly, employers have the right to set their own conditions for monitoring workers, and if workers agree to these techniques (and they are legal), then that arrangement is a voluntary contract. If people sign contracts with "private life" clauses, such as those governing an employee's "moral turpitude" or physical appearance, that is their business. Learning to read the fine print is a matter of personal responsibility. Libertarians have a problem with involuntary social control, but not when people accept such conditions voluntarily in a free market for labor.

# The Social Democratic Point of View

Social democrats object to polygraphs and other such instruments for different reasons. For them, a lie detector is a technique of management power—an unfair practice through which employers control employees. A worker's humanity is denied by these intrusions. Social democrats oppose intrusions into the private thoughts and history of workers—sometimes even to the point of appearing to let the inmates run the asylum.

Why do corporations use lie detectors? A key reason is to save money from employee theft. But often, as in employment screening, they are not catching those who have committed an offense, but screening those who are judged "likely" to commit an offense. The criteria of who is likely to commit an offense is fertile ground for employment discrimination. By eliminating all possible sources of trouble, good people are denied jobs.

The social democrat also is likely to emphasize the relative lack of validity of these machines. Not only can people discriminate, but also faulty technology can produce inequality. It is important not to overlook the fact that instruments used to scrutinize private lives, regardless of the justification for doing so, can simply be flawed. While we do not discuss the extent to which lie detectors are accurate, more innocent people are judged guilty than the reverse, and polygraph evaluation is less accurate in "real-world" settings than in laboratory studies.[23] Polygraphs are considered sufficiently suspect that the American Psychological Association prohibits members from administering tests.[24] Psychologist Leonard Saxe suggested that it is "shocking that such unreliable measures are being used to decide the fate of innocent people."[25] Senator Edward Kennedy termed them "twentieth-century witchcraft."[26] Often polygraphs are attacked because some people are highly anxious at having to take the test (or because their children are ill or they are going through a divorce); however, as noted, if a person's own responses are being compared to each other, this generalized anxiety should cancel itself out.

Besides debating when employers investigate the private lives of employees, *how* they do so is particularly salient to social democrats, since a faulty instrument may be used simply for an employer's convenience. Some social democrats charged, given their level of inaccuracy, that employers used polygraphs solely because they were easy and cheap to administer. They are a "quick fix" substituting for more careful background checks. As Montana Democratic congressman Pat Williams suggested, the popularity of lie detectors is because

> They're convenient. They save employers money that otherwise would have to be spent creating good personnel practices and a good personnel department. It's a lot easier to give five dozen employees a lie-detector test than to do a good personnel check on them. There's a line in a song by the Western singer named Tom T. Hall, "If you hang 'em all, you'll get the guilty." Unfortunately, some American businesses have found that it's cheaper to hang them all than it is to really seek out the guilty.[27]

Beyond this concern is the belief that employers can use lie detector tests to fire those workers who are honest but troublesome (such as being active in unions), refuse the sexual advances of their supervisors, or are members of minority groups. These machines are seen as a means of arbitrarily firing people. One former government employee noted, "if you don't have the right WASP profile and weren't born in a medically sealed bag which was opened just before the polygraph, you won't pass."[28] When private aspects of one's life make termination more likely, such as lacking the "right" profile, saying that someone failed the polygraph is simply easier than justifying in more depth potentially actionable and discriminatory reasons for dismissing the employee.

In some instances, lie detectors were used deliberately to fire workers whom management wanted fired. Consider this account from a former manager of a Southern department store chain:

> According to Blews, his district supervisor told him that blacks "just don't work out" and ordered him to dismiss two black women workers. Blews said that when he re- fused, the supervisor remarked, "We'll have to show you how our polygraph test works around here." The women were subsequently fired after their test results indi- cated "a sign of a possibility of deceit." His bosses also turned down the only two blacks whom he had ever recommended for management trainee positions, again on the basis of the polygraph test.[29]

There is evidence that blacks fail preemployment polygraph tests more often than whites. Critics of the test suggest that this is not because blacks are more likely to lie but because the races may react to stress differently. Failing a test can have long-term consequences if a new employer learns of old test results. It bothers the social democrat that the fired worker can only appeal with difficulty. After all, the company can claim that the firing was due only to the fact that the machine (or its operator) claimed that the worker was a thief. For the social democrat, this places too much power in the hands of private employers, and it is no wonder that social democrats were particularly pleased when Congress passed strict regulations banning routine use of the polygraph. People may still be fired for unwarranted reasons, but doing so will no longer be abetted or disguised by a flawed instrument of social control.

## The Conservative Point of View

Not all conservatives support using lie detectors. As noted, conservative Utah senator Orrin Hatch sponsored the bill that former president Reagan eventually signed, limiting lie detectors, and many successful companies have never used them. However, it is probably fair to suggest that conservatives are more sympathetic to the private use of lie detectors than are other groups. Remember that the conservative believes that human beings are naturally imperfect and that various forms of social control are justified as a result. They may be tempted to believe that "If you have nothing to hide, you have nothing to fear."[30] Conservatives are also likely to believe that employees can have character flaws that should be screened out and support polygraphs as a means for doing so.

The conservative (and the libertarian, too) believes that employers know their own best interests without direction from Congress.[31] If the technique were not effective, it wouldn't be used. The conservative notes that thefts from employers hurt profits and can bankrupt small businesses. Larry Talley, the vice president of Risk Management for Days Inns of America, reported that in 1976, the last year before his company used the polygraph, he lost more than $1 million from employee theft. Since instituting the polygraph in 1977, Days Inns lost no more than $115,000 each year. He noted further, "Especially in the hotel, day-care and nursing-home industry, companies have been sued for hiring people who later committed crimes against a guest or a patient or someone in their care. If used properly, polygraphs help screen out such people."[32] With large liability judgments, companies avoid taking chances on employees. Employers will attempt, and always have attempted, to judge the honesty of their employees. Why shouldn't they develop a relatively objective, unbiased, accurate test (the polygraph), rather than use an idiosyncratic interview that people can easily manipulate? The conservative suggests that polygraphers be licensed, and standards for examiners established, to make the tests better and fairer. A licensing standard may protect employers from liability suits and would increase the public confidence in the power of these machines to get the "truth."[33]

Ultimately, the conservative says, the lie detector can help to stem the tide of lawlessness and immorality. For example, one study found that one-third of all applicants lie about their job credentials.[34] These tests may reek to some of totalitarianism, but others find it a bracing breath of discipline. Consider the words of polygraphers R. J. Ferguson and A. L. Miller:

> Complacency and toleration, with respect to crime and moral conduct, is the deadliest of diseases. If a deadly disease is not checked, death results—in this case, the death of a nation. No matter how hard it is to accept, a democracy such as ours, like less libertarian systems, cannot grant all freedoms to individuals and leave none for itself to use in the interest of its own preservation.[35]

Conservatives are willing to give up some freedoms that the libertarian prizes, for their own prize of social order. The lie detector is but one tool in this effort.

## Social Control and Social Research

Do you know any college students who hide their on-campus behaviors from their parents? People who cheat on their boyfriends or girlfriends? Someone who pretends to be better off financially than he or she actually is? Someone who lies about what he or she really does at work? People's private lives can contain some amount of *dirty data*, or secret information, which, if revealed, discredits them and brings about various punishments.[36] Impression management theories assume that individuals control, to whatever extent possible, the information that they reveal about themselves. It makes perfect sense that people work hard to keep their secrets off-limits, particularly when they have something to hide. Of course, one person's concealed dirty data is another person's

buried treasure; identifying an individual's secrets is not just a busybody's guilty pleasure or a task for law enforcement, but can also be a business enterprise. Betrayed
spouses, worried parents, and victimized employers pay private detectives handsomely
to gather other people's dirty data. How do private detectives do this work? What is
their work like? What ethics accompany a job investigating people's private lives?

David Shulman (the coauthor of this book) has researched the investigative
methods and ethics of private detective work.[37] Shulman was drawn initially to studying private detectives to learn how they managed deceptive subjects. Shulman believed
that social science research has some parallels to private detective work. Both interview
informants, gather paper records, and observe people with and without their knowledge
in order to construct accounts of people's real attitudes and behaviors. Private detectives, given that many of their subjects are involuntary participants in their "research"
and have something to hide, must worry about people's honesty more than social scientists do. As a consequence, private detectives use research techniques designed to
thwart people's attempts to mislead them. Shulman felt that social scientists might benefit from learning about those techniques.

Shulman's concern with respondent honesty was also an immediate one. When a
private detective told him during an interview "that if bullshit was music, I'd be the
philharmonic," he worried about whether he was in the midst of some "virtuoso" per-
formances. To gather his data, Shulman pursued a qualitative approach. He interviewed
private detectives and observed them conducting investigations. He participated in a
training program at a private detective agency to witness how new operatives were
taught the investigative ropes, and he also reviewed case files and field reports. His
strategy of combining case files, interviews, and observation was intended to *triangu-
late* information—not only because the more data the better, but also because different
sources of information help researchers avoid being misled. By combining information
from different interviews, reviewing files, observing detectives at work, and comparing
depictions from his respondents to published scholarship on private detectives,
Shulman could cross-check his data against different sources.

It is also useful to ask whether Shulman, or other ethnographers, should go further to validate the information that their informants provide. Private detectives and social science researchers play by different ethical rules. It is unlikely, for example, that a
social scientist would be allowed (if he or she wanted) to polygraph interviewees to
check whether they made false claims during their interviews. Are researchers required
unnecessarily to be gullible when they doubt an informant's honesty? Does etiquette
require accepting people's representations at face value, even at the price of diminished
accuracy? Conversely, what should social scientists be willing to do to guarantee veri-
fied information? Should researchers go as far as private detectives? Would you conduct covert surveillance to see if someone is working as hard as they claim? Where
should researchers draw the line to acquire accurate information?

People clearly have many motives for trying to control what impressions other
people have about them. Yet, we may not be fully aware of how many methods exist
that circumvent our control over our own personal information, allowing others to learn

the secrets that we hide about ourselves. Private detectives are keenly aware of the *performance vulnerabilities* people have, of the social actions individuals take that expose or leak hidden information. Some examples include private detectives tapping inevitable byproducts of dirty data, such as drug paraphernalia, mandatory paperwork (credit reports and income tax returns), or people's carelessness in being visibly intoxicated or falling for an agent's fake undercover identity. Private detectives' strategies reflect a practical knowledge of how performance vulnerabilities are distributed socially, which informs their investigative techniques. For example, do you think about whether you are throwing away embarrassing or incriminating information? One respondent, to his regret, did not, as this private detective recounted:

> In one instance, we literally ended up with a credit report on someone. They had requested a copy of their credit report and then discarded it in the trash. . . . Just threw it in the garbage and it went out on the curb and we're going through the dumpster and oh well, well, look at this. And considering it was one of these situations where it was a divorce case, the husband was pleading . . . the wife wanted certain things and certain amounts of money and property, and he was saying, "I don't have that kind of money," he was hiding assets and of course here along with his credit report is also a bank statement which in part lists a couple of accounts which he's denying exist. And he knows that there are people looking into this because it's being contested and it's a long, drawn out very bloody divorce. He knows that people are looking and he throws this out full in the trash. It never occurred to him that somebody might pick up his garbage and go through it.[38]

Because private detectives use deceptive methods that scrutinize people without their knowledge or consent, their investigative techniques raise ethical questions. People might be naïve (or stupid) enough to make incriminating evidence available; that does not mean that the professionals who go looking for it lack accountability. Or does it? Popular culture's image of private detective work is often of deductive geniuses (Sherlock Holmes) and jaded heroes (Sam Spade, Phillip Marlowe). However negative portrayals of real detectives also exist, which cast them as agent provocateurs, union busters and wiretappers for big business. This nasty image, for example, persists in today's action films, where all corporations (who invariably are up to no good) have an evil private security staff that exists solely to commit felonies and attempt murder.

Private detectives are certainly aware of the different ways that people can perceive them, in terms of the methods they use and the clients for whom they work. One investigator, complaining of being perceived as "someone who will do anything for a buck," commented:

> I was trying to solve a murder case on one particular assignment and another particular assignment, I was trying to get a guy off on an armed robbery beef. I'm the prosecuting team one day, and on the defense team the other day . . . because I mean guys who are friends of mine are in bars, you know they're going, are you on a good assignment now or are you on a bad assignment now? And that's why people don't trust private eyes. It's not who pays you more; it's who pays you first.[39]

What legitimates prying into people's privacy? Shulman explored the accounts that private detectives give to justify the controversial job of investigating people's private lives. Accounts are "stories and narratives" that reconcile peoples' "untoward" behavior with social expectations.[40] Shulman found that private detectives stressed three different thematic accounts to justify their investigative work: *means/ends* justifications, *technical-legal* justifications and an *ethic of neutrality*. While a private detective might hold more than one of these views, each represents a distinct way to justify private detective work.

Private detectives who use means/ends justifications depict themselves as instruments of justice who combat criminals. Targets of investigation commit serious transgressions (adultery, drug dealing or use, insurance fraud, or stealing) that must be punished. An employee who commits a crime deserves being exposed, just as do criminals in the streets. One private detective, when asked about how he felt during a recent undercover operation, replied:

> It didn't bother me when I did it. . . . Hey those people are dealing drugs on the workforce! You have people working cranes; you have people working on big machines. If they're there under the influence of any type of drugs or alcohol, you know they shouldn't be there. You know, you're out there for the safety of the people.[41]

Shulman believed that this view emerges from private detectives thinking of themselves as quasi-public law enforcement agents. Thus, invading a person's privacy is justified when acting against behaviors that threaten or harm people. Since many private detectives were in public law enforcement before becoming private detectives, this justification for investigative work is comfortable and familiar. These private detectives also favor working cases with clear criminal targets. One private detective, who moved from an agency specializing in investigations of adultery to one specializing in recovering fugitives, compared his old job unfavorably:

> Here we specialize in surety recovery work, bail theft investigation and prevention. I am much more satisfied and comfortable in doing that kind of work. These are people that are facing. . . . they've been charged with a crime, a serious crime in most instances, and have fled from lawful prosecution.[42]

A private detective once described the necessity of lying in investigations, saying, "If you call someone up and say, 'Hi, would you mind telling me where your brother is, so that I can put his ass in jail for the next five years,' you won't last too long in the private detective business."[43] While people may dislike lying in the abstract, acting deceptively to catch someone who ought to be in jail, as a concrete example, is justifiable to private detectives (and probably to many of this book's readers).

Alternatively, private detectives who use technical-legal justifications, focus solely on whether a given investigative technique is legal. *When and who* a technique is applied to is a less relevant consideration. In this view, there are no *moral issues* involved in investigating people's private lives as long as legal techniques are applied to do so. That a technique is legal presupposes its morality; the issue then becomes staying within the bounds of the law when performing investigations. Anything legal goes, anything illegal does not. As one investigator commented, "I will do my best to avoid breaking the law. I may get right to the edge of it, but I try to stay away from that. It's not so much morally; it's my fear of being locked up. Other than that, I will do almost anything and everything I can to get the job done."[14]

In *ethic of neutrality* accounts, investigators stress the professional, dispassionate conduct of their work. Private detectives are trained, have expertise, and are state-licensed—professional qualifications that should make them neutral and should prevent unethical investigations. From this standpoint, using investigative techniques is justified; a professional's detachment assures that subjects who are behaving faultlessly will be exonerated, and that anybody who is guilty will be detected. Whether investigative techniques themselves ought to be used, or even if they are unpleasant or harmful to experience, is a nonissue.

Consider, for example, this private detective's description of his work on an insurance investigation:

> There are certain riders in policies. I had a case I worked on in (names a state). A woman was killed as a result of an auto accident, a roll-over. . . . She recently applied for a policy but the policy has a smoker rider in it. So, I'm up there investigating, interviewing the beneficiary which is her husband, asking questions, did she smoke or not? The guy is kind of freaked out. "Why are you asking this kind of stuff? My wife died in an auto accident." "Yes, yes, I know." These are very touchy and sensitive cases and I've had people break down and cry on them. The idea is that the woman was found to be a smoker during that contestable period; do you know they don't have to pay off the full death benefit? They'll refund the premiums paid to date. They're cold-blooded; they don't care.

Here professionals are simply neutral conduits of information. If the ends the information serves are "cold-blooded," that label describes the client, not the investigator. Of course, there are exceptions to this rule. For example, private detectives will often examine why someone wants to locate a missing person. Would the private detective end up helping to violate a restraining order (that explains why the person is difficult to locate)? Does the client appear to be mentally unbalanced, such as a celebrity stalker?

Some professionals earn a good living by transcending people's efforts to hide their private activities. In as much as we worry about contemporary surveillance technologies and professionals, like private detectives, who can make society too transparent, we must also recognize that there are good reasons to collect dirty data (and for private detectives to have work). Individuals make contractual commitments to other people that require honesty, from subjects in research studies who are assumed to volunteer truthfulness if participating, to employees who guarantee their loyalty to employers. If private detective work constitutes social control, underlying that social control is suspicion of an initial breach of trust. Don't employers and spouses have the right to know if they are being cheated?

# Work and Organizational Control

Most workers do not have the luxury of being their own boss; control is part of a hierarchical workplace. As anyone who has been their own boss can attest, hierarchy is not always bad. It is nice to know from where one's next check is coming. Yet, our bosses have expectations of us and may attempt to manipulate us in ways that are in their interest, but not ours. What concerns do the classic sociological theories raise about workplace social control?

Functionalists and conflict theorists disagree about the utility of the hierarchical control of workers that is so characteristic of today's capitalistic enterprises. The functionalist points to the enviable success of Western capitalistic economies. The factory system, for example, is an orderly, efficient system, which when coupled with vigorous collective bargaining, can preserve basic rights of workers. Workers are not slaves, but they do need to be directed. Without control of labor costs, goods would be too expensive for consumers, and, eventually, workers would be unemployed. Managers are, from this perspective, necessary for the successful use of labor—as is securing the "right" kind of workers.

Conflict theorists have a different view. They note that the accident of birth has a considerable influence on whether you will be giving or taking orders throughout your work life. They agree that capitalistic enterprises often make a profit—but for whom and on whose shoulders? Is it fair that some, with access to capital, should control the destiny of others, particularly when those with access to capital do not engage in productive labor themselves? They invest, instead of working. Some workers find their humanity demeaned by the desire of bosses to make a profit—through working long hours, being exposed to unsanitary working conditions, or having to submit to lie detectors and other identity investigations. Control of workers is where capital does great damage to the human condition.

Interactionists note that the relationship between management and labor is not fixed. In fact, it is always negotiated in practice. The precise amount of time workers have off, their opportunities for conversation, and their personal autonomy result from local, situational conditions. This, of course, downplays the conflict argument that the negotiating groups may have quite different amounts of power. Interactionists have tended to ignore the conditions of the economy that lead to these decisions, but recently interactionists have argued that the structure of the economy has "interactional" effects because managers and workers assume *images* or *symbolic meaning* of the economy and organizational structure in their interactions.

# *Questions*

1. What aspects of someone's personal life should employers be allowed to know? Should employers be told if someone has a past drug addiction or if he or she is being treated with antidepressants?

2. Should employers be able to deny employment because of obesity, smoking, sexual orientation, and controversial political beliefs?

3. Are the benefits of bureaucracy worth the risks they pose to individual autonomy and choice?

4. Should employers be allowed to read e-mail and track employees' Internet use without employee consent?

5. Should lie detectors be used to screen applicants for employment?

6. Should the federal government prevent the use of lie detectors to screen applicants for employment?

7. If your professor found a final exam stolen, should students in the class be given a polygraph test?

8. Are private investigators providing a legitimate service for society? Would this be a career in which you would be interested?

9. What might a private investigator discover about you that you wouldn't want your parents to know?

10. If a lie detector could be made perfectly accurate, when should it be used?

## For Further Study

Abbott, Andrew. *The System of Professions.* Chicago: University of Chicago Press, 1988.

Ekman, Paul. *Telling Lies: Clues to Deceit in the Marketplace, Politics, and Marriage.* New York: Norton, 1985.

Jackall, Robert. *Moral Mazes: The World of Corporate Managers.* New York: Cambridge University Press, 1985.

Lykken, David. *A Tremor in the Blood.* New York: McGraw-Hill, 1981.

Martin, Joanne. *Cultures in Organizations.* New York: Oxford University Press, 1992.

Nippert-Eng, Christena. *Home and Work: Negotiating Boundaries Through Everyday Life.* Chicago: University of Chicago Press, 1996.

Perrow, Charles. *Complex Organizations: A Critical Essay.* New York: Random House, 1986.

Shulman, David. "Professionals' Accounts for Work-Related Deceptions." *Symbolic Interaction* 23 (2000): 259–281.

Smith, Vicki. *Managing in the Corporate Interest: Control and Resistance in an American Bank.* Berkeley: University of California Press, 1990.

Strauss, Anselm. *Negotiations.* San Francisco: Jossey-Bass, 1978.

## Notes and References

1. Everett C. Hughes, "Work and Self" in Everett C. Hughes, ed., *The Sociological Eye* (Chicago: Aldine, 1971), pp. 338–347.

2. For discussions of the meaning of the concept of professionalism, see Ernest Greenwood, "Attributes of a Profession," *Social Work* 2 (July 1957): 45–55; Julius Roth, "Professionalism: The Sociologist's Decoy," *Sociology of Work and Occupations* 1 (1974): 6–51.

3. See Andrew Abbott, *The System of Professions*. Chicago: University of Chicago Press, 1988.

4. Emile Durkheim, *The Division of Labor in Society* (New York: Macmillan, 1933).

5. Max Weber, *From Max Weber: Essays in Sociology*, Hans Gerth and C. Wright Mills, trans. and eds. (1919, reprint, New York: Oxford University Press, 1946).

6. Anselm Strauss, *Negotiations* (San Francisco: Jossey-Bass, 1978).

7. Arlie Hoschilds, *The Managed Heart* (Berkeley, CA: University of California Press, 1976).

8. Cited in Laura Pincus Hartman, "The Rights and Wrongs of Workplace Snooping," *Journal of Business Strategy* 19 (May–June 1998): 16.

9. Cited in Todd Raphael, "Does HR Want to Be A Digital Snoop?" *Workforce* 80 (2001): 96.

10. For a recent review of such arguments in organizational theory, see S. Ackroyd and P. Thompson, *Organizational Misbehavior*. (London: Sage, 1999).

11. Paul Ekman, *Telling Lies: Clues to Deceit in the Marketplace, Politics, and Marriage.*

12. Clarence D. Lee, *The Instrumental Detection of Deception: The Lie Test* (Springfield, IL: Charles C. Thomas, 1953), pp. 11–14.

13. Daniel Jussim, "Lies, Damn Lies—and Polygraphs," *Nation* 214 (December 21, 1985): 683.

14. Guy Halverson, "'Honesty Tests' Replace Lie Tests in Job Screening," *Christian Science Monitor*, December 22, 1988, p. 10.

15. Ibid., p. 665.

16. K. R. Murphy, *Honesty in the Workplace*, (Pacific Grove, CA: Brooks/Cole 1993).

17. K. B. Slora, "An Empirical Approach to Determining Employee Deviance Base Rates." Pp. 21–38 in J. W. Jones (ed.), *Pre-Employment Honesty Testing: Current Research and Future Directions* (New York: Quorum Books, 1991).

18. "Lie Detectors Can Make a Liar of You," *Discover* 7 (June 1986): 7.

19. Constance Holden, "Days May Be Numbered for Polygraphs in the Private Sector," *Science* 232 (May 9, 1986): 705.

20. Jussim, "Lies, Damn Lies—and Polygraphs," p. 682.

21. Ibid., p. 39.

22. Irving K. Kaler, "A Mole Among the Gerbils?" *Newsweek* 105, March 11, 1985, p. 14.

23. Holden, "Days May Be Numbered for Polygraphs in the Private Sector," p. 705.

24. Stephen Dujack, "Polygraph Fever," *The New Republic* 195 (August 4, 1986): 10.

25. Donna Demac, "Sworn to Silence," *The Progressive* 51 (May 1987): 32.

26. "Lie-Detectors: Bearers of False Witness," *The Economist* (March 12, 1988): 31.

27. "Bar Lie-Detector Use by Private Firms?" *U.S. News & World Report* 100, February 3, 1986, p. 81.

28. Demac, "Sworn to Silence," p. 32.

29. Jussim, "Lies, Damn Lies—and Polygraphs," p. 682.

30. Lykken, "A Tremor in the Blood," p. 40.

31. "Lying in Congress," *Fortune* 116, December 7, 1987, p. 186.

32. "Bar Lie-Detector Use by Private Firms?" p. 81.

33. Jussim, "Lies, Damn Lies—and Polygraphs," p. 684.

34. Halverson, "'Honesty Tests' Replace Lie Tests in Job Screening."

35. Lykken, "A Tremor in the Blood," p. 38.

36. Gary T. Marx, "Notes on the Discovery, Collection, and Assessment of Hidden and Dirty Data." Pp. 78–113 in Joseph W. Schneider and John Kitsuse (eds.), *Studies in the Sociology of Social Problems* (Norwood, NJ: Ablex, 1990).

37. Most recently in David Shulman, "Professionals' Accounts for Work-Related Deceptions," *Symbolic Interaction* 23 (2000): 259–281.

38. Shulman, "Professionals' Accounts," p. 271.
39. Shulman, "Professionals' Accounts," p. 265.
40. See Marvin Scott and Stanford Lyman, "Accounts," *American Sociological Review* 33 (1968): 46–62.
41. Shulman, "Professionals' Accounts," p. 266.
42. Shulman, "Professionals' Accounts," p. 267.
43. Shulman, "Professionals' Accounts," p. 259.
44. Shulman, "Professionals' Accounts," p. 270.

# CHAPTER ELEVEN

# Health:
# Are Americans Too Fat?

■ People are often taught, in forming opinions of others, that "looks aren't everything" and that "beauty is only skin-deep." We are supposed to evaluate people by the content of their character and not by the shape of their body. Baloney! The evidence of our own eyes contradicts this lesson. Cars sport "no fat chicks" bumper stickers and children are sent to summer "fat camps." People live in dread that family and friends will notice and comment on a recent weight gain. Corporations pay higher salaries to thinner men than to overweight ones.[1] Americans spend more than $33 billion a year on weight loss programs, diet aids, and low calorie foods.[2] The presence of eating disorders, such as anorexia and bulimia, rising numbers of liposuctions, and surgical stapling of stomachs illustrate an even more dramatic and relentless pursuit of thinness. Despite what we are taught, are people really only as good as they look?

Many have noted the symbolism—the stereotyping—that people in U.S. society apply to the overweight. In our society, the overweight are often viewed as lacking self-control and willpower, and as being physically unattractive, unhealthy, and weak. Life-long pressure to avoid gaining weight and the negative treatment that people encounter when they are overweight have been described as the "tyranny of slenderness."[3] The World Health Organization defines health as a "state of complete physical, mental and social well-being."[4] Is being overweight actually "unhealthy," that is, incompatible with a person's physical, mental, and social well-being?

Sociologists know that what people perceive as healthful or harmful depends on numerous factors, many of which are not strictly speaking, medical.[5] Consider that a patient in a U.S. hospital will hear a doctor blame germs for a patient's illness, while in a remote Mexican village, a *brujo* (witch doctor) may hold a magical curse responsible. Though illness indisputably can have biological components—no one denies that prolonged oxygen-deprivation and severe blood loss are grave medical emergencies—our cultural background also influences our perceptions of health and illness. To denigrate overweight people in U.S. society as "unhealthy" contrasts, for example, with the fact that some cultures have historically viewed being fat as desirable, such as in the paintings of the seventeenth-century Flemish painter Peter Paul Rubens. Being fat was associated with power and wealth in men, since they could afford to indulge in excess consumption. Heavier women, who now confront a radically thin vision of female beauty, were, in turn, once perceived as having the most sexually attractive body type.[6] Take that, Kate Moss!

People also have long associated what is "healthy" with what they define as morally good and what is "unhealthy" with what they define as morally improper. Some religious conservatives asserted that AIDS is God's punishment for homosexual promiscuity, applying a vision of religious morality to explain disease and to classify "healthy" and "unhealthy" lifestyles. Cultural interpretations of what is "healthy" also change over time, as do society's techniques for healing the sick. America's first president, George Washington, died in part because to treat a severe cold, his doctors drained most of his blood, and barbers, not doctors, once performed surgeries.[7] Children received medical checkups from chain-smoking doctors, who might also urge their mothers to start smoking in order to lose weight, actions unimaginable today.

Beyond examining how different cultural and moral lenses affect how people think about health, sociologists also study *social epidemiology*, which refers to identifying how health and disease are distributed throughout a society. According to epidemiological research, Americans are now heavier than ever before. Body Mass Index, or BMI, is a mathematical calculation used to determine whether a person is overweight. The BMI is obtained by dividing a person's body weight in kilograms by their height in meters squared. Presently, 55 percent of all adult Americans—97 million people—are classified as being overweight. People who are severely overweight, who weigh at least 20 percent more than what their weight should be proportionate to their height, are classified as "obese." Twenty-five percent of Americans are now obese, with the highest rates among African Americans, Hispanic Americans, women, and the poor.[8]

To understand how and why illnesses spread, and to explain patterns in who gets sick and with what diseases, epidemiologists look to social factors such as culture, economy, geography, gender, race, and technology. Sociologists, like epidemiologists, analyze how societies are organized in order to explain patterns of health and illness. For example, that Americans en masse are heavier than in the past shows the immense agricultural, scientific, and technological success of the past century. Instead of failing to produce enough to eat, we have generated a vast array of foods, made the distribution of high-fat diets more available to consumers, created labor-saving technology, and seen the widespread use of automobiles.[9] These societal innovations have helped make mass obesity possible. Providing abundant food, ironically, can clash with other needs of a society, such as optimizing personal health and physical fitness. Dan Glickman, the U.S. secretary of agriculture in the Clinton administration, in discussing the health risks associated with obesity, stated, perhaps with some irony, that "the simple fact is that more people die in the United States of too much food than of too little."[10]

There are also cultural and ethnic traditions that strongly encourage children to eat, as stereotypes of plate-filling Italian and Jewish mothers illustrate. Television encourages us to be sedentary, advertisers whet our appetites, and fast food and snack food businesses tempt us with cheap, convenient, and "supersized" portions. Businesses, insurers, politicians, and public health officials are now debating taxing high-fat foods. So although being overweight refers to an individual's biological condition, it is also a social phenomenon, through which sociologists can explore commercial, cultural, medical, and political dimensions of U.S. society.

The interactionist, conflict, and functionalist perspectives offer different ways to think about health in general, and weight in particular, as sociological issues. Interactionists explore the nature and variety of cultural definitions for what being "healthy," "sick," "fat," or "thin" are. They note that there are no inherent, universal cultural meanings or labels associated with either being overweight or thin. People's physical appearance constitutes a master status, an individual characteristic that other people emphasize in deciding how to interact with them.[11]

Who defines what an obese or normal weight is? Could we ask, for example, whether Americans are "too thin" rather than "too fat"? Some sociologists are concerned by the power of health and medicine as social institutions. Medical professionals are now exerting influence over many areas of life that were formerly handled by families, courts, churches, and other social institutions. For example, a child that was once labeled unfocused and unruly is now given a medical diagnosis, such as hyperkinesis or attention deficit disorder, and treated with medications. Referred to as the *medicalization of deviance*,[12] this phenomenon is relevant to weight—should a person's size be judged by medical professionals, such as nutritionists, psychologists, and physicians? Is there really one "right" size for one's health? The act of judging what a person should "ideally" weigh reveals a connection between individual autonomy and social institutions, such as the health care system, which claim expertise and jurisdiction to label someone "too fat."

Conflict-theory-oriented sociologists examine the connection between health and social inequality, researching how a person's health benefits or suffers under particular economic and social arrangements. They investigate issues, such as the cost of prescription drugs, unequal access to health care, the medical consequences of hazardous workplace conditions, and the impact of business practices that promote or lessen health, such as health clubs or tobacco advertising. A conflict theorist, for example, might examine obesity levels in the population in relation to the marketplace. For businesses that profit from getting people to consume as much food as possible—such as fast food, snack, soft drink, and diet food producers—obese people are desired customers. It is no coincidence that Coca-Cola, Hershey, Kraft, and Slim Fast Foods helped sponsor the recent Annual Conference of the North American Association for the Study of Obesity.[13] There are profits in pounds, ranging from selling consumers more food to getting them to buy weight-loss products.

Functionalists examine how different social institutions act in unison to fulfill social needs. A critically important societal function is to optimize and preserve individual health. Although an enhanced ability to treat medical emergencies is the most vivid demonstration of modern medicine, a major functional role of the health care system is preventative, based on providing people with behavioral guidelines that help them manage ongoing illnesses and prevent future medical problems. Health professionals often propose dietary rules and suggest standards for what people should weigh in order to meet this goal. Diet, in relation to a person's weight and health, connects medical professionals with the regulation of an individual's daily behaviors. The desire to curb obesity must be measured against the right people have to decide what and how much they want to eat and weigh.

Just as the weight of Americans is changing at an unprecedented rate, the institution of health care in the United States has also undergone a dramatic transformation. We have seen a change in the past forty years from doctors who were basically solo practitioners—family doctors—to the situation today in which it is more common for doctors to be affiliated with hospitals, clinics, health maintenance organizations, or group practices. Whereas patients used to pay their doctors directly, today this is rare. Even though, unlike many industrialized nations, we do not have socialized medicine, we do not have a free market in medicine either. Most bills are paid by third parties— government, health plans, insurance plans. You may well have no idea how much your last medical encounter cost, and, had you known, you might have become sickened. When the first author's son was hospitalized for two months, it might have cost the family two years' worth of salary, which fortunately they did not have to pay.

What is referred to as the "crisis of health care" is really a set of several economic crises. How do we contain costs, make sure that everyone's health insurance is covered, protect doctors from court settlements arising from "honest" mistakes, shield patients from incompetent doctors, and see that medical care is distributed fairly? The bitter debates in Congress over health care and proposed changes to Medicare reveal how complex and controversial any government-mandated changes in health care are, and also the extent to which the costs of medical care affect us all.

## ▪ Question:

*Are Americans too fat?*

> *A high school guidance counselor once turned to an overweight*
> *student and announced, "I'd rather be dead than look like you."*
> —National Education Association, "Report on Size Discrimination"

Does society have the right to dictate how people should act toward and regard their own bodies? On what basis should we insist that individuals follow health-related advice that other people create and claim is in their best interest to obey? Is it reasonable to insist that people who are "too fat" have a disagreeable appearance or lack self-control and that they must change in order to become more socially acceptable? In addressing the question, Are Americans too fat? we must consider the issue of what being "too fat" means and explore the social construction of being overweight as a public problem.

How a problem is defined sets the tone for how people think about the problem. If you view being "too fat" as a medical diagnosis, then you might adopt a therapeutic orientation and language, and argue that obesity is a health problem to eradicate, like cancer or diabetes. If you view being "too fat" as an aesthetic matter, equating being fat with being morally flawed, then deciding that Americans are too fat is a value judgment. Here we examine the question of whether Americans are too fat from different viewpoints—the medical one, as a potential issue for government action, and the aesthetic one, as a question of cultural values.

If one examines the question from a medical perspective, to be overweight is to be unhealthy, and to be obese is to invite an early death. Doctors argue that obesity causes at least 300,000 excess deaths a year in the United States and that obesity is a leading cause of unnecessary death.[14] William Dietz, the director of nutrition at the Centers for Disease Control, stated, "Obesity is an epidemic in the U.S., the likes of which we have not had before in chronic disease."[15] Twenty-five percent of all Americans under nineteen are obese or at risk for obesity.[16]

Imagine if 25 percent of all children—millions and millions of kids—contracted an illness that was commonly recognized as a chronic and degenerative disease, such as multiple sclerosis—there would be dramatic and widespread calls to action to address the problem. To many doctors, obesity is a rampant, serious, and degenerative illness, a medical time bomb that is chipping away at millions of people's health. To heal and preserve health is a moral imperative. Curbing medical costs is also important, and the estimated costs to the public health budget of treating obesity's medical consequences will "by 2020, run into the hundreds of billions, making HIV look, economically, like a bad case of the flu."[17] From a health-oriented perspective, Americans are too fat for their own and the general public's good, and to stem the tide of obesity, social institutions, led by government, must act.

Of course, people often engage in risky behaviors, such as drinking and smoking, which few, even tobacco companies today, deny have adverse health consequences. Overeating may cause health problems—but people seem to choose to do so. We have all seen obese people consume staggering amounts of food without anyone forcing them. How does the view that obese people bring their condition upon themselves complicate a health-oriented entreaty that Americans are too fat?

Sociologists often emphasize the "agency" that individuals have, claiming that people have the power (the agency) to bring about their own destinies. This agency is not absolute, as we know, also, that social institutions play an important role in determining people's fates. This debate over the balance between personal agency and institutional structures is relevant to exploring the responses that people have as to whether Americans are too fat. Arguing for limiting public involvement is easier when you view individuals as ultimately deciding to overeat. This view suggests the responsibility and solution to obesity involves individuals. People are less sympathetic when they think that an illness is caused by the affected individual's irresponsible behavior, such as drug-related illnesses, lung cancer, and sexually transmitted diseases. Why should society devote resources to solve a problem that people can control on their own?

Consider different reactions to this journalistic account of a medical crisis facing a morbidly obese man:

> Here in the ghastly white light of modern American medicine, writhed a real-life epidemiological specter: a 500 pound twenty year old. The man whom I'll call Carl, was

propped up at a 45 degree angle, the better to be fed air through a tube, and lay there nude, save for a small patch of blood spotted gauze stuck to his lower abdomen, where surgeons had just labored to save his life. His eyes darted about in abject fear. "Second time in three months," his mother blurted out to me, as she stood watching in horror. "He had two stomach staplings, and they both came apart. Oh my God, my boy. . . ." Her boy was suffocating in his own fat.[18]

This distressing account can simultaneously evoke both sympathy and revulsion. Perhaps we wish Carl well and feel sympathy for him and his mother; but we might also hold Carl responsible for his predicament and resent that our medical resources are expended on him because he can't eat responsibly. If people do not view obesity as an illness, perhaps one with a genetic origin, and instead perceive obesity as an individual choice, then they might think that tax dollars should not go to combat regrettable outcomes of personal irresponsibility.

Alternatively, what if we view individuals' obesity as strongly influenced by the actions of social institutions, such as schools, advertising, cultural values, even people's ethnic and racial affiliation, and wealth? James Hill, an epidemiologist from the University of Colorado, claimed that "being obese is a normal response to the American environment."[19] How do we explain and act toward obesity if we consider being overweight as not an individual problem, but created by social factors?

If the obese lack self-control, obesity might also be a racially or ethnically blind phenomenon, such that the chance of being obese is equal for men and women of all races and ethnic origins, if we assume that all groups have equal self-control. Is obesity an equal opportunity offender? Alternatively, we might think that being overweight is associated with affluence, since richer people can afford to eat more than poorer people. If we agree with either claim, we are in error. Obesity in the United States is strongly correlated with being poor and with being an ethnic and racial minority. As journalist Richard Klein noted, "You get fatter in this country as you get poorer, thinner as you get richer . . . what you weigh it turns out, has as much to do with what's in your pocket as what's in your food."[20] Regarding racial and ethnic variations in weight, historian Peter Stearns noted:

> The United States is a very segmented society when it comes to eating and diet goals. If a melting pot in some respects, in matters of body shape, the ingredients most definitely have not yet melted. . . . African Americans and Hispanic Americans are much more likely to be overweight than are whites or Asians and, as we have seen in the case of African Americans, the rates of increase have been greater as well.[21]

Addressing whether Americans are too fat also means identifying which Americans are "too fat" and why. If obesity occurs in patterns, then it may be reasonable to infer that heavier populations are exposed to influences that predispose them to obesity more than other groups. Sociologists explore broad patterns in what happens to people, such as why some types of people are discriminated against more than others, some populations achieve college degrees in the greater numbers, or in this case, why some groups are more likely to be obese than others.

Analysts "explain getting fatter as you get poorer and thinner as you get richer" in several ways. Excluding the unproven and unpleasant claim that some populations have more or less willpower, predisposing factors include limited access to physical facilities; commercial targeting of high-fat, inexpensive foods to minorities and the poor; inadequate education about obesity's medical risks and nutrition; and cultural values that view weight management and body types differently.

Examining the distribution of obesity with these factors in mind underlies the perspective that social institutions can legitimately intervene to combat obesity. In other words, if one claims that Americans are too fat because existing social conditions help to make them that way, then individual actions alone will not reduce obesity levels. For example, one could argue that schools should integrate nutritional lessons, provide low-fat meals, and introduce mandatory physical fitness programs for students.

Although health concerns are one reason for considering Americans too fat, cultural standards also underlie this conclusion. Certainly, the verdict of popular culture is incontestably that "one can never be too thin." For example, only 10 percent of the people portrayed on American television are overweight while 55 percent of actual Americans are.[22] If they are even present, consider how overweight people are depicted in magazines, movies, and television. Weight-related stories in magazines emphasize triumphant accounts of celebrity weight loss and inventories of dieting strategies. Movies and television cast heavy people primarily as comic relief, villains, nonentities, and objects of pity or disdain. *Baywatch*, once the world's most-watched television program, didn't exhibit obese lifeguards in Speedos rescuing swimmers. Whether right or wrong, American culture promotes some physical appearances and censors and scorns others. At present, mass culture depicts a world that is unremittingly hostile to "fat" people. With few and partial exceptions ("Roseanne"), anyone who is overweight is unattractive, and by that measure, anyone who is remotely heavy is "too fat." Thus, we followed Oprah's various attempts to get her weight "under control." Oprah, not to the contrary, some have speculated that minority populations are heavier because they are less influenced by existing cultural pressures to be thin than white women are.[23] According to one analyst, what some obese populations may actually need, such as African American women (44 percent of whom are obese), are "a few more Black Kate Mosses."[24] And, in this sense, as well as others, Oprah, although no Kate Moss, is a role model.

One must be wary of popular culture promoting ideal models of thinness. There is some evidence that eating disorders, depression, and steroid abuse can result from attempts to realize unrealistic images of a "desirable" appearance. In what one might call the "*Beverly Hills 90210* effect," psychologist Anne Becker reported that the introduction of cable television programming in Fiji in 1995, which included *Beverly Hills 90210*, produced an unprecedented increase among Fijian teenage girls in both dieting and vomiting to lose weight. By 1998, in a culture where dieting to look very thin was never common, Becker reported a fivefold increase among Fijian teenage girls in vomiting to control weight, that 62 percent of girls had dieted in the last month, and that 74 percent now reported feeling "too big."[25] Even toys help socialize children into ideals of physical appearance that are laughably different from the physical appearance of most human beings. Barbie dolls offer physically improbable depictions of female bodies, and male action figure dolls have such heavily muscled upper bodies that it would be aerodynamically and physically impossible for an actual male to have such a chest and stand upright.

What stakes are involved in choosing to value some appearances over others? Perhaps, as some argue, promoting a cultural ideal of thinness is functional for enhancing individual health. Alternatively, there are discriminatory and human costs to cultural promotions of thinness. Overall, considering whether Americans are "too fat" raises questions about individual autonomy over one's own body, the cultural values affixed to body types, and how social institutions should respond to public health. Answers to these questions translate into strikingly different policy initiatives, as is evident in the contrasting approaches of conservatives, libertarians, and social democrats about whether Americans are too fat, and what, if anything, to do about it.

## The Libertarian Point of View

The libertarian belief in individual freedom includes a person's autonomy to eat as much or as little as he or she chooses. To the libertarian, people should be as free to be "virtuous," such as staying physically fit, as they are to pursue "vices," such as choosing to forgo exercise. What matters to the libertarian is not what an individual chooses to do (as long as one avoids harming others), but that no government actions infringe on the decision how to act. From this viewpoint, whether Americans are too fat is irrelevant from a public policy perspective and no excuse for government intervention. People who are too heavy choose that path, and government should not force them to eat less or exercise any more than they desire. Libertarians resist any government efforts to that end.

Libertarians oppose proposed initiatives to increase taxes on foods with a high-fat content, which they see as using the tax code for social engineering. They are deeply suspicious of such government intervention, which they view as a means of imposing new taxes and restrictions on individuals. Writing about government initiatives to lessen obesity in the *Libertarian,* columnist Vin Suprynowicz communicated the libertarian view about the ultimate motive of such regulation:

> Make no mistake, this will not end with a few "Eat your vegetables" TV ads, any more than the anti-smoking campaign ended with tobacconists required to print the "Surgeon General's warning" on every pack—any more than gun control ended with a $200 tax on each machine gun back in 1934. Based on just those precedents, we can now expect to see "menu calorie averaging" requirements, penalty taxes, and coordinated state and federal "health cost liability lawsuits" against the evil fast food behemoths, based on how much "excess fat" they supposedly cram down the throats of unwary Americans. Why? Because hamburgers, fries, and a Coke kill more Americans than car crashes, legal alcohol, or swimming pool drownings? Of course not. To identify the next likely candidate for this sequence of gentle federal ministrations, all one has to do is apply Willie Sutton's Law: "That's where the money is." [26]

To impose these taxes also strikes at two principles that libertarians hold dear—not to interfere in the free market and not to restrict individual choice:

> In recent months, the "fat tax"—a new federal tax that would be levied against high-calorie and high-fat foods—has been endorsed by several organizations as a solution to a national "obesity epidemic.". . . . But such suggestions ignore the right of Americans to choose what they want to eat—and the right of restaurants to serve it. Says Mr. Dasbach [national director of the libertarian party]: "What you eat, and how much you eat, are matters of personal preference and personal responsibility," he said. "Our eating habits shouldn't be the government's business—and bureaucrats shouldn't be allowed to micromanage our menus or tax our Twinkies in the name of so-called public health."[27]

For libertarians, individuals are responsible both for choosing how much to eat and for managing adverse consequences of that decision. Though at an individual level, people may want help losing weight, the issue of whether Americans are too fat is simply not the nation's business. As Jeanne Jacobs noted:

> Many overfed folks need help sticking to the Stairmaster and staying away from the Rocky Road. Spokesdieter Monica Lewinsky (she finally found a job!) may not be sufficient inspiration. But do you really want the health police shouting "drop the chalupa!" in your kitchen?[28]

It is bad enough to have the government police your bedroom, but should they police your kitchen as well?

## The Conservative Point of View

Conservatives place great stock in traditions that they view as effective in restraining people from their worst impulses. To a conservative, mass obesity represents sloth—an abandonment of moral values, such as physical fitness and self-control, that help bring about and sustain a disciplined, ordered, and productive society. What is most distressing to conservatives is that mass obesity means that too many people are "letting themselves go" in an epidemic of unrestrained gluttony. The issue is one of moral character.

For conservatives, government should not regulate business enterprises, for example, by raising taxes on fatty foods or by restricting the advertising and marketing of "junk" foods. Rather than ban or tax fast food, individuals should develop enough self-control to forgo second and third helpings. Edwin Fuelner, president of the Heritage Foundation, explained the argument:

> Fewer and fewer people seem willing these days to take responsibility for their own behavior or to accept the fact, sad as it is, that every ill that befalls us isn't necessarily a consequence of somebody else's negligence. . . . To imply that our cravings for things we enjoy are simply a product of advertising and "marketing" is to place humans on the level of animals, helpless to act contrary to our physical appetites. So long as we

pursue this nutty line of reasoning—that everybody else is responsible for our actions and their consequences—we will invite the government to intrude further and further into every detail of our daily lives.[29]

Though conservatives and libertarians both agree that government should not restrict business operations in order to curb obesity, conservatives do view obesity as symbolizing a problem, unlike libertarians, who view judging obesity as an individual decision. Conservatives are concerned about the physical and psychological consequences of gluttony, such as whether obese people are less effective citizens, since their excess weight handicaps them physically and, to many, demonstrates laziness and a lack of self-control. For example, some professionals who are too heavy, such as police officers and firefighters, may be unable to perform their duties at an optimal level. When many jobs have mandatory physical fitness requirements, such as law enforcement and military work, and because people perform physical labors with less fatigue when they are in shape, epidemic obesity threatens workplace efficiency. The health consequences of obesity may also relegate a vast amount of the American population to a draining infirmity. For parents to ignore obesity in children worsens the problem in the future and also promotes the wrong moral message.

Heritage Foundation analyst Robert Rector suggested advocating a "stronger work ethic" to solve the problem.[30] People must prioritize getting in shape, so schools should renew mandatory physical education classes. Families should turn off the television and take their kids outside to exercise. People should learn about appropriate foods and amounts to eat and gain self-control, working primarily through the social institutions of the family and school. These institutions should also have a primary role in inculcating social values that will reduce obesity. While some might fear the negative consequences of such messages, such as stigmatizing overweight people, conservatives fear worsening the effects of obesity and laxity by softening that view. Conservatives view obesity as a form of individual irresponsibility, and they reject government regulation of business as the cure for those detrimental impulses.

## The Social Democratic Point of View

Social democrats are staunch advocates for the possibility of governmental intervention against obesity. In this view, government's proper role is to eliminate discriminatory barriers to people's quality of life, including any exploitative profit-taking by businesses that bolster those obstacles. Rather than thinking that all individuals have the free choice to decide to "let themselves go," social democrats argue that the ability to "choose" to be overweight or slim depends on the resources that individuals' social context affords them. In that sense, social democrats notice that a disproportionate number of the obese are members of minority groups and are economically disadvantaged. Poorer people must eat inexpensively, making cheaper high-fat, fast food diets an option. A person who must balance multiple jobs may be unable to structure healthy meals and exercise routines into daily life. Affluent people may live near recreational fields or gyms and may be able to exercise more easily. Knowledge of what foods to eat or to avoid, and of the health consequences of obesity may not be widely available to people with less education.

Social democrats also argue that businesses profit by working actively to produce patterns of consumer behavior that encourage obesity. Continually urging people to "supersize" their fast food portions and to consume high-fat and sugary foods encourages people to act in self-destructive ways. Imagine advertising campaigns extolling the virtues of drinking your tenth beer in one sitting or of smoking two cigarettes at once. To social democrats, urging people to buy a 64-ounce "big gulp" soft drink, when a typical single serving is 8 ounces, is similar. Social democrats are angered when businesses profit from encouraging people to engage in self-destructive behaviors that help aggravate public problems. In this sense, social democrats feel that business enterprises that encourage eating too much junk food are just like businesses that promote alcohol consumption, cigarette smoking, and gambling. As Dr. Kelly Brownell, head of Yale University's Eating Disorders Program put it, "To me there is no difference between Ronald McDonald and Joe Camel."[31]

Similar to government regulations that restrict tobacco advertising, social democrats encourage curbs on businesses that profit by encouraging overeating. One suggestion has been to introduce "a fat tax where foods with a high fat content are taxed at a higher rate. In an ideal world, the government would subsidize fruits and vegetables and tax foods with more than a certain number of grams of fat."[32] The Center for Science in the Public Interest has said that a "fat tax" is not enough and called for a ban on "junk food" advertising and for mandatory calorie labels on restaurant menus.[33]

A larger question is to ask what responsibility, if any, businesses should have for the consequences of people choosing to consume their products. On one side, that businesses encourage consumption of their legal products does not force people to purchase them, nor to use them in harmful amounts—that decision is a matter of individual responsibility. Why act against businesses by holding them responsible for people deciding to indulge themselves? However, social democrats argue that some business practices promote behaviors that produce health-related and financial costs, yet those businesses disown any obligation to alleviate the consequences of the damage that they have helped create. Shouldn't businesses have to help solve the problems that they helped cause? If businesses gloss over the health-related implications of their products and market them aggressively, particularly to people who are defined as lacking alternatives, isn't it in society's best interests to lessen the resulting damage?

Social democrats also attack what they perceive as a separate social inequality associated with obesity—discrimination against the overweight. A panel convened by the National Institutes of Health recently wrote that "There is increasing physiological, biochemical and genetic evidence that being overweight is not a simple disorder of willpower as it is sometimes implied."[34] If the hereditary predisposition to being overweight is a causal factor, then obesity might owe more to genetics than to free will. If an inherited tendency toward obesity is also aggravated by a conducive social environment, the obese deserve not condemnation, but support. From this perspective, obesity is more an illness to sympathize with than a reprehensible personal choice to censure.

Reactions to the overweight can be intense and overwhelmingly negative, moving writer Natalie Angier to note:

> Some slurs are considered worse than others. Insults to a person's race, ethnicity or religion rank as completely unacceptable. Making fun of a woman for being female or a gay person for being homosexual may be somewhat less taboo. Children are taught not to point at a handicapped person and only the most callous would jeer at a down-and-out drunk. But a fat person is fair game. People who would never publicly confess to racism have no qualms about expressing revulsion for the obese.[35]

For social democrats, any unequal and discriminatory treatment against a group should be opposed. Government must act against "size" discrimination socially and enforce laws against employment discrimination based on weight. Michigan is presently the only state in the country that explicitly includes "weight" as a protected classification, like race, sex, and religious affiliation.[36] The impact of social discrimination against the obese also produces intense feelings among those affected. One study of forty-seven morbidly obese people who lost weight through surgery reported the following:

> Every one of the 47 people said that they would rather be deaf, or have dyslexia, diabetes, bad acne or heart disease than be obese again. Ninety-one percent said they would rather have a leg amputated. Eighty-nine percent would rather be blind. One patient said: "When you're blind, people want to help you. No one wants to help you when you're fat."[37]

Fat also has been referenced as a feminist issue, one that calls for action against cultural values that define an idealized femininity using an exacting and uncompromising physical standard. Social pressures to attain a "desirable" female body type may produce eating disorders and low self-esteem, in part to avoid the stigma associated with an overweight appearance. For the social democrat, rampant obesity calls for restricting business practices that encourage overeating, preventative education strategies, reducing the stigmatization of the overweight, and ending economic and social discrimination against obese people.

# Obesity and Social Research

Can you recall a situation where self-consciousness held you hostage? Where you worried intensely about how you looked, perhaps causing you fearfully to check and recheck a mirror to scrutinize and polish up your appearance? Every day includes pressures from the social interactions that we anticipate having with others. For many (just recall high school), each day offers anxiety-filled opportunities to worry about how one looks, from wondering if we are wearing our clothes well, to fretting if we've covered up a pimple, to checking if the spinach from lunch isn't stuck to our teeth.

Sociologists use the term *impression management* to describe the strategic actions that people take to manage their physical appearance and personality in anticipation of other people's reactions. Occasions of self-consciousness help us think about impression management, since at such times we have an acute awareness both of having to engage in impression management and of our marked sensitivity to how others appraise us.

There is a long tradition in social science of studying how people present themselves to others, particularly the steps they take to avoid being treated badly. Though there are times when we all may feel vulnerable to being judged negatively, individual characteristics intensify our risk of being disparaged socially. For the obese, social life is a particularly painful battleground of impression management, because excess weight encourages salvos of abuse, starting in childhood and continuing into adulthood. Consider one child's recollection of lunch in elementary school:

> One day, schoolmates started throwing food at [a "fat" student] as she sat at a table at lunch. Plates of spaghetti splashed on her face and the long greasy strands dripped onto her clothes. Everyone was just laughing and pointing. They were making pig noises.[38]

Obese people describe a social landscape filled with the possibility of encountering affronts: at home, at work, and in public space.[39]

Erving Goffman used the term *stigma* to describe a "deeply discrediting characteristic associated with an individual."[40] Stigmas may be immediately apparent to others, such as a facial disfiguration, or be traits that one can camouflage or hide from others, such as being an ex-mental patient or a "deadbeat" dad. The obese have an overtly discrediting stigma because their weight is impossible to disguise and brings forth an adverse reaction. Apart from the health consequences associated with carrying excess weight, social scientists have actively researched the consequences of obesity as a social identity. In the parlance of impression management, being obese is a "spoiled" identity or a "stigma."

How do people with spoiled identities manage the impressions they give to others? People who are handicapped physically, such as the blind or paraplegic; or who are openly gay; or who have controversial political opinions; all share the necessity to adapt to those social circumstances that can make everyday life more difficult. Deciding what identities warrant "spoiling" and how to treat people with spoiled identities is also a litmus test of a society's divergence in cultural values—its tolerance—and represents an endless cause of social conflict. Who, and on what basis, deserves scorn? Can spoiled identities ever be "unspoiled"? For example, under what conditions do people really see an ex-prisoner as being able to transform from "convicted criminal" to "citizen"? When does a "drunk driver" become a "driver"? People might support or decry obesity being a spoiled identity, including seeing different degrees of appropriateness as to when stigmatizing obesity is useful or to be denounced. By considering the problem from the perspective of those with this spoiled identity, we can address how they themselves attempt to "unspoil" their identities through different action strategies.

How do sociologists learn how stigmatized people think about and react to their identities? One method is to spend time with them. Again, this rather obvious technique of sociological investigation is known as *participant observation* or *ethnography*. In using this technique, sociologists can enter a community or group by pretending to be a member, by joining as an actual member, or by informing the community or group that they wish to spend time with them. Although journalists also sometimes observe people or groups, the sociological observer typically is interested in more than merely describing the setting to readers; he or she wants to discover sociological principles that transcend the observational setting.

In his article "Organizational Approaches to Shame: Avowal, Management and Contestation," sociologist Daniel Martin analyzed the different stigma management strategies that Overeaters Anonymous (OA), Weight Watchers, Inc. (WW), and the National Association to Advance Fat Acceptance (NAAFA) offer their respective members. To gather information, Daniel Martin conducted in-depth interviews with members of all of these groups to learn what *they* think about the stigma of obesity. He also relied on participant observation by gaining twenty-five pounds and attending weekly meetings at Weight Watchers, in order to experience being overweight as a social identity. For example, he participated in the anxiety of "facing the scale," which all Weight Watchers members must do—he had to get weighed in the semipublic context of each weekly meeting. By sharing some of the experiences of Weight Watchers members and by interviewing obese NAAFA and OA members, Martin garnered the subjective understandings of the individuals and organizations that he researched.

Martin learned that each organization provides their members with distinctly different guidelines about how to define the social identity of being overweight. Members of OA use the metaphor of addiction to define an obese identity. They learn to view obesity as a compulsion to overeat, much as organizations like Alcoholics Anonymous define drinking as an overpowering addiction. Members of OA must "avow" a compulsion to overeat and acknowledge that they have "hit bottom" in having an utter lack of self-control with food in order to redeem themselves from their addiction. They avow their compulsion in meetings with fellow members, garner support from such disclosures, and appraise their shamed identity as involving suffering from and needing to conquer an addiction.

In contrast to OA members, WW's shame management strategy does not attempt to deny, contest, or embrace the experience of being overweight, but to contain it through dieting and weight loss. Here, excess weight results from failing to follow rational steps, such as sensible diet and self-control. The shame of weight is best managed as a problem to solve using a programmatic set of lifestyle changes, which is, of course, WW's commercial product. Where OA avows a dramatic problem with self-control and hence with weight, WW uses the rhetoric of rationality and education, arguing that WW programs offer skills for exiting an overweight identity.

In contrast, NAAFA offers members a direct refutation of being shamed by weight, arguing that the obese should accept themselves for who they are and fight determinedly against any forms of "size discrimination." Members of NAAFA avidly reject that obese people should have a spoiled identity and urge them to contest any efforts to attach shame to being overweight. Consider a NAAFA member's reaction to a supermarket display for a diet product:

I was shopping and all of a sudden I found myself in front of this huge section of Slimfast products. And all of a sudden the idea came to me, (shouts) gee, I don't have to use the entire card [NAAFA business card]. So I just tore the bottom half of the card off, the part that had the NAAFA address and left the part that said "Do something about your weight, accept it." And I just stuck it on the shelf, sort of like behind one of those little plastic place cards and said "there."[41]

Members of NAAFA take the most confrontational approach to stigmatization, urging obese people to reject negative labels and to fight back against social shaming, embracing their body type. For them, fat is, in effect, a civil rights issue.

Individuals do not define themselves in a vacuum. The social organizations around us provide frames for self-identification. Martin's research demonstrates how organizations associated with overweight people help shape members' understandings of what an overweight identity should be. People can be taught different interpretations of a given identity, running the gamut from viewing being obese as suffering from addiction, to seeing one's obesity as a different, but perfectly acceptable lifestyle. Of course, organizations have vested interests in cultivating particular understandings in their members. Just as OA preaches redemption, WW sells weight-loss strategies for profit, and NAAFA urges "fat activism." Naturally, these frameworks for defining an overweight identity reflect each organization's vested interests.

A final point in research on obesity as a social identity is to consider whether women must confront the stigma of obesity more than men do. Martin cited membership statistics that indicate that 95 percent of WW members are female, as are 78 percent of NAAFA members and 85 percent of OA members. This disproportionate number of female members led him to conclude that these groups are "women's organizations," and that his analysis is therefore of "women's shame." Certainly his informants viewed "body shame as exclusive to the experience of female members," and one group leader described it in the following way:

Men are not as shameful about their bodies. They don't care if they are thirty pounds overweight; they go ahead and take off their shirts at the beach anyway. Women just aren't able to do that—we're ashamed to wear bathing suits and show off our cellulite or flabby legs or varicose veins at the beach. We are overwhelmingly told that we can't do that, that we must be thin.[42]

Feminist thinkers have also claimed that weight ideals oppress women more than men. While acknowledging that many women feel this point keenly, we should also question whether the shame men might feel is fully considered. Men may feel shame at their bodies but feel less empowered to admit having to manage that shame, particularly by joining an organization that is widely considered a "woman's organization." The male experience of bodily shame may not be fully explored, since it is more socially acceptable for women to discuss and monitor their appearance than it is for men. This point certainly doesn't lessen the importance of studying how women are affected by ideals of thinness, but it does call for fuller consideration of how obesity's stigma affects men. An overweight man could be just as reluctant to take his shirt off at the beach as an overweight woman, yet feel more pressure to remove his shirt regardless.

## Government Action, Public Health, and Obesity

Sometimes we are victims of our own success. In our society, more people die from overeating than from starvation. Comparing our position with societies around the globe, we ought to be grateful and perhaps ashamed that obesity is a problem that we must confront. Can one imagine a debate about a national need to lose weight in Haiti, Ethiopia, or Bangladesh? It is a national luxury to question whether Americans are too fat—a developed nation's privilege in a world of countries where many starve to death.

As Americans become increasingly fat, different policy initiatives are debated to affect individual decisions about what and how much to eat. For some, society has a lot to gain from such steps. With health costs high, and incidence of diabetes and other weight-related diseases skyrocketing along with the public waistline, the issue of whether Americans are too fat has taken on an increased urgency. However, integrating this sentiment with concerns for individual and business autonomy and for developing strategies for holding people responsible for their own actions creates thorny problems.

For the libertarian, the only problem is when people cannot decide on their own courses of action. People don't have to make good, moral, or even rational decisions, as long as their actions avoid harming others. Each person should be free from having other agendas infringe on his or her own. The libertarian questions the right of the government or medical establishment to dictate weight-related decisions for individuals. The libertarian can live with people being "obese." If obese people can live with that decision, we have no right to prevent them from doing so.

The conservative emphasizes traditional values, such as exercising self-control and avoiding the biblical sin of gluttony. We must all be called upon to embrace some self-restraint in order to adhere to our social values. Conservatives fear the lessons that obese children learn by failing to have values of self-discipline imparted to them, as well as living in a society with endless physical reminders that its citizens cannot control their own appetites. Fat is "civic immorality."[43] Social institutions should respond to threats to the social good—to conservatives, fat imperils not only public health but moral health as well.

The social democratic perspective deals most directly with the question of whether Americans are too fat, arguing for urgent government action to reduce obesity, but also, paradoxically a willingness to prevent discrimination because of weight. Social democrats think that the government should regulate business practices and also provide the resources to fund educational initiatives on issues of nutrition while simultaneously fighting prejudice against those who are obese.

If a libertarian argument won the day, producing no government action on these fronts, obesity might increase even more, continuing to produce staggering health costs. Yet, protecting individual autonomy and acknowledging individual responsibility is important. Why should a person support obese people if doing so only exacerbates a problem? Why tax high-fat foods when many people eat them in moderation and don't want to pay for that privilege? As with other issues, deciding how to protect people from a perceived harm is anything but simple.

## Questions

1. Are *obesity* and *overweight* medical, political, or social terms?

2. Is obesity in America a grave public health crisis?

3. Do obese people lack self-control?

4. Why might minority and poorer populations have higher levels of obesity than other populations? Is the concept of obesity racist or elitist?

5. Should the mass media promote cultural ideals of physical fitness and thinness?

6. Should the government raise taxes on high-fat foods in order to combat obesity?

7. Should companies be able to discriminate against "fat people" in hiring? Should they be able to do so if the job involves meeting the public (receptionists, restaurant servers, flight attendants)?

8. What steps, if any, should parents take to prevent obesity in their children?

9. What is your own ideal weight? Why?

10. Would you date a "fat" person?

## For Further Study

Bordo, Susan. *Unbearable Weight*. Berkeley: University of California Press, 1993.

Bray George A., Claude Bouchard, and W. P. T. James. *The Handbook of Obesity*. New York: Marcel Dekker, 1997.

Goffman, Erving. *Stigma: Notes on the Management of Spoiled Identity*. Englewood Cliffs, NJ: Prentice-Hall, 1963.

Martin, Daniel. "Organizational Approaches to Shame: Avowal, Management and Contestation." *The Sociological Quarterly* 41 (2000): 125–150.

Millman, Marcia. *Such a Pretty Face: Being Fat in America*. New York: W. W. Norton, 1980.

Schwartz, Hillel. *Never Satisfied: A Cultural History of Diets, Fantasies and Fat*. New York: Free Press, 1986.

Stearns, Peter. *Fat History: Bodies and Beauty in the Modern World*. New York: New York University Press, 1997.

# Notes and References

1. Irene Hanson Frieze, Josephine E. Olson and Deborah Cain Good, "Perceived and Actual Discrimination in the Salaries of Male and Female Managers," *Journal of Applied Social Psychology*, January 1990, pp. 46–68.

2. E. A. McLean, "USA Snapshots: Where the Diet Bucks Go," *USA Today*, August 2, 1994, B: 1:1.

3. Susan, Bordo, *Unbearable Weight* (Berkeley: University of California Press, 1993).

4. World Heath Organization, *Constitution of the World Health Organization* (New York: World Health Organization Interim Commission, 1946), p. 3.

5. John Macionis, *Sociology* (Upper Saddle Rive, NJ: Prentice-Hall, 2001), p. 538.

6. These two points are made in Peter Stearns, *Fat History: Bodies and Beauty in the Modern World* (New York: New York University Press, 1997), and Hillel Schwartz, *Never Satisfied: A Cultural History of Diets, Fantasies and Fat* (New York: Free Press, 1986).

7. The George Washington example is cited from Tim Curry, Robert Jiobu, and Kent Schwirian, *Sociology for the Twenty-First Century* Upper Saddle River, NJ: Prentice-Hall, 1997), p. 391.

8. These statistics, and the BMI description are from "What Is Obesity," published by the American Obesity Association, an association of public health specialists. "What Is Obesity" is available at the web site, www.Obesity.Org. The National Institutes of Health and National Heart Lung and Blood Institute, "Clinical Guidelines on the Identification, Evaluation, and Treatment of Overweight and Obesity in Adults" supplement this information June 1998.

9. Greg Crister, "Let Them Eat Fat: The Heavy Truths about American Obesity," *Harper's*, March 2000, p. 44.

10. Cheryl Wetzstein, "America's Quiet Epidemic," *Insight on the News*, Dec. 28, 1998, 14:i48, p. 41.

11. Everett Hughes, *The Sociological Eye*. (New Brunswick, NJ: Transaction Press, 1984).

12. Peter Conrad, "Medicalization and Social Control," *Annual Review of Sociology* 18 (1992): 209–232.

13. Greg Crister, "Let Them Eat Fat," p. 46.

14. Cited in "What Is Obesity," The American Obesity Association.

15. Cited in "What Is Obesity," The American Obesity Association.

16. Greg Crister, "Let Them Eat Fat," p. 42.

17. Greg Crister, "Let Them Eat Fat," p. 42.

18. Greg Crister, "Let Them Eat Fat," p. 41.

19. Greg Crister, "Let Them Eat Fat," p. 41.

20. Richard Klein, "Big Country: The Roots of American Obesity," *The New Republic*, September 19, 1994, p. 28.

21. Peter Stearns, *Fat History: Bodies and Beauty in the Modern West* (New York: New York University Press, 1997), p. 136.

22. David Croteau and William Hoynes, *Media and Society & Industries, Images and Audiences*. (Thousand Oaks, CA: Pine Forge Press, 1999).

23. Susan Averett and Sanders Korenman, "Black-White Differences in Social and Economic Consequences of Obesity," *International Journal of Obesity* 23 (1999): 166–173.

24. Greg Crister, "Let Them Eat Fat," p. 45.

25. Cited in John Macionis, *Sociology*. Upper Saddle River, NJ: Prentice Hall, originally reported in "Eating Disorders Jump When Fiji Gets Television," *Toledo Blade*, May 20, 1999, p. 12.

26. Vin Suprynowicz, "Time for a Fat Tax on Wendy's, McDonalds?" *The Libertarian*, June 3, 2000.

27. From the Libertarian Party press release, "Hide the Ham: Health Fanatics Want to Slap a 'Fat Tax' on Your Favorite Foods," December 8, 1999.

28. Joanne Jacobs, "They'll Tax Your Cheeseburger and Lecture You to Boot—The Fat Patrol is Closing In." *San Jose Mercury News*, January 6, 2000.

29. Edwin Fuelner. "Suing Elsie the Cow," Heritage Foundation WebSite, September 11, 1997. Address: www.heritage.org

30. Cheryl Wetzstein, "America's Quiet Epidemic," p. 41.

31. Hanna Rosin. "The Fat Tax: Is it Really Such a Crazy Idea?" *The New Republic*, May 18, 1998, p. 18.

32. Hanna Rosin, "The Fat Tax," p. 18.

33. Cited in the Libertarian Party press release, "Hide the Ham: Health Fanatics Want to Slap a "Fat Tax" on Your Favorite Foods."

34. Gina Kolata. "The Burdens of Being Overweight: Mistreatment and Misconceptions, *The New York Times*, November 22, 1992, p. 38.

35. Natalie Angier, "Why So Many Ridicule the Overweight," *The New York Times*, November 22, 1992, p. 38.

36. Reported in the National Education Association document, "Report on Size Discrimination," October 7, 1994. This document may be found at www.Lectlaw.com/files/con28.htm

37. Gina Kolata, "The Burdens of Being Overweight," p. 38.

38. National Education Association, "Report on Size Discrimination."

39. Multiple sources inform this summary, including Marcia Millman, *Such a Pretty Face: Being Fat in America* and the National Education Association, "Report on Size Discrimination."

40. Erving Goffman, *Stigma: Notes on the Management of Spoiled Identity*.

41. Daniel Martin, "Organizational Approaches to Shame: Avowal, Management and Contestation," p. 141

42. Martin, Daniel, "Organizational Approaches to Shame," p. 138.

43. A nice turn of phrase used in Daniel Martin's "Organizational Approaches to Shame."

# CHAPTER TWELVE

# Social Movements/Collective Behavior: Can Civil Disobedience Be Justified?

■ *"We shall overcome,"* says the old spiritual that, in time, became the anthem for the Civil Rights movements. This hymn symbolizes the crucial role that groups of citizens can have in our social system, where people have the right, perhaps the obligation, to protest when they feel that the government, social institutions, or their fellow citizens are acting unjustly. Throughout U.S. history, people have attempted to change government policies; as evidence of the Constitution's effectiveness, most of those organized efforts have occurred through social protest and lobbying—not gunfire.

Although Americans like to think of themselves as having a representative democracy, this is only part of how policy is made. Elections are not the only means by which citizens do—and should—influence their government. The First Amendment to the Constitution recognizes the right to assemble peaceably, and petitioning the government for redress of grievances is a protected way to bring about change. The right to free speech also allows alternative ideas the opportunity to grow into persuasive words, arguments, and debates. The organized form that these constitutional freedoms often take is through social movements. A *social movement* is a collection of individuals who organize together to achieve or prevent some social or political change.

Throughout U.S. history, a remarkable array of social movements has existed: from the International Workers of the World to the National Association of Manufacturers, from the Animal Liberation Front to the Women's Christian Temperance Union, from the Promisekeepers to B'nai B'rith. These movements reflect libertarian, conservative, and social democratic ideologies, as well as others that are incompatible with democratic ideals. The goals and ideas for which these groups choose to fight are astonishingly diverse. Some groups organize to promote change and others (called *counter-movements*) to oppose it. Sometimes, after change occurs, such as after the 1973 Supreme Court decision that legalized abortions, the roles of opposing movements and organizations switch. Now "pro-choice" groups fight to keep things the way they are, while "pro-life" groups fight to change state policy. Should the Supreme Court ever overturn *Roe* v. *Wade,* their positions would change yet again.

Obviously, social movements differ considerably in their structure, tactics, ideology, goals, and national origin; they also have violent and nonviolent incarnations. Some social movements are organized centrally, with a strong and effective hierarchy. This hierarchy may be open or secretive, democratic or authoritarian; it may employ different tactics—persuasion, letter writing, voter registration, civil disobedience, or violence. Today, through the Internet, social movements have an enhanced capacity to learn effective tactics from one another, ranging from lessons in how to "spin the media" to "how to hang yourself in effigy (carefully)."[1] Technology also has enabled social movements to coalesce into more hybrid groups and has provided a medium (the Internet) that constitutes a mass distribution system for delivering a group's message. The same promotional flyer that was once posted on street corners or stuck under a windshield wiper can have a worldwide distribution today.

Depending on perceived need and effectiveness, people within a social movement may change their approach over time or spin off violent or nonviolent branches of their group. Some terrorist organizations—for example, the Irish Republican Army or the Palestinian Liberation Organization—renounce terrorism when they perceive it is in their interest to do so; other groups may become frustrated working within the political sphere and choose to become more militant, such as some U.S. antiabortion groups and offshoots of the militia movement. In the United States, groups that engage in forceful action (violence or civil disobedience) are more successful in responding to repressive treatment than "meek" organizations.[2] Radical groups (such as ACT UP or Earth First!) also serve a valuable purpose for less militant groups (Gay Men's Health Crisis or the Sierra Club) with the same concerns by making the latter groups appear more reasonable in contrast.[3]

Sociologists have proposed numerous theories to explain the emergence of social movements. An early approach suggests that individual members of social movements all have psychological characteristics in common. These theorists, such as Gustave LeBon, see a social movement as fundamentally irrational, as are its participants.[4] Other theorists emphasize that social movements serve a psychological need for individual members. These approaches, however, in their haste to characterize participants, can ignore what the movement is fighting for. While one can reasonably suggest that people who are active in social movements may have different preferences from those who are not, this does not explain why a movement exists or why it arises when it does. The temptation to label individual participants and their social movements as irrational can detract from understanding why social movements writ large emerge and persist.

One explanation for their emergence is the existence of "strain" in society.[5] When a problem (a strain) is recognized, groups are likely to coalesce to deal with it. This strain may be an "objective" problem (such as the existence of guns) or a "perceived" problem (such as people feeling deprived as compared to others). Such a theory has considerable appeal because it recognizes that social movements respond to societal stimuli. Yet, some charge that strain theories rely too heavily on a simple cause-effect analogy. The problem exists, and then a social movement arises to meet it.

The difficulty is that there are many potential "problems" but only a few prominent social movements. One could envision groups, for example, mobilized to get bicycle riders off city sidewalks or to stop double-parking. Why do some social movement causes thrive while others never do? It is by no means clear that social movements emerge only to confront the most pressing problems that a society faces. Sociologist Barry Glassner suggested, for example, that a "culture of fear" can cause people to label some problems as requiring collective action in complete lack of proportion to their seriousness, such as attempts to combat pseudoissues like "road rage."[6] Spurred on by a sensationalist media and individuals with vested interests, fear can inspire collective action around arguably nonexistent or trivial problems.

Once started, what makes a social movement survive? *Resource mobilization theory* helps explain why some movements succeed and others do not.[7] As the name suggests, access to resources is crucial to an aspiring movement. No social movement can grow until a committed group of individuals is willing to acquire and use resources. In the broadest sense, these resources need not only be material objects, but also can include mobilization of the press, recruitment, and use of members' social networks. These mobilizers may, at first, be outsiders, with the expertise and resources to assist in the mobilization of a movement, such as the members of the Communist Party of America who visited southern states during the 1930s to organize textile workers.

Typically, social movements that are oriented toward change do not have the material resources of governments or those in favor of keeping the status quo. But one advantage they do have is their ability to use "bodies" in collective behavior. Sociologists examine the collective identity or shared status and relations that individuals feel as part of participating together within social movements.[8] A social movement's collective identity bestows an individual affiliation with a movement's claims, tactics, effectiveness, and recruitment. Social movements develop "frames," or interpretations of collective identities and the "cause," that are designed to appeal to potential adherents and constituents.[9] Movements need to construct narratives that are plausible and involving. A social movement is a cultural organization as well as a political one. Mobilization is crucial to successful movements.

*Collective behavior* is the behavior of large numbers of people—behavior that typically is unstructured and relatively, although not always, unplanned. Crowds, mobs, demonstrations, sit-ins, and pickets lines are instances of collective behavior. While social movements may not have much cash, they have supporters, and these supporters can make a strong argument by their mere presence.

Some people argue that crowds are, by their nature, irrational (they have a "group mind") and subject to contagious mass behavior,[10] but an alternate view sees collective behavior in a more positive light. According to the emergent norm theory,[11] crowds are not as uniform as they might appear from a distance. For example, participants may have different motives for being present: from some looking for violence to others hoping to find love; a few hoping to pick a pocket, while still others are expressing a deeply held conviction. This approach to collective behavior suggests norms develop through the interaction of the group. A crowd situation is often ambiguous, with most participants uncertain what they should be doing. As a result, a few outspoken members can define proper behavior by setting a framework for action. Even though the majority of the crowd may not feel strongly, participants will typically acquiesce since at the moment it seems proper. This approach to crowd behavior is set squarely within the interactionist tradition because it suggests that what is happening is uncertain until defined by the dynamics of social contact.

Whether social movements and collective behavior are helpful or harmful depends on how you evaluate their methods and goals. Functional sociologists are more cautious than conflict sociologists about endorsing the idea of collective behavior because it may provoke a radical restructuring of a social system that may not need fixing. Conflict theorists are more enthusiastic about such behavior and hope for the radical restructuring of relationships among classes and social institutions—something that would disturb functionalists, who often believe that many cures, particularly revolutionary ones, are worse than the diseases that they replace.

# ■ Question:

## *Can civil disobedience be justified?*

Does true freedom mean the right to say "No!" whenever one feels like it? For some, this is precisely what freedom implies, and, for those individuals, civil disobedience comes easy. The issue of what constitutes civil disobedience has been complex for philosophers, political theorists, and jurists. We will use a simple and rather straightforward definition of the term: "Anyone commits an act of civil disobedience if and only if he acts illegally, publicly, nonviolently, and conscientiously with the intent to frustrate (one of) the laws, policies, or decisions of his government."[12] Surely no society can long exist if every citizen could pick and choose which laws to obey. For example, what would happen in the United States if paying taxes became completely voluntary?

Of course, civil disobedience does not mean disobeying laws generally; it is a subset of all law breaking. Among the criteria usually proposed to differentiate civil disobedience from other criminal activity is that, in addition to being performed in public view, it is derived from moral principles, it avoids harm to others, and frequently the lawbreaker willingly accepts the punishment meted out by courts.[13] It is this last feature of civil disobedience that may differentiate some recent U.S. protestors from the tradition of true civil disobedience, since many of these people attempted to avoid the punishment they might otherwise have received. Scholars differentiate between "pragmatic" and "conscientious" civil disobedience, and suggest that the former seeks to avoid punishment when possible.[14]

The history of civil disobedience is a lengthy one, populated with numerous distinguished names. Socrates and Antigone both refused to obey the state on moral grounds. Saint Augustine pointed to the Gospels as justification for civil disobedience to immoral laws. More recently, the example of Mahatma Gandhi in the campaign for Indian independence has proven to be an attractive model for many pacifists. Gandhi freed India from British rule with a minimum of violence; he succeeded because he embodied moral authority and was backed by millions of protesting Hindus and Moslems.

In the United States, too, civil disobedience has had a long history. In 1755, Pennsylvania Quakers opposed taxes levied by the British to fight the French and Indian Wars. Some might consider the Boston Tea Party to be an act of civil disobedience although the protestors were not arguing that a law was immoral but that it was passed without representation—that the process was immoral. Throughout the Revolutionary War, acts of civil disobedience targeted the British. Throughout U.S. history, some people of conscience have refused to pay taxes for wars they considered immoral or unjust. Perhaps the most sustained period of civil disobedience during the nineteenth century concerned the opposition to acts that condoned slavery. Northern abolitionists who strenuously opposed the fugitive slave act aided and abetted slaves in winning their freedom.[15]

The twentieth century has also witnessed considerable civil disobedience. The Civil Rights movement, and its most prominent leader, Reverend Martin Luther King, used the inspiration of Gandhi to organize nonviolent civil disobedience. Civil disobedience continued throughout the decade of the 1960s with protests against the war in Vietnam, including sit-ins, draft card burning, and tax protests. During 1971, the IRS recorded a peak of 1,740 returns from war tax resisters (and a remarkable 70,000 households resisted the federal excise tax on telephone bills in 1972 and 1973).[16] Although the amount of civil disobedience declined during the mid-1970s, by the end of the decade and into the 1980s, protest aimed first at nuclear power plants and then at nuclear arms production.

Currently, active groups practicing civil disobedience (sometimes with a mix of other tactics) include ACT-UP against AIDS, People for the Ethical Treatment of Animals (PETA), and Earth First![17] Recent protests against the World Trade Organization paralyzed Seattle in 1999, and acts of civil disobedience against the Navy bombing of the Puerto Rican island of Vieques led President Bush to phase out future bombing. Groups also protested injustice by blocking traffic (as was done in Miami during the Elian Gonzalez case), causing massive inconvenience to travelers. Philosopher Gerald Kreyche, surveying the "plethora of protests," sarcastically called for another social movement, the New Protestants, to "protest the protests!"[18]

Most of the social movements mentioned so far are considered generally to be "progressive," but the right also participates in this kind of activity. During the 1980s, extreme right-wing tax resistance protests sprang up.[19] One can think of parts of the militia movement of the 1990s as involving civil disobedience, standing up to perceived unjust federal authority, although stockpiling weapons and practicing attacks suggests that civil disobedience is not all that is in mind.[20] Still, for many among the far right, the incidents at Waco and Ruby Ridge provided a clarion call for future civil disobedience. Perhaps the largest civil disobedience movement currently is Operation Rescue—militant pro-life activists intent on shutting down abortion clinics, aligning themselves with the abolitionists of 150 years ago. Anyone can claim a moral objection to laws he or she dislikes.

Even if participants do not gain immediate satisfaction, they do get publicity for their cause, exposing the ideas of their social movement to those who were otherwise unaware. This represents, in the words of the Russian revolutionary Pyotr Kropotkin, "the propaganda of the deed." The act, whether or not effective in achieving the group's ends, communicates a message.

# The Libertarian Point of View

Libertarians believe individual freedom is the ultimate value; as a result, they see civil disobedience as profoundly moral. A "libertarian strain" is said to connect opposition to government policy.[21] Protest is moral, not so much because it prevents the application of an unjust law, but because the individual stands up to an oppressive government. Although libertarians do not support random or continual lawbreaking, the content of the law that is broken is not as critical as it is to social democrats. The libertarian treasures the rebel who refuses to accept the rules of society. In the words of Texas columnist Molly Ivins:

> Only half the reason the Constitution of the United States is a great and living document is because the founding daddies were among the smartest sumbitches who ever walked. . . . The other half of the credit goes to 200 years' worth of American misfits, troublemakers, rebels, eccentrics, mavericks, anti-Establishmentarians, (and) outsiders.[22]

The most profound American theorist of civil disobedience was Henry David Thoreau, the nineteenth-century Massachusetts transcendentalist and inspiration to many contemporary libertarians. Following the lead of his friend Bronson Alcott, Thoreau refused to pay the Massachusetts poll tax as a matter of principle. Thoreau's immediate objection to the tax was Massachusetts' indirect support of slavery and the U.S. government's expansionist war with Mexico. These were only symptoms of something larger, however. Thoreau made clear that his opposition was really an opposition to all government. In July 1846, he was stopped in Concord by the local constable who asked him to pay the tax he had not paid for three or four years. When Thoreau refused, the constable jailed him. By the following morning, an anonymous friend had paid his tax, and Thoreau went on his way. His night in jail led to Thoreau's 1848 lecture to the Concord Lyceum, "The Relation of the Individual to the State," now better known as "Civil Disobedience." Thoreau rejected the coercive power of the state, writing:

> I heartily accept the motto, "That government is best which governs least;" and I should like to see it acted up to more rapidly and systematically. Carried out, it finally amounts to this, which also I believe—"That government is best which governs not at all;" and when men are prepared for it, that will be the kind of government which they will have. . . . It is for no particular item in the tax-bill that I refuse to pay it. I simply wish to refuse allegiance to the State, to withdraw and stand aloof from it effectually. I do not care to trace the course of my dollar, if I could, till it buys a man or a musket to shoot one with—the dollar is innocent—but I am concerned to trace the effects of my allegiance. In fact, I quietly declare war with the State, after my fashion, though I will still make what use and get what advantage of her I can, as is usual in such cases.[23]

What, then, is Thoreau's theory of government; are we to live in blissful anarchy? Thoreau's idealistic answer is that individual conscience must take priority over the state. For Thoreau the consent of the governed depends on each individual law and can be withdrawn at will:

> The authority of government, even such as I am willing to submit to . . . is still an impure one: to be strictly just, it must have the sanction and consent of the governed. It can have no pure right over my person and property but what I concede to it. The progress from an absolute monarchy to a limited monarchy to a democracy, is a progress toward a true respect for the individual. . . . Is a democracy, such as we know it, the last improvement possible in government? Is it not possible to take a step further toward recognizing and organizing the rights of man? There will never be a really free and enlightened State until the State comes to recognize the individual as a higher and independent power, from which all its own power and authority are derived, and treats him accordingly.[24]

The ultimate power in a social system, should, for the libertarian, belong to the individual. Some libertarians even claim that their theory of government is profoundly antimilitaristic because it rejects the need for collective force. Libertarians note that many leftist nuclear war protestors see no contradiction in government forcing individuals to support other programs. That is, many of these "hypocritical" protestors accept government power as essential. Frederick Foote, a libertarian law student, argued that a weak state is not a warlike state:

> Laissez-faire capitalism, in contrast (to socialism or a welfare state), is the only social system that consistently upholds individual rights and bans the use of force against peaceful citizens. It is the only system under which no group, however large, can use force against another group, however small. *In theory and practice, laissez-faire capitalism is the only social system fundamentally opposed to war.*[25]

The extent to which libertarians disobey laws varies; some, despite their rhetoric, are model citizens. Others try to do whatever they can to remain free of government entanglements. While voluntary compliance with the Internal Revenue Service is extraordinarily high, the IRS can enforce their will. It takes a brave, committed, masochistic, or foolish person to stand up to this might. Yet, despite the difficulty, libertarians believe it is the mark of a free citizen to pick and choose which laws to obey,[26] and on occasion to say, "I won't." While you may pick and choose which laws you will obey, other free citizens may choose to isolate you if they think you have made a poor decision; this threat produces cooperation and social order.

## The Social Democratic Point of View

Civil disobedience is a problem for social democrats because they believe in the power of the state to do what is morally right and to enforce equality. Whereas libertarians believe that self-motivated civil disobedience is morally justified, the social democrat examines the goal of the disobedience and the nature of the opposed government. Moreover, the social democrat is likely to welcome a collective social movement more than the libertarian, who focuses on individual actions.

The nature of the government is critical to social democrats. Political scientist Hanna Pitkin wrote:

> If it is a good, just government doing what a government should, then you must obey it; if it is a tyrannical, unjust government trying to do what no government should, then you have no such obligation. . . . Legitimate government acts within the limits of the authority rational men would, abstractly and hypothetically, have to give a government they are founding. Legitimate government is government which deserves consent.[27]

This sense of moral absolutes is found throughout social democratic writing. Social democrats believe equality and justice are concepts worth protesting for. The social democrat does not like all government, only moral ones.

Consider the words of the former chaplain of Yale University, William Sloane Coffin, an outspoken supporter of civil rights and opponent of the war in Vietnam:

> Too often we forget that majority rule can never be equated with the rule of conscience. After all, the majority of our citizens have in the past supported slavery and child labor, and today still support various forms of racial discrimination, sex discrimination, slums, and a penal system far more punitive than curative. . . . [We] must recognize that justice is a higher social goal than law and order. . . . Rarely do the powerful ask which side is struggling for greater justice; rarely do the powerful see what is clear to me, that a conflict for the emancipation of a race or a class or a nation has more moral justification than a law to perpetuate privileges. In other words, the oppressed have a higher moral right to challenge oppression than oppressors have to maintain it.[28]

In war-tax protest, this issue is sometimes phrased as the hypocrisy of "praying for peace and paying for war." The problem with this approach is, Who defines what is moral?

Consider the comments of the Reverend Martin Luther King:

> [A] just law is a law that squares with a moral law. It is a law that squares with that which is right, so that any law that uplifts human personality is a just law. Whereas that law which is out of harmony with the moral is a law which does not square with the moral law of the universe. It does not square with the law of God, so for that reason it is unjust and any law that degrades the human personality is an unjust law.[29]

King suggested that to disobey an unjust law reveals deep respect for *law*. But such a belief does not really solve the problem. As we know from the history of religious strife, human beings do not easily interpret God's law. Some churches discriminate against African Americans because of how they interpret the Bible; should those churches engage in civil disobedience to prevent racial integration? Should citizens who are against abortion because of their moral principles stand in the doorway of abortion clinics or prevent them from being built, as others do at nuclear power plants? These are difficult questions for social democrats to answer, since presumably their position does not justify all forms of disobedience. If citizens share a belief in what is moral (the abolition of slavery or the prevention of nuclear war) and they can agree on which tactics help them reach that goal, then civil disobedience is morally right—both in provoking the government to act and in raising moral issues in the minds of others.

Social democrats see civil disobedience as a moral drama—an action designed to persuade and to lead to further action. David Carlin, Jr., a Rhode Island state senator, saw civil disobedience as a form of political theater. Civil disobedience is essentially a theatrical performance, a public action carried out in full view of an audience and with that audience in mind. Like a good play, it will exhibit character as well as plot. That is, actors will make the audience understand not simply the significance of their act of disobedience, but the significance also of the characters performing the act; for unless we understand the characters, we will not be able to appreciate their actions. In this particular play the characters, of course, will be those of exceptionally good persons—the saints or moral heroes.[30]

From this perspective it is not surprising that religious people are frequently publicized for their activity in civil disobedience. Religious leaders give a movement moral credibility by indicating that the protest is founded on justice and human values, not in selfishness.

## The Conservative Point of View

Because of their love for order, civil disobedience presents a troubling moral issue for conservatives. A government must lose all shred of moral authority and democratic process before the conservative will concede the right to disobey laws. Laws in a democracy are enacted with the consent of the governed. If citizens oppose the laws, they can elect different politicians in the next election, operating within accepted political channels. Because a political democracy allows us to change leaders, some legal authorities, such as Alexander Bickel, see all civil disobedience as coercive in its ultimate attempt to sidestep the electoral process.[31]

As one judge commented,

> Every time that a law is disobeyed by even a man whose motive is solely ethical, in the sense that it is responsive to a deep moral conviction, there are unfortunate consequences. He himself becomes more prone to disobey laws for which he has no profound repugnance. He sets an example for others who may not have his pure motives. He weakens the fabric of society.[32]

If someone believes the legal process is sacred (or nearly so), then any disruption becomes a serious breach of order. These people who civilly disobey the law may wish to define their action as obeying a higher law, but Cornell University philosopher Stuart Brown, Jr., contended that lawbreaking is lawbreaking:

> The very notion of a justified case of (civil disobedience) seems to imply a contradiction. It seems to imply the possibility of a legally permitted case of lawbreaking. For if civil disobedience, which is lawbreaking, can be justified, then surely the law ought to permit it where justified. But the law logically cannot permit lawbreaking. It logically cannot take the position that in the course of a public protest the breach of a valid law is no breach. . . . The moral beliefs and convictions of a man absolve him from obedience to the law only where the law itself allows.[33]

The conservative emphasizes the responsibility that citizens have to abide by the laws they helped to enact by their votes. It is too tempting for people to structure their sense of outrage and impassioned morality on the basis of whether their side has prevailed in a fair political struggle. Just as the majority may not always be right, it need not always be wrong, and there should be a strong presumption that it is correct. The conservative is likely to reject claims that the United States is not truly a democracy and not worthy of support from its citizens. Philosopher Sidney Hook saw the social democratic vision of civil disobedience as "sour grapes":

> It is characteristic of those who argue this way to define the presence or absence of the democratic process by whether or not *they* get their political way, and not by the presence or absence of democratic institutional processes. The rules of the game exist to enable them to win and if they lose that's sufficient proof the game is rigged and dishonest.[34]

Of course, if a person believes he or she is fighting for basic moral principles, a defeat would only support his or her questioning of the legitimacy of democratic institutions.

Conservatives also maintain that civil disobedience affects everyone in the society in that it costs the taxpayers money that could be spent elsewhere. Consider tax protests. If tax protesting ever reached significant levels, nonprotesting taxpayers might have to make up the difference that the government loses by not being able to collect taxes from everyone. Rather than preventing the government from spending money on military weapons, these protestors might only insure that everyone else's taxes will be proportionally higher. At the present time, such redistribution of the tax burden has little practical effect, but it could. Likewise, protests of all kinds, and particularly those that involve civil disobedience, cost taxpayers money for police, court proceedings, jailing, and sanitation. One protest in Minneapolis against the Honeywell Corporation, which makes guidance systems for nuclear missiles, resulted in the arrest of 577 people. It is estimated that this protest cost local taxpayers at least $40,000[35]—money that might have been used for social service programs. For conservatives, civil disobedience is an affront to public order and, as such, conservatives can be expected to oppose it. The morality of a social movement's cause has little weight against the morality of a nation's legitimate social institutions.

# Moral Development and Social Research

For most students today, the 1960s is not vivid as an age of protest and civil disobedience. It is simply a historical period in which they had no part and must be relived through books, movies, and music. In the aftermath of the AIDS epidemic and September 11, the slogan "Make Love, Not War" sounds quaint and a bit musty. The first and perhaps the most significant of the protest movements of the 1960s was the Free Speech Movement at the University of California at Berkeley. Students in 1964 conducted an illegal sit-in at the campus administration building, demanding to have a wide variety of speakers on campus. As a result, many were arrested.

Norma Haan, a researcher at Berkeley, was curious about the moral reasoning of those involved in this controversy.[36] In order to learn how students justified or condemned the free-speech movement, she sent questionnaires to three groups of students: students who were arrested during the protest, students who were members of conservative and/or Republican groups, and a random cross-section of Berkeley students. In this survey, she asked the participants to provide moral justifications for a set of hypothetical situations and specific moral questions about the sit-in ("Do you think it was right or wrong for the students to sit in? Why, or why not?").

The hypothetical and actual moral reasoning responses divided into six moral reasoning categories that psychologist Lawrence Kohlberg developed.[37] Kohlberg believed that individuals progress through six stages of moral reasoning, with the first two, mainly egocentric, primarily characteristic of childhood. Stages three and four, termed "conventional" moral reasoning, focus on the role of authority in determining proper action. Stages five and six, "principled" reasoning, return the responsibility for moral judgment to the individual actor—suggesting either that the rights and duties of individuals be respected (stage five) or that transcendent moral principles be observed (stage six). Kohlberg believed that individuals proceed through these stages sequentially until they reach their highest level of moral reasoning. He suggested that only a small proportion of people would ever base their reasoning on transcendent moral principles. Haan differed from this approach to some degree because she recognized that the context of reasoning is important. It was her concern for context that makes this study of moral reasoning fall within the interactionist approach. Moral meanings can change depending on what is happening around you. (We must also be cautious in judging a person's capacity for moral reasoning from their answers to hypothetical issues.)

Haan's methodology might perhaps be called an "experimental survey." She compared the reactions of three different groups of subjects to two types of moral dilemmas (actual and hypothetical). She hypothesized that there should be systematic differences between a person's reasoning about real situations and about hypothetical ones. Even though this was not the focus of the analysis, she was also able to examine differences among those with different attitudes toward civil disobedience. Haan attempted to incorporate the advantages of survey research and of experimental research. Specifically, she used a broad sample of subjects who responded to a large set of questions that allowed her to contrast responses of groups of subjects. There is at least one weakness in her research method. Because the questionnaires were mailed to subjects, only half of the potential subjects responded and perhaps those who did were only half-hearted in their responses. And by lumping subjects into large groups, some of the meanings of their personal situations may have been lost.

Haan's findings supported the importance of context in moral reasoning. Focusing on students who engaged in civil disobedience and were arrested (the group most pertinent to the arguments in this chapter), Haan discovered that 63 percent, a clear majority, showed an *increase* in their level of moral reasoning when discussing their justifications for civil disobedience during the sit-in as compared to their responses to hypothetical moral questions. Among the broad cross-section of Berkeley students, 54 percent of those who displayed "principled" reasoning sat in, whereas 60 percent of the nonprincipled did not—a finding that is on the borderline of being statistically significant. This finding suggests that students with "high" moral reasoning ability were the most likely to put their beliefs into action through civil disobedience. Part of the argument for this increase of moral reasoning is that these protestors were developmentally ready to increase their level of moral reasoning, and this dramatic event provided the impetus for positive change. Of course, this developmental readiness is hard to measure in advance, and, furthermore, there is no certainty that the moral reasoning of these students will remain high. Even more troubling is the uncertainty that these stages of moral reasoning are actually hierarchical. Who is to say that "principled" reasoning is better than "conventional" reasoning? Conservatives would not agree that a belief in the power of legitimate authority is undesirable and would suggest that the conclusions are influenced by the author's political perspective.

Haan's research implicitly supports libertarian theory by suggesting civil disobedience is characteristic of students who have higher levels of reasoning. Also, by suggesting that the rationales for civil disobedience are "better" than those for other moral problems, this implies that civil disobedience is a profoundly liberating and moral enterprise.

# Social Movements and Civil Disobedience

What is the relationship of the individual to the state? Is government based on the consent of the governed, and when must that consent be given? Do people have the right to press for change outside formal political channels? Widespread civil disobedience seems to provide evidence that all is not well—that a sizable number of citizens are rejecting the traditional lines of authority. Although these actions may not come from an individual conscience but rather from a political movement, this does not deny their morality. Social movements can educate individual citizens and then provide a channel through which they can express their new grievances.

It is important to remember that the issues on which people might engage in civil disobedience do not neatly fall in any one corner of the political arena. Abortion, school prayer, and pornographic bookstores can provide as potent a motivation for direct action as nuclear power plants, racism, or military buildups. The theoretical underpinnings of civil disobedience are tied to how a person perceives the state. To be willing to engage in acts of civil disobedience, a person must concede that in some cases government authority is limited. In a democratic system, philosophical conservatives would not agree with this, notwithstanding the support of supposedly conservative groups for such action. The social democrat, with an absolute code of morality based on equality and justice, places some organized resistance above a government's right to crush that resistance; libertarians place any resistance over the government's right to intervene. For the libertarian, civil disobedience proves that individuals are still free; the bonds of consent to the government can be broken at any moment.

We might consider a social movement to be like a collective individual. By bringing individuals with shared values together, a movement can express views more forcefully than any single individual. In time, if the movement proves successful, it comes to speak for all of its members, even though there may be some within the category that the group supposedly represents who would disagree with specific claims. The National Organization for Women (NOW) is often said to speak for women, but this is obviously a loose use of the word "women." Likewise, the Christian Coalition does not represent all fundamentalist Christians. Yet, the existence of such groups allows the social order to function, dealing with these groups as brokers for their constituencies.

In a society as large and diverse as ours, it is impossible to deal with citizens as individuals. The ideals of libertarianism function far better in a small state than in a large one, in which individualism must be sacrificed in some measure. A social movement as a voluntary collection of like-minded individuals provides a means by which some principles of libertarianism can be incorporated into a nation-state. The existence and vitality of social movements can provide legitimacy to a democratic government and permit this government to maintain the consent of the governed by providing an avenue for the expression of dissatisfaction.

## *Questions*

1. Is civil disobedience ever justified? If so, when?

2. Are people who engage in civil disobedience criminals? Why or why not?

3. Is there any circumstance in which you would refuse to pay your income taxes to protest a government action?

4. Was Thoreau right in saying that the government that governs best, governs not at all?

5. Should people who oppose abortion blockade clinics?

6. Is the U.S. system of government sufficiently democratic to make any form of civil disobedience inappropriate?

7. Should protestors accept the punishment they are given, or should they use whatever legal techniques they can to avoid being punished?

8. Should social movements organize and direct acts of civil disobedience?

9. Should religious leaders organize acts of civil disobedience?
10. Was civil disobedience justified in the South during the Civil Rights movement of the 1960s?

## For Further Study

Barkan, Steven. *Protesters on Trial: Criminal Justice in the Southern Civil Rights and Vietnam Antiwar Movements.* New Brunswick, NJ: Rutgers University Press, 1985.

Gamson, William. *Talking Politics.* New York: Cambridge University Press, 1992.

Glassner, Barry. *The Culture of Fear: Why Americans Are Afraid of the Wrong Thing.* New York: Basic Books, 1999.

Hook, Sidney. "Social Protest and Civil Disobedience." *The Humanist* (1967): 157–159, 192–193.

Lofland, John. *Polite Protesters: The American Peace Movement of the 1980s.* Syracuse, NY: Syracuse University Press, 1993.

McAdam, Doug. *Freedom Summer.* New York: Oxford University Press, 1988.

Morris, Aldon. *The Origins of the Civil Rights Movement.* New York: Free Press, 1988.

Polletta, Francesca, and James Jasper. "Collective Identity and Social Movements." *Annual Review of Sociology* 27 (2001): 283–305.

Thoreau, Henry David. "Civil Disobedience." This essay can be found in many editions of Thoreau's writings.

Weber, David R., ed. *Civil Disobedience in America.* Ithaca, NY: Cornell University Press, 1978.

## Notes and References

1. "Creating a Dot-Commotion," *Foreign Policy*, November 2000, p. 105.
2. William Gamson, *The Strategy of Social Protest* (Homewood, IL: Dorsey, 1975).
3. Kimberly D. Elsbach and Robert I. Sutton, "Acquiring Organizational Legitimacy through Illegitimate Actions: A Marriage of Institutional and Impression Management Theories," *Academy of Management Journal* 35 (1992): 699–738.
4. Gustave LeBon, *The Crowd: A Study of the Popular Mind* (London: T. Fisher Unwin, 1896), pp. 54–56.
5. Neil J. Smelser, *Theory of Collective Behavior* (New York: Free Press, 1962), pp. 47–66.
6. Barry Glassner, *The Culture of Fear: Why Americans Are Afraid of the Wrong Thing.*
7. John D. McCarthy and Mayer N. Zald, "Resource Mobilization and Social Movements: A Partial Theory," *American Journal of Sociology* 82 (1977): 1212–1241; J. Craig Jenkins, "Resource Mobilization Theory and the Study of Social Movements," *Annual Review of Sociology* 9 (1983): 527–553.
8. See Francesca Polletta and James Jasper, "Collective Identity and Social Movements," *Annual Review of Sociology* 27 (2001): 283–305.
9. David A. Snow, E. Burke Rochford, Jr., Steven K. Worden, and Robert D. Benford, "Frame Alignment Processes, Micromobilization and Movement Participation," *American Sociological Review* 51 (1986): 464–481.

10. Le Bon, *The Crowd*, pp. xiii–xxi.

11. Ralph Turner and Lewis M. Killian, *Collective Behavior*, 2nd ed. (Englewood Cliffs, NJ: Prentice-Hall, 1972), pp. 21–25.

12. Hugo A. Bedau, "On Civil Disobedience," *Journal of Philosophy* 58 (1961): 661.

13. William Sloane Coffin, Jr., and Morris I. Leibman. *Civil Disobedience: Aid or Hindrance to Justice* (Washington, DC: American Enterprise Institute for Public Policy Research, 1972), p. 14; Charles Colson, "The Fear of Doing Nothing," *Christianity Today* 31 (May 15, 1987): 72.

14. Jay R. Howard, "A Comparative Analysis of the Civil Disobedience of Operation Rescue and Martin Luther King's Civil Rights Organization," *Free Inquiry in Creative Sociology* 21 (1993): 177–187.

15. Although the example of John Brown and his raid on the federal arsenal at Harper's Ferry reminds us that the struggle against slavery involved what we would today label "terrorism," that "terrorism" can be justified if it was part of a just cause, as some of the founders of the Republican Party argued.

16. John Junkerman, "Why Pray for Peace While Paying for War?: Tax Resisters Seek the Path of Conscience," *Progressive* (April 1981): 16.

17. John Leo, "Today's Uncivil Disobedience," *U.S. News & World Report*, April 17, 1989: p. 64.

18. Gerald Kreyche, "Methinks They Doth Protest Too Much," *USA Today* 188, May 1990, p. 98.

19. "A Blue-Collar Tax Revolt," *Newsweek*, March 9, 1981, p. 33.

20. Jill Smolowe, "Enemies of the State," *Time*, May 8, 1995, pp. 59–69; Tom Morganthau, "The View from the Far Right," *Newsweek*, May 1, 1995, p. 36–39.

21. Katha Pollitt, "Subject to Debate," *The Nation* (June 5, 1995): 784.

22. Molly Ivins, "Up the Rebels," *The Progressive* 51 (November 1987): 28.

23. Henry David Thoreau, *Walden and Civil Disobedience* (Cambridge: Riverside Press, 1960), pp. 235, 252.

24. Ibid., p. 256.

25. Frederick C. Foote, "No Nukes—No Consistency," *The Freeman* 33 (1983): 461.

26. Burton Zwiebach, *Civility and Disobedience* (Cambridge: Cambridge University Press, 1975), p. 150.

27. Hanna Pitkin, "Obligation and Consent—I," *American Political Science Review* 59 (1965): 999.

28. Coffin and Leibman, *Civil Disobedience*, pp. 3–4.

29. Martin Luther King, "Love, Law and Civil Disobedience," *Civil Disobedience in America*, David R. Weber, ed. (Ithaca, NY: Cornell University Press, 1978), p. 215.

30. David R. Carlin, Jr., "Civil Disobedience, Self-Righteousness, and the Anti-Nuclear Movement," *America* (September 25, 1982): 153.

31. Rodney Clapp, "Christian Conviction or Civil Disobedience?" *Christianity Today* (March 4, 1983): 31.

32. Charles E. Wyzanski, Jr., "On Civil Disobedience," *The Atlantic* (February 1968): 59.

33. Stuart M. Brown, Jr., "Civil Disobedience," *Journal of Philosophy* 58 (1961): 672–673.

34. Sidney Hook, "Social Protest and Civil Disobedience," *Moral Problems in Contemporary Society*, Paul Kurtz, ed. (Englewood Cliffs, NJ: Prentice-Hall, 1969), p. 169.

35. Wayne Wangstad, "Protest Runs Up Hefty Bureaucracy Bill," *St. Paul Pioneer Press* (October 25, 1983): 8A.

36. Norma Haan, "Hypothetical and Actual Moral Reasoning in a Situation of Civil Disobedience." *Journal of Personality and Social Psychology* 32 (1975): 255–270.
37. Lawrence Kohlberg, "A Cognitive-Developmental Approach to Socialization," *Handbook of Socialization*, D. Goslin, ed. (New York: Rand McNally, 1969).